Contents

iii

Building & Managing a World Class IT Help Desk

Bob Wooten

Osborne/McGraw-Hill

New York Chicago San Francisco
Lisbon London Madrid Mexico City
Milan New Delhi San Juan
Seoul Singapore Sydney Toronto

Osborne/**McGraw-Hill**
2600 Tenth Street
Berkeley, California 94710
U.S.A.

To arrange bulk purchase discounts for sales promotions, premiums, or fund-raisers, please contact Osborne/**McGraw-Hill** at the above address. For information on translations or book distributors outside the U.S.A., please see the International Contact Information page immediately following the index of this book.

Building & Managing a World Class IT Help Desk

1234567890 CUS CUS 01987654321

ISBN 0-07-213237-x

Publisher	Brandon A. Nordin
Vice President & Associate Publisher	Scott Rogers
Acquisitions Editor	Steven Elliot
Project Editor	Madhu Prasher
Acquisitions Coordinator	Alex Corona
Technical Editor	Rod Sharp
Copy Editor	Carolyn Welch
Proofreader	Paul Tyler
Indexer	Valerie Robbins
Computer Designers	Tara Davis
	Michelle Gallicia
Illustrator	Michael Mueller
Series Design	Peter F. Hancik
Cover Design	Greg Scott
Cover Illustration	Stephen Quinlan

This book was composed with Corel VENTURA™ Publisher.

Acknowledgments

Without a doubt, this book could not have started, let alone been completed, without the absolute support of my wife, Donna. She provided the inspiration to write it and the love to finish it. As I sat behind a computer screen over many months, she raised and cared for our two small children, Max and Elizabeth. She never complained and always supported me and for that I will be forever grateful.

Brantlee Lemmink is a wonderful person with many great ideas for the proper creation of a Help Desk. She began her career as a Help Desk agent for me and is now in a new organization responsible for building and running her own world class Help Desk. Her time, effort, and input were invaluable.

I also want to thank all those at Osborne/McGraw-Hill who helped me complete the book. From Steve Elliot to Alex Corona to Madhu Prasher to Carolyn Welch and everyone else behind the scenes, these superb professionals offered guidance and editorial advice that turned my collection of ideas into this extremely effective book on Help Desks. Rod Sharp was also very instrumental in providing me with ideas and the experience to fine-tune my thoughts throughout the book.

Last, I want to thank all the associates and customers I have had the pleasure to work with over the years. They have given me a wide variety of experiences from which to draw upon for this book. Who would have known that those episodes of complaints, constructive criticisms, and indeed some appreciation could have shaped a book like this one? Thanks specifically to Tom, Jess, Paul, and MK for their help over the years.

Preface

Help Desks are the face of the IT department. They are typically the first and longest lasting impression a computer user receives. Because of this, it is crucial that they receive the attention and resources to efficiently and effectively operate and serve the customer. Until recently, Help Desks did not exist in many organizations and those that did were mostly by-products. Today, Help Desks are widely recognized and established. I encourage you to make the most of your Help Desk. Allowing it or requiring it to be only reactive is a waste of resources. The people on the front line can see things happening that others cannot see. Using these people wisely will make the organization and you more successful.

This book was written primarily from an internal customer, computer user perspective. The acts of customer service, however, transcend organization charts and mission statements. Whether you use a computer or need help with a broken refrigerator, contacting someone else for help can be frustrating. Finding the person who recognizes your needs, has the ability to help you, and carries through with it, brings a sense of satisfaction despite bad beginnings. Your company can stand out from the others by continuing to be the one who wins over others in need of help. This applies to customers who pay you for the service or not. It applies to customers who work in the same company as you do or to those who only use your services or products.

If you are new to the Help Desk area, I welcome you. You will soon see that this is a world of challenges but they all can be overcome by using the items discussed in this book. If you are a veteran of the Help Desk's wars, congratulations. I urge you to push the group to new places. Many of the items covered here are examples of new places that are outside of everyday Help Desks. They can be natural extensions and have been successful in places I have been.

To both the new and old, I wish the best of luck to you!

Introduction

For fourteen years, I have worked in, designed, built, staffed, trained, read about, and been trained on Help Desks. It was my first career in the Information Systems industry and will always be my pride and joy. I have seen many people describe aspects of Help Desks and while all have very good points, I have never seen one that described the Help Desk adequately from start to finish.

So one night I set out to write this book to talk about the Help Desk world from the idea stage through to its existence as a must-have in the organization. It begins with a section on defining a Help Desk and the reasons businesses have created them. Assuming that the reasons apply to your organization, the book starts with the list necessary to actually open up shop. With the Help Desk up and running, the next section is on sustaining operations and overcoming common pitfalls of Help Desks. It takes a brief detour for those who already have a Help Desk but do not like it so it talks about how to turn around a failing Help Desk. Finally, the book shows you larger uses of a Help Desk that are proactive and that contribute mightily to the corporate climate.

This book is not technical in nature but conversational. I tried for an experienced, common sense approach versus formulaic, scientific methodology. The book is designed for those who do not even know what a Help Desk is as well as for a company that already has a Help Desk. It is for CIOs, IS department heads, business managers, or entry level IS associates who are looking for a way to make a name for themselves in the organization. Most of all, it is for those who recognize the importance of customer service in the IT world.

You will note that I spend more time presenting options than I do dictating exactly what you should do. That is completely on purpose. Believe me when I say I have some specific preferences. Because there are so many ways to set up Help Desks and incorporate them into the business, I think it is far more valuable to give you choices that allow you to customize your operation instead of dictating exact ways of operating.

To give you a heads up on what to expect, there is a "What to Look For" section at the beginning of each chapter. This section lists major topics the chapter will cover. At the end of each chapter is a "Quick Recap" section. This section asks you high-level questions that serve as a review of the chapter. It is intended to make you think about how the information in the chapter could apply to your unique situation.

Following each major part, there is a checklist of items to help ensure you are moving in the right direction. This is a good place to make sure you understood the ideas presented in that part and how you can use them in your Help Desk.

About the Author

Bob Wooten is Vice President of Consulting Services for a nationwide IT services firm. Prior to that, he was manager of information technology services and operations at a national wholesale distributor with more than 9,000 employees. He has more than 14 years experience in the IT field, and directs a staff in such varied capacities as systems and database administration, networking, applications development, asset management, telecommunications services, and Help Desk staffing and training.

PART I

What Is a Help Desk and Why Would I Want One?

CHAPTER 1

Help Desk Concepts

The business world today is changing and the importance of technology is increasing rapidly within that world. Technology has become a crucial element in the success of a business and, in many cases, how technology is used can make or break a company. Whether it is telephones, fax machines, PCs, or the Internet, technology continues to evolve. It's getting cheaper, faster, smaller, and easier to use. To get cheaper, faster, smaller, and easier, the components that make up this technology are getting more and more complicated. These technological advances make our lives simpler and more productive, and corporations will gain mightily from these technologies as they can conduct business more profitably and efficiently.

The one constant in the use of technology in the business world is the need for someone to keep it up and running. Help Desks are that constant. A Help Desk of some type is needed for the basics like phones or word processing packages, or for complicated things like Enterprise Resource Planning (ERP) packages and global networks linked by the Internet. Beyond keeping the actual hardware and software available, users need to know how to use this technology. Better yet, users should be able to concentrate on their jobs and not have to think about the tools they're using. For example, I am not worried about how the keyboard is attached to my PC right now; I am more interested in getting my thoughts and experience into this book. A world class Help Desk lets you focus on your job at hand without caring about the technology you're using.

The IT world can be a confusing place to outsiders because of its terms and acronyms. I sometimes wonder if it's on purpose to keep people thinking that the IT world is special and unique. To help overcome some of the confusion surrounding these terms, this chapter will explain some of them and how they are used. Other concepts will be addressed as they relate to the chapter they come up in. So hang on.

What to Look For

- The definition of a Help Desk as it fits in any organization
- The different connotations of Help Desk names, and the people who work on a Help Desk, the people outside the Help Desk who need its services and support, and how they reach it to resolve problems
- The important distinction between a call, an incident, and a problem

Defining a Help Desk

For purposes of this book, we will define a Help Desk as *a formal organization that provides support functions to users of the company's product, services, or technology.* Let's break this statement down and analyze it phrase by phrase.

A formal organization that... Support can be a full-time job or part of someone's job; for example, a programmer may also take phone calls with questions on the software he or she is coding. But a Help Desk is an organized effort with an expressed purpose. A Help Desk can be staffed by one person wearing many hats or by literally thousands of people supporting scores of functions in the business.

...provides support functions... This can be reactive, as in "I sit by the phone and wait for someone to call," or proactive, looking for ways to make users more productive and effective in their jobs. Support can be break/fix, as in "my printer jammed," training, as in "the correct way to enter a purchase order on the system is...," or behind the scenes administration, as in "keeping the network up all day every day."

...to users of the company's products, services, or technology. The users (or customers, to sound friendlier) are the ones calling or are in need of the services you provide. The products, services, and technology are the point of the need. It may be a product your company manufacturers, a PC, printer, software, or telephone.

Help Desks are not as well known as applications development, database administration, or network management. You cannot get a college degree majoring in Help Desk; for that matter, I have never even seen a college class on the topic. I worked for years in a Help Desk before I could get my mom to understand what I did. Granted, I didn't mind that she told her friends, "My son runs the computer department," for lack of a better explanation!

What you see is the recognition of the Help Desk profession. The Bureau of Labor estimates there are over 450,000 Help Desk professionals now employed. The Help Desk Institute feels this number is closer to 560,000, which will double in the next ten years. College majors may not exist for a Help Desk career, but certifications and professional organizations are popping up all over. It is even fair to say that if you consider yourself a quality IT shop that will expand into the electronic commerce arena, you are behind the times if you don't have a formal Help Desk in place. You are behind because service, for customers or technology, has taken over electronic commerce and those businesses that cannot deliver quality customer service will not succeed in the long term.

Understanding Several Help Desk Names and Terms

I will use many terms interchangeably throughout this book, not to confuse you but because they have become so mixed together in their use today. While some have distinct differences, some do not. There is a glossary for a long list of terms related to a Help Desk, but following are some I use quite often.

Help Desk, Support Center, and User Support

I started above, and will use throughout, the name *Help Desk* to describe the person(s) or group that functions to support your department and company. Personally, I dislike the term because it's old-fashioned and doesn't give the credit a well-oiled department deserves, but it is the most popular. Once I was in a position to name the group, I used the term *Support Center*. Even this name is supportive or reactive but it's a bit more fashionable than Help Desk. (It did draw many comments towards *Sports Center,* however, which is not necessarily a bad thing.) We then decided to go to Customer Services and finally to Technical Customer Service. Other terms I have seen are Support Services, User Support, Technical Support, Competency Center, IS Support, Customer Care, and on and on. Mix in the words Support, Help, Customer, User, Technical, and Service and somewhere you will get a good name!

Associates, Agents, and Employees

For a long time, if you worked in a company you were considered an *employee.* Lately, I have seen a trend away from that term towards the more favorably regarded *associate.* It's supposed to sound more like you are a part of the big picture and not just a person employed by an impersonal corporation. You won't see the word *employee* here but you will see *associate* and *agent* mixed throughout. I distinguish between the two by using *associate* when I am writing about a person's career and personable traits and *agent* when I am referring to his or her role within the Help Desk itself. If this is confusing, you can go with the assumption that the two are interchangeable.

Customers, Users, and Callers

I will use a mixture of these terms when referring to the people outside the Help Desk who need your services or help. The term *customers* denotes a group of people who need extra care and should make you feel more inclined to help them with their problems. *Users* might be an accurate term because they *use* your product, but it does not promote the "I care for you" feelings a Help Desk agent should have. *Callers* may call you on the phone, but they could just as well walk up to your desk, e-mail you a question, or fill in a Web page. The point is they need you. Again, these terms will be used interchangeably throughout the book.

Calls, Incidents, and Problems

What could be the difference between these terms? For routine conversations, there really isn't any. It is more important to distinguish between them when we speak of measurements and call management packages. The book will take some time to distinguish between them when it specifically matters.

A *call* is any contact from a customer to the Help Desk. It is not limited to telephone conversations, but includes e-mail, faxes, Internet chat, voice mail, and walk-up traffic. An *incident* is a driver of the call. Incidents are the occasion that makes the caller recognize the situation. A *problem* is the root cause of all this mess. Recognizing the distinction between these terms can really affect the outcomes of measurements and call tracking. You can see this distinction in Figure 1-1.

Let's walk through an example. You stroll into work one morning and walk past two of the associates in the IT department. They're on the phone and making notes frantically. As soon as they put the phone down, it rings again. You whisper to one of them asking what is wrong. She replies that there are PC hardware problems. It seems that some of the PCs in the building are experiencing slowness. Walking over to the other associate, you ask the same thing. He replies that he is working on some software issues. Microsoft Office keeps hanging up on people. Although it seems odd to get this many calls so early in the morning, the associates seem to have it under control, so you head to your office to begin your own day.

All is not under control, however. Left completely in this state, the root problem will not be resolved and eventually the whole building, including you, will have its computing service come to a halt. Why? Because the IT associates are not working on the *problem*, which is a faulty server, instead they are answering phone *calls* and working on the corresponding *incidents*.

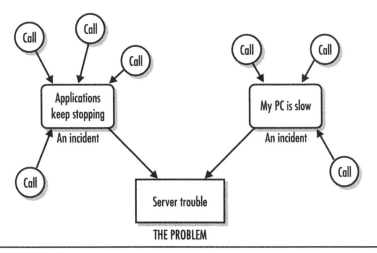

Figure 1.1   Calls, incidents, and problems

The *calls* are each phone ringing, the guy waiting by the agents' desk to try and reach them, and the voice mails stacking up. The call is the contact by the customer into the Help Desk. A call is not technical; it happens every day in businesses across the world. In our example, the customers would tell you the problem is what they called in and that is correct…from their view. From the view of a Help Desk, the problem may lie elsewhere.

The *incidents* are what the two IT associates have narrowed down their calls to—PC slowness and software hanging up. It is good they were able to focus their efforts on these two incidents, but they are not done.

They are not done because the *problem* has not been reached yet. Eventually someone will discover that the incidents are related and are the result of a faulty server in the computer room. Until that problem is fixed, the calls will keep coming and more incidents will be found.

This scenario really points out many topics for building and managing a Help Desk. We will cover all of them throughout the book, but it's good to recognize now. Whether it's a central place to call, training agents to resolve problems, having a manager discover that multiple calls are related, or communicating out to customers that a problem exists and is being worked on, the Help Desk brings enormous value to any organization that uses technology.

Calls, incidents, and problems. Which are you measuring and which are you working on? I will go into more depth on this in the measurement chapter and when I discuss call management packages. You can see from here that just talking about calls or problems can have several different connotations. This example is typical of problem resolution in Help Desk incidents.

Quick Recap

- How does this description of a Help Desk fit your desire to build or run one? Will yours be formal and managed as the definition intends?

- Have you picked a name for your Help Desk yet? The book will go over the need for this later, but there is no reason not to start thinking about it now.

- Do you care about the differences between customers and users? Will it make a difference in your company for the people who need the Help Desk's services to be referred to in a particular manner?

- Do you understand the distinction between calls, incidents, and problems? If not, re-read that section because as it will play a big part in future chapters. Remember that calls are each contact into the Help Desk, incidents are what prompted that particular call, and problems are the root reasons that started it all.

CHAPTER 2

Why Do I Want One?

Companies create their own formal Help Desk for a variety of reasons. The key word is *formal*. Help Desk functions exist in all companies and at all levels. Looking over at the person next to you and asking whom to call for an insurance question could be a function. Stopping a person in the hallway to figure out how to make the copy machine staple can be a function. Pulling out a manual (does anyone really do this?) to develop a whiz-bang spreadsheet fulfills the function of a Help Desk. You must have some inkling as to its need since you are reading this book. This chapter will go over some of the common reasons for a Help Desk's existence in an organization.

What to Look For

- There are many reasons to create a Help Desk. The value it will bring to your organization can be seen through increased effectiveness in your associates, your processes, and your customers' satisfaction. Many of these reasons will be discussed in detail in this chapter.

- A Help Desk will allow your associates to perform the job they were hired to do. They can use the Help Desk to resolve computing issues so they can remain free to continue their own job responsibilities.

- A Help Desk also creates a central repository of knowledge for the company as a whole. Instead of pockets of knowledge being spread out across many of your associates, this knowledge can be accumulated in the Help Desk for easy referral and transfer.

- A Help Desk can also provide a centralized database of technical experience to help multiple groups do their jobs better. Help Desk agents can access this database for their work, or for anyone in the company who needs the Help Desk's services and support.

- You may be looking into building a Help Desk because the current environment does not give you the level of services you need. Your computing services are critical to your business and if you cannot get the help you need, you will have to come up with new ideas to get it from somewhere else.

- A Help Desk is the first impression many people get of the IT department and the company. Establishing a professional group devoted to providing technical customer service can leave lasting, positive impressions on your customer base.

Reasons to Create Your Own Help Desk

There are seven primary reasons a company goes to a formal Help Desk. We will look at each one individually for more details. A Help Desk does the following:

- Lets associates perform the jobs they were hired to do
- Provides synergies from a central organization handling computer-related issues
- Creates a physically centralized repository of knowledge
- Provides help when current computer help methods are not meeting expectations
- Provides customers or users their first contact into the IT department
- Bridges the technology gap between end users and "super technical" associates
- Helps keep technology use consistent and aligned

Allows Other Associates to Perform Their Own Jobs

All companies need their associates to do the jobs they were hired to do, not fixing the tools they use for the jobs themselves. Paying high salaries for programmers to reset passwords is not very effective. Conversely, having administrative assistants answer business rules questions within your software may not be wise for the business either. These local support providers, the associates whom others go to with computer problems, are typically not experts and provide answers based more on their own experience rather than on formal training. "I don't know why but it worked for me last time," is a phrase used often when local associates support their peers. Even when correct, their answers are short term in nature and may not align with the long-range technology plans of the organization. It's when the "fix" is not correct that more problems are created. What works on one PC may very easily mess up something when it's performed on a different PC. Before too long, companies will have multiple people discussing a problem and their experience with it and none of the associates will be performing their own jobs.

Provides Synergies from a Central Organization Handling Computer Problems

Another good reason for a Help Desk is the synergy you get from its centralized focus towards resolving computer problems and issues. *Central* here does not necessarily mean physical. Help Desks can span multiple sites; it is how the Help Desk is organized that I am referring to.

It can be very costly for a company with many locations to train its associates in every facet of the business. Total Cost of Ownership is a popular phrase that speaks to reviewing all costs involved in ownership, specifically beyond the acquisition price. Gaining efficiencies by pooling resources to solve problems helps reduce this cost of ownership and gives you a higher return on your investment. Help Desk agents can be involved in the technology or software development stages so they can have a thorough understanding of the behind-the-scenes of a product. The ability for the Help Desk agent to understand the inner workings of the technology is vital to supporting it effectively. Conversely, the users of the technology will usually only receive training after it is released. The users have the advantage of using the technology in their work every day, but the Help Desk can at least know "why" the technology works like it does.

Creates a Physically Centralized Repository of Knowledge

A strong advantage a formal Help Desk offers a company is its knowledge. The Help Desk agents are constantly in touch with the customers and quickly gain valuable insights into how things are going in the field. A Help Desk, even if staffed in multiple locations, can store its knowledge in a centralized database. This database lets Help Desk agents access prior problems and solutions to quickly resolve problems that occur over and over. This database can be as simple as a file folder, an Excel spreadsheet, or a full-blown call management package. Call management packages will be discussed in great detail later. For now, just consider them as software that allows agents to enter calls in an efficient manner.

This physical repository helps resolve both the easy and the hard problems. For the easy ones, a review of the database can give good feedback to trainers on topics to teach the users. By educating users on simple resolutions to problems, you can empower customers to better help themselves. For the harder problems, the database can show trends that help systems administrators and programmers resolve the root cause or design new programs with a similar focus.

Current Computer Help Methods Are Not Meeting Expectations

It may be that you currently use Help Desk services from an organization and they are not meeting your expectations or are too costly. Bringing that functionality in-house can sometimes reduce the costs and/or give you a better understanding of what your business needs as it moves forward with technology.

For example, the business may have contracted with its software supplier for their support group. At another time, they contracted with a hardware reseller to provide support for the various types of hardware deployed. Each of these contracts should have included specific details on service levels and escalation procedures. That looked good on paper at the time and the business felt like they were covered.

Over time, the different business units began noticing a decrease in call resolution times and felt they were not being taken care of. The legal group reviewed the contract but found the service providers were performing just within the requirements of the contract. Maybe the business had shifted priorities since the contract signing and the terms were no longer adequate. If the service provider could not expand its services to meet the business needs, a change would have to be made. One option is for the company to bring all or most of that support in-house, and build its own Help Desk.

Provides First Contact into the IT Department

Your customers' first and ongoing contact with the IT department will primarily be through the Help Desk. You want that contact to be professional, efficient, and effective, and devoting part of your organization to it is a superb way to achieve this. The Help Desk will be staffed with associates dedicated to providing customer service in a technical world. Their focus is entirely on this goal and results in higher levels of satisfaction among your customers.

This applies even to a smaller IT organization. An example could be a five-person shop. One person manages the group, three more are programmers, and one is a technical engineer. They're always either in meetings or deep into projects for the business. What do users do when they have a problem? Call IT? In this group, the phone may go unanswered for a while until someone returns from a meeting or lunch. At other times, the programmers are behind closed doors concentrating on producing high quality code within the time frame allowed them. Being interrupted throughout the day by users is counterproductive to their programming mission. This attitude might spill over into the conversations with the caller and produce unneeded antagonism between the parties. Now the business has unhappy customers with problems and longer lead times on its programming efforts. In this example, you can see why the Help Desk should be a strategic part of your plans and not a by-product of the services you offer.

Bridges the Technology Gap Between End Users and "Super Technical" Associates

Help Desks allow a focused entry point for customers to interface with the IT department. Help Desks also allow this interface to be as "customer-friendly" as possible. Super technical people, computer geeks, are not known as extroverted, people-friendly people. This is a broad generalization, but it typically holds true over a large population. When customers need help and can only explain their issues in business or general terms, the interface can be cumbersome. Trying to accurately relate "my computer is throwing up" to a technical problem can be trying. Relating it in a friendly manner can be even more so.

Help Desk agents are absolutely used to this type of conversation and can handle it in stride. They are trained to provide customer service. They realize that users do not know all the right terms and are OK with that. The Help Desk can serve as a translator and allow the customers and IT department to speak well with each other.

Helps Keep Technology Use Consistent and Aligned

Help Desk agents cannot enforce consistent technology use all by themselves. They can help greatly in this process, however. Agents can see what works and what doesn't work in the field and can communicate this information to others. The communication can go out to customers in the form of Best Practices and helpful hints. The communication can come into the IT department with popular technology uses and ideas for better ways to roll out new technology.

Without a Help Desk, technology is designed, purchased, and installed in whatever manner the person that is asked is experienced in. This "experience" may be in the form of something they heard or something they tried on their system at home. You wouldn't want a salesman to recommend a cheap PC to help keep costs down if it wasn't stable or loaded with the correct operating system. Formal Help Desks, with a central focus, keep technology use consistent and aligned.

Quick Recap

- There are many reasons to build a Help Desk. Can you literally write down the reasons you are looking into it?

- A Help Desk can provide a central place to research information pertinent to the IT world. Can you see how this will benefit your company?

- How do your customers view their contact with your business's IT department? Are they greeted in a customer-friendly manner? Is there room for improvement?

Action Plan Checklist

❑ Solidify your own definition of a Help Desk so you can explain it to others.

❑ Understand the basic differences between calls and problems.

❑ Understand all the reasons this Help Desk is being built and the benefits it provides.

PART II

I Want a Help Desk.
Go Create One.

CHAPTER 3

Identify the Drivers

The first driver, or major influencing factor, in creating a Help Desk comes from the people or organization requesting its creation. Many IS folks have begged and pleaded for a formal Help Desk and have been given the opportunity to build one. Other IS folks have been performing their jobs and have been told to create one. Yet more people have been hired specifically to come in and bring up a Help Desk within the company.

Regardless of the initial request, the expectations have been established and you are responsible for creating a Help Desk and are expected to have it fully functional as soon as possible. What was once a wishful thought has turned into a large task that could affect your career. You may be able to staff your Help Desk with existing personnel or you may hire associates solely for this purpose, including your management team. Neither case has to be a problem as long as you start with the basics. Your Help Desk is an organization, and as such, will be influenced and will operate as one. The key elements of an organization are shown in Figure 3-1.

The People

The foundation of any organization, but especially the Help Desk, is its people. Good people will overcome a majority of poor decisions and will find ways to do an effective job despite obstacles. Bad people will tear down the best of processes and ruin relationships. Buy an expensive tool to improve customer service or the efficiency of a process and good people will make it work. Bad people will not use it and its return on investment will be lost. We will spend much time discussing the people in a Help Desk and how to make the best use of them moving forward.

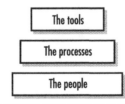

Figure 3.1   Major elements of an organization

The Processes

People will work hard, but good processes allow that energy to be focused in the right direction. You need to pay attention to the processes you implement, as they can really help or hurt the Help Desk. Too much bureaucracy will slow them down and ultimately hurt the customer. Your associates will also spend as much time trying to get around the processes helping the customer. Properly implemented plans and procedures make the work easier and more productive.

The Tools

Tools only take the people and processes and make them more effective. Good tools can speed up processes, make agents more knowledgeable, and lower the cost of doing business over time. A good tool mixed in with bad people or bad processes will not work. It may disguise bad issues, but it will not overcome them. Bad tools will simply be unused or used very ineffectively.

In addition to people, processes, and tools, there are many other factors you need to consider when building your Help Desk. At the same time, there are drivers you need to coordinate or align. Drivers are people or situations that guide or *drive* you to organize in a particular manner or operate in a certain way. You can see the drivers depicted graphically in Figure 3-2. *Alignment* is a term used to describe a situation in which two or more entities have matched their expectations or definitions of a service or product. When these parties are aligned, they work with each other to achieve common goals and objectives. Without alignment, the actions of the parties are not coordinated and goals will not be met or will require much effort to do so. The alignment of your Help Desk with each of the following drivers is paramount to its continued existence and success. If you already have a Help Desk, check to make sure it is as aligned as it should be. Six months later, check it again. This practice is always relevant and should not be ignored.

What to Look For

- Senior management alignment is critical to the short- and long-term success of your Help Desk. Alignment must exist between the management team

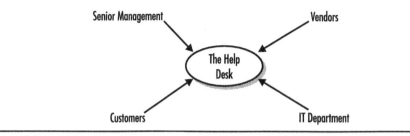

Figure 3.2   Driving factors of the Help Desk

and your Help Desk, and it is essential that you achieve it as early as possible. Alignment among senior managers themselves is also important so that everyone agrees with the intended direction of the Help Desk. This may not always be possible, but you should try to build shared goals and expectations for the Help Desk among managers.

- The rest of the IT department will have an impact on your operations and success. You need to be aligned with them as well. The department has somehow managed to exist without you in the past and your new entry needs to be understood. Roles and responsibilities can be communicated to ensure everyone is on the same page.

- The vendors that have designed, sold, installed, and supported your technology can help you develop a very effective Help Desk. Working with your vendors can help you leverage resources to achieve the goals you set for yourself.

- Last but not least is the alignment of your Help Desk with its customers. You must understand them and their needs to move forward effectively. Without customers, the entire need for a Help Desk goes away.

Senior Management

The senior management referred to here are the people who approve the creation of the Help Desk. Unless you are just so in tune with the thought patterns of your managers, it would hard to run full force with simply, "Max, I want a Help Desk." Right after "No problem," you should probably ask them what they want it to do. Will it support the whole organization or just parts of it? Will you support all the technologies or just certain software or hardware? Are you staffing in full or using outsourcing partners? Somewhere in there is the question of how much you can spend. To be successful, you must understand what the approvers want from this new venture.

This is not a one-time deal, either. The initial discussion should take some time to ensure alignment. Be cognizant of senior management's schedules and be prepared when you begin. If they are not completely sold on the idea or different managers have different ideas but are willing to try it, you must be good from the start. The worst of all things is to get closed down before you even begin.

How to Find Them

It is doubtful that there is a sign in the lobby pointing to "Senior Management." You know you want to talk to them, but how do you find them? If you are already an employee of the company, odds are you have some idea of who they are. If you are new to the company, you will likely have no idea.

A good place to start in either case is to talk to the person who hired you or who is your boss. This person may be part of the senior management team and your journey has begun. He or she can introduce you to the team, help get you started, and identify the major players. Job titles can exude grandiose meanings but the person have less impact on the company and its direction than someone with a lower-sounding title. Aside from titles, some senior executives will have much visibility to and from the Help Desk and should not be overlooked. For those managers who are more remote in their impact, they can be put on the list to speak with but at a later point in time.

Interview Them Separately

One thing I suggest for these initial discussions is to first conduct them separately. Don't get the management team together in one room (I never could if I wanted to), but instead set up appointments with each one. The purpose of this is to get their individual feedback without others around. This way you get their honest and sincere input and don't have to worry about potential grandstanding that can occur when a group of people are asked their opinions.

When you conduct the interview, divide the communication into three parts: educating the manager, educating yourself, and setting expectations. Have your questions written down so you don't forget anything, but don't keep your head down and read strictly from the list. Be conversational and pay attention. Go for more details when you can, and go lightly when you sense frustration. You don't know when you will get another shot at this, so make the best of it while you can.

Educating the Manager

Lead off with a brief explanation of why you are there. Don't talk down to the manager but don't assume he knows much about the technical aspects of your business, either. The key is to start off on the right foot and make him an ally. A common way to win over others is to show them they are needed. You can achieve this by soliciting their opinions and feedback. Some examples of what to communicate in your discussion include

- "I have been chartered with starting an IT Help Desk. Were you aware of this?" This clearly states why you are there and begins to bring them into the process. If the manager is not aware, it might be a good opportunity to explain what a Help Desk is and what it can provide to the business.

- State your goals. Show the executive you have a plan and know where you are going. Watch his body language or tone of voice. You don't want to get too deep. For example, if he seems to be technically savvy, it is OK to talk about some of the tools and services you want to offer. Otherwise, stick to higher goals and objectives.

- State your timelines. "I hope to have this in operation in two months." Again, keep an eye on how attentive he is.

- Finally, end with, "Does this sound like stuff that makes sense? I believe the company needs this service, but I am interested in how you see it." Again, bring the executive into the process and get his feedback on what you are doing.

Educating Yourself

The real reason of the interview is to understand where the executive is coming from. Find out his expectations and experiences. Some of your questions might include

- "Have you had experience with Help Desks before?"

- "What worked well during that time?"

- "Where were opportunities for it to have been done better?" These questions help educate you on the executive's prior experience. They can show you how much he knows about the topic and how much he has paid attention to these services in the past.

- "What does your department need most from the IT department?" You might get a laundry list of items that do not relate to the Help Desk, but it shows you what services and products are important to him.

- "Do you have any recommendations of others I should speak with?" This gains you several things. First, it gives the executive an out from future conversations on Help Desks. If you get a "Yeah, talk to Chip from now on. He is my main guy on computer stuff," you know he wants out. His mentioning other people's names does not necessarily mean that, though. If he gives you names from his group, it shows you his department uses technology, and this is good to know. You also gain if you get names outside his group. Add these to the list for future conversations.

Setting Expectations

Conclude the meeting by establishing expectations for further interaction. It may be a lot, or it may be none. Either way, depart with both of you knowing what to expect.

- "I am finishing off my plan with additional input from the other executives. Then we can all get together and go over the presentation."

- "Would you like to get back together for more details?" The rubber meets the road here. Don't take it personally if the answer is no or inconclusive. You need to know who is important to keep up with and who doesn't really care. Don't give up on them, but don't concentrate on them either.

Present Your Findings Back to the Group

After you have gathered all the individual feedback, you can present your findings to the combined group. The names of the people who gave you each statement or idea are not as important as the ideas themselves. This combined forum will also serve as an approval process for all the managers to hear the information and accept it as presented.

After you get senior management aligned, you will put more concrete plans together and check back in again. This is all before you have answered the phone once. Be confident in your abilities and thought processes but also be aware that this senior management piece really is important. Obviously, it matters more for a new Help Desk of 500 associates than for a Help Desk of 1, but you never know how fast that 1 can turn into 500.

The IT Department

Working your way down from senior management, you now reach the rest of the IT department. Alignment here is just as important as it is with the senior management team. Only in this case, the alignment does not result in funding and approval, but in daily functionality and effectiveness. The Help Desk will reside in the IT department for the duration, and how it interacts with the existing groups is critical.

The roles and responsibilities of the Help Desk as they relate to the IT department need to be clearly delineated and communicated. Issues such as the ownership of escalating problems or the testing of software before it is released can rest in several IT areas. An effective organization does not want issues to be dropped between the cracks or duplicated by multiple people, so get as many of the questions answered ahead of time as possible.

The end result of this planning effort needs to be communicated to all associates in the department. Just because the department heads understand doesn't mean that all the associates will. You are introducing a new group of people into a department and they are taking on a role visible to the rest of the company. For them to succeed, they must fit in quickly with the existing associates. This is best achieved by effective and ongoing communication.

A Help Desk brings many advantages to an IT department. The Help Desk can have considerable influence on future issues and decisions through its constant interaction with customers and users. As the department works on its project plan for the coming year, it should include some members of the Help Desk. The Help Desk agent may not be able to decide every piece of technology that is coming, but he can ask questions to guide where the technology plan is headed. The technology's impact on customers, the need to train customers on the technology, and how the technology will interface with existing, deployed technologies are important issues that should be addressed before final decisions are made.

Vendors

Your vendors are the companies and individuals who sell you the products and services that keep your Help Desk running. If your company has not had a Help Desk until now, the vendors supplied the separate departments and customers with their technologies.

The technology vendors are a driving factor in the creation of your Help Desk because they can influence which services you are forced to design and which ones they can participate in themselves. If your vendors are strictly "providers of product," you will need to design and build all the services yourself. However, if the vendors offer services along with their products, you can look to them to offset some of the services you would like others to perform. In today's world of shrinking hardware prices, there is not much margin to be made on hardware alone. For this reason, hardware vendors are looking for more lucrative markets, and service is definitely one of them.

Another potential partner in the technology chain is the value added reseller (VAR). Their mission is not only to sell technology to companies but to add value on top of that. An example can be seen with a server. A vendor can sell you the server or you could pick one up at their retail store. A VAR will sell you the server and other amenities you may want such as asset tagging it, testing it in your environment, or even helping you install it. There is a price for this service, but it may be well worth your having the VAR do it.

Customers

This sounds easy enough to know, but to be truly successful, your Help Desk must fully understand the total impact and expectations of your customer base. You should begin by asking yourself several questions. As you gather the answers to these questions, you may find that you have multiple groups of customers with different issues. As this happens, you may want to document your findings and create customer profiles or outlines. These can come in handy when you set up your organization and create service level agreements. Service level agreements are contracts between the Help Desk and its customers. The contract outlines the processes and procedures for interaction with the Help Desk. Its purpose is to set proper expectations for both the customer and the Help Desk. We will devote more time to service level agreements in Chapter 12.

The basic things you need to find out about your customers are

- Who are they?
- Where are they?
- What do they want?
- When do they want it?

Who Are They?

In a reactive world only, it would be easy to discover who your customers are. You wait to see who calls and they obviously are your customers. Taking a step towards proactiveness, you could review the call logs that anyone may have retained and see who called in the past. These call logs may be actual databases or notepads or notebooks. For lack of anything else, you could talk to the people in IT who used to take the calls. They are bound to be able to list for you the names of frequent callers or locations.

Let's go further and not wait to see who calls or who has called. This is a good step to take, but it should not be the only one. Obviously, if your Help Desk will support only internal associates, the identification can be as easy as pulling out an associate roster from the HR department. If there are external customers, you can meet with sales people or production associates to help you find your potential customer list.

Internal Versus External Customers

Your customers may be internal fellow associates in the organization, or external customers of the company itself, or both. There are similarities in each instance, but there are definite differences as well. (In this book we will concentrate on internal customers, but see the text marked with the External Customers icon for information relevant or unique to external customers.)

External Customers *The differences between the two can have a strong impact on your Help Desk. For example, external customers are probably paying for your service and have high expectations and low tolerance levels. Internal customers will also, but they cannot walk away from the situation as easily as an external customer can. Upsetting an internal customer is bad and will get higher managers involved. Upsetting an external customer may result in loss of revenue and ill will towards the whole company. You should strive to avoid both situations, but you may act and react in different ways based on the customer's position.*

Customer Versus Consumer

I also want to recognize a distinction between customers and consumers that author Bob Lewis has discussed frequently in *Infoworld's* "IS Survival Guide." According to Lewis, customers are the ones who pay for your services and consumers are the ones who use them. His argument is that you must keep both in mind as you proceed through the IS world. My tack is a bit different, and I feel it comes down to semantics in the end. As you are setting up your Help Desk you need to keep the expectations of your bill payers in mind for they are key to your survival. However, I also think it is important to maintain the mindset that your end users will ultimately determine your success and career survival. Their willingness to use your services and recognize them as invaluable to their business will keep you in business for as long as you want. Ultimately, you should always acknowledge the executives or shareholders that allow your organization to exist but you should also stress the day-to-day focus on your users as your customers.

Interview All Levels of the Customer's Organization

No matter how you define them, you must go after all levels of the customer base. When interviewing customers to understand their needs, it may be much more convenient to meet with higher level managers to get the information. They are on top so they should know the most about their aspect of the business, right? The answer is yes and no. Yes, they know about *their* aspect of the business. No, they do not have the best grasp of *all* levels of the business.

A store manager will give you great feedback on the importance of the system being up and fast and accurate. You will also get extremely valuable information from the shop floor workers on the importance of a particular printer or desktop device. The manager might think of that, but it probably would not register in his mind unless you specifically asked him. Because the odds are that all levels of the customer base will call you at one time or another, it is good to know each angle of the business from the beginning. There will be opportunities to prioritize how you arrange that, but at least you will be setting up shop as informed as you can be.

Where Are They?

Your customers may all be located in the same facility or spread out in hundreds of locations across the country or world. This is a huge factor in the formation of your Help Desk. If everyone is in the same facility, you need to set up more for walk-up traffic and your hours can easily mimic those of people in the rest of the building. Staffing levels can be affected if your customers are all co-located with the Help Desk. At the same time, co-located customers will probably require some deskside support. You will need to plan for some of your agent's time to be spent away from the phone and at the customer's desk.

The more remote locations you have, the more phone and e-mail traffic you will have, and tools to handle these calls will increase. Customers across time zones require that you align your support hours to their business hours more creatively. If your customers are located in different countries, they might speak different languages. Staffing now takes on interesting challenges.

The physical location of your customer base may change over time, so allow flexibility when you organize your Help Desk and its processes. Handling phones and work hours are the same acts regardless of location. It is how you are forced to handle them that is impacted.

What Do They Want?

Another basic question but one full of issues. You must be careful to balance your customers' "needs" against their "wishes." You must also check in with the executives who allowed you to create the Help Desk to ensure that their needs are aligned with those of your customers. Matching up these expectations is absolutely critical to the success of your Help Desk. It doesn't matter that you are staffed 24 hours a day, 7 days a week; if your agents cannot answer questions, you will be deemed (correctly) a failure. On the other hand, a team of expert agents working eight to five o'clock cannot help business operations that work the midnight shift.

Needs by Technology Usage

Gartner Group's classification of a company's use of technology can also help you determine what your customers want and need.

Try to determine where your company fits in this model. I say "try to determine" because I doubt your company's mission statement mentions anything about this. It is important though to gauge as best you can where your company sits because this could affect the success of your Help Desk. The speed in which your customer base brings in new technology will help you in multiple areas. It will tell you how fast and constant your internal training must be. It helps you know if you must hire agents quickly or at a slower pace. The Gartner Group classification also lets you know if you need to hire people with a broad range of experiences or if you can hire entry level agents and ramp them up. Moreover, your Help Desk must be aligned with the company's corporate direction. If they use

Gartner Group Classifications

Type A	Aggressive user of technology; always uses bleeding edge; recognizes short life span of technology
Type B	Less aggressive but recognizes the importance of technology
Type C	Slow user; only takes technology once it is widely accepted in the industry

bleeding-edge technology, so should you. If customers are using voice-over IP (VoIP), they are in the Type A category. If they are just bringing in Pentium PCs, they are deeply in the Type C classification, and you probably won't need as many of the newest gadgets to successfully run your Help Desk. Believe me, you will still have challenges in the Type C organization; they will just be different from Type A's.

Needs by Available Skill Set

You can also evaluate your customers' needs by viewing their skill set. They may need PC break/fix help. Their skill set may be at the computer illiterate stage, which means your staff will have to answer questions on how to change the background color or address issues such as memory management or IRQs. If your customers are power PC users, they will require a higher level of PC skills from your Help Desk because they already know the easy stuff. As power users of any hardware or software, they will be pushing it to extreme boundaries. They will find bugs in the software that a lot of people would not, or find ways to connect devices that others would not think of. This is fine; you just need to be ready for it at staffing time.

Keep Checking In

This alignment is not a one-time event. You must check in regularly to ensure your team is performing services the business expects. Don't let the results of this check-in hurt your feelings. I say this because you need to recognize quickly if your grand plans moving forward do not line up with what your customers want. I have done this before and it is much better to adjust plans than to constantly battle an implemented idea.

When Do They Want It?

Knowing the answer to this question helps you decide staffing hours and the level of skill set required during those times. If your customers work around the clock, they will probably expect support to be available around the clock. If their business is open during the day but some people work late, they may want support but the Help Desk doesn't have to be fully staffed or staffed with your best agents. The in-office staff may be able to answer the easy questions and can beep an on-call agent for the harder things. Times of day matter but don't forget days of the week either. Holidays? Do yours align with those of the customer?

One trick in this might be to look at when the management of the customer works. Never openly express this, but when the customer's management feels they need to be there, you really do too. Now, I am not discounting late-night shifts who may have truly legitimate support needs. Their function may be as important as those working during the day. I'll bet that if it is a large group, management will be there. If it is a smaller group, you obviously have a smaller customer base at that time and can afford to have a smaller Help Desk staff in the office as well.

Add Some Needs of Your Own

You absolutely must understand the needs of your executives and customers. At the same time, you should be bringing in some needs of your own. They may be personal goals and objectives or they may be needs you know the organization and customers want but don't realize yet. Good for you and go get them; just don't allow them to override the specifically mentioned needs of those who pay you! Some examples of goals you should set for yourself include the following:

- Be a communication and information hub
- Recognize issues and pull together the right resources
- Promote technology and its tools and services
- Remain flexible
- Maintain a proactive workload
- Work yourself out of business

We will discuss each of these goals in the following sections.

Be a Communication and Information Hub

One goal you should strive to achieve is to make your Help Desk the hub of communications in the business, at least for IT-related information. Your group touches every computer user and is privy to the direction in which both the users and IT are going. The Help Desk becomes very valuable if it can match the two together and help each to be informed. Whether it is upcoming upgrades, recurring hardware problems, or the effects that physical inventories have on the system,

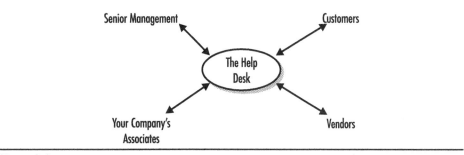

Figure 3.3   Communication and information hub

the Help Desk is in a prime spot to route information throughout an organization. Figure 3-3 denotes the flow of information going into and out of the Help Desk. It also expands from just the IT department to all associates in the company.

These are two examples of ways the Help Desk can communicate information to the organization. By doing this, you appear knowledgeable of world and local events and can be seen as a partner and ally of the business and not just techno-geeks.

Real-World Example

One way our Virginia Help Desk shared information was through hurricane status reports. Each summer hurricane season begins and threatens the eastern coastline. Because many of our stores were located on the East Coast, we used pictures and weather predictions from the Internet to keep our associates informed. Although the local news could do the same thing, it was interesting to see our Help Desk agents make hurricane charts available for everyone to see. I knew our efforts were successful when the CEO of the company asked me to provide him with hourly updates of any approaching hurricane. With that information, he was able to work with the facilities manager to determine what additional steps needed to be taken to protect the campus. The HR director was able to determine staffing hours and the conditions under which the associates came to work.

Real-World Example

Another example of the Help Desk as a communication hub was informing associates of an impending phone company strike that could have affected phone and data service in our business and personal lives. Stores knew that phone repairs would be delayed and downtimes extended. The strike did indeed take place, but we were as prepared as we could be. Stores that were due to open could either speed up plans to install new lines or communicate to others that their opening may be delayed. When there was downtime the Help Desk did not have to take the brunt of the blame because the business knew the phone company would be slower than normal in resolving issues.

Recognize Issues and Pull Together the Right Resources

Remember the calls to the IT department about slow PCs and frozen applications when we described calls versus incidents versus problems in Chapter 1? This was an example in which resources were working for the customer but not in a combined effort. A formal Help Desk gives you the ability to pull together resources to tackle multiple angles of a problem.

A Help Desk all by itself will not give you this ability, however. It needs to be structured correctly with management and proper procedures to get you to that point. Help Desk agents working together can recognize when there are patterns within the incoming calls. With that knowledge the agents can pull together other resources if necessary to work on the solution. Your goal in creating a Help Desk is to recognize issues and get the root problem solved.

Promote Technology and Its Tools and Services

The Help Desk is in a prime position to promote technology to its customers throughout the company. The agents can quickly recognize areas where customers can benefit from technology and should use this opportunity to further advance the proper use of tools and services. The following lists some ways you can promote technology to your customers. These methods are not mutually exclusive, so you can explore and implement all of them over time.

- Use what you support
- Interact with users to show them how they can resolve issues on their own using technology

- Train users on the technologies
- Include examples and suggestions while customers wait on hold
- Hold technology fairs
- Create an innovative Technology Users group

Use What You Support

The biggest testament to any claim of a good thing is to see the proclaimer actually using the thing itself. Think about a chef in a restaurant. You see menu items that sound appealing, but you aren't sure how good they taste. Wouldn't it help boost your confidence in any item if you saw the chef eating it himself? Seeing your doctor work out at the gym reinforces the value of exercise far more effectively than if he were to sit on a stool proclaiming that exercise is good for you.

The same applies to technology use. Don't just roll out new desktops and printers to customers and tell them it will be better for them. Install the devices in your Help Desk, too. Agents can support these devices better, and customers can also see that you are using the same tools they are. If your Help Desk is using product A but makes customers use product B, you will create questions in people's minds. If customers see the Help Desk using the same tools and software to get their jobs done, it helps customers feel more confident that technology can help them as well.

From a positive standpoint, customers will think they are using strong technology if the IT department is using it. From the "misery loves company" view, customers will know that any problem they are experiencing is being felt by the Help Desk agents as well.

You can promote the shared use of technology in several ways. First, make sure it is visible on desks or in common areas. When customers approach the Help Desk or take tours of the building, they may not help but notice that the agents are using the same tools they are. This subtle display works better than simply proclaiming to the world that "We use what you do, too!" Another subtle, yet helpful, way to communicate this shared use of technology is to bring it into conversations with customers. For example, "Yeah, I see that problem too on my desktop," informs the user that not only has the agent heard of the problem, he has seen it himself as well. These are not loud, boastful claims, but they let customers know that the Help Desk can relate to their issues and problems. This creates a foundation from which you can promote the use of technology to your customers.

Interact with Users

You have an opportunity to teach technology while your customers are on the phone. Take some time to educate callers during the same phone or e-mail interaction they use to report a problem. This is a good time to make a point in a casual fashion, as if you are sharing a secret with them. An example is to use the phrases, "I just fixed it by … Did you know that you had access to this too by doing …?" These phrases have multiple advantages. First, you are informing users that you are indeed going to take care of their problem. This gets you by the "don't call me for this stuff" phase. Second, users learn how they can resolve the problem themselves and save time and a phone call the next time the problem happens. Last, you get callers used to looking for ways to resolve issues with the technology and becoming better informed about the services they have available to them.

Train Users on the Technologies

Probably one of the best ways to promote technology is to train users on it. If they can feel comfortable that this evil computer stuff can be easily handled, they will be more likely to use it in the future. If they can see that the technology can help them be more productive and efficient, they will go from reluctant use to a proactive request to use it.

The training can be formal, such as in a classroom environment, or informal, such as sessions with users at their desks. One example is how to change toner in a laser printer. This is basic stuff that does not require deep technical knowledge but may intimidate infrequent computer users. If the Help Desk can show people how to do this themselves, users will feel that much more comfortable around technology. At the same time, the Help Desk has eliminated many more calls to the agents on how to change a cartridge. No one will claim that changing toners is a giant leap for computer use, but it is another item to add to the foundation of empowered users in technology.

Related to the issue of technology training is training people how to use and apply technology in their business. It is good to know how to create tables or change fonts in a word processing application. Even more important is teaching users how to use this technology in their business. Take the word processor, for example. There may not be much need for a store manager to know how to use it when his administrative staff knows how. However, if you can educate him on the uses of it, the word processor becomes more valuable. You can show him how he can use list merges to quickly create mass mailings to advertise his business or promote upcoming sales. The Help Desk will have now spurred his creativity to think of even more ways to use technology to help his business. The Help Desk will also have created another partner and advocate of the Help Desk's effectiveness.

Include Examples and Suggestions While Customers Wait on Hold

If your phone system allows you to play messages while callers are on hold, use that opportunity to insert messages about technology. This medium is good for many things and promoting technology is one of them. You can inform the caller of examples of systems and processes that help out other customers in certain situations. Use it as a "Did you know that …" session with the caller. It may not stick with everyone but if it reaches even one caller every so often, you will have received a good return on a low-cost investment.

Hold Technology Fairs

What better way to promote technology than to display it right in front of people? Invite key customers to a demonstration of the latest technologies the business and IT department have deployed. Set up dates and times for senior management and other executives to attend. Make sure you gather people who can make decisions on the technology as well as those who would use it on a daily basis. Both sets of people can help promote the technology when they return to their locations.

Don't just have the technology sitting on a table, however. Connect it so the demonstration is live. Get a real user of the technology to work with it and speak about how it helps him in his business. The more people can see the tool in action, the more likely they are to see its benefit.

Either in a separate section of the fair or set up for another day, hold a technology fair for technology that is about to be implemented into the company or technology that exists in the marketplace, even though you have no plans to install it yet. This exposure to technology is good for non-IT people to see. It can also create some problems, as in, "Why don't we have that yet? It could really help me." The overall return is positive, though. If that is their reaction to new ideas, then when the time comes for you to budget for it, they will be more likely to approve it.

Create an Innovative Technology Users Group

Don't think you and the rest of IS are the only ones who can think of good uses of technology. The customer base who uses the technologies every day can be very creative when it comes to making things work in their business. They may not even be tools and services you know of or support. Before you go yanking them out of the business because they did not meet standards, review how they're used.

Reach Out to a Wide Audience   You may want to reach out to customers to proactively find out how technology is being used in the workplace. Seek out those customers who are innovative in finding tools or implementing them in ways that were not part of the original design. By doing this, you will have learned more and could possibly include it into your standard offerings. The technology itself does not have to be extravagant. You are looking for how it is being used that is not part of the normal operation within your company. To the outside world, the use may be mundane or even outdated, but if the technology is productive in your company, you want to be aware of it.

Spread the Word   Remember the goal to be a hub of information? Finding good ideas and spreading them around to the rest of the company helps everyone. Don't take credit for them; this is not the point. Instead, announce the creator of the idea to give him or her the credit. If customers don't see you as the bad guy, they will be more apt to tell you of other things going on. Know that these things are happening despite your wish to know all. By learning of these implementations, you at least have the opportunity to incorporate them into your databases or modify operations to make them work even better.

These are just some ways the Help Desk can play a part in promoting technology. Be judicious in its use, however. You don't want to be labeled a "use technology for technology's sake" kind of person. Technology must be used in ways that are real and valuable to users. The Help Desk must truly believe in technology or customers will see through the hype.

Remain Flexible

Time changes many things, and technology and customers' needs follow suit. If your Help Desk is rigid in its actions, it will quickly lose its effectiveness for customers. The following list itemizes several key areas that must be flexible in the Help Desk's design. They must be reviewed on a periodic basis to ensure their continued alignment with the Help Desk.

- Organizational structure
- Call routing procedures
- Standards
- Policies
- Agent skill sets

It is also important to review the technologies that are brought into the Help Desk. These technologies should be implemented in such a way that the Help Desk does not lose its flexibility or is forced to act in a certain way strictly because of the technology itself.

Buying a phone system could be an example. Automated phone systems are good technologies that can really help a Help Desk function more effectively. However, if it is rigid in its design and cannot be modified for many different situations, it may become more of a hindrance than a help. It would be bad if your Help Desk needed to be organized in a certain way with agents working in different groups but the phone system could not route calls in that way.

Organizational Structure

When you first begin, you have to organize your Help Desk somehow, and you do it with the knowledge you have at the time. It is important to keep watching the company and its customers to ensure your structure is still aligned with the way business is being conducted.

For example, you may have organized the Help Desk to work a certain number of hours that matched the business hours. Over time, the business may have expanded into different time zones and now works essentially longer hours. If you keep the staff coming in as you always have, you will not be providing office hours to the western users at the same hours as the eastern users.

Another example is if your company moves from a central mainframe environment to a client server setup. If this happens, the skill set of your agents will need to change to keep up with the technology. This environment is typically harder to support, so the organization chart may need to change also. Where you had a general pool of agents working on hardware problems before, you may now need a more specialized group to address server issues versus PCs or smarter desktops.

Call Routing Procedures

Call volume will be the main driver behind changes to your call routing procedures. Blindly requiring more and more callers to contact the Help Desk with no proper routing plan will lead to customer dissatisfaction. If you find through customer feedback that your routing scheme creates confusion or makes callers go through many people to get to the person they want, you need to change your routing procedures. What was effective at one stage of the Help Desk development can be cumbersome and counterproductive later on.

Standards

We will address standards later on in the book, but for now think of standards as establishing a common, approved list of hardware, software, and processes that should be used in the company and that will be supported. This list can include types of PCs, databases, or preferred vendors to use in certain situations. They are useful for ease of support, allowing quicker integration of new technology, and may allow for better discounts on pricing of items when arrangements can be made.

Standards Need to Be Current   Archaic standards do more harm than good. Standards by themselves can make customers rebel, but when the standards are out of date and do not apply to the current state of technology in the business, customers will flat out ignore them. On top of that, the Help Desk or whoever set the standard will lose credibility, and future initiatives will have a tougher time winning approval.

Old standards are hard to support as well. As the technology gets older, it will tend to break down more often. This begins an ineffective cycle. The vendor of the old technology will slowly (hopefully) phase out their own support of the product as they roll out newer and better ideas. Interfacing the older technology with newer technology will become more difficult, or maybe even impossible. New software might need more memory in the PC, but if your standards do not call for that much memory, the software may not work.

Beyond that, your recruiting efforts may begin to suffer as new recruits come to regard your organization as behind the times. Why should they work in your company when other companies are offering newer "toys" that require more marketable skills?

Review Standards Frequently   The type of organization you are in (remember Gartner's A, B, and C types?) should determine how often you review your standards list. If the company is constantly on the edge of new technology you will need to review your list more often than if the company is slow to implement new things. The key is to stay in touch with the business, the customers, and their needs and modify your standards when you find them out of alignment. Don't keep the standards list a secret, either. Publish it and keep it in front of the customers.

Policies

For the same reasons your standards should remain flexible, so should your policies. Policies are rules on how the game should be played, and as the game progresses, the policies and rules need to be reviewed. Sometimes this even means the addition of new policies or the complete deletion of existing ones. For example, if your company uses only a text-based e-mail system, you might have policies on the correct use of e-mail. There would be the standard ones about using e-mail for business only, whether e-mail could be reviewed by others, and maybe some about who could send e-mail to whom.

Now, what happens when your company goes to Internet e-mail that can have attachments with large space requirements or virus potential? If the policy is not flexible and reviewed often, the company will not be able to address prominent issues with this type of mail. It would seem perfectly acceptable for an associate to download large files of pictures and the like. Until the policy is revised to deal with this type of action, the company will be using resources to overcome problems it did not deal with in the past.

Agent Skill Sets

The Help Desk must maintain existing agents' skills as well as the attributes it looks for when hiring new people. As the IT standards evolve over time, so should the Help Desk's skills. This flexibility is required from both the Help Desk management and the agents themselves.

Management Is Responsible Management must always concentrate on updating and upgrading the skills of its staff. Allowing agents to remain in one technical area as the industry and your own company move forward to new areas will produce ineffective work from the agents and a loss of value to your customers. There will be no clear sign that the skill set is slipping against the technologies. However, you may be able to see it in the form of longer times to resolve problems and more frequent transfers of calls from one part of the Help Desk to another.

So Are the Agents The agents are in this requirement, too. They cannot remain inflexible and refuse to learn new skills. There are many instances of someone who has many years of experience in a technical area and is considered an expert in that field. What happens when the IT department replaces that technology with something else? Now the agent is an expert in a field with no one in it. This can lead the agent to evaluate whether he wants to remain in the company or move to another company where he can regain his expert status. If he decides to stay, he must embrace the new areas he will work in and strive to become the resident expert all over again.

Certifications If you track the skill sets of your agents by certifications, it may be easier to follow the skills of your Help Desk as they relate to the needs of your customers. We will speak about training and certification later, but it is important to note here. Training is not bad and it should not be ignored. The fear that well-trained agents will leave your company for better opportunities elsewhere is no reason not to train them. In fact, it's the lack of training opportunities, rather than too much training, that causes people to leave a company. Training broadens associates' skills and abilities and this breadth provides you more flexibility to tackle new issues that arise in the future.

Maintain a Proactive Workload

The executives and customers will surely load you and your group up with tasks and objectives. It is crucial that you find the time and resources to be proactive in your actions as well. Just as communicating events is proactive and helpful, so must you find other things to help your customers in their jobs. No one wants to just sit around and wait for the phone to ring. Challenge yourself and your agents to seek out core issues to resolve. Be seen as a leader, not just of people but as an advocate of the business as well.

Look for Ways to Enhance Efficiency

Always keep looking for ways to improve the business. The Help Desk is in a very favorable position to see how the business is doing and where its strengths and weaknesses are. Use that information well. An effective Help Desk can point people to training needs in a division or location. It can share Best Practices with its customers on the proper way to use technology. You won't need to come across as a business expert that can fix all the problems, but you can use the data you have gathered to let others come to the same conclusions you did.

Get Vendors to Be Your Eyes and Ears

One good way to stay proactive is to get your vendors to stay on the lookout for you. They are a prime resource for you to provide a third-party review of events that are taking place around you. These events may be internal, such as multiple people in the department getting quotes on technologies or services, yet the people do not seem to be aware of the others' work.

The events may be external. For example, vendors can provide you with product updates or new features about to hit the market. Manufacturers can give you ideas about their particular product lines, and resellers can provide options that cross multiple manufacturers. You may not need to rely completely on this input, but it can help serve as a guide or an item to balance other's thoughts off of.

Fix Issues Not Yet Reported

The Help Desk agent typically dives into hardware and software issues when a customer has a question or need in that particular area. Sometimes the agent can find a problem that was not called in, but was in the same general area. Resolve the customer's issue, but don't lose sight of the other problem. Go back to it and verify that it is indeed a problem. If it is, get the right resource working on it.

A great gain for the Help Desk is to resolve issues before anyone else even knows they were there.

Work Yourself Out of Business

Yikes, I am just getting started and you want me to fire myself? Am I supposed to sabotage the operations? No, of course not! I am not talking about firing yourself and your associates. In this section, we will look at how you can maintain an effective organization, even though some of the following methods may sound counterproductive to the obvious existence of the Help Desk:

- Allow customers to help themselves whenever possible
- Strive to reduce problems before they occur
- Do more with less
- Outsource where appropriate

Allow Customers to Help Themselves

The Help Desk should not have a goal to be needed by its customers. The best goal is that the Help Desk provides assistance to the customer base and the customers do not even recognize it. Does this sound funny or contrary to other information you have read? It shouldn't. The agents should always be there if necessary, but they should seek ways to empower the customers to help themselves. Provide them with alternate ways to obtain information. Provide the rest of IT and the business with information to make the product and services better so support is not needed for day-to-day issues.

You can help customers help themselves in a variety of ways. The Help Desk can document and distribute training material and Frequently Asked Questions and answers. It can create a Web page to inform customers on proper processes and best practices. Look for automation opportunities. If customers are always calling the Help Desk for certain things, see if the task can be automated or provided to the customer in a protected way. For example, resetting passwords is a common call into a Help Desk. If a program can be run from a screen or even a phone system, customers can reset their own passwords and not need to directly involve the Help Desk. Using technology to compensate for human intervention will be a theme expressed many times throughout this book.

Finally, analyze all the rules and procedures to ensure the IT department has not created bureaucratic processes that slow down the customer without providing more value overall. By reducing the need to "get permission" to perform certain tasks, you have empowered the customer more and reduced calls to the Help Desk at the same time.

Reduce Problems Before They Occur

Another strategy to reduce call volume is to work on reducing the core root of problems instead of just fixing the symptoms over and over. An industry term for this is call avoidance. Figure 3-4 shows the different stages of calls and problems, but also points out your primary goal.

Solving the call is a short-term fix that helps the customer for the moment. Fixing the problem that caused the call is lasting and ultimately more effective in the long run. Here are some suggestions for how you can fix underlying problems:

- Make time to discover the root cause
- Get as much detail on the problem when it is called in as possible
- Review call logs to uncover trends
- Have a contest to discover the root cause of long-lasting issues
- Talk to your agents

Discover the Root Cause   A Help Desk agent's world is constantly moving and changing. His primary mission seems to be to fix as many calls as fast as he can. As soon as customers hang up, there is another call, e-mail, or fax waiting for the agent's attention. In this environment it is extremely difficult to fix problems instead of calls.

Therefore, you need to modify the environment to tackle the deeper issues. This doesn't have to be drastic. Instead, it could be as easy as giving agents a break from the phones every couple of hours. During this time, they can focus on open issues with more concentration than when they are being interrupted by ringing phones or people standing over their shoulders. For this to happen

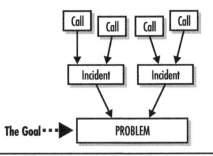

Figure 3.4   Calls, incidents, and problems revisited

best, the agents should be allowed to leave their desks and work from a different desk. Some agents may feel more comfortable and productive at their desks and that is fine. It will just be more trouble when people walk up and need their help and the agents tell the customers they are busy. To get around this problem, the agents should move to a common area that has all the available tools. Taking this time away from the hectic environment of the Help Desk helps agents investigate and resolve the root causes of problems.

How you staff the Help Desk can come into play here as well. If you staff the Help Desk with just enough people to answer the phones in an acceptable way, you will be forced to live with recurring problems for long periods of time. If you hire more agents, even one more, to answer the incoming calls, you will have an opportunity to devote more resources to nagging problems. Do not think of this as overstaffing because all agents will be busy and productive. The group will just be able to move people around to focus on different aspects of problem resolution without adversely affecting incoming call support.

Showing the agents why this deeper research is important and how it will lead to greater things will help give them more incentive to do the work. They shouldn't worry that fixing a problem that produces an extra ten calls a week will cause them to lose their jobs. Instead, they will have fewer calls to answer and more time to spend on training or other projects. Along with this, give your agents credit for finding solutions or even clues to a solution. Self-satisfaction and reduced call volume are terrific incentives; good, old-fashioned recognition is even better. The impact of the problem can help you decide how public to make the acknowledgment. Some "attaboys" may be simple e-mails of thanks; others may be as big as a memo to senior management and the customer base that was affected. Make the agent a hero in the minds of the people who will no longer be impacted by the now-solved problem.

If you can help it, don't develop a "clear the logs" attitude. This attitude comes about when certain problems have lingered around for so long that you decide they will never be solved. You tell the agents to live with the temporary solution or workaround as the normal course of action. Once deleted, the history of the problem is lost and must be re-created if the need to resurrect it develops.

Get as Much Detail on the Problem When It Is Called In   Again, in the hurried world of a Help Desk agent, it becomes real easy to hear what you need to hear to answer a question or fix a problem. To resolve an underlying problem, it is necessary to get as much information from the caller as you can.

Think about taking your car into a mechanic for repair and leaving a note on the windshield describing the problem (see Figure 3-5).

Dear Sir,

My car is not working right. After some amount of driving it just cuts off. Please fix and I will be back later to pick it up.

Figure 3.5 A note to the mechanic

Odds are that when you returned to pick up your car, it would still have a problem, if it was even looked at in the first place. With no name or phone number, the mechanic could not call you for more information, either. The interaction between you and the mechanic would have been far more productive if your note had included a more detailed description of the problem as in Figure 3-6.

With this additional information it is easier to determine that the car ran out of gas but had no other problems (besides the driver). This extreme example is used to test your empathy with the plight of a customer. Help Desk agents can come up with the funniest stories of "stupid user" calls that easily rival this example in its obvious answer.

The simple goal of this method is to ensure that frontline agents get as much information as they can when the customer calls in. Record it in your call log so it can reviewed later by the agent or by others if necessary. If your agents are new, provide them with a template of questions that must be answered before they allow a customer to hang up or leave. Call management software will automatically give you this template, but if you do not have this feature, you will have to create one on your own. It doesn't have to be formal, but it should be used and reviewed. There is a drop in effectiveness every time a second-tier support person or group has to get back with the frontline agent to follow up on details that are missing from the logged call.

Dear Sir,

My car is not working right. After many hours of driving, the car starts to sputter and eventually it cuts off. I have a bright light on my dashboard that looks like a gas tank whenever this happens. I call a tow truck and they fix it every time. You can reach me at 555-1414 if you need more information.

Marc Tredeau

Figure 3.6 A better note to the mechanic

Review Call Logs to Uncover Trends   Now that you have captured the details in your call logs, you can begin your trend analysis. This review can uncover very valuable information that would not have surfaced otherwise. As soon as your Help Desk is staffed by more than one person, you will start disseminating information, and the work to combine it all gets harder. Unless you have effective internal communications, one agent may not know that another agent has been receiving the same issues he has. One problem could be causing several calls, yet the Help Desk overall does not recognize the calls as having any commonality.

The review process can yield good clues to the root problem. For example, looking at the locations calling in may show that a particular server or piece of the network is faulty and needs to be looked at. Similar calls at the same time of day or year may reveal a batch job that is corrupting data. Even finding the trend of a particular customer calling in repeatedly on issues may show you that they need some job or system training no one in the business has noticed. If the caller always gets his answers from the Help Desk, he may look productive to his manager but he really is a drain on company resources.

Accuracy is therefore extremely important when calls are logged. What may appear to be dreaded administrative work for a busy frontline agent may be a gold mine of treasure for other IT associates tasked with researching causes of problems. Those agents working on a problem will have wasted much time in research if they find out late in their work that the problem was not really happening in the location or manner in which it was logged.

This accuracy is also important from an ongoing training viewpoint. If a new agent is reviewing call logs for a solution to a problem he has and he finds one, he should use it. What happens if the solution was wrong? The agent has now implemented a bad fix to a problem. The problem will remain unresolved, and the customer will lose confidence in the agent. The agent will lose faith that any other solution found will be accurate or work as well. Worse yet, the initial problem may have been compounded in scope with the introduction of the bad fix. For all the reasons mentioned above, time should be taken to review solutions in your own database. Once found, a bad solution should either be fixed, clarified, or removed completely from the database.

Have a Contest to Discover the Root Cause of Long-Lasting Issues   There will be times when a problem has existed for so long that agents' careers have come and gone without anyone finding the root cause. Yet if the Help Desk is still dealing with the problem after all this time, it is worth investigating the root cause. For these types of issues, consider having a contest to fix the problem.

Tell your Help Desk agents and managers, other IT department members, and even your customers about this contest. Give them all the information you can on the particular problem, including examples and what work has been done to date. Have a gift certificate for dinner or some other prize for the person who can find the root cause first. The prize does not need to be, and should not be, too extravagant. You don't want an environment where people intentionally don't resolve issues in hopes of getting a larger prize later on. Make it fun, don't have a lot of rules, and encourage people to help each other. The contest is productive and can actually teach people about technology along the way. If the problem gets solved, it will be worth the price of a gift certificate!

Don't have time for this type of problem hunt? If you answer yes, it probably means you feel as if you don't have time to train, either. You are encouraged to find time for this event even if it is not formal or rewarded with a prize. Otherwise, you will remain busy working on calls that will keep coming in based on the same root cause.

Time is important and the phones don't stop ringing, it seems. So have these contests during slack times of the day or year. Maybe Friday afternoons bring in a slower call volume. Perhaps the winter months are slower for the business and therefore slower for the Help Desk. Whatever the case for your Help Desk, pick the best time for the agents to participate. You should watch that they don't spend all day troubleshooting the problem. To get around this, impose time limits. Give all the participants a certain number of hours to devote to this exercise. You do have a Help Desk to run and serving your customers must always be a high priority. Just recognize that this work also serves your customers, just in a different way.

Talk to Your Agents   Many fancy tricks and practices can help you fix problems at the root level. One basic but very important practice is having regular conversations with your Help Desk agents. These conversations can increase the agents' morale and also provide clues to other things at the same time. Ask your agents what types of calls come in most frequently and if they have any thoughts on why the calls are occurring. Don't just go through the motions—as you will only be wasting your time and theirs. Sometimes the most innocent remarks can trigger thoughts that can work wonders towards resolving long-standing, open issues.

Not all calls have a sinister, deep problem awaiting an unsuspecting customer and Help Desk agent. Unless you take it to an extreme, many times there is a fluke occurrence of a problem that will never repeat itself, but still generates a call. Other times, lack of complete, comprehensive training is the root cause. The point here is to go after the type of training that can reach the most people with the highest return on your training investment.

You may find that the best way to uncover training opportunities is to provide the call logs to the group responsible for providing the training. Let them look through the calls to uncover trends or groupings of calls that training can solve. You may need to help them understand any codes or categories you have implemented in your call logging routine, but after that they should easily be able to find issues to work on.

Do More with Less

Doing more with less means figuring out ways to provide more services and capabilities to the company and customers with fewer resources. This could mean eliminating cost, time, or people from the budget. When kicking off a campaign like this, it is easier on morale to work towards reducing the rate of growth in these resource areas instead of eliminating them entirely. People may be far more helpful in this goal if they are confident it will not endanger their jobs in the process.

Reduce Headcount Within the Help Desk   Headcount is always looked at during these times because it is easy to see and measure. Don't necessarily pursue a staff reduction campaign, but if your company is growing at a rate of 15 percent a year, work on ways to reduce headcount growth within your Help Desk by 10 percent, then 5 percent. Try to achieve a lower growth rate in your Help Desk as the rest of the company is expanding. This shows that you can grow with the business but do it more effectively (if you indeed are).

You can use ratios to measure headcount. Whether it is calls per agent, devices per agent, or customers per agent, capture the information now. Over time, while you are implementing your ideas, keep track to see if the ratios go up. For example, at the beginning you may have been able to support 200 customers per Help Desk agent. As the company grows and your processes mature, you may recount and find that you are effectively supporting 300 customers per agent. If so, communicate it aggressively to senior management. Show them that as the company or some technology is growing, your staff is growing more slowly. Management loves to look at headcount because of its high impact on the budget in many areas. Being viewed as an effective manager of this expensive and valuable resource will help you get more from senior management when you need it.

If you find the ratios slipping the wrong way, you will ultimately need to communicate this to senior management as well. Perhaps not as aggressively as with the good news, but you must convey that you at least are aware of the situation and have plans to overcome the trend. There is more respect for people who communicate conditions under any circumstances than for those who speak up only when there is something good to report.

Last, ratios are good to have around at budget and hiring times. If you have successfully communicated your headcount strategy based on ratios and senior management has approved your assumptions, it will be significantly easier to gain more resources when those ratios are over or under the plan. Don't hire or buy blindly on the ratios, but use them as reminders that, if nothing else, it may be time to look for more resources.

There are five main ways to get more things done with fewer resources:

- Work smart
- Use technology wherever possible
- Train agents and customers
- Take time to do it right the first time to prevent re-work
- Outsource where it makes sense

We will examine each of these strategies in the sections that follow.

Work Smart   There are many common sense issues we talk about throughout this book and getting your agents to work smart has to rank up there in its sensible approach. However, it would probably amaze you to find out how many processes you will have over time that are done merely because they were always done that way. The approach at the time of their implementation was not necessarily incorrect, but maybe it does not apply as tightly now as it once did.

For example, when a Help Desk started it may have had an agent who walked to people's desks in the building when they needed a PC fixed. Over time, the building turned into a campus of buildings and the agent still walked around. Fortunately, the company excelled and grew its offices across town. Depending on what else was happening in the Help Desk, no one may notice that the same agent is now driving around town fixing PCs. This is not necessarily bad but it is definitely a process that needs to be reviewed. You could look at how the agent's schedule was managed to ensure that he took care of all known problems in one building before he moved to the next. A smart process would implement a scheduling plan that routed the agent from problem to problem with his drive time factored in.

Working smart does not just imply performing a job intelligently. It also means working within a process that is developed intelligently. That travelling agent may be able to fix PCs with the best of them, but if the process he works under is flawed, his overall impact on the business will be devalued.

Use Technology Wherever Possible   For the most part, tools run on and on without needing reviews and salary increases and morale-boosting events. They run day and night and don't complain about their desk location or who sits next to them. The speed with which technology can process, store, and recall information is not even comparable to that of the best of Help Desk agents. Inserting technology into selected processes will allow greater amounts of work to be done without adding more people.

An example may be to put your documentation of processes on an intranet. The information is available at the agent's desk, and he can remain at his desk when he needs the information, rather than having to walk somewhere to get it. This technology is also easily updated and eliminates the need for someone to make and distribute copies of the updates to everyone who needs them.

Technology needs its own version of reviews, complaint processes, and upgrades. They come in the form of maintenance, system errors, and hardware and software upgrades. These can be expensive depending on what is needed. However, where there are opportunities to implement certain technologies for redundant and mundane tasks, it is wise to do so. This will free your existing agents for more creative work to help your customers and company be more productive.

Train Agents and Customers   A good way to get more work from existing people is to continually train them. This does not stop at the agents; it extends to the customers who need and use your computing services as well.

Training provides three advantages to your goal of doing more with less. First, it educates users on ways to do things that they did not know how to do before. This saves them time in the trials and errors of figuring out the process or technology. The quicker users can achieve what they set out to do, the quicker they can get back to their jobs and be productive, or more productive, again.

Second, the training exposes trainees to resources or avenues of information they may not have seen before. For example, if you point agents to a particular Web site for some hardware specifications and training, they will learn what they need to know on that subject. What this also does is show them that there are Web sites with good, relevant information. Now, when they have a question on something similar, they may use the Web site as a resource to find the answer.

The third advantage training offers is the inherent morale increase among your agents and customers. They may not show it outwardly, but investing time, money, and energy to train them shows them you care about their future. You may be doing it just to get them to do their jobs better, and they know that. However, they will also see their own skills increase and feel better about themselves within the company and the marketplace overall. This inward motivation is good and should provide them some extra energy in doing the jobs they set out to do.

The timing of this training can go a long way towards doing more with less. If you can plan certain training to occur right before events that normally trigger a large volume of calls, you get a quick return on your training investment. Examples could include technology implementations, year-end processing, or physical inventories.

Do It Right the First Time   Do it right. What a basic concept! Doing it right the first time is still basic, but it is not thought about as much. Think about this. You decide to make a cake for your spouse's birthday. You are almost done baking it when you realize you forgot a main ingredient. Without it, the cake won't rise. You toss it, mix in ALL the ingredients this time, and bake again. The cake finishes in time for the surprise party and everyone enjoys it.

What happened? The end result was just what was needed…a great tasting cake for your spouse. We could call that a job done right. What we would not call it is a job done right the first time. Depending on the situation, the costs could be small or large. You could have increased cost in time, money, and people. You could also have lost the opportunity to be doing something else. In the cake example, the cost of not doing it right the first time was in lost ingredients and the time lost that could have been spent decorating the cake more elaborately or wrapping a gift.

The business world brings a higher cost factor in most anything it does. Time is money and re-work only adds to time. Therefore, it follows that if your Help Desk is redoing work a second or third time, it is costing the business more money than is necessary. There are some other costs to not doing it right the first time, such as:

- If the Help Desk agents are spending time fixing a problem over and over, they are not working on other customers' problems.
- More staff is needed to handle the extra load of calls.
- Customers get frustrated when one problem always leads to another.
- The perception of the Help Desk is greatly diminished and its value to the business comes into question.

All this could be prevented with a careful approach to processes and procedures. Teach the agent the value of getting it right the first time and the results will begin appearing shortly thereafter.

None of this should undermine the importance of following up with your customers. Doing something right the first time may sound as if it eliminates the need to contact the customer after a problem has been resolved, but this is not necessarily true. Your solution to the problem could be right on, but the customer found something else. It may not be real important to the customer, but a followup call from the Help Desk agent to make sure everything is still fine would uncover that. The customer service points you could gain by following up on customer calls are well worth the time it takes to do it.

Outsource Where It Makes Sense

Sometimes there are opportunities to do more with less by simply letting someone else do the work. Finding low value added work that can be done by someone outside the organization is definitely a way to reduce headcount within the Help Desk. An example may be traveling to remote sites to fix hardware. If your Help Desk conducts large-scale customer satisfaction surveys as part of its mission, you may find that contracting with a firm to do this for you can help. As an aside, you may also get a more objective view of the work you are measuring.

At the same time, outsourcing work may reduce costs as well. When you factor in all the costs to recruit, hire, train, and compensate an associate, it can be cheaper to contract with an outsourcing partner to do the work for you. You need to consider many other issues when getting into an outsourcing arrangement, and we will cover these in several parts of the book. Suffice it to say for now that you should review your processes and services over time to see if there are ways to get other people to do some of the work for you. Don't do this to shirk responsibility, but to get as much value from your in-house agents as possible.

Quick Recap

- Do you have a good plan to find the senior management team and to know what to say to them when you find them? Are you aligned with your senior management team, and is the senior management team aligned within itself?

- Is the rest of the IT department on board with your plans for the Help Desk? Do you feel comfortable that everyone understands their roles once the Help Desk begins operations?

- Your vendors can help you in many ways. Have you identified your main partners and how they can help you in the future?

- How about your customers? Finding all of them can be tricky but is absolutely necessary. Are you comfortable with the technologies they use and the processes they are expecting from you?

- You should be adding some goals of your own to the mix. Do they align with the ones already in place between the Help Desk and its principal drivers?

- The information flow through an organization can make things easy or much harder than they should be. Are you ready to help facilitate this?

- As a vital IT department member, the Help Desk should be one of the strongest promoters of technologies. Do you have a plan on how to achieve this?

- Do you agree that one of your goals is to work yourself out of business figuratively? Even if you don't like the phrase, can you understand why it's good for your company?

CHAPTER 4

Defining the As Is

Up until this point you have been having conversations with people around their wishes and needs for the new Help Desk. You have probably debated some points and nodded your head politely at others. It is now time to go deeper and investigate the actual environment of your company and its customers. This process is called defining the As Is and represents the current state of affairs your Help Desk will be inheriting.

What to Look For

- Defining the As Is environment is very important to the effective design of your Help Desk. It helps you create a strong foundation of services that will be aligned with your customers.

- Many questions must be answered to better understand this environment. The first is finding out whom the customers have called for help up to this point. Learn what issues they called about, what services they were receiving, and what technologies they were using. You will need this information to provide appropriate services to your customers.

- Learn what methods they used to reach this help. They may have called or e-mailed or just walked up to the person. Find out if these contacts occurred at all times of the day or only in certain peak periods.

- Problems result when processes do not flow easily. You will need to know what customers did when their calls were not answered immediately.

- It is important to know what customers like and dislike about the help they currently receive. This information is essential to learning which processes to continue providing and which ones to never implement.

- The environment and culture of the company will shape your Help Desk in many ways. It will provide rules on how to act and expectations of what to wear and when to work. Your Help Desk needs to blend right in with these expectations.

The Importance of Defining the As Is Environment

Defining the As Is environment is important for many reasons. You took the time to interview the key drivers that will influence the Help Desk. This part of the process helps you understand what actually exists. The interviews had some of what exists and some of what they expect in the future.

Establishes a Foundation

The As Is provides the foundation from which your whole operation will form. This information will let you know the things that need to be fixed, the things that need to be done away with, and the things that need to be kept just as they are. Just as you want to fix issues that are broken, you don't want to tinker with things that are running just fine. Change for change's sake is not worth the time and energy. There will be plenty for you to do to prove your worth without changing the good stuff.

Helps You Get it Right the First Time

You will be defining many processes and procedures when you design the Help Desk. Instead of starting with a clean sheet of paper and hoping you understand all the issues out there, why not start with some notes? It would be impossible to organize the Help Desk and its agents without knowing what kind of customer expectations await you. Without knowing the technology that has been deployed, how could you know what skill sets you need in your agents? The goal of this deep discovery phase is to learn all you can and prevent as many surprises from springing up as possible.

Exposes Legal Matters

The As Is process helps you uncover any legal matters that may exist in the company or customer base. There may be contractual agreements with customers to provide a particular type of service in a particular way. It is one thing to design a process that is inefficient; it is entirely another to design one that is against the law. There may be service or maintenance contracts with vendors that don't terminate for months and years. If you design your Help Desk to provide those services, it won't be illegal but it will certainly be duplicating dollars to pay for that same service.

Questions That Must Be Answered

Assuming you understand the importance of this process and are ready to dig in, let's go over the main questions that must be answered to best understand the As Is environment. These questions are geared towards understanding the needs of your customer, but some also look at the situation surrounding the coming Help Desk. Getting the answers to these questions will put you in a perfect position to build your world class Help Desk.

Whom Did Customers Call for Help?

When customers needed computer help, to whom did they turn? Odds are they called one of three groups: someone in IT, a local expert in that area, or an outside partner as shown in Figure 4-1. While the goal is that customers will now call you, this research can help you in many ways. If nothing else, you will learn who else in the organization has computer knowledge.

The IT Department

Customers may have called someone in the IT department when they had trouble. Assuming you are creating a new Help Desk, this means the customers were interfacing directly with someone who was hired to do other technical work. Perhaps they were programmers, or LAN administrators, or network analysts. This experience was probably not optimal. The customers typically met a technical person who had other work he felt was more "pressing" to get done. The technical person was also pulled away from this work and had to go back to it at another time. The good thing about this scenario is that you have valuable information at your disposal under the same roof. The help provider is part of the IT team and you can get data more readily from him than from other providers.

Local Experts

Customers could have asked the person sitting next to them when they had a computer question. Or, they could have gone to the locally recognized "expert" and asked for help. The word "expert" has quotations around it because it does *not* imply a formally trained IT person who happens to work in another department. This "expert" has just worked with the product enough to know most of its nuances and the tricks of the trade.

An example could be Susan, the executive administrative assistant. All day long Susan works in Microsoft Office developing spreadsheets, memos, and presentations for the vice president. Because she spends so much time in these

Figure 4.1   Where customers go for help

applications, there are not many situations she has found herself in that she cannot resolve. She has attended a training class in Intermediate MSOffice, but that was a few years ago.

Word around the water cooler is that Susan is the one to go to with PC application questions. If she doesn't know the answer right off, she will work on it for you until she resolves it. This is a very common situation and is not terribly bad. At least not for the people who benefit from Susan's help. What about the expectations of Susan's boss for her work? What about the times she works long hours just to help someone else? Odds are this is not what her boss wants her doing all day long.

Knowing the local "experts" is a very beneficial piece of information for you to find. They can help you prepare for the type of problems the Help Desk will run into and who calls them in. They may even keep a knowledge database that can be used to quickly solve problems. This database may be a notebook somewhere, but don't turn down good information when it is in front of you.

Handle these local providers carefully if you want them to continue helping you over time. If you come in with the attitude "I am in charge now. I am a professional who will handle this better than you did," you will set the stage for a cold shoulder when you really do need their feedback. Being the new sheriff in town is okay, but gather up a posse of help instead of doing it alone.

There also may be experts in the company who are more subject matter experts (SME) than someone who just happens to sit close by. These people work in the environment to provide support where it is needed. For example, the purchasing agent in the logistics department could be considered a SME for any purchasing-related issues. Similarly, certain people in the finance department would be SMEs for accounting or budgeting questions someone may have. The title of SME probably does not exist anywhere, but those needing help will learn who these people are over time.

Outside Partners

The third option for people to find computer help without a Help Desk in place is outside resources, such as formal service providers contracted to resolve certain types of issues, or vendors and resellers who help customers out to maintain good working relationships. Get a copy of all contracts and agreements that have been established with these partners. There is typically a price tag associated with these services, so you need to understand the terms of the agreement early in the process. By reviewing the contracts, you may also find that there are discounts available if a formal Help Desk is in place. The partner can afford to do this by counting on the formal Help Desk to reduce the call volume the partner would have been forced to handle in its absence.

The terms and quality of work may be quite acceptable for areas of the business and you can leverage off this for the initial phases of the Help Desk design. Outsourcing partners gives you the opportunity to pick the areas you want to provide services for and the ones that can wait until you have achieved some success.

Qualifications for Providing Help

A good by-product when asking the "Whom did you call" question is learning the qualifications of the people providing that support. Did most of the daily issues require a strong technical associate in the IT department or was Susan the admin assistant strong enough for the job? Surely, this answer varies by type of call, but find out as much as you can about the skill sets used by those providing support before your Help Desk existed. This information will be invaluable to you when you sit down to write out job postings or job descriptions. You would not need to hire a ten-year veteran of IT departments for the Help Desk if a self-trained associate in the marketing department could easily handle 90 percent of the calls. Conversely, you would not be wise to hire a team full of entry level associates mixed in with interns if the calls were all handled by outsourcing partners and systems administrators.

The qualifications of the providers is important to understand. First, they inform you whose input to value more when discussing existing issues and processes. They also give you an idea of where potential problems exist. For example, Susan the admin may give one answer to a question that contrasts with someone else's answer. If it is just a different way to resolve a spreadsheet problem, that is probably okay. If the answers contradict corporate policy or guide a user down a path that will corrupt data, there will be deeper repercussions.

What Did Customers Call About?

Customers contact providers for two reasons: services and products. Service will include buying or installing something, fixing it, or removing it. In the case of the Help Desk, the product will be technology, whether it is hardware, a database, or an application.

Services

The services customers are accustomed to receiving need to be reviewed by you. You will have to decide whether to incorporate these services into the Help Desk or point the customers somewhere else.

One option you may have in this area is the customer's desire to perform the service themselves. For example, they may have software available to write their own reports from your business systems. This is a service a Help Desk can undertake in its responsibilities. However, if the customer wants to keep this ability and it is not part of your planned core competency, it would be beneficial to all concerned to allow the customer to keep this service.

On the other hand, customers may be accustomed to purchasing their own PCs and printers because there was no one else to do it. Some might not have felt comfortable doing it because they did not understand the technology but they had no choice. By interviewing them and getting this input, you will find a good opportunity to add value to the customer by the Help Desk taking on the service.

Technology

Next, find out what technologies your customer base has that they need help on. At some point you will need to differentiate for them which products you will support and which ones you will not. You may take on their PCs, printers, and scanners but not assume responsibility for their telephones and unique software applications. Don't discourage anything at the beginning; allow them to list everything they can. Save this information for future reference as your Help Desk grows in skills and aptitude.

You have two angles of attack when researching the technologies of your customers. One is an actual list of technologies they use and the other is the competency they have using them. We will cover the competency part first because it will impact how you gather the technology list.

Customer Competency in Technology Use   It will be great to know what technologies the customers have called for help on in the past. What is equally good to know is their skill levels in using the products. Their ability to use the technology will translate directly into their ability to resolve certain problems that arise. That ability then directly translates into the skill sets required of your Help Desk agents.

Extremely savvy customers who know everything about their product is not a sign that you don't have to have smart agents; in fact, just the opposite is true. Smart customers can fix the easy issues. Smart customers need even smarter Help Desk agents to get to the bottom of issues they themselves cannot fix. This can be tough as the customer works in the technology every day while your Help Desk agent only deals with it when there are problems. To battle this, you may need to organize the Help Desk into specialized groups where agents can dedicate training to the technologies that require the most attention.

The main advantage you can derive from your customer's technology competency at this stage is knowing how much help they can provide in listing the technologies out in the field. Taking it further, reasonably technical customers may be able to list the technologies, but they may not be able to give much detail about them. Some customers may refer to everything as a computer and be quite content to know that much. This is okay; in fact, it helps your job security for a while. You just need to know it up front.

List of Technologies The quickest way to find out the competency of your customers in their technology is to ask their help for an inventory. Go after equipment lists and asset information if it is available. Find out how old the systems are and what kind of maintenance contracts are on them. It will make a tremendous difference if your customers use high-powered PCs or dumb ASCII terminals. At this early stage of the game it is important to get a good feel for the lay of the land and the effectiveness of the system's use. If the inventory comes back with vague listings and references that don't line up, you should be alerted to the customer's skill level. Be careful to discern between a lack of understanding and a lack of time to compile it, however.

You also need to discover what software the customer is running. Your choice of support options will be affected if the customer is running a "home-grown" software package as compared to a business package available in the market. Home-grown software will more than likely require more support than an off-the-shelf or shrink-wrapped application. Most purchased applications come with options for support and maintenance. However, if your company has made extensive modifications to the software after it was purchased, finding readily available, affordable support for it will be more difficult. Odds are that even in a company that has programmed its own software, there will be niches of purchased software also.

Whether you ask customers to document the technologies themselves or you need to visit each customer site to get the information you need, you must get a firm handle on what is out there. Your customers may not have the time or technical knowledge to give you the level of detail you need to make good decisions, so you must be prepared to get it in some other way. Here are two sample questionnaires you can use to start the process. The first one, shown in Figure 4-2, is pretty generic and is best used when your agents are doing the work themselves. It serves more as a reminder sheet than a survey.

If you are sending the survey out to the customer to complete, you will need to make it more of a questionnaire than a few sections with blank spaces. Figure 4-3 shows a form more suited for this purpose.

Technology list for: _____
As of: _____

Desktops
> *Pentium II PCs*
> *3 Pentium II laptops*
> *All are running Windows 2000*

Software
> *Office 2000 on all desktops*
> *DME Corporation's accounting package and inventory mgmt are installed on respective halves of the PCs.*
> *There is a miscellaneous assortment of other packages they will send us once documented. I have a concern that there may be legal licensing issues here.*

Printers
> *2 HP Laserjet IV printers on the LAN*
> *2 are directly connected to PCs*

Servers
> *1 NT 4.0 server networked to the PCs*
> *Customers are complaining about repeated hardware failures so we may need to replace.*

Networking
> *Cabling in the building is brand new.*
> *There are 2 switches with the router connected back to HQ over a 256k frame relay line supplied by MCI.*

Figure 4.2   Customer technology survey

Once you get the form back, you can judge by the customer's response how much more detail you need. It may be significant enough that you need to send someone out to the customer's site. In any case, if the customer has technologies or models you are not familiar with, ask them to send you a manual your agents can study. If the manual is not enough, you may need to purchase that device or get a vendor partner to loan you a demonstration model so you can learn more about the product.

While these surveys are being returned, it is important to keep a running list of the findings. Categorize the technologies as best you can and add to the list as more surveys come back. Perhaps you could put some designation next to each item reminding you of technologies you are comfortable with versus those you need more training on and those that will become standard offerings. In the end, you will have a good picture of the technology landscape and can build the skill sets, standards, and support plans to best support it going forward.

Technology survey for _____   Completed by: _____

As of: _____

Hardware:

1.   What type of desktops are used in your organization? Please include manufacturer, model, quantity, and a general idea on when they were purchased. Any asset tags would be appreciated as well.

2.   What printers are used in the organization? Please include manufacturer, model, quantity, and a general idea on when they were purchased. Any asset tags would be appreciated as well.

3.   Any other special hardware like scanners, copiers, etc.?

4.   Do you have any servers in the company? Please include manufacturer, model, quantity, and a general idea on when they were purchased.

5.   What type of networking equipment do you have? This would include routers, switches, terminal servers, hubs, etc. Again, please include manufacturer, model, quantity, and a general idea on when they were purchased.

Software:

1.   What software applications are in use in the organization? Please break down by clients or servers. We will need software name, # of licenses, and a general description of their business use.

Networking:

1.   How are your locations connected together? Who is your carrier, what are the quantity and speed of lines, and what protocol is used?

Miscellaneous:

1.   Please include any other information that may be relevant to this survey. We would like to know all computer-related technologies you have so we may best serve you in the future.

Figure 4.3   Customer technology questionnaire

You will also need to start thinking of a plan for the technologies you will not support. This plan needs to include how you will communicate this list, what are the reasons for it, and how you will recommend the customers should get support. The good news is that they have not had a Help Desk before yours so they could just continue on as before. Even better is if you can provide a more effective support plan for them even if it is not your Help Desk that does it. This shows the customers you are not abandoning them, but actually helping them get better support.

Getting all this information from internal customers is significantly easier than getting it from an external customer. At least with internal customers you can find someone higher in the organization who can require them to sit down with you.

External Customers

For external customers, this is not so. If you send them a survey, they may or may not respond. It would probably be difficult to send an agent to each site to do the work as well. A way to obtain this technology information is to make it a prerequisite when external customers first sign up for your Help Desk services. Just as they will want from you a list of services and contacts, you should expect a technology list from them. If they return a patched-together list of technologies, it's okay because these technologies will be the ones you support. If the customers later say they have more products and you need to support them, you can ask for that list and give the customers an estimated time on when you can pick it up. The key is to get the information while both of you are negotiating the structure of the support plan.

Whether your customers are internal or external, it is wise to audit them periodically. An audit is recommended no more than once a year to validate the list of technologies you think are deployed compared to what the customer actually has. A good time to conduct this audit is when the customer calls in. If you have an asset management database, you can keep track of when the customer was last audited.

Tip

Use a different term than audit. It sounds very formal and maybe even oppressive. When discussing the audit with your customers, refer to it as "checking my records" or "validating what I show you having." This might help your customer be more cooperative.

When the customer calls in for a support issue and it has been awhile since he has been audited, take advantage of this opportunity to check what equipment he has. You don't need to make him answer before you help him with his problem, but it should serve as the opening of communication between you and the customer. Then you can call him back after a few days to follow up on the information.

How Did Customers Reach Anyone?

Researching whom the customers called for help will help you answer the question, "When you needed to contact someone for help, how did you reach them?" The information you need will come in the form of contact medium and timing.

Contact Medium

Contact medium is a fancy way to describe the method customers used to contact the help provider. It could have been the telephone, fax, or e-mail. The customer might have walked downstairs to the local "expert" or completed an Internet questionnaire for an outsourcing partner. The medium is obviously a critical piece of information you need to design the Help Desk you are building.

The medium will aid you in organizing the Help Desk and in understanding technologies to consider implementing. If all the customers are used to phoning in their problems, you may organize the Help Desk with call takers and problem fixers. As the call volume increases, you may find opportunities to implement phone system technologies to help you route the calls to the correct agent to resolve them.

On the other hand, if you find that all your customers would walk to the Help Desk with issues, you would not need to purchase fancy headsets for the agents to help them with long phone conversations. It may point you to installing electronic display boards throughout the building to disperse information to the customers and save them walk time. If customers could look at a status board to see the LAN was down, they would not waste time walking to the Help Desk to report the problem.

Timing

By researching timing issues, you may learn the patience levels of your soon-to-be customers as well as the hours of operation you will need to establish with your Help Desk. This alignment is important to best satisfy the customers' needs.

Patience Levels   Unless you unleash some psychological testing on your customers, you will not directly learn how patient your customers are. What you can discover is the amount of pain they will endure before they get upset. How? Ask them what they do when the system goes down. Do they wait five minutes, get some coffee, then return and hope all is better? Do they complain loudly to anyone who walks by that the stupid computer is down *yet* again? What if the problem occurs real close to quitting time? Does the customer decide this is fate and head for home, or will he stay and demand that someone fix the problem before *anyone* goes home? In addition to these questions, you need to find out if the provider can work with customers remotely or must be in the office at any given time.

The situation will drive much of their patience but it is good to keep in mind. This pain threshold will help you design communication parameters and escalation procedures.

Hours of Operation   Research that does not hint at psychological profiling is finding out when customers are at work and when they call their provider for help. Do they need help from eight to five o'clock or at all times of the day? Are there more calls in the morning or in the afternoon? Aside from volume, are there critical business functions that must occur at certain times of the day, week, or month that will demand a higher level of support than at other times? Finally, do customers dial in from home and work late at night or at any other nonbusiness hours?

Answers to these questions will factor heavily in the design of your Help Desk. They will point you to staffing levels and office hours. If the business requires 24-hour support, even a low volume of calls would overwork one agent. Nice, easy business hours with heavy volume would require more agents as well. The criticality of the business will help determine the times you actually have staff at the desk. If agents can walk customers through possible solutions over the phone, you can spread your staff farther and wider by allowing them to work from pagers or cell phones. If the customer's issues could result in millions of dollars of exposure or other significant impacts, you may need the staff closer to home (as in the office).

What Processes Were in Place to Facilitate This Interaction?

We are getting closer to an overall understanding of what awaits us once the Help Desk is created. The thing we are missing is the interaction piece. There are some questions that must be answered so we can best understand how the customers dealt with the Help Desk in daily activities. The questions include:

- What if no one was there when a customer needed a problem solved?
- How was communication handled between the customer and the help provider outside of calling in a problem?
- How were priorities handled?

No One Was Available When a Customer Needed a Problem Solved

Finding out what actions a customer took when there was no one to help them with their problem will give you good information about their patience levels, as we discussed earlier, and the need for Help Desk staff at certain times.

Let's say Mitch could not figure out how to make Microsoft Project work the way he wanted. He asked around and learned that Beth in Finance was a whiz in Microsoft applications. He found out what floor she worked on and headed her way. Once he got there, he discovered Beth was out for the day. He was really in a hurry so he started asking around again for help. After several others tried in vain to help him, he gave up. All he could do was wait for the morning and hope that Beth would be in.

These customers are great to have. They try for help but if they cannot get it, they wait until they can. Not all are like that. Some may be used to leaving messages on voicemail or on a note stuck to someone's desk. They accept that no one is immediately available, but do assume that they will be contacted at the first possible moment. This "leave a message" medium is good to learn so you can transfer it into your Help Desk operations.

One person on one occasion does not make a complete case for how to staff a Help Desk, but if the trends continued in that way, you could realize which applications were deemed more mission critical than others. From there, you ensure that you have staff trained in those technologies available during the same hours the users are at work.

How Communication Was Handled Between the Customer and the Help Provider Outside of Calling in a Problem

This communication piece is to understand how the customers and help providers interacted when there was not a problem actually being reported. Three examples include problem status, coming events, and knowledge bases.

Problem Status   Once the customer asked someone for help and the problem was not solved while he stood there or waited on the phone, how did he get the ultimate answer? The provider may have been in the "I am only doing you a favor" mind-set and will let you know the answer only when you call back to find it out. After all, the provider's job is not to help you on any problem you run across. On the other end, the provider may have been a contracted hardware repair organization that has agreed to follow up with customers with a status report every hour.

Coming Events   This communication works both ways. From the help provider to the customer it would include informing them of scheduled downtime or other events that would impact the computing services of the customers. Without a formal Help Desk, this communication is probably not high on the list of the providers.

Communication could also take place from the customer to the help provider. It could be in the form of telling the provider of special work nights where many people would be using the computer during odd times. This would be beneficial to alert the providers to not schedule system maintenance or to be available for questions. Again, without a help function dedicated to the cause of customer service, this type of communication may fall on deaf ears. After all, why would an administrative assistant care about another department working late?

Knowledge Bases   Knowledge bases are places, physical or logical, where information about certain issues is stored. Typically there are databases where people have entered information about things they have run into. This will be helpful if you can find any existing knowledge bases that someone has kept for prior computer issues.

The data may be kept by either the help provider or the customer. The help provider might have logged calls from the customers in case the issue came up again. The customers may have kept information for the same reason. In that case, it may be in the form of "helpful hints" or "computer reminders."

This is beneficial to you because it can give you a head start on the common issues your customers have encountered over time. You can see who calls, what they call about, and possibly find out hints to resolving issues you might not have been aware of.

How Priorities Were Established

What are the current expectations about call prioritization? Are the customers used to a "who screams the loudest" methodology or "who has the best job title"? If someone called in a problem in the morning, were they used to being answered by the afternoon? Were there any priorities at all, or was it just first in first out? You may find that prioritization in an informal setting occurred only if a higher job title got involved. Why would the resident Microsoft Office expert who was an administrative assistant to Finance care about fixing a problem for Human Resources if she got busy herself? She probably would not unless her boss or the HR boss instructed her to do so. And if that happened, politics may get involved and everyone gets unhappy.

Priorities involve escalations much of the time. Do the customers expect the help provider to escalate their problem higher in the organization if it has not been resolved after some amount of time? Does the very nature of the call imply other managers will be informed? Formal Help Desks provide a much easier and more effective method for this to happen. Again, if helping others is only a part-time job, it will get only part-time attention. External service providers will have more concerns than a local "expert," but even then the attention may be split among many other customers. At this stage, understand what the customers are used to and incorporate that into your initial planning.

What Do Customers Especially Like and Dislike?

This information gives you a good feel for customers' wishes and expectations. You can gain this knowledge by reading between the lines of their answers to these questions:

Question: "Whom did you call when your PC had problems?"

Answer: "I called our outsourcer, Ray Computing. It took them forever to call me back, though. We always tried to fix it ourselves before bothering to call them."

Discovery: You know there is an external partner who may have historical data for you. You are also reminded that callbacks are important and will show an immediate improvement over the current situation.

Question: "I noticed the "low toner" light is on your laser printer. Who puts in a new one?"

Answer: "Again, Ray Computing. They come in once a week to see if things like that need replacing. It would be much quicker if we could keep a stock ourselves and just do it."

Discovery: Another tick mark for the external service provider. It may also be an opportunity to empower the customers to take on some work themselves. This could reduce their waiting time, reduce the cost of the service provider doing it, and prevent a low-value added function to enter the design of your Help Desk.

Question: "What hours do you work?"

Answer: "The advertising group works from 7:00 A.M. to 6:00 P.M., Monday through Friday. There is weekend work about twice a year but we don't mind too much. I tell you, though, the IT department seems to always be available. We tease them about how they leave early, but when I call them on their cell phone, they respond immediately and resolve my issue within minutes. I don't know how they get into the computers from wherever they are but they do."

Discovery: OK, you picked up that there is infrequent weekend work you may need to plan for. You know the hours they work, which may impact your staffing hours. And finally, you know they appreciate a quick response regardless of whether the staff is in the office or not. All good things to keep in mind as you get closer to the design phase.

The other way to discern customers' likes and dislikes is simply to ask them. Your question could be direct such as, "What do you like and dislike about your computing help?" The other way is to get them to be more of an owner of the process. Include them in the design phase or at least in the appearance of it. For example, "If you were building a group to do all those things we have been talking about, what would you change? Also, what would you keep the same?" Now you have given the customers the direct ability to express their thoughts on how things should work.

This method of asking has the advantage of putting some extra work on the people you are talking to. It is easy to say, "I hate when this or that happens." See if you can get them past that and to suggest what they would do about it. Don't appear clueless and that you won't be able to fix it without their help, but it is nice to see what they come up with. It may be an extremely enlightening idea that will help greatly, or it may force them to sit back and admit to not having an answer. Their inability to fix the problem in their own mind is fine. It may just show them that the solution is not as easy as they think it is.

What Is the Environment Like in Which the Help Desk Will Be Placed?

Look around and see what departments surround you and will impact you. Is the development staff close by physically or logically? Their ability to help you with issues will be very nice and your ability to reach them easily will come in handy. Same goes for networking, systems administration, or LAN managers. Physical location will help determine how you transfer calls. For example, if all resources you need for help are in another building, you will have to develop a process for getting their calls and details differently than if they were in the office next to you. Phone calls and e-mails will have to take the place of a quick walk down the hall.

Is the Executive group close by? They may expect a very formal work environment, so group pizza parties each Friday may be frowned upon. Bells and alarms going off when certain system thresholds are reached may cause disturbances to the very people you don't want to disturb.

Help Desks are typically noisy places to work. The sharing of information and teamwork in resolving problems points to an open work environment that uses cubicles more than offices. Because of this, the daily noise levels are loud regardless of extra bells or alarms. If nothing else, there will always seem to be phones ringing. Positioning one Help Desk agent next to the legal department and its quiet demeanor may work fine. However, a Help Desk of 300 agents may need to be far removed from anyone else who needs to think. (This is not a slam on Help Desk intelligence; it is quite the opposite. Help Desk agents can think logically and creatively under the worst of conditions.) Your Help Desk may start with one agent and you may not need to worry about all this; however, it is suggested that you plan for the success of your Help Desk, and anticipate growing its headcount to much more than the original agent.

Regardless of the closeness of other groups, it is wise to acquire furniture that is designed to keep noise levels down. Foam walls and wall designs can absorb or deflect noise to keep conversations and other factors to a minimum. This need is magnified when the location of the Help Desk is in close proximity to other departments or individuals.

Company Culture and Your Help Desk

While researching all of this, you will begin to see the culture that exists at the company. If you are already an associate you may know it well, but this exercise will show you angles you might not have noticed before. What are the patience and tolerance levels when things go wrong? You will start seeing that some groups need every problem solved immediately and others are less dependent. Some areas have good budgets and can afford to pay for high levels of support. Others may have limited resources and can only hope someone will help them when needed.

You can determine the company culture by speaking with many different people. Talk to people on each end of the organizational chart. Speak to data entry clerks and shop floor workers. Talk to middle managers and department heads. Glean as much as you can from your initial conversations with the senior executives. These can be casual conversations; in fact, don't walk around with a clipboard asking questions. The answers you get may be different from reality because you may be viewed as a "spy" reporting back to the boss. The input you get will be far more valuable if it is viewed as coincidental or without major ramifications.

Culture will tell you many things about the design of the Help Desk. As an example, it will tell you not only the hours the business works, but the hours the business expects. This can be far different. Business hours may be 8:00 to 5:00. However, it may be viewed negatively if you leave before 5:30 or 6:00.

Another example is dress code. There may be a written policy that business casual is accepted. Understanding that there is an expectation that business casual does not apply to managers, or that the CEO approved the policy but doesn't like it, may get you to act differently. You may not change, but you are least making an informed decision when you create your own dress code expectations.

You can get a handle on these unwritten expectations only by speaking with people. Designing your organization with this in mind will give you a higher chance of succeeding than if you just sat down and wrote out a plan.

Don't dismiss the importance of culture. Fast-paced, high-growth companies need an entirely different set of services than laid-back, informal organizations. Aligning yourself and the Help Desk with the proper mind-set will save you numerous problems down the road.

Quick Recap

- Why is defining the As Is so important? Can you answer all the questions presented in this chapter off the top of your head? That is saying a lot if you can. It might be saying a lot if you just think you can.

- Who provided the computer help for the customers? Were there more local "experts" than you thought there were? Hopefully, the help providers kept some information on the type of calls they took and how they were resolved. Don't be surprised if they did not.

- Do you know the technologies you will need to support? There will probably be some you will not be able to support right from the beginning, so you need a plan to handle and communicate that.

- What hours does the business work? Do you know yet what hours the Help Desk will work? You don't need an exact layout yet, but you should have all the information you will need to make that decision.

- Do you have a communication plan in mind? We will speak about call routing and internal communication ideas in the next chapter, but you need to have a feel for what the company and customers are used to. You will have to meet that need and improve on it in the future.

- The customers will be more than willing to tell you what works and what doesn't. Do you have a plan for how you can go after this information?

- If you are already in a company that wants you to build a Help Desk, you probably know the environment and culture. If not, be thinking about the people you can talk to who will give you the information you need.

CHAPTER 5

Define the Help Desk Processes

It is now time to put everyone's ideas into a plan and draw the blueprint for the Help Desk! This plan will serve as the foundation for everything else you develop over the life of the Help Desk. Getting it right from the beginning will save you time and money over the long run.

What to Look For

- Moving to the "To Be" world involves the actual design of many of the processes your Help Desk will practice. The processes will inevitably change over time, but you should get it as right as you can from the start.

- Designing your call flow is very important. There are many ways to do it and some will be discussed here. This is a foundation piece of the Help Desk process so you need to generate some ideas after this part.

- Problem handling makes up the core of your Help Desk's function. This design will set the stage for the agents to operate within the Help Desk. Without proper problem handling, customers will quickly grow frustrated with your Help Desk.

- Communication between all parties is a must for the Help Desk. It begins with internal communication and points out from there. The Help Desk must be able to pass along information effectively to achieve its goals.

- Everyone needs to understand their responsibilities from the beginning. Your agents will understand what is expected of them as you hire and train them. You will also need to communicate these responsibilities and expectations to your customers and the rest of the IT department.

Now it's time to put it all together and design the Help Desk and the processes within which it will operate. The company needs to start seeing action from you. Talking about it has been fine; now they want to see something real.

Because you were picked to start up or fix this Help Desk, you probably have some ideas on how you want it to work. You have the benefit of interviewing senior management and a sampling of the customer base to understand their needs and expectations. Last, you also know how things have worked up to this point to give you a foundation. The following lists the primary items you need to include in your design:

- Mission statement
- Determine the services the Help Desk will provide

- Define standards
- Hours of operation
- Call routing
- Problem handling
- Notification
- Customer responsibilities
- IT department responsibilities
- Internal communications

We will cover each of these in detail in the following sections.

Mission Statement

A mission statement is a declaration of the ideals you hold for your organization. It is written and distributed so others in your organization, and those dealing with your organization, can also understand and practice these ideals. The mission statement should set the direction of the Help Desk. It will describe the purpose of the Help Desk's existence and how you fit into the business. Several steps are involved in the mission statement life cycle:

1. Creating it
2. Publishing it
3. Reviewing and revising it

Creating a Mission Statement

Mission statements can be one phrase or paragraphs of thoughts and goals. Some people take weeks of brainstorming to formulate them; others take several minutes to write down what they already hold true. Bring people and their ideas into the process. If you get other people involved in the mission statement, they should come away with some sense of ownership around its message.

To ensure that this process does not take months and many people's valuable time, you may want to answer the following questions and ask the same questions of the people from whom you want input:

- What goals do we want to achieve in the workplace?
- What goals do we want to achieve outside the workplace?

- Whom will we interact with in the workplace?
- Whom will we interact with outside the workplace?
- Are there particular ways and methods we want to employ to achieve these goals?

These questions are very basic but they go after the complete foundation of the mission statement. What do you want to do, with whom will you interact, and in what manner do you wish to do it?

Many mission statements capture ideals around customer service, reaching corporate goals and alignment, personal and professional growth of the associates, and maybe some thoughts around contribution to the community. Wow! That's some heady stuff, especially for those who can get it in one phrase or sentence. There are no strict rules or requirements for formulating a mission statement but here are some guidelines you should follow:

- Keep it simple.
- Keep it realistic.
- Don't set unattainable goals.

There is nothing wrong with a statement of "Be the Best" if that is all you can come up with. Just make sure you come up with something because mission statements are worth having. A formal mission statement does not have to be the first formal step you take in designing your Help Desk processes, but you should write one early in the process. Here is a sample mission statement:

IT Support Center
Mission Statement

Our mission is to support and service the customers of DME Corporation
with any computer problem or request in a timely and professional manner.

The mission statement in the preceding illustration sounds kind of bland and uninspiring. It is short and makes a good point, but will it lead your associates to work hard and with enthusiasm? How about this one instead?

DME Help Desk
Mission Statement

- To provide quality customer service to the system users of DME Corporation
- To act in an ethical and professional manner in all interactions we encounter
- To provide a challenging workplace for associates to further their personal and professional careers
- To continually look for new ways to use technology in the business to increase profitability and productivity

---

This mission statement has more of a bite! It describes a mission to help customers. It describes a mission to help the Help Desk agents help themselves. Last, it directs the agents to help the business itself become stronger and better.

Publishing the Mission Statement

The previous example of a mission statement would look good on the Help Desk wall or in front of the business leaders. Whether you print the mission statement and hang it on a wall or you print it on display cards for everyone's desks, you must make sure the document is visible. We are talking physically here but visible in the back of everyone's mind also applies. You may publish it only as a reminder to people of your goals or you may distribute it everywhere and practice its words constantly. To test whether the statement has made it into the agents' minds, quiz them every so often. They do not need to know the answers verbatim, but they should respond with the general principles. If your agents are unclear about the statement's goals and objectives, you need to do a better job publishing it.

Reviewing and Revising the Mission Statement

A five-year-old mission statement may be perfectly applicable to the business, but you won't know unless you review it periodically. You should review the mission statement to ensure its alignment with your goals once a year or after any major technology or customer shift. Get other agents involved, as well. Just as they helped in creating it, they can have good input into editing it if necessary.

You should avoid modifying your mission statement too frequently. This may be okay in the beginning when you are still figuring things out, but after a while the mission statement should be able to stand strong overall without many changes. Goals in life change as marital status, children, and jobs change, but your mission in life probably stays pretty constant. Help Desk processes are not as important as your life, but its goals, if well conceived, should be constant as well.

Determine the Services the Help Desk Will Provide

Mission statements express lofty goals of support policies, customer and associate care, and corporate beliefs. Documenting your Help Desk's services is an important and required part of the design process. Without such documentation, you have no place to start the design process and no way to tell customers what you can do for them. The good thing is you have a starting place determined for you already. Remember those senior managers who gave you this job? They probably expressed some wishes and guidelines for you to follow. Now put these wishes on paper. You spoke to customers too, so add their ideas to the list as well. You also had some of your own goals so put them in there, too. See? This wasn't that bad. Here are some examples of services your constituents may have included or you can look at adding:

- Help us bring newly acquired companies onto our computer system
- Keep up with the hardware and software we have
- Keep track of any changes to the technologies as they happen
- Train customers on simple procedures
- Fix any hardware problems at the customer's site
- Hook up hardware once it is purchased
- Buy the hardware for me to begin with
- Coordinate resources to get things done
- Test hardware and software before it is installed or when changes are made
- Add and delete users on our network
- Write basic reports for customers
- Answer questions about our hardware and software
- Help install other technologies the R&D group comes up with

That is a pretty extensive list to choose from, but it does get at the needs of your customers and if effectively done, will show everyone the value of your Help Desk. As you begin comparing your list of services to other organizations' services, you may find that they don't line up well. Let's take one quick moment to line up the services listed earlier with more industry-aligned terminology (Table 5-1).

Phased Implementation

Many Help Desks will not be funded to start with such an aggressive list of services. Perhaps the executives wish to see a proof of concept before they invest significant dollars to the group. The recent budget cycle may not have had enough funds to cover all these ventures, either.

If this is the case, you may want to institute a phased implementation of Help Desk services. By phasing in the Help Desk's services you gain two benefits. First, you allow yourself to learn from each phase and can fix any problems before you are consumed by the next rollout of services. Second, the business has a chance to see your Help Desk in action before it invests even more dollars in you. Put this plan into a document so you can "shop" it by the executive. Once you get his agreement on

Customer Request	Translates to ...
Help us bring newly acquired companies onto our computer system	Acquisitions integration
Keep up with the hardware and software we have	Asset management
Keep track of any changes to the technologies as they happen	Change management
Train customers on simple procedures	Conduct training classes
Fix any hardware problems at the customer's site	Field service for hardware repair
Hook up hardware once it is purchased	Hardware and software installation
Buy the hardware for me to begin with	Procurement
Coordinate resources to get things done	Project management
Test hardware and software before it is installed or when changes are made	Quality assurance
Add and delete users on our network	Simple LAN administration
Write basic reports for customers	Simple programming
Answer questions on the software we have	Application support
Answer questions on the hardware we have	Hardware support
Help install other technologies the R&D group comes up with	Technology implementations

Table 5.1 Customer Needs Translated to Help Desk Terminology

the basic idea, you will need to go into much greater detail to actually make it happen. The resulting document could look something like Figure 5-1.

We will go into more detail of this services plan in Chapter 11. At this stage the plan doesn't have to be too detailed. Your goal is to plant the seed of what you can do to add value to the organization, and this can serve as a trial balloon for senior management approval. Your time to put it all together is coming soon, but after they approve the plan.

You must take this services document back to the senior management team for a periodic check-in. It is imperative that you and the executives are tightly aligned throughout the life of the Help Desk. They need to see if you heard them correctly and what other drivers added to their list. After all, this group will be the one funding you, and you need their OK from the beginning.

Define Standards

This is the time to document and prepare for the standard technologies you will recognize. *Recognize* is used here because there are several actions that can happen with these technologies and some layers of detail even within that. This list comes directly from the As Is surveys you conducted with the customers.

There may be standard technologies you will install as well as support for the customer. These technologies make up the basic foundation of the Help Desk's services and are used throughout the company or are installed in high profile sites. This would include most of the hardware that is deployed as well as the software installed for it.

There might be another level of technologies you recognize but will not support directly. Either it is not in your planned skill set or is not common enough to justify staffing for it. Because it is used in some instances, it is still of value to the company that you help with the support. You can do this by pointing the customer to a contractor who will provide the support and maintenance.

Still, there may be technologies you found in the As Is process that you will not support and are not part of the technology plan for the company as a whole. This may be software that was purchased by one customer to run one process unique to him. It might even be a copy a neighbor gave him that had some neat stuff on it. In this case, the software might be illegally copied and could pose a risk to the whole company. You should not support this kind of software. If anything, you should make some effort to get rid of it altogether.

In all the cases above, it is worth your time to maintain a database of the technologies. What was not directly supported one day, may turn into a company-wide initiative to deploy the next. A database of who has it will be valuable in the rollout of the software to others.

**DME Help Desk
Service Offerings Time Table**

Phase One
First 6 months
Support of PCs and printers
Support of applications

Issues
Will use this time to get our own operations in order and well understood.
Do not see taking on any more work than this for the first six months.

Resources
2 Help Desk agents including myself

Phase Two
6 – 12 months
Asset management
Change management
Procurement of hardware
Quality assurance
Simple LAN administration

Issues
We want to move to the areas that affect us more than other areas so we can
have some control over or input on how they work. We will need others'
assistance in making it work effectively but this should not be a problem.

Resources
1 additional agent for more administrative tasks
1 agent for the quality assurance
1 more agent for the anticipated increase in workload

Phase Three
13 months and on
Field service for hardware repair
Field service for installations
Technology implementations
Acquisitions integration

Issues
We feel the Help Desk will be stronger in hardware-related issues and that
will bring the most value to the IT department. For this reason, our focus
will start shifting to more hardware issues and how we can have the most
impact on them.

Resources
3 additional agents for traveling to customer sites
1 additional agent for the technology integration
1 additional agent for the increase in workload with the increase in customers

Figure 5.1   Service offerings phased implementation

Your documentation of standards will need to include your plans for each of these actions. It will need to be explicit and very clear so your customers fully understand what you plan to do and not do. Be careful that your recognition of the software does not create an expectation among customers that you will support it. It will be very easy for customers to assume that because they told you about something existing, you are now responsible for its upkeep. Again, clear documentation of standards should address this as good as can be hoped.

Hours of Operation

Discussions have been taking place between you and your customers over when they need computer support. Armed with this information, it is time to decide when you will actually offer the Help Desk services to them. This can be done in two ways: in office and after hours. In office are the hours the Help Desk agents are at their desks, ready to take calls. After hours support can be provided by beeper or cell phone.

As with staffing levels, you must determine if office hours will be made available any time a customer needs them, or for the majority of that time. Remember Beth, the associate who knew Microsoft Project? She was not available when Mitch needed help. What if Mitch needed that work done that night for an important presentation in the morning. Beyond the fact that he should not have waited until the last minute, he needed support at that time.

Factors in Establishing Office Hours

Two main factors that will influence your office hours will be the hours of the customers using the services and technologies you support and the number of agents you are allowed to employ.

The Hours of the Customers

The most important factor in determining the hours of the Help Desk is to align them with the working hours of your customers. This does not have to be an exact match but there should be some logic applied if they are not.

For example, the business may assemble toy parts during the day and use the overnight hours to load the trucks for distribution. The customer surveys show you that the computer use is heaviest during the assembly stages, lighter during the initial phases of truck loading, and dramatically lower once the loading process is underway. In this case, your agents should not work around the clock, but should probably leave once the initial loading phases are complete.

The Number of Agents You Can Employ

You can also shape your office hours by the number of agents you employ. It should be obvious that you cannot provide 24-hour office coverage with only two agents. Some people may think they can get by with it, but it will not last for long. To also keep a longer lasting Help Desk, it is not wise to have your agents on the phone every hour of every day. No matter if you staff for a ten-hour day or an eight-hour day, the agents will need to take a break every so often. If your company is big on work productivity, this break does not have to be 30 minutes in the cafeteria. It can be just off the phone working on a training session or reviewing the call log for escalation needs.

If the company's budget calls for you to have a limited number of agents who cannot cover all the time periods you feel you need, you must make the best use of what you have. If the Help Desk gets good reviews over time for effectiveness and efficiency but gets poor grades on being available during off hours, you will need to communicate this to the executives. They can then decide if additional agents are worth the cost of no one being available to answer calls.

After Hours Support

Points can still be gained with the customer community if the after hours support process is efficient. After hours support here means that the agents are not in the office but are available by beeper or cell phone. If an agent can respond to a call within 5 to 15 minutes, the caller shouldn't have too many complaints. What you must monitor is the frequency of the after hour calls. Once you reach a certain load, it will be more advantageous to be in the office after all.

Using technology to help extend "working hours" is also a good idea. For example, if you normally hire an agent to work late shifts to monitor file saves or batch processes, you may have an opportunity to let technology do that work for you and bring the agent into a more normal business shift. System management packages can be installed to watch for certain parameters on the system and can contact someone if the parameters are out of range. A file save process that dies because of a bad tape error could be programmed into technology that beeps an on-call agent with the tape error message. Then the agent can fix the problem remotely or come in if needed. This would happen only in error conditions and would not require a full-time, in-office staff.

Ultimately, the nature of your customer's business will shape your Help Desk's office hours as much as anything else. Businesses that run 24 hours a day, such as hospitals, will require far more responsiveness from your Help Desk than a bank or retail store that is open only during defined daylight hours.

Call Routing

Designing how calls will come into your Help Desk is a large part of the work. From this, many other pieces will fall into place including organizational setups, staffing levels, technologies, and many other things. This is probably the most important part of the Help Desk design process because it is the first real interaction between the agents and the customers. Call routing done correctly can prevent confusion on the part of your customers and help ensure a smooth and efficient Help Desk process. In this section, we will cover

- The definition of call routing
- Planning ideas
- Various options to facilitate calls

This is the mere beginning of the call routing process, but it will help get you acquainted with what is available. There will be much, much more covered through many chapters to follow.

Call Routing Defined

The *call* in call routing will mean any form of contact initiated by the customer into the Help Desk. As discussed earlier, this can be telephone, fax, voice mail, e-mail, Internet, and walk-up traffic, to name a few. Although e-mail and walk-up traffic are not "calls," enough similarities exist among all of these forms of contact to allow this stage of the design to combine them together.

The *routing* in call routing is the directing and processing of the calls through the system. It addresses what a call does once it comes in, where it goes from there, and where it ultimately ends up. This may all be in the same place, or it could be in several different places throughout its life cycle within the Help Desk.

Planning Ideas

The easiest place to begin is with the wealth of data you collected from your As Is assessment of the customers. Start with where the customers are used to going to get computer help, and let that be the beginning of the design. Judging by their tolerance for waiting for help and the overall criticality of their needs, you can start sketching the different ways you can facilitate their calls.

If all your customers use the phone or e-mail for computer help, there is not an urgent need to set up an elaborate Internet solution from the outset. Do not discard your ideas just because they are not in place currently for no one may have thought of them before. After all, you are supposed to be bringing some value and new ideas to this process!

Aside from your bringing in new ideas, the business and customer base will evolve over time and ideas like an elaborate Internet solution may quickly come into the forefront. Internet solutions are good to have in high call volume environments or when you have a sophisticated customer base. They are also good when you have a comprehensive knowledge base to share with your customers, or your Help Desks are decentralized and information needs to be shared easily.

We have not covered the actual skill sets of your agents and their organizational setup yet, but it is not too early to be thinking about the overall makeup of your Help Desk. For example, can you get by with a pool of generalists who have a wide range of technical knowledge and skills but are not real deep in many areas? Are your customers so sophisticated and broad in their needs that you will have to dedicate multiple teams of experts deep in knowledge but narrow in function? Again, this will be the subject of an entire chapter soon, but file this away while you are going through all this.

Don't let panic kick in yet thinking about all the variations of ideas you could implement to begin the Help Desk. There will be a pilot phase where you can test all kinds of scenarios. To be sure you are as good as you can be on Day One, you will test each kind of call, each way you route it through the system, and all the other plans you have so thoughtfully crafted before the first real customer calls you for help. Do take this planning seriously enough to be as close to how you want it on the first try. These plans are so intertwined that to change an aspect of one will usually change aspects of several others.

Routing Options

How do you plan on handling the calls coming in? Who answers the phone and are they the ones who will work on the problem? Will you offer a toll free number or will customers incur long distance charges to reach you? Can a customer walk into the Help Desk and ask for help as easily as someone e-mailing an issue? This book will go over more options in subsequent chapters, but at this point you need to have a good feel of the path an incoming call will take. For a general overview, your choices include the following:

- Calls go straight to the Help Desk
- Calls are taken by a dispatcher and routed
- Calls are handled by phone technologies, then routed

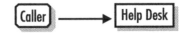

Figure 5.2   Direct call routing

Straight to the Help Desk

The easiest, cheapest, and most straightforward routing of calls is to route the customer base directly to the Help Desk as shown in Figure 5-2.

The caller has a problem, contacts the Help Desk, and is connected to an agent to help with the issue. For small Help Desks, this is definitely the way to go. Small is determined by the number of agents you have, the number of customers you support, and the different types of technology you will support. As your call volume increases or the complexity of the calls gets deeper, you should look at other options, but not until then.

This strategy implies that your Help Desk staff is made up of generalists. If any one agent can take a call on any given topic, he or she must have enough general knowledge of the technologies to have a chance at resolving it. If you find that the agents are increasingly receiving calls they cannot solve on their own, you need to change to a different model. The agents will be frustrated that they are unable to help, and the customers will be even more frustrated that no one can take care of them or that they must be passed around to multiple people before an answer is given.

There is one decision at this stage that will be the object of future debates and that is whether to give customers each agent's direct phone number or provide a Help Desk number any agent can answer. Customers generally want to have each agent's number so they can call whom they want when they want. This is good, especially if they have a follow up issue or need someone familiar to help with an ongoing or recurring problem. It is also good to provide if you are on the "anything the customer wants" path of Help Desk service.

The downside to giving customers each agent's number is that your newer agents or those in training will never get called. Think about it. If your server was down and you needed it fixed immediately, would you call LuAnn who helps you all the time, or someone named Jim whom you have never heard of? Jim may well be far more qualified but customers tend to go with those agents they are familiar with. If this process continues over time, LuAnn will be burned out with call overload and Jim will be sitting around not being used or not trained as much as you wanted. There is no right or wrong choice; you just need to see what works best in your environment.

Using a Dispatcher

Inserting a call dispatcher between the caller and the Help Desk can help you route the calls to the correct group based on the nature of the problem. The dispatcher can either front end every call or be brought in when you reach a certain number of calls in queue. The dispatcher can also proof incoming e-mails and faxes and give them to the right group. Figure 5-3 shows a diagram of this method.

The advantage of this setup is, again, the funneling of calls to the most appropriate agent or group. Callers will have a better chance of speaking with the person most able to resolve their issue on the first try. A dispatcher is also beneficial if you need a human voice on the line instead of a machine. Customers may complain about needing to speak to a person for that touchy-feely service experience. Last, dispatchers are good in high call volume Help Desks that need someone always available to answer the phone.

The disadvantages of a call dispatcher in the middle of the routing include additional salary cost and the possibility of handling the message incorrectly. Unless you can find someone who wants to work for free, the dispatcher will add cost to your salary budget. Interns or temporaries may fill this position well for a lower cost if you need to get around this, but they may not have the knowledge or ability to route calls correctly. Interns and temporaries are also more likely to leave than regularly hired associates. Turnover will cause you more training and ramp up time.

Have you ever played the game where a group of people sits in a circle and one person whispers a phrase or topic to the person next to him? Each person then whispers the message around until the last person gets it. That person then speaks the message out loud and everyone can see how much the message was garbled or translated. To some degree this can happen in a dispatching scenario. The dispatcher may interpret a caller's problem incorrectly, and actions subsequently happen that should not have happened. To overcome this, the customer may have to repeat his problem over and over each time someone new gets involved. The customer may also feel that he has to go through a lot of red tape to get his call handled.

Another scenario is that the dispatcher may have heard the message correctly but sent it to the wrong group for resolution. Now the caller must explain the problem again to someone else who responds by saying the problem is not his to fix. Then he redirects the caller to the correct agent, and the caller has to describe the problem all

Figure 5.3   Call routing with a dispatcher

over again. This is not a pleasant experience for anyone and creates a hostile environment that has nothing to do with why the caller called in the first place!

You can overcome both of these message concerns by hiring dispatchers somewhat familiar with the services and products you support and training them in your processes and environment. Once hired, treat them as an asset to your organization. A common problem with interns and temporaries is that they can be excluded from company events or communications. Because they are not on the payroll, it seems that many other "niceties" are also left out. This cannot be the case with your dispatchers. As the front end to the customers, they must be knowledgeable and competent and not a "temporary" person biding his time each day. Their courtesy on the phone, combined with a working knowledge of the situation, will win over most customers and make the Help Desk call as enjoyable as a Help Desk can be.

Phone Technology

Very similar to the dispatcher process is the insertion of technology between the caller and the Help Desk. Figure 5-4 replaces the dispatcher in Figure 5-3 with technology.

The technology can perform the same functions, though obviously not as personally, and is in place at all times on all days. It carries the same issues as all other automation, such as not needing the HR management that a person does, and typically has a lower cost over time. The initial budget expense will probably be more and may not be worth the investment for a beginning small Help Desk, but it is a critical and much needed investment for long term growth and customer service. We will speak more of this later.

A benefit of this strategy is that it allows callers to route themselves. You can present them with a menu of options and the customer can choose where he wants to go. With some technology, callers can even resolve the problem themselves and not be routed anywhere. You may have seen this yourself when you call your bank or stockbroker and are allowed to move account balances and change features over the phone without speaking to a single person.

A negative to this strategy is that if callers get confused they may choose the wrong option and be routed to the wrong group of agents. Now the process has to kick in and transfer the customer to the correct place. This will not be viewed as the customer's fault but the fault of having to use this darned system to get help. Be sensitive to this and ready to show an upset customer the value the technology

Figure 5.4   Call routing with phone technology

brings. Be steady with the technology, though; most customers will come around and learn how to use the system if it really is deployed correctly. Don't be tempted to yank the whole thing out at the first sign of trouble. But after a long period of problems, you may have to reconsider.

If the "machinery" of this strategy gets too much for customers, you can always bring the dispatching option into the middle somewhere. Now the system can prompt customers for a dispatcher or the technology route if they are comfortable with it. Stay flexible with your planning as it evolves and don't fall too deeply in love with one approach with customer dissatisfaction all around you.

Problem Handling

Remembering the difference between calls and problems, you need to define the process around how you handle problems. Along with call routing, this part of your design is the foundation upon which all other processes will rely. You must take time to think this all the way through.

Why Problem Handling Is So Important

The design of your problem handling process is critical to your Help Desk. Handling problems efficiently and effectively is, after all, the primary reason for the Help Desk's existence. While the Help Desk may take on new responsibilities over time, what it does with the problems it gets will forever define its success.

The Customer Is Depending on You

When a customer contacts the Help Desk, he is counting on the agent to resolve whatever issue he is bringing up. If the customer felt that the agent would not know what to do or just wouldn't do anything, the customer would not waste his own time turning the issue in. How many times would you take your laundry to the cleaners if when you returned, they denied even knowing you had left it? How many times would you come back if they knew you left it there, but they had just forgotten to do anything with it? The Help Desk is the same way. Internal customers may not have a choice for some length of time, but poor handling of their problems will eventually lead them to complain loud enough that changes will be made.

A Good Problem Handling Plan Can Last Forever

Agents will come and go, technologies will change, even the customers will move to different areas, but your plan for managing the problems can last throughout. This is not to say that you must get it absolutely right the first time, but you should make that very thought your goal when you sit down to design the plan. Soon, we will go over all the steps necessary to manage customers' problems and issues in such a way that your Help Desk will be considered world class. Take the time to apply your situation inside these parameters and see how well they fit. Before you open up shop, there will be a pilot period where you get to test all your plans and processes before all the customers experience them. But again, strive to make your first design pass the vast majority of the harshest of tests.

A Bad Plan for Handling Problems Will Take a Long Time to Forget

A customer's first interaction with your Help Desk will leave a lasting impression that can give you a head start with their confidence or dig you a hole that will take forever to get out of. Make your goal to be the hero of the moment (that is all it lasts in the Help Desk world) rather than the goat of the year. Manage each customer as if he is the president of the company with a huge issue even though he is the newest hire on the sales force with a simple logon question.

If you see problems with your plans, don't hesitate to leap into the process and revise it wherever necessary. Bad processes can eat away at time, resources, and money very quickly and will result in poor customer satisfaction. You probably won't get it all right the first time, so be ready for the inevitable hole in the process and be prepared to fix it. Communicate this throughout the Help Desk as they may find the problems before anyone else, anyway.

Managing Problems

There are seven issues to work through as you look at problem management. Each step needs rules within it to ensure the Help Desk is operating as you need it to.

1. Tracking the problem
2. Recording it
3. Prioritizing it
4. Escalating it
5. Transferring it
6. Resolving it
7. Reporting it

Tracking the Problem

It may seem odd that the first part of your plan is to design how to track the problems before you even plan on how to receive one. Thanks for trusting there is a reason.

The reason for designing a tracking plan first is that this part of the process will define many elements of the following steps. Its design will provide needed input into each of the steps and can help it flow smoothly or struggle to move along. Some components of the tracking plan itself are in the following list:

- Tools for tracking problems
- Problem identification
- Problem status
- Problem severity
- Problem history

Tools for Tracking Problems   The first thing you need to know is what tools you will have available to track problems. The amount of technology you can incorporate into this part of the process can greatly determine the lengths to which you can track the problems. Tracking problems can be done with notepads and pencils or it can be done with software that costs hundreds of thousands of dollars to implement. Throughout this section, the issues around tracking problems can apply to either end of the tool spectrum. We will cover ideas as if you have an electronic system, not to discourage you from implementing the ideas but to show you the advantage an electronic system can provide. If you do not have a package already, Chapter 15 will discuss call management packages and will list several different options and varieties.

Problem Identification   Here we are not talking about recognizing that there is a problem; that is the part the customers play in our world. No, problem identification means assigning a name or number to each problem that comes in so it can be identified and followed throughout the Help Desk life cycle. By life cycle, we are referring to the processes the Help Desk is involved in from the initial discovery of an issue until it is fully closed, measured, and reported.

Identification can be as easy as assigning an increasing number to each subsequent call (1 then 2 then 3) or a combination of alpha and numeric characters that are coded to mean different things. *HW123* could mean the 123rd hardware problem and *7825-NY* could mean the 7,825th problem logged from the New York office. The important thing to remember is that the identification scheme needs to allow for a large number of items that all remain unique. Identifying a problem as "that server problem from yesterday" is only as good as the next time a server problem happens. Software is good for this because it will assign an ID # based on sequences you set up.

Category	Explanation
Pending review	Problems have been worked by an agent but are waiting on a second tier group to review.
Transferred	A problem has been transferred to another agent or group, but that receiving entity has not picked it up yet.
Re-opened	Problems were once closed but have been re-opened for some reason.
Need customer feedback	An agent needs more information about a problem from the customer. This status helps an agent show he is not sitting on a particular problem in case management wants him to hurry and close it.

Table 5.2　Examples of Problem Categories

Problem Status　As you track a problem through the system, it is necessary to assign a status to it for quick reference and inquiries. This status will show the problem's place in the life cycle. *Open* and *closed* are the two most basic examples of problem status. Open means the product has not yet been resolved and closed means that it has. This status can help an agent know what his items are to work, assist anyone who reviews the open list to better prioritize the problems, and provide one cut at grouping the problems for measuring and reporting needs. Basic measurements could be how many problems are still open after 30 days or how many were closed during the month.

You may want to create more statuses than open and closed. Table 5-2 shows some variation of these statuses.

You can use additional statuses to describe the lifecycle placement of the problem. As you begin taking calls and handling problems, others may present themselves to you.

Problem Severity　In different sections, we have spoken about prioritization. A way to quickly designate the priority of a problem is to assign it a severity level. Severity levels allow another way to group problems together so that agents or managers can review open problems to make sure they are receiving the correct resources and attention.

Severity levels can be very simple. *High*, *medium*, and *low* are examples of severity levels. A quick look at problems flagged as high could show a manager all the issues that should be being worked with some degree of intensity.

Other severity levels may be more descriptive in their intent. If you have created service level agreements with your customers, more descriptive levels are good to include as in these examples:

- Business halted
- Business interrupted
- Mission critical
- User affected
- Top priority

More important than just assigning a severity level to a problem is making sure everyone understands what that severity level means. Is *business halted* more critical than *mission critical*? There is no way to know unless each level is described and the expected actions explained to those reading and assigning them. So if we took some of the previous examples, we could create an action form like this one to help our agents understand the priority of the problems.

Business halted

Definition:	Entire location or customer process is stopped where no one is able to work
Action:	Immediately notify Help Desk Manager
	Bring in second tier support group for assistance
	Work problem as highest priority until it is resolved
	Follow up with customer every 15 minutes

Business interrupted

Definition:	Many portions of the business are affected; workaround processes exist
Action:	Immediately notify Help Desk Manager
	Work problem as high priority
	Follow up with customer every hour

User affected

Definition:	Issue outstanding in which a single user is unable to perform his computing function
Action:	Work problem
	Bring in second tier support after 12 hours
	Notify Help Desk Manager after 24 hours if problem has not been resolved

This action form is basic but it begins to share your expectations with the Help Desk agents. You can expand this form with more times and exact points where others should be brought into the process or informed of the problem.

You will also want to share this information with your customers. There are times when they can help the agent with the severity level in case the agent does not recognize a situation correctly. You will need to watch out for the customer who claims the problem is halting his business just to get the most attention, but that should be relatively easy to spot.

Problem History   So, we have been tracking problems and watching them go from open status to closed. What do you do with them at that point? Do they simply get deleted from the database or are they kept? If they are kept, how long do you keep them?

The method of logging these problems will drive this decision some. If all problems are written down in a spiral notebook, it may become quite cumbersome to store a bunch of notebooks after many months of taking calls. Even if you have storage space for all those notebooks, it is doubtful that you would ever go back through them to locate a problem's resolution to create reports. For written notes, you should not store them for more than a few months. After that the storage is not worth the effort. For electronic storage, I would keep the problem logs for years. There may be opportunities to purge some of the data, such as if your company completely disposed of a particular kind of hardware, but otherwise the data is too valuable to just throw away.

Keeping this historical data can help you solve future problems and report on your Help Desk's efficiency and productivity. Most call management packages use your historical data as one way to help an agent solve problems. For example, the package can see that turning the monitor off and on fixed a certain type of call and when the package sees this problem entered again, it can advise the agent that this fix has worked in the past. Therefore, the more history you have, the more potential solutions for problems will be available.

Historical data is also good for reports. Reporting on the Help Desk and its effectiveness can be very beneficial, or maybe required at times, to show senior management or your customers. If you keep a long history of problems, you will be better able to show trends and other measurements. Obviously, if you keep only two weeks worth of data, you will be able to show only two weeks worth of trends. This may be an issue if your company has any kind of cyclical business that may push more work towards the Help Desk at one time of year than during other times. If your company sold swimming pools, there is a chance that the summer months bring more business, which will more than likely bring more business to the Help Desk.

Recording the Problem

What information do you want your Help Desk agents to record when they first hear of a problem? Where do they record it once they know what you want? These are the questions you need to answer in this section. Remember to tie this back to the plans you have made during our tracking discussion for this is THE time to get all the information you will want to track throughout the problem life cycle. It will be wholly impractical to call your customers back one day and ask them, "When you called the Help Desk last week, what was it about? Did we happen to tell you the resolution? Did we tell you how we categorized it by any chance?"

At the very least, you need to capture enough information to resolve the problem. Depending on the problem, this would include the caller's name and a way to reach them, where the problem is occurring, and when it happens.

If you are building a database of issues, you could add much more information to help you track trends and add to knowledge bases. This might be asset information, business situations where this problem comes to light, and customer impact.

This information can certainly be recorded manually with a notebook and pen. This is definitely the cheapest method, but it is hard to manage and is less effective than recording the information electronically. This book will take a long look later on at software packages to help you log problems.

Prioritizing the Problem

Prioritization of calls is very important and should be well understood by the Help Desk staff. The goal is to answer the question, "Which problem should an agent work on next?" Job titles may win the day or quantity of customers affected may bring a problem to the top. Your conversations with senior management will come in handy here to help you with these decisions. There will always be exceptions, but you really need to document the rules around problem priorities. You can best perform this function when combining it with the severity level concept we mentioned in the tracking section. Common factors that determine a call's priority include

- Age of problem
- Status of caller
- Breadth of impact
- Effect on productivity

- Classification of call
- Timelines affected
- Relation to major corporate initiatives
- Time of day, month, or year
- Repeated nature of problem
- Quick win

Age of Problem   A common way to prioritize a problem is based on the length of time it has been open in the Help Desk. Taking a "First In, First Out" methodology, this priority concentrates on the date the problem was entered and resources people to work on the oldest item. All things being equal this is not a bad approach, but it ignores many other important factors if done by itself.

Just as this priority method calls for the oldest call to be worked, it is also important to recognize when a problem is so old it is not worth prioritizing. There may be cases in which the environment surrounding the problem has changed so much that the problem is no longer valid. For example, a problem in a purchasing screen may have caused errors to occur at a certain point. If over time, the programming staff has made enhancements to the purchasing module, the problem may not even exist anymore.

Managers should take time to review call logs for old problems that have not been worked in quite a while to see if the issues remain. If not, you can delete the problems from the log. Odds are that the original caller has moved on if the problem has not been followed up on. This periodic "cleansing" can also help the morale of agents who feel their call log is overwhelming and insurmountable.

Status of Caller   Time for politics. Prioritizing by the caller's status or job title tells your Help Desk agents to work on the problems in an effort to please certain people. True customer service would not rest on this scheme, but there are times when this definitely comes into play. When the CEO comes down and asks for a report, people usually jump. The assumption is that the CEO's use of the report may return more value than working on another problem. This is not necessarily the case, but it is logical for agents to make that conclusion.

In times of heavy workloads or staff shortages, it is perfectly fine for a manager to politely inquire as to the importance of the "important" caller's problem. This conversation will also allow the manager to communicate what else the Help Desk is working on so the customer can understand you are not just trying to get out of working on their problem. In fact, it needs to be made clear that the Help Desk is not looking to refuse their call, but to properly align it with the priorities of the company. The hope is that the person will recognize the intent and not take it personally. Just in case, it is not recommended that a front line agent do this. The message would be received better from someone viewed as having a bigger picture of things.

How does an agent know who a caller is in the big picture of things or which job title is more important? This knowledge can be gained through experience. Experience takes time so you may also want to run through the organization structure during an agent's initial training times. The best approach would be to actually introduce the Help Desk agents to senior management and key customers but that may be hard to facilitate. Without that option, you will need to communicate the key positions and how everyone interfaces with one another.

Breadth of Impact   Breadth of impact prioritizing takes into account the effect the problem is having across the company or on a customer's location. This method focuses resources on a problem impacting many users versus one. For example, a location with many down devices would be worked on versus a location with one. Software that affects the customer's ability to place orders in a retail store will take precedence over a bug in a seldom used report.

Your job is to educate your agents on the hardware, software, and the business processes that have the largest impact on the company. Even if it is only a high level view that points out the big pieces of the business, this training can help the agents make a good first cut at a problem's priority. Any one problem can have a wide variety of impacts on different customers. Figure 5-5 demonstrates how one problem can create very important and very unimportant issues for others.

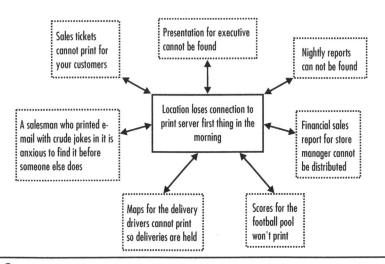

Figure 5.5   A problem can have a widespread impact on your customers

This method can be very subjective when the impact of the problem is widespread. End users will tend to think their problem is big and will have trouble understanding why you are working on someone else's issue over their own. This method is also more naturally used. Fire fighters go to bigger fires versus smaller ones, and fires near hospitals or heavily populated areas versus remote areas.

Effect on Productivity   Similar to breadth of impact is prioritizing by the problem's effect on productivity. This allows the priority to increase when a problem shuts down a process or user versus only impacting them versus the customer just noticing something doesn't look right. A term used in this case is "workaround." If a workaround exists, it means a problem is real, but the customer can continue doing business by allowing for it in some way. However, the workaround should be reviewed to judge how complicated or painful it is. True that a workaround can reduce the priority of a problem somewhat, but the mere existence of the workaround should not prioritize the issue completely.

You also run into the issue of who determines if a workaround exists. The customer may volunteer that he can continue working throughout the problem or he may insist that all work stop until the problem is resolved. Experienced agents can show their creativity and knowledge of the business processes by suggesting workarounds themselves. Depending on how the workaround is presented and the mood of the customer this can go over very well or not so well. At best, the customer learns another way to get things done and can appreciate the value that the agent brought to the situation. At worst, the customer gets mad at the agent for not understanding the business and wants the agent to stop thinking and start working on the resolution. At this point, "I fully realize that, Spencer, but I wanted to give you something to work with while I get all the resources available to help," may be the only reply. Suggestions are the way to go for even if they are wrong, the agent will learn why the idea will not work.

An example might be a person working on a weekend whose PC dies. If he only needed access to the system, he may be able to use a PC on someone else's desk. If this is the case, he has a workaround. However, if the information he needs resides on his PC, there may not be a workaround. Customers are not always ready to concede their problem is not terribly important so it helps to know the business environment to prioritize this way. This should always be a short term resolution, however.

Classification of Call   The very nature of the call may determine its priority within the queue. There are many classifications of calls. For example, you can have problems being reported, questions being asked, or requests being made. One is not always higher than the other because the issue underlying each classification helps determine the call's priority. At first glance, it may appear that problems are highest with maybe requests next and questions last. However, if the problem is a printer that jams every once in a while and the question is how to back out a large check printed in error before month end processing runs, the question may outweigh the problem.

Timelines Affected   The importance of a problem may increase because of the effect it has on timelines of related events or issues. An example is someone working on a presentation. If the presentation is weeks away, it may not be a big deal if the software locks up. If the person is making small changes right before speaking to hundreds of people, the timing is critical and the problem escalates in importance.

Another example may be a store that is unable to reach the central servers. This is a serious problem and needs attention. What happens when there are multiple stores down? First, you could look for common factors to help in bringing them back up. If it appears though that there is not a common thread between them, they might be worked one at a time. Prioritizing based on affected timelines may come into play if one of the stores is opening for the first time that day. It may be more important to the business that that particular store is fixed first so it can have more positive first impressions on its customers.

Everyone seems to need their work done right away when they contact the Help Desk because it's a major issue. You and your agents must figure out which problems are more timely than the others. The best way is constant communication and education. Later on in the chapter, we will discuss the benefits of a strong internal communication plan. In this priority scheme and many of the others, communication goes a long way to help determine the best path. Your agents will stay in the loop more and can make better decisions when helping customers.

Relation to Major Corporate Initiatives   Problems that occur in parts of the business may be higher in priority when there is a lot of focus on that business segment. A major marketing campaign may be rolling out to get everyone's attention on a new product coming in a few days. If hardware that runs the assembly line dies, it is a big deal. If that assembly line is producing this new product, it is probably an even bigger deal. This priority method works only if the agents are well-informed of corporate initiatives and goals. Again, internal communications allows this to happen. It is always nice to resolve high priority problems without involving Help Desk management or senior executives. Problems solved at the

Help Desk agent level allow the senior management team to continue to focus on strategic direction and larger business problems while the agent resolves technology issues at a more tactical level.

Time of Day, Month, or Year   The priority of a problem can be affected by the timing of its occurrence. There are times when a problem is escalated merely because of the time of day, week, month, or year. Server slowness on a regular Tuesday is an annoyance and should get the attention of the Help Desk. Server slowness on the last day of the fiscal year will be higher in priority so the financial accounting and any other year end work can be performed. If your company performs cycle counts at the end of each day, a problem in cycle counting will slowly increase in priority as the day goes on. Publishing calendars that show IS and Help Desk events as well as corporate events can help agents understand what times of the day, month, and year are more crucial than others.

Repeated Nature of Problem   Recurring problems should bubble up in priority over time. As part of your call reduction campaign, you should be watching for problems that consistently generate calls to the Help Desk. This focus helps reduce calls and shield customers from problems that continually require assistance from the Help Desk. Otherwise, these problems will eventually leave a bad impression of the Help Desk and the whole IT department.

External Customers   *When external customers are involved, recurring problems may leave such a bad impression that customers look elsewhere for not only technical support, but for another company to do business with as well. After all, if your company cannot fix problems, how can it fix other issues that crop up on the business side?*

Even the smallest problem that does not have a major impact on the corporation should be reviewed if it happens on a very frequent basis. It may not become the top thing you work on, but it should be noticed.

Use your agents to help identify repeating problems and then enlist their help in resolving them. Perhaps you can give it to an agent as a side project to research the root cause. Have a contest where on slower call volume days the agents see who can find the cause of the problem first.

Quick Win   Sometimes a problem can rise in priority merely because it can be resolved in a short amount of time. Used a lot during "clean up" times, quick wins allow call log quantity to be reduced because some effort is made to fix the quick and easy problems regardless of their impact on the company.

This load relief can help in a couple of ways. One way is that it helps unburden the agent whose log was cleaned up some. It can weigh on anyone's shoulders to know that every day when they come to work, there is a mountain of things to do. Another advantage to this priority scheme is that it shows the customers movement on problems. It may not be the problem they would have picked, but at least something they turned in came back out. The downside of this scheme relates to that point of customer expectation. The customer could wonder why the agent had time to fix a simple, small problem but couldn't work on the hotter, high priority ones. For this reason, you shouldn't advertise this scheme too often, if ever.

You also need to manage this process. Perhaps you have "quick win" days where the agents go after the problems they can solve fastest. The important factor is that this philosophy does not become the standard operation procedure for your Help Desk. Only solving easy problems will, by nature, leave out the hard ones that are probably more critical to the business to begin with. It also generates an overall atmosphere of laziness. If your whole goal is to work easy things, your agents will begin to slack off in their processes as well.

Priority Summation   As you can tell from the previous list, there is no one set way to prioritize all the calls coming into the Help Desk. Know that you will have a variety of priority processes. Some calls fit into one category, while others seem to have a hard time fitting in anywhere. The key is to recognize all the factors that come into play as you manage a problem workload, and work towards resolving them in a common sense manner. Then communicate this recognition to the agents and customers so everyone understands the strategy.

Escalating the Problem

How long should an agent work a problem before informing others about it? Do you want an agent to spend days on a problem that could be solved by a second tier agent in minutes? How about a location that is down and the agent works on it for hours even though he has not been trained on it? All these questions get answered when you design an escalation procedure.4

The first consideration is deciding where to escalate issues. The biggest factor in this decision is the impact of the problem. If the problem is relatively local and does not reach out to many people, the escalation path may resemble the one in Figure 5-6.

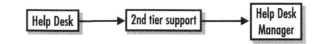

Figure 5.6   Basic escalation path

However, if the problem is a down system that has been unavailable for a long period of time, other parties may need to be part of the escalation path. When designing this path, you also need to plan who will be the escalator both in terms of deciding to do it, and who communicates to whom. Figure 5-7 shows a more complicated escalation plan that may more closely resemble a company. We will go over the factors of deciding when to escalate in a moment.

Escalations are tied together with priorities. Knowing the priority of a problem will help agents know when to escalate the problem. Escalating doesn't necessarily mean giving the problem to someone else; it may just mean informing a higher level manager that the problem is out there. That manager can then make decisions around other actions based on his knowledge of the issue or the environment around it. A problem should be escalated for the following reasons:

- Service level agreements call for it
- The customer is escalating the issue through other routes
- The problem has a high profile impact on the customer
- Agents are not able to solve the problem on their own

Service Level Agreements Call for It   A good reason to escalate an issue is because you are supposed to. If you have agreed upon service levels with your customers or management team on when the Help Desk will escalate issues, you must act appropriately. What's left is how high up the problem is escalated and at what time interval.

For example, you may have in your agreement that any Code 1 problem that has been open for more than four hours be escalated to the Director of IT. Now

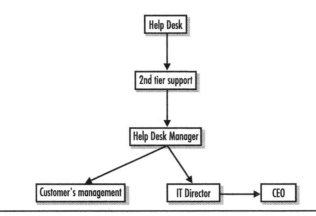

Figure 5.7   A more complex and complete escalation path

when an agent sees this situation, he automatically knows he is supposed to tell the Director of IT that the problem exists and has reached this stage.

An advantage an electronic system like a call management package brings you is that it can be the process that recognizes when problems reach certain levels and need escalating. Based on the rules you provide it (like a service level) it can perform several different tasks such as sending e-mail, transferring the problem to someone else, or performing other actions you designate.

Customers Are Escalating the Issue Through Other Routes   Another reason to escalate a problem is when you see the customer doing the same thing. Take a store clerk calling in a problem to the front line Help Desk agent. If the agent feels the clerk will be escalating the issue to her manager, it might be appropriate for the agent to inform the Help Desk manager. This feeling can come from the general mood of the clerk on the phone or can be as blatant as the clerk saying that she is taking the problem to her manager. The thing you are trying to achieve is preventing your management from getting blindsided on an issue from the customer. Your manager will look far better if he can answer complaints with, "I know of your issue and feel comfortable we are working it correctly." rather than with, "Oh really? I will have to look into it and see what we are doing."

One thing I do not advocate is reacting strongly to a customer who threatens to go higher in the chain. Sometimes an agent will hear, "You aren't working this good enough; I am going to tell your boss!" It is wise to inform your boss that this issue is coming and the circumstances around it, but not to react much to the customer. It is perfectly acceptable to accommodate the customer and say it is OK for him to escalate however he wants. This shows a feeling of confidence that the agent is doing all the right things on the problem and is not afraid of the issue being told to others.

There is a fine line between notifying higher levels of management when issues are getting escalated and when the agent can handle things on his own. If you have to err, err on the side of overcommunication, but try to find the balance. Communicate regularly to the agents on the appropriate times you wish to be brought into a problem, and when you feel comfortable that they are handling it as you would like without your assistance.

High Profile Impact   Problems should be escalated to others when the impact on the customer or company is very visible or counterproductive. This type problem should stand out to the agents but your internal communication plan will continue to bolster this.

An example of this could be your company's Internet site that takes sales transactions from your customers. If the Internet site were to begin having problems, there is an obvious need to get it up and running quickly before it affected your customers. Any customer who wished to use the site and could not would be upset. This is a high profile issue because in an electronic commerce world it is difficult to know what business you may have lost, perhaps permanently, when the site is down. Your customers may take their business to your competitors if they continuously run into problems conducting business with you. If you make them use your Internet site and it is problematic, this loss of business will most certainly occur. This is extremely bad press and must be treated as a top priority.

Agents Cannot Solve the Problem   Escalation of a problem should also occur if the current agent working on its resolution cannot solve it after some time. There doesn't have to be an exact time limit per agent per problem, but there should be a range of times based on the type of problem where an agent should move the problem to someone else. It makes sense that the higher the profile of the problem, the more quickly the problem needs to get into the hands of the resources that can fix it.

Whether it is their skill set or their lack of understanding of the circumstances around an issue, good agents will realize when they have encountered something they will not be able to bring to closure. The proper thing to do in this situation is to make the next level of the Help Desk aware of the problem, describe how the problem has been handled up to this point, and provide any other pertinent information. If the trends are showing you that an agent is having a hard time figuring out how to solve a problem, you should implement some procedures that allow you to review their open issues every so often to see if problems need to be escalated.

This review on your part should not be viewed as a negative thing. For newer agents, this could be explained as mandatory until they feel more comfortable with the business and its processes. For more experienced agents, present this as a more casual exercise to help keep you in touch with what is going on. It is not personal; you are just getting an overview of the current support issues.

Escalation Overall   Escalating a problem can happen for many reasons. It is imperative that the Help Desk understand when escalations are needed or required. Escalation does not have to be done by the agent handling the problem, either. Someone else who sees what is transpiring and realizes its impact on the business can escalate the problem. This is not, or should not, be done in a "tattletale" fashion to get anyone in trouble. Instead, it is done in a manner that helps everyone involved better understand what is going on.

Everyone wins when a problem is properly handled. The wins include

- Customers feel confident that the Help Desk understands the urgency of their issue and will resolve it more quickly.

- Management is better prepared if confronted on the topic.

- Customers get a more positive impression of the Help Desk and its processes.

Transferring the Problem

For some reason, problems may need to be transferred to someone else because of your organizational setup, the skill set of the agent originally working it, or perhaps the original agent is out sick and the problem needs to be worked. Your processes need to be defined and communicated to the agents. Can an agent just call the next person and let go? Who lets the customer know the status or the resolution?

No matter how you establish that you want problems to be transferred, you must always keep the following rules in mind:

1. Someone must always own the problem. Whether it is the original agent who took the call or the associate who ends up with it, the problem must clearly and constantly have a recognized owner. Unless the problem will be worked for weeks or longer, the owner remains the original taker of the call. This person had the initial contact with the customer and knows as much detail as anyone.

2. The associate receiving the transfer must clearly acknowledge that he has taken over the problem. Without this expressed acknowledgement, there is a big opportunity for the problem to lie in wait between two groups with neither knowing the problem is sitting idle.

3. All known details of the problem should be passed to the next person. It is a waste of time for the receiving person to not be brought up to date as much as possible before working the issue.

4. Inform the customer that the transfer has taken place. This does not have to be a formal announcement but can easily come during a follow up conversation. "Hey Lane, I just wanted to let you know that Vicky, our systems person, is now working your issue and should have an answer for you soon." This fact allows the customer to see movement on his issue and lets him know where it stands.

A terrible customer service sin is to let a problem slip through the cracks. You need to take great care that someone always owns the problem and is responsible for seeing it through. Another advantage for call management packages is that they can handle the transfer process for you, complete with notifications, acceptance, detail passing, and ownership. Any time you hand something from one person to the next, there is always a chance it will fall through. Don't let that happen to you.

Resolving the Problem

Now you need to resolve the problem. Without a resolution, all the prior steps are really pointless. You will have spent much time working on it, and the customer will not have a solution to the issue he called about. This is certainly not the place to describe how to fix every technical problem, but there are some points to consider. First, to what depth do you want certain agents solving problems and what do they do once they are done?

Referring back to the description of calls, incidents, and problems, you can see that there are levels of issues to resolve. Depending on the severity or time-criticality of an issue, you may want your agents to resolve incidents and pass on the root problem for others to review. This might be the case for front line groups with high call volumes. *Front line* is a term to describe the agents who take the incoming calls. They are the front line because they are nearest the customer (not the enemy!). You want them fixing the easy stuff so they can get back on the phone for the next caller. If you have only one support group, they must resolve the problem at its root. If they do not resolve the root problem, your call volume will not go down and you will make no long term progress. Someone at sometime has to work the cause of the calls so they will stop.

Reporting on the Problems

Measurements will be reviewed in subsequent chapters, but at this stage you still need to know what information to capture during the whole problem handling process. You may want start and completion times, a list of everyone who worked on the problem, or lessons learned from the experience. The agents need to know this expectation from the beginning so they can get the information you need. So when you are designing the tracking model, think forward to typical reports your senior management, customers, IT department, and Help Desk agents may want and need to view the operations. Chapter 13 covers measurements and reports for various parties.

Real-World Example

Our IT department set up a Quick Response Team that was made up of programmers who reported to the applications group but their sole focus was on resolving software problems turned in by the Help Desk. The Help Desk filtered incoming problems, worked the ones they could, and passed the ones they could not resolve to this QRT group. QRT was trained and experienced in application level troubleshooting and could get to the root cause of a software problem more quickly than a Help Desk agent who was constantly on the phone. The QRT was a very successful organization model.

Once a problem has been resolved, you should have some processes in place for quality assurance and customer satisfaction. Perhaps the agent calls the customer back after several hours to see if everything is still OK. You could do surveys here as well to get information on the whole process, and not just the problem resolution itself. I will speak more on surveys later as well.

Notification

The next phase the Help Desk needs is a notification plan. Where escalation means notifying those higher in the chain, notification is simply communicating information anywhere along the chain of involvement.

This type of communication helps keep everyone on the same page, makes them feel part of the process, and projects a sense of confidence to anyone dealing with the Help Desk. Three questions will guide you in creating an effective notification plan:

- Who needs to know the information?
- How will they receive this notification?
- When is this information released?

We will discuss the answers to each question within the following list. The list is made up of major events that should trigger the notification process. It will be important to make note not just of the trigger events, but also the who, how, and when related to each one. There will be different answers depending on the type of event.

- Coming events
- Planned downtime and outages
- Problem statuses
- Outside news

Coming Events

Much like a calendar does, it is important that the Help Desk notify affected parties of coming events. Coming events are items within the company you need to know about. Examples could be software upgrades, lease expirations, or new processes being implemented in the Help Desk. As with other notification items, coming events helps the customers plan their own workload so that it is aligned with what the Help Desk is communicating.

Who Needs to Know of Coming Events

The hard part at times is knowing all the parties who need to be involved. Software upgrades certainly impact the customers who use that software. At times, they could also impact the associates who rely on the outcome of the software applications. For example, upgrading the spreadsheet software on the server would affect the entry people who use the spreadsheet. It would also impact the managers who need the spreadsheets to make business decisions. Although you should not communicate this type of event to anyone who has ever seen a spreadsheet, you should nonetheless keep these factors in mind.

A good way to build this knowledge of whom to call so you don't have to figure it out every time is to establish primary contacts within your customer base. These primary contacts will pass the message along to others in the organization. The contacts may be picked because of job title importance, or the responsibility may go to someone who has the time to communicate upcoming events quickly. It is recommended that you let the customer pick the contacts along with your suggestions on who might work best.

How They Should Be Notified

Coming events implies by its very name that the event has not happened yet. Because the communication takes some time to reach the receivers, a tool that can reach many people easily is recommended. E-mails and Web pages come to mind where phoning and faxing do not. One e-mail message can be typed and sent to massive numbers of people at once but it takes much longer to fax something to many locations.

When to Notify People of Coming Events

The length of time that the notification needs to precede the event is driven primarily by the scope of the event itself. The goal is to give people time to prepare for whatever it is you are telling them. If you are informing them of a lease expiring for their desktop, they will need some amount of time to decide how they want to handle it. This time would be measured by the time it takes to order and receive a replacement. If you are informing people of a software upgrade that will render old documents irretrievable, you should definitely give more notice. The people will need to either print or archive the documents somewhere or work with other tools to translate the information into the new software.

Planned Downtime and Outages

It is absolutely crucial to inform everyone when you know of downtime in the system. This downtime can either be when the system is completely unavailable for use or when it will be so affected that using it will be extremely cumbersome. It is bad enough when unplanned outages hit the system and force the customers to scramble. When the outage is known ahead of time but not communicated, it is worse. The scramble remains the same, but the hard feelings of not being told only add to the frustration.

Who Needs to Know of Planned Downtime

Notifying customers and management of these types of events cannot be overemphasized. Don't take chances when deciding whom to inform. If there is a chance that a planned event could reach out and affect a group of people, tell them.

It is far better to set an expectation that something may happen even if it doesn't in the end. From a confidence view, it is OK to not communicate an event to people whom you are absolutely sure will not be affected by the event. There is no need for others to worry about the stability of the system when it won't impact them. Otherwise, you should always err on the side of overcommunication.

How They Should Be Notified

Just as with coming events, people should know when downtimes are scheduled. Therefore, the same methods of communication apply. Use tools that reach a wide audience with ease of effort. You may also include this message on the front end of your phone system if that is possible. This way you catch all people who call the Help Desk.

When to Notify People of Planned Downtime

Again, depending on the system that will be down, you should give as much lead time as you can. One server going down that will affect 100 people deserves some attention. A Web server that will impact thousands deserves more advanced notice. With something as important as a system going down, you should communicate the message several times. For example, you can first inform the parties as soon as you know a date. Then, as the downtime draws closer (and people can remember), you can send out another brief reminder. Finally, the day before the downtime, send out one more "Do you remember that …" communication just to be sure.

Problem Statuses

Problem statuses are updates to the customer who called in a problem that was not resolved during the initial contact. Anything still open after that first interaction will have a status. These statuses should have distinct and defined meanings and are set up in advance of the Help Desk taking calls. Examples of statuses could be as easy as Open and Closed or include some in between like Transferred to …, In research, Pending customer follow up, Needs more details, and so on.

Communicating a problem status to customers should not be as simple as saying, "Your problem is still open. We will let you know when it is no longer open." The hard part is determining how much detail you give your customers. Do you give them only a "We're working on it" notification, or do you tell them exactly who is working the issue and what pieces of code are causing the trouble? Do customers want to know that the router configuration had wrong parameters set or only that the parameters are working correctly now?

The individual customer or the priority of the problem can help you answer these questions. Some customers want to know exactly what happened. This is not bad; in fact, it may help the customer recognize the problem if it happens again and it shows the customer that the Help Desk is on top of things. No matter how much detail you provide, always describe what the next steps will be in your notification. This includes when you will follow up again, what the customer should do in the meantime, and what you will be doing as well.

Who Needs to Know About Problem Statuses

The quickest answer to this question is that you should communicate the status of a reported problem to the person who reported it. There is no doubt that the person who contacted the Help Desk with the problem will always want to know the status of it.

You know that quickest is not always the path to the best answer and that is true in this case. Sometimes, there are more parties that should be notified. For example, if a problem is really important and has high visibility, you may want to notify higher management of the status. They will have an interest in issues that may impact people. Other associates in the company may be aware of the problem but not recognize its importance. This type of communication is close to escalation, but you are not transferring the problem to higher level managers; you are just making them aware of it. You can be confident that once you bring them in, they will typically stay in until they see a resolution.

Continuing on the theme of notifying others, you should also communicate a wide scale problem to a larger audience if the issue will impact them. This communication will usually come in the form of, "We are aware of a problem that affects you when…. Be advised to … when you see it." This is a proactive step you can take and it shows your customers that you understand business situations and how one issue can affect seemingly unrelated issues. Depending on how you announce this status, it may also prevent future calls to the Help Desk because when people notice the problem, they will know you are aware of it and won't feel it's necessary to report it.

How They Should Be Notified

When you are notifying a single person or group that turned in the problem, you should correspond in an individualized manner. E-mails still work, but phone calls do, too. If the status is ongoing and has not changed much from the last communication, an e-mail works fine. When the situation has changed and there is a new development, a phone call may work well. This allows the receiver to interact more and both sides can better understand where the other is.

If you are communicating the problem status to a larger audience, you should revert back to the mass communication tools such as e-mail or Web pages to disseminate the information.

When to Notify People of Problem Statuses

The "when" of status updates is best determined by the criticality of the issue. When both business and productivity are heavily impacted, status updates should happen regularly. In some cases this could be every hour and in others it could be weekly. For example, when systems are down and no one can work, hourly updates will work. If a screen in a software application acts up every once in awhile and the cause is unknown, weekly updates are fine. If the problem has been open for weeks, hourly updates will become more of a bother than a help. "Lynn, I just wanted to tell you the problem you called in six months ago is still open. We don't know when it will be fixed," is not the most helpful or effective conversation you will ever have.

Set the expectation of when statuses will be delivered definitively from the beginning so the agents understand your goal. It is much easier to do something because it was always done that way versus modifying behavior after some period of time. You also want the customers to understand the goal so they feel comfortable that you are working on their problem even though they haven't heard from you in the last five minutes.

Outside News

Outside news are events that are occurring outside your company but will have some impact on your business. Approaching storms, union strikes, or even expected hardware shortages are all examples of news the business may be interested in knowing about.

Who Needs to Know About Outside News

The parties that should be notified are definitely those that will be impacted but this could be expanded to all customers as well. The communication is not "Myrt, there is a hurricane headed your way, good luck!" Rather, it could be "Myrt, that storm seems to be headed your way. Remember to cover your computers in plastic and unplug all the power when you leave. Good luck and let me know if we can help." This notification is informative (the storm is coming), gives your customers some planning steps (unplug the computers), and expresses goodwill on their behalf (good luck).

Assuming others may want to be kept up to date, you could notify other parties about the news. Although the phone company strike may only be in the western region, other customers may need to know in case they are trying to reach a location in that region.

How They Should Be Notified

The closer the news is to happening will determine how you notify the customers. If the storm is still days away, you can afford to publish the news in a large scale manner such as a Web page or e-mail. If the phone strike is imminent, you may want to contact the customer personally. This way, you know they'll get the message. When you are communicating to other parties that will not be directly involved, it is OK to publish the news on a Web page or through some other medium they visit frequently.

When to Notify People of Outside News

Notification of outside news is very similar to notification of coming events or planned outages. The key is to stay ahead of the news and give the parties time to plan for its result. As you get closer to the event, send reminder notifications in case someone forgot or did not receive your earlier communication.

Customer Responsibilities

The interaction between a customer and the Help Desk is not a one way dialogue. Just as the Help Desk has procedures and processes, so does the customer. It is important that you educate customers on what is expected of them for the most effective and positive exchange with a Help Desk agent. Customers have eight main responsibilities:

- Contact the Help Desk with any problem encountered
- Establish a single point of contact
- Seek training on basic computer skills
- Review documents or FAQs before contacting the Help Desk
- Have as much detail ready as possible when contacting the Help Desk
- Go through the right channels
- Deal with the Help Desk agent in a professional manner
- Be a resource for the Help Desk

Contact the Help Desk with Any Problem Encountered

This responsibility may sound unworthy of listing due to the common sense nature of it. However, you would be surprised how often problems are not called in. Three reasons include

- The customer may feel that someone else has already informed the Help Desk of the problem so there is no need to do it themselves. For problems that are large in scope, there can be a tendency with some people to just live with it until it is resolved. They feel confident that other customers have reported the issue so it will just be a matter of time before it is fixed. There are two problems with this line of thinking. First, no one else may have noticed the problem and therefore no one at the Help Desk is working on resolving it. Second, if the Help Desk knows that many people are experiencing a problem, it could increase its priority. Each time someone calls, the Help Desk can realize how large the problem is becoming.

- The thought that the problem is so small that it is not worth the time to look up that Help Desk number and turn the problem in. This sounds like "That figure is wrong but I know the right amount and the total comes out like it should anyway."

- The fact that the customer may feel stupid having run into it. This could happen when the customer runs an application incorrectly and finds a hole in the program. To turn the problem in would be to tell that agent that they used a program incorrrectly. "Why in the world did you do that?" should never leave the mouth of a Help Desk agent, at least not in front of the customer.

Catching people in the act of doing something wrong or making them feel dumb is not a part of any Help Desk mission. When customers do not want to turn in their problems this points to a major issue in how the Help Desk is operating and this should be fixed immediately. Small problems can lead to large ones and it is far better to find them when they are small. The customer may have seen a wrong number in one screen and discarded the impact. However, if that same calculation is corrupting data elsewhere, the problem is larger than it first appears. You need your customer's help for this.

Establish a Single Point of Contact

Having the customer establish a single point of contact into and from the Help Desk is a very valuable process to implement. *Single* really can be more than one; the point is to limit the number of people who call the Help Desk with issues. In fact, you may want to start with two contacts so the location can have a backup in times of vacation or at other times when the first contact cannot be available.

This action has a ripple effect across the company. Take for example a company with three locations and ten associates. If all ten associates called the Help Desk every time they had a question or issue, the Help Desk would be forced to staff for that volume. There would also be a need for phone lines to handle the potential of all those callers. When the customers did call, there would be a chance of ten callers competing for a limited number of agents.

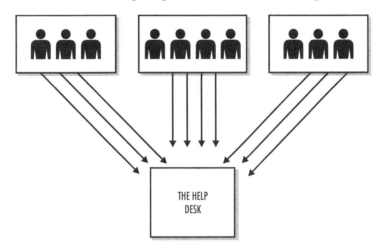

With a single point of contact at each location designated as the computer contact, the volume into the Help Desk would be decreased as shown here:

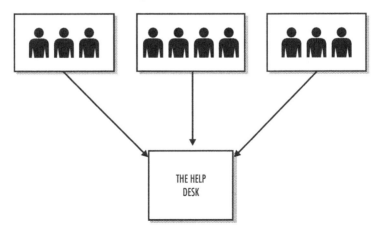

Benefits

This frees up phone lines, the agents themselves, and the customer's time waiting on hold for an agent to answer. This also funnels knowledge into central resources and allows that location to have more computer-friendly associates closer to home. Locations do not have to be physically different buildings, either. Points of contact can exist within the same building but represent different departments or large groups of users.

This example does not appear to help much with three locations and ten associates. Can you imagine the savings though if there were 300 locations and 10,000 associates? Perhaps you don't need to institute this policy with a small customer base, but you probably cannot survive without it as the base gets larger.

Enforcement

This is a good strategy, and on paper it will produce very positive results. How do you enforce it when customers continue to call regardless of their having a designated contact or not? Assuming you have corporate or senior management buy-in, there are three steps you can take to help the process along. In order of importance, they are

1. Make sure the caller knows there is a contact at this location. If he is not aware of the contact, help him this time but suggest he go to the contact before he calls the Help Desk. If the caller was aware of the contact, ask why he didn't seek out the contact. It may be as innocent as the contact was out that day (remember the need for a backup?) or as guilty as his not wanting to find the contact to report the problem. Hopefully, by your asking the question, the caller will be more likely to at least try for the contact next time around.

2. Show the customer and their managers how all these different callers are impacting them and the Help Desk. Remember that they will be more interested in its impact on them than on you. All these different callers mean more associates are spending more time phoning in to the Help Desk rather than doing their own jobs. And if the Help Desk has to increase its staff, your customers will soon pick up the additional cost.

3. Show regional or corporate management metrics that demonstrate the quantity of callers by location. They can see for themselves who is playing by the rules and who is not. If one customer site is particularly worse than the others, you may not have to literally point them out yourself. The reader of the report may see it and go after its resolution himself.

If you can get the data, you may also look to see if the locations that are playing by the rules are more profitable or more efficient in some areas than the ones who allow anyone in the building to call the Help Desk. You don't explicitly say the single point of contact plan is responsible, but you can let it sit out there on the report for others to make their own judgement. Table 5-3 can show you an example of how measuring call volume can help you in proving your point.

Again, provide this report as a "continuing metric we are tracking in the Help Desk" and let the audience decide if the plan should be better enforced in any particular location.

4. Implement or increase charges to that customer. If you are billing your customers for your service, this may be an opportunity to increase their costs if they continue to use your services. You could implement a fee for a certain quantity of callers and a higher charge for any callers over and above that limit.

5. Worst case is to reduce or cut off the services to that customer. This should be the last resort, and you should invoke it only if you feel so strongly about the merits of the single point of contact. If the strategy is working for the rest of your customers, it may be politically better to just allow the customer to use multiple contacts for the good of "customer relations."

Provide Training on Basic Computer Skills

The single contact will learn many tricks of the trade in a short amount of time if all the computer problems and questions are routed through him. Don't let that be his only form of training, though. Take a proactive stance and create a formal training curriculum for all computer contacts or, for that matter, all customers. Whether you bring all contacts into the Help Desk for training or you send them documentation through the mail, get them up to speed on as many common issues as they can handle. This responsibility rests primarily with the customers, though. Although the Help Desk can make some classes available, it is up to the customers to attend classes and educate themselves.

Location	Calls	# of Callers	Gross Profit%
Raleigh	56	3	26%
Greenville	47	2	28%
Columbia	42	35	16%
Monterville	25	3	23%

Table 5.3   Incoming Help Desk Calls by Location

The training should not just center on when to call but also on how. You could hold discussions around the best use of phone calls compared to e-mail or Internet chat groups and so on. You should also speak about what information to have before the Help Desk is called. Again, this is a major responsibility of the customer on our list, so we will speak more on it later in the chapter.

Last, the training should provide resources to help customers solve problems on their own. It is good to hold classes, but show your customers that you have provided (have you?) other ways for them to get information as well. This may include Web pages, published training manuals, or computer classes offered outside the company.

Resolving Problems Without Help Desk Intervention

Fixing problems without assistance from the Help Desk has several benefits. The immediate return is the resolution of more and more problems in the field without the direct involvement of the Help Desk. This should result in faster turnaround times, which get the end user back to being productive faster. The contact should not work on problems for long periods of time, however. This runs counter to the creation of the Help Desk to keep all associates productive in their jobs. The contact's role is to resolve easy-to-fix problems or answer questions that aren't necessarily computer related. This strategy allows the Help Desk to concentrate on the more difficult and complicated technical problems. Many times a customer will call on process related issues that are actually better solved in the contact's location, anyway. For example, a new finance officer in a store may inquire of the Help Desk when to process credit memos. Although the agent may have an idea, this type call should be handled by a contact within the location or on the business side of the company.

Building a Bench for Future Help Desk Agents

Another benefit of this contact training is that it provides opportunities for people who might want to work on your Help Desk in the future. For example, there could easily be times when the contact begins to like the computer role more than the job he currently holds. It then becomes in the company's best interest to move that person into a job he enjoys. Don't advertise this benefit publicly, however, because the business may assign people to be a contact as a way of getting rid of them in hopes the Help Desk will hire them one day.

Review Documents or FAQs Before Contacting the Help Desk

Whether a location has implemented a single point of contact or not, people contacting the Help Desk should do some homework first. It is not productive for anyone if customers call the Help Desk when the answers to their issues are available on their desks, be it on a Web page or in a book. The time they spend calling the Help Desk, waiting on hold, speaking to an agent, and getting the answer could be far better spent performing the jobs they were hired to do.

Now it is first up to the Help Desk to design, provide, and educate the customers on the location and use of these materials, but it then falls to the customer to use them.

Have as Much Detail Ready as Possible When Contacting the Help Desk

In Chapter 3, we spoke about reducing problems by getting as much detail as possible on problems when the customer calls in. This responsibility can lie just as easily with the customer as with the Help Desk agent. The following list outlines the key components of information the customer should always have before contacting the Help Desk:

- Time and date of the problem
- What they were trying to do when they noticed the problem
- What actually happened leading up to the problem
- Hardware, software, and database information
- Examples of the problem's outcome
- Whether it can be duplicated
- Impact of the problem

Time and Date of the Problem

Most customers do not wait days, or even hours, to call in a problem they have experienced, but it does happen. Perhaps the caller found the problem on a Saturday but because it wasn't that important, he waited until Monday to call it in. When the customer does place the call, he is responsible for bringing up the fact that the problem actually occurred over the weekend. The agent should not assume it was the same day, and it does not hurt to ask for the date, anyway.

Time and dates are important because other events unknown to the customer may have been occurring at the same time to cause the problem. For example, the programming group may have been installing some new software patches at the same time the customer noticed a problem on his computer screen. If the agent was aware of this timing and knew of the programming group's plan to install the new software, he could more quickly narrow down his cause of the problem.

What They Were Trying to Do When They Noticed the Problem

Sometimes it is as helpful to know the intent of the customer's action going into the problem as it is the result of the problem. From this information, an agent might be able to determine the path the customer took even if the customer cannot remember. This path leading into the problem can provide good hints at how to fix it.

It can also provide a good opportunity for the Help Desk agent to conduct some training. "I was trying to enter an order on the inquiry screen," may be invaluable to know from an agent's standpoint. Can orders be entered on that particular screen? If not, the problem is not the software, but the way in which the customer is using the software. This example provides the agent a quick answer to the "software" problem as well as a training opportunity to inform the customer on the proper place to enter orders and the use of the inquiry screen in question.

What Actually Happened Leading Up to the Problem

"I was just sitting there and the PC started making crackling noises," is an example of how customers turn in issues to the Help Desk. Replace *PC* with some other noun and *crackling noises* with some other adjectives and the example becomes more commonplace.

More than likely something transpired right before the PC started making crackling noises and the agent needs to find that out. The customer is responsible for informing the Help Desk of the events leading up to the problem if he wants the problem resolved. Without the customer confessing to the Coke he spilled into the PC, the agent and the customer are going to spend far more time than they should in tracking down the cause of the problem. Eventually, some technician will find the dried up Coke inside the PC so the customer will only save face until that time.

The issue on the agent's side of the conversation is to "help" the customer explain everything that happened. A good way to do this is to de-personalize the situation. Instead of saying, "You didn't spill your lunch in it, did you?" try "I wonder if anything was spilled on it." The agent will have eliminated two uses of *you* and turned the caller into an observer instead of a direct participant. Even if the customer wimps out and states that someone else may have spilled the Coke, the agent will have received the information he needs and can begin working towards a solution.

On a more innocent note, knowing what the customer did or saw before the problem was noticed is very good information for the Help Desk. It is not required but it is an enormous time saver for all involved. The goal is not to persecute the caller, but to truly solve the problem more efficiently. This goal will best be achieved if the environment between the customer and the Help Desk is conducive to it. If there is antagonism or an "us versus them" attitude between the two parties, this open communication will not happen. This is yet another reason the Help Desk must continue to stay aligned with the business so it can understand how to fit in and be seen as a team player.

Hardware, Software, and Database Information

"I was on the computer in the other room when the screen showed some message, then the whole thing cut off," offers some help to the Help Desk agent but not much. "I was at the PC with asset tag F3402 on it when I got an error message. I couldn't write it down fast enough but I was in the sales entry screen when it happened," is significantly better and will go a long way to being resolved more quickly than the first example.

For hardware problems, the customer should get as much information about the hardware as he can get before he calls in. This could include asset tag information if available, manufacturer, and model numbers. The Help Desk agent can quickly identify the configuration of the system or other problems with that specific piece of equipment or manufacturer.

Customers should also be aware of software and database related information—such as exact screens or applications that were running, software versions, and anything else pertinent to the problem—and include it in their initial contact with the Help Desk. Error messages are especially critical to communicate to the Help Desk. With this information, Help Desk agents can quickly look into the application to find what generates that particular error message.

Examples of the Problem's Outcome

The customer should try to make examples of the problem available to the agent. This may not be possible in hardware cases, but is extremely nice for questionable data on a report. The customer can fax or e-mail the report to the Help Desk agent, and they can then review the information together while looking at the same piece of paper.

There are too many variables when the customer just claims a report is wrong without anyone else looking at it. The customer could have misread a number, thought the report was something it was not, or even have reviewed a report that was from a different time period than expected. If reports have time/date stamps on them, agents can go after problems with more detail. Why a customer's account receivable balance is "wrong" may be due to when the report was actually run, not when it appeared on the caller's desk for review.

The more examples of a problem that can be produced, the better the Help Desk agent will be able to narrow down the problem. Some data issues are caused only if certain circumstances are met. This type of problem is extremely hard to find. If the customer can show multiple examples of the problem, the set of circumstances can be more easily seen and ultimately rectified.

Whether It Can Be Duplicated

A direct correlation to producing multiple examples of a problem is the customer's ability to duplicate the problem on demand. Being able to duplicate a problem is extremely valuable to a Help Desk agent. If we revisit Marc Tredeau leaving his car at the mechanic for repair, we can see why duplicating the problem is important. Imagine taking your car in to repair a funny noise. Invariably, when you arrive at the garage, the noise stops. The mechanic will make efforts to find the problem, but without being able to hear the noise himself, it will be hard to do. Now, if the car will make that noise every time you perform a certain action, you can re-create it for the mechanic and he can go right to the spot of the noise.

The same analogy holds true in the Help Desk world. Watching an application blow up at a certain point every time will help the agent and subsequent people fix it much better than a sporadic problem. If the problem cannot be re-created, that is OK, but the customer needs to have as much detail on what happened leading up to it as possible. This makes the steps we have discussed earlier that much more critical.

Regardless of the customer's ability to re-create the problem, the problem should still be turned in. Perhaps the agent has seen something similar from other customers, and this last call bring the clues into place. From another angle, the problem still exists whether it can be duplicated or not, so it needs to have the Help Desk look at it.

Impact of the Problem

Communicating the impact the problem is having on the customer or the business is an important element in helping the Help Desk agent prioritize the call. Especially if the agent is new, the call may not be recognized as a high priority merely by the facts of the problem specifically. The customer can help his own cause by explaining to the agent what the problem is affecting. The customer might exaggerate the impact of the problem to move the escalation, but it is better for that to happen than for a critical business application error to sit idle in someone's call log for hours or days without being worked.

Advantages of Being Prepared

The more information you have, the better. This could serve as the mantra for customers calling into a Help Desk. Agents quickly become adept at ciphering through information to glean out what is germane to the problem as in this example:

> "My PC, labeled DME asset# 5342, hangs up every time I try to install the latest copy of Office 2000 on it. I tried it on another PC and the same problem happens."

> **is better than**

> "My PC, labeled DME asset# 5342, hangs up every time I try to install the latest copy of Office 2000."

> **which is better than**

> "My PC, labeled DME asset# 5342, hangs up a lot."

> **which is better than**

> "My PC keeps getting stuck."

The agent will ultimately get all this information out of the customer but it will take some time and patience from each side of the conversation.

Transitioning to an automated help process is also easier for the Help Desk when customers gather and prepare information before they call. When customers deal directly with an agent, they can get by with not being prepared because the agent will just have to walk them through all the scenarios. With an automated process that has no Help Desk agent involved, the customer must provide details for the process to help provide recommended solutions. For example, there is software that prompts a caller for information and will then respond with answers based on historical knowledge regarding that type of problem.

Even without automation, a well-informed customer will help himself get back on track. Explaining to your customers that gathering and preparing information is not just for the Help Desk's own good will hopefully encourage them to be better prepared when they report problems.

Go Through the Right Channels

An ongoing source of frustration for front line service providers is when customers decide for one reason or another to skip them and go to other sources. Customers may do this for political reasons thinking they are above the front line, or because they think someone else will give them a quicker and better answer.

It is important to properly communicate the expectations regarding the routing of calls. If there is a single point of contact in each customer location, that person should be contacted first. From there the customer could contact the Help Desk. If escalation is needed, the Help Desk agent should inform both Help Desk management and others designated in the plan. Figure 5-8 shows both the incorrect and correct way to contact someone for help.

This practice should not be a part of normal customer behavior. The Help Desk is set up to handle requests from the computer users and will work most effectively when the procedures are followed. It is up to the Help Desk to make this channel effective and useful for customers, but the customers should do their part, too. If you see a customer continually going around the Help Desk to someone outside the process, don't just try to make him stop. Ask why it is happening and see if you can fix it. A better working process is always more effective than a process that is required because of some rule.

Deal with the Help Desk Agent in a Professional Manner

Under no circumstances should a customer interact with a Help Desk agent in anything less than a polite and professional manner. Yelling and screaming at

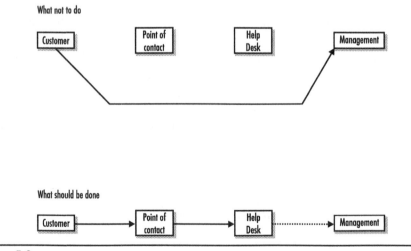

Figure 5.8   How to use the right support channel

someone on the phone will not get a printer unjammed or a phone line back up. It is fair to think that it will only prolong the issue if both sides are working under some form of duress. A clear expectation between all parties should be established that everyone is on the same team and rude behavior will not be tolerated. There will be times when frustration seeps into a conversation and this should be recognized. Here, we are talking about behavior that is over the line. If the conversation would not be held if other people were present, it should not happen at all.

People interact better with one another if they know each other or have at least met before. If there are opportunities for the Help Desk agents to meet their customers, it would be worth the time and energy. Maybe it is a visit to the customer's location or inviting the customer to spend time at the Help Desk to get this going. Customers spending time in the Help Desk can be very beneficial. It allows the customer to experience what the agents go through and shows them how hard the agents work to resolve issues.

Be a Resource for the Help Desk

The Help Desk and the customers should be on the same team and have common interests in each other's success. Just as the Help Desk has responsibilities to its customers, the customers have some responsibilities to the Help Desk. These responsibilities are not requirements as the customer does not *owe* the Help Desk anything, but they should do their part to help the Help Desk agents when needed. This help really comes into play in two areas: training and references.

Training
A good way for Help Desk agents to learn their support role and to best align with the business is to be trained within the business. There are many advantages if the Help Desk can partner with a customer site. The agents can see the technologies in actual use as opposed to reading about them in a manual. They can also see the business processes and how they interact with the technologies.

The customers should also want to be a part of this training. Although it could be seen as a drain on resources and a distraction from the day-to-day business, it has many long-term advantages. First, the customers get better trained agents that they will deal with on the other end of the phone one day. They also get an ally in the IT department. Having met each other, the customer and the agent should have a better chance to get along or at least understand what each other is going through.

The Customer Should Be a Reference Source for the Help Desk
The Help Desk should be an expert in the systems and technologies used in the business. The truth is that the people actually using the software every minute of

every day will know the operations at a much closer level. The agents might know the behind-the-scenes workings better, but the customer typically has the advantage on how to use the software. Because of this, the customer can be a good source of information for the Help Desk when it runs into problems it cannot resolve.

A strong compliment to pay someone is to ask their opinion on an issue because they are seen as an expert on the topic. When a customer is called by the Help Desk to help them with a business issue, it should be viewed as positive and complimentary, not a pain to deal with. This should not be abused, but a call every once in a while will not hurt anyone. This resolution path between the Help Desk and a customer should be used only when the Help Desk and the customer have a good history and working relationship. The tides could change if that customer begins to feel that the agent is not learning and should know this stuff anyway, so care should be taken to prevent this from happening. If nothing else, spread these types of calls among several customers.

Setting up this contact between the Help Desk and the customer should be done on a personal level. It does not have to be formal and should really evolve over time. For example, after helping Mary Louise with a PC problem, an agent could close the conversation with, "Hey, while I have you on the phone, do you have a minute to answer a question? I have a purchasing problem that I would like your opinion on." Then the agent could proceed with finding out any more clues that Mary Louise could help with on that problem. Ending with a true "Thank you," the conversation will have started a foundation for that agent to get together with Mary Louise on future problems if necessary. Other agents should not now start calling Mary Louise as that relationship was not meant to be used that way. Nor should you post on the Web page that Mary Louise is available for other customers to use for help too!

IT Department Responsibilities

It is important to establish a strong game plan for the roles and responsibilities of the Help Desk and the rest of the IT department. This is even more important if the IT department was the help provider before you were brought in. All the players in the IT department need to be on the same page and operating as a team so their effectiveness can be viewed and felt by the customers. Figure 5-9 shows how Help Desk activities are just one part of an IT department.

IT departments can be organized in many ways and can include many varieties of job functions and expertise. Because they can vary so widely, it is hard to list

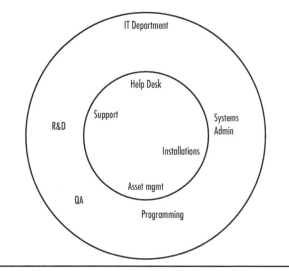

Figure 5.9   The Help Desk is one part of the IT department

the responsibilities definitively for each section. For the purpose of the Help Desk's interaction, let's look at four groups that may exist in one form or another in an IT department. They are

- Systems administration
- Research and development
- Applications development
- Quality assurance

Systems Administration

Systems administration consists of groups of associates that are responsible for keeping mainframes, servers, and networks up and running. This group needs to work closely with the Help Desk because when calls come in to that location or when a group is down, the systems department is usually brought in to help. The interaction works the other way too as the systems group must communicate to the Help Desk when downtimes are scheduled so preparations can be made with the users. It is a waste of time for agents to work on an issue only to find out that the systems group was conducting an upgrade and that was the cause of all the problems.

Research and Development

Depending on the size of your IT department, you may have a formal organization that looks ahead to new technologies or an informal collection of people that do it in their spare time. In either case, the Help Desk can provide valuable insights into this process.

The Help Desk's natural ability to know what is working in the field and what needs improvement can aid the R&D group to focus on certain areas. Whether it is the need for a new model printer because the current model breaks frequently, or the need for wireless connections for remote users, the Help Desk can show the IT department how it can increase its value to the business.

Working the other way, the R&D group needs to regularly communicate with the Help Desk to inform it of upcoming plans and implementation requests. As with the systems administration group, the R&D people can have a major impact on the Help Desk and its incoming calls. The R&D group and the Help Desk should make every effort to share information on a consistent basis.

Applications Development

The applications development group can be part of the full-time staff in IT, or an outsourced group that provides development when needed. As with the previous two groups, these teams need to work well with the Help Desk.

Applications development programs new tools and software for customers to use in their businesses. The new tools and software could include enhancements to an existing system, or a completely new module to support a new line of business being implemented. Each of these examples impacts both the end user and the Help Desk. Notice of impending changes therefore needs to flow to the Help Desk, and information and feedback from the customers need to flow to the applications development group.

Quality Assurance

Quality assurance groups test the deliverables of the IT department. They can test software that is being developed or hardware about to be implemented. Their value lies in their ability to catch problems before the customer is impacted by them. Some IT departments do not have a formal group that does this testing but instead requires the actual people developing or implementing the product to perform the task. A formal QA group provides a more objective view of the product and frees up the developers and implementation teams to develop and implement instead of formal testing.

A strong QA group makes the Help Desk's job considerably easier. Each problem or inconsistency they find before a product goes live is one less problem that a customer will encounter and call the Help Desk on. If you can, you may want the two groups to cross train with each other. The quality assurance analysts can see the typical ways that a customer uses a product and can therefore test future products with that style in mind. Help Desk agents can benefit the QA group by adding their knowledge of the system and business into the testing process.

Internal Communications

With all the focus on your customers, it can be easy to forget your own people. They need to be updated with information as much as anyone, so don't forget them. This information is not just about upcoming releases or product changes, but it also includes corporate performance reports, the direction of the department, or even how external economic changes will affect the company as a whole. Depending on the information you need to convey, there are many ways to spread the word:

- E-mail
- Department or group meetings
- Offsite meetings
- Day starting or ending meetings
- Change of shift meetings
- Severe problem recaps
- Board postings
- Newsletters
- Web page
- Calendar

E-mails

E-mails are a good way to reach large audiences at once with messages that are straightforward and don't require much interaction. These can be good for informing the group of the company's monthly performance reports or for recaps of meetings and presentations. E-mails also do well for delivering "attaboys" to the group. *Attaboys* is a term used to describe congratulating someone on a job well done. Carbon copying the rest of the Help Desk or IT department gives the associate more recognition for his performance.

Department or Group Meetings

Sometimes it is important to share information face to face and allow the group to interact or share ideas. Getting all of them in a room is good to get some back and forth on topics affecting the group. This form of brainstorming can produce good results and thoughts but it needs to be monitored. Healthy debates could rage for hours if allowed. This department meeting needs to also communicate other issues so limit the debate when necessary.

You will want to publish an agenda of the meeting ahead of time. If your audience knows the topics you will speak on, they have time to prepare themselves in case they have questions or concerns about it. Always allow time for questions and answers anyway in case your agenda didn't cover all they wanted to know.

Hey, who is answering the phone while you are all in this meeting? Having it late at night might solve that problem but then you are cutting into your group's home life and that may cause other problems. While "all at once" is nice for a consistent message to be delivered, it is hard to do in the Help Desk world. You need to either split the groups into shifts so the phones can be covered or inform the customers so they can be prepared. The customers may debate it, but keeping an informed Help Desk is in their best interest, even if they don't realize it.

The frequency of these meetings is determined by the rate of change in the group or by factors outside the group. You should regularly schedule this type of meeting once a year or even quarterly if possible. As the company begins new initiatives or new technologies have been implemented, you can arrange for intermediate meetings to bring everyone up to date on what is going on.

Offsite Meetings

To add a different twist to any of the meetings discussed previously, consider having a few offsite meetings. Rent a conference room in a hotel close by and conduct the meeting away from the office. This usually gets everyone in a more laid back frame of mind and people can interact in a more relaxed manner. This is not recommended constantly as it would get expensive, but it does help when done once in a while.

Offsite meetings are especially good for planning, budgeting, and other strategic types of interactions. During these times, you want your group to be particularly sharp and full of good ideas. The best way to do this is to make the setting more comfortable and conducive to thought provoking ideas. Conversely, gathering everyone out of the building just to give project status updates is more expensive in time and money than it is probably worth.

Day Starting or Ending Meetings

For problem status and event planning, hold quick meetings with your various Help Desk managers or associates every day. The meetings shouldn't last more than 5 to 10 minutes, and you will be informed of open or approaching issues before senior management can hit you with them. Daily meetings naturally take up time, so try to keep them quick and to the point, but do have them every day. Have them even if you are not in that day. This gets everyone used to showing up, and the real key is the communication of issues regardless of where you are. If you need to go deeper into a particular status, just keep the managers or agents that are directly involved so the others can get back to work.

You should hold this meeting either first thing in the morning or last thing at night. The alignment of your schedule with your managers or key associates will tell you which one is best for you. Because this is a time-consumer every day make sure you have all the right people attending and none of the wrong people. Everyone may want to attend because they can hear good stuff or be seen by the right people, but these are the wrong reasons. Experience will show you if you have all the right people. If you do not have the right people, topics will not be covered as they should be, or you will have someone sitting in the meeting who never speaks because his topics are never brought up.

8:00 Meetings

Having this meeting first thing in the morning catches you up on the events of the previous evening. First thing should really be 15 minutes or so after the group gets in. This way they have time to get status reports from their own people or check their systems and processes for errors. Without this time to get informed themselves, their updates to you will be worthless. Morning meetings also allow the attendees to communicate work that will be done during the day in case it impacts anyone else. You can even discuss coming vacation times for the attendees so everyone can best know where everyone else will be in case of an emergency.

Before You Leave at Night Meetings

Another way to update the group is to have everyone check in before they leave at night. These night meetings are useful for priority checks because you know where everyone is leaving their open issues. If Harvey is leaving and he tells you of a problem that is more critical than he thought it was, you can have him stay or pass the necessary information along to someone else. You could have a morning and evening meeting, but that is probably overkill. Unless your customer base is extremely sensitive to open issues such as hospital equipment or 911 phone systems, one update meeting is plenty and works well.

Change of Shift Meetings

Regardless of the time of day, if you have shifts changing, you should have a quick meeting to bring the incoming group of agents up to speed. This is a perfect time to discuss problems that are still being worked or look for things that were supposedly fixed earlier. This meeting helps prevent problems from falling between the cracks just because one group went home and someone else is reviewing the open call list.

To make this exchange of information as good as it can be, you can create a formal checklist that is completed by the departing group to give to the incoming group of agents. This standard checklist will remind the departing group of all the questions they need to answer and will help them formalize their thoughts a bit more. This checklist can also be used throughout the next shift as it works its way through problems. When all open issues are resolved, the checklist can be filed for future reference.

An example of the need for a shift change meeting is a machine crashing in the late afternoon. The systems group worked the issues and brought the machine up right before the Help Desk day shift went home. As the first night shift group arrived, the machine was just coming up. If the two shifts met and the day shift informed the night shift of the problems, the night group could be more vigilant in monitoring the machine's status and would be able to recognize problems sooner than otherwise. What might have appeared to be something small in a normal situation will alert the agents to more potential trouble with this communication. They can also know who was working the issue originally and contact them directly for a quicker resolution.

Severe Problem Recaps

Morning and night meetings cover the status of issues happening on a regular basis. Severe problem recaps review a recently resolved major issue and the events around it. The purpose of a problem recap meeting is to fully understand the surrounding actions and reactions from a problem with a wide range or deep impact on the organization. Examples could be server crashes, extended downtimes due to data lines, or software bugs that corrupt data. When you hold these meetings you need to have everyone who was involved in the problem in attendance. I suggest you go after

- A description of the problem
- Dates and times of actions
- What was done to resolve the problem
- Any work left to be done
- Impact on the customer
- Lessons learned on how to get better

The results of this meeting should be documented and kept for future reference. Figure 5-10 is an example you can follow and build upon.

If the same problem or a similar problem were to happen again, you will want to check this document for trends within the technology and among your staff. You will want to know especially if the lessons learned from prior events were not heeded. These results are also good to have if you need to present them to senior management. You need to show them you are in charge and are doing things proactively to prevent future problems where possible.

Board Postings

For information that does not need to be immediately delivered, use white boards or electronic display boards if you can afford them. This media is great for displaying statistics or other general information that is not critical in nature.

Newsletters

Newsletters are good ways to distribute historical information, such as performance updates, and upcoming projects. You can fill the pages with comments from management on how they are seeing things progress or light topics like whose birthday is that week or month. This media is more time-consuming than a lot of the others, so you need to make sure it is worth it. If the agents read it every once in a while or let a couple of newsletters stack up before they open them, you may want to re-visit the idea. If they are reading it actively, look for even more items to put in the letter.

Severe Problem Recap Form

Production Server Crash

March 12, 2001

Problem description

Monday, the production server crashed. The hardware was fine but it locked up and was unavailable for 3 hours.

Action date and times

4:00 A.M.   The early shift agent performed her routine server checks and saw that the server was not responding. She immediately beeped the LAN Admin on call.

5:30 A.M.   The LAN Admin returned the beep and quickly realized the problem. The faxing software was upgraded earlier the night before and must have caused the lock up.

5:50 A.M.   The old version of the software was reinstalled and the server was reset. Users were allowed back on the system by 7:00 A.M.

7:00 A.M.   Verified with various users that they could log on fine and were able to work.

Resolution

The faxing software was reloaded to the prior version. Once this was done and the server was reset, everything was fine.

Any work left to be done

Need to better test the faxing software in the environment in which it will be installed

Schedule a new time to reinstall the software and communicate to the HQ campus

Reinstall the software

Customer impact

Luckily, we found the problem before the users did. A dozen or so calls were placed before the server was completely fixed but it was up soon after. Customer impact was therefore deemed minimal.

Lessons learned

We need to test upgraded software BEFORE we send it out live.

The monitoring of the system by the early shift Help Desk worked beautifully.

The LAN Admin did not respond to the beep well at all. The importance of this needs to be reiterated to all on call agents.

The evening shift should escalate system problems to the Help Desk manager if the Admin staff does not respond in a timely manner.

Figure 5.10   Severe Recap form

Web Page

A Web page is a good way to get the benefits of a newsletter but with the updating capability of e-mail or a display board. It can reach anyone with a browser so the agents can find out information they need without getting up from their desks. This is another "pull" information delivery system in which the audience must *pull in* the information to get it. This means the information must not be time-critical because you do not know when it will be read, if at all. This makes Web pages good for the same type information that newsletters bring.

Quick Recap

- Do you understand the current environment and have you documented it? You need to know where things began to know where to take them. The As Is should have you very informed.

- A good place to start is developing a mission statement. Will yours be long and detailed or short and to the point? How will you distribute its message and intent?

- What are the services you will be offering to your customers? Will you be prepared to offer them from the beginning or will you need time and resources to develop your ideas?

- Standards must be defined at this stage of the process. Do you have a handle on what technologies you will support or allow someone else to support?

- The hours your Help Desk will be available is important to establish. You need to make sure these hours are properly communicated and fit in with your customers' needs.

- How will calls come into the Help Desk and what happens to them once they arrive? Take the time to draw a flowchart and run it by several people to make sure you have thought of all possible options.

- Taking the call is a good start; do you have the plans drawn for handling the problem? As with call routing, a flow chart will make things easier to see.

- You need a plan to communicate within the Help Desk. Do you feel comfortable that you have everything lined up for information to flow freely through the Help Desk and its associates?

- Your customers are part of the process. Do you have a list of items you feel the customer should be responsible for in your environment? If they are allowed to work completely without standards or processes, it could make for a long Help Desk experience.

- The IT department is also part of the process. Have you held a meeting to acquaint everyone with the roles and responsibilities of the Help Desk and how it will interact with the other groups?

- Do you have some plans for how you will communicate internally about issues? As long as there is even one person other than you, there will be a strong need for communication.

CHAPTER 6

Budgeting

Although you must know your customers and their needs to be successful, the extent to how well you can service them is driven by the budget you are allowed to work with. We hope you had significant input into the budgeting process, but in many startups the budget may have been determined at the same time the decision to proceed was made. This could be dangerous as this budget amount was probably made in a "spend no more than $x" mode versus a "how much do they need to be successful" mode. We will address how to best use your budget later, but for now we will assume your organization is progressive enough to have involved you at the beginning and go after some of the decision points you must make.

The other main consideration in the budgeting process is the type of Help Desk you are building. If your Help Desk is part of the corporation, you may not be forced into a balanced budget, but will be tasked with staying within the expenses you listed during the budget calculation. If your Help Desk operates independently from a corporation, then you will probably need to maintain a balanced budget or at least be able to explain why its income did not cover expenses. For our purposes, we will stay in the middle of these two types. We will spend a good deal of time covering income sources and will also go over expenses. From there, you should be able to contrast your own situation with the material in this chapter.

What to Look For

- If you are creating your first budget for the company, it is important to know how they want the budget completed. You must understand if the budget needs to balance at the end and how much detail will be required. Once you know the rules of the game, you can really work on the budget itself.

- There are several types of income sources. You need to understand which ones apply to your Help Desk budget. Basically, who will be funding the Help Desk and its operations?

- There are many cost factors to consider when preparing your budget. This chapter will go over some of them.

- Budgets are typically not approved without some discussion and debate. There are some strategies that may come in handy for your budget to work.

- Some organizations would rather invest in people over tools. Some the opposite. Which one fits best in your organization?

This chapter will begin with a sample budget in Figure 6-1 showing income and line item expenses. I will refer back to this example as the chapter continues.

Total Income	$ 525,000
Expenses	
Dues	1,500
Facilities	100,000
Insurance	56,000
Maintenance	27,000
Meals	15,000
Office equipment	25,000
Office supplies	8,000
Outsourcing contract	45,000
Salaries	350,000
Software licenses	33,000
Taxes	98,000
Training	20,000
Travel	50,000
Total Expenses	$ 827,000
Over / Under	$(302,000)

Figure 6.1   Sample Help Desk budget

Know the Rules of the Game

Each company handles its budgeting in different ways, so it is important that you research how your budget is expected to work. These rules may be published or just "understood." They may be actual rules with penalties for nonperformance or guidelines to help along the way. Don't downgrade the importance of these distinctions; your employment may hang in the balance.

Balanced Budget vs. Running a Deficit

The first rule to understand regards the balancing of your budget. Specifically, you need to know if your budget must be balanced at the end or if it can run at a deficit. A balanced budget means that the income stream equals or exceeds the expense stream. If the expenses of the Help Desk are greater than the income, then the budget is in deficit. Basically, the Help Desk is spending more money than it receives. Obviously this cannot happen in the truest business sense, but it can look that way on paper. The income is most likely enhanced by the company so that the Help Desk can continue operations. In the case of our budget example, DME's Help Desk is running at a deficit and will have to be resourced through other corporate means.

Need for Exactness

Once you understand this, you can begin itemizing your line items and providing budgetary numbers for each of them. To understand the need for exactness in the numbers, find out what happens if any one line, or the whole budget, comes in higher or lower than expected. This reaction may be written in policy somewhere, but find out the unwritten rule as well. It may be that senior management does not care for complete accuracy and is only looking for an overall picture for the company. On the other hand, they may look to the budget process as an exact science and require strict adherence to its figures.

Padding the Numbers

In either case, do not include high padded numbers in your budget. By this, I mean bumping your numbers up to cover for any oversight or mistake you may encounter down the road. For example, if you think travel will be $20,000 for the year, make that your number. Don't make it $40,000 in case you are wrong. Also, don't do it because you know budgets are always cut and you want to ensure you get your $20,000. Integrity is a virtue to always strive for and that includes the budget process. If you find your budget getting cut in places that are important to the Help Desk, get with your management team to understand their reasoning. This meeting can also give you a chance to make your case on why the line should not be lowered. I will talk more on getting your budget approved later in this chapter.

Income Sources

One item to consider is your source of income. Many companies include this as part of a corporate expense while others bill out the Help Desk's services to the customers who use it. We will look at three options:

- Corporate sponsorship
- Chargebacks
- Professional services

Corporate Sponsorship

If your corporation's core business is not computing, your income will probably be an expense line item in the overall budget. Revenue comes from the core business and some percentage of it is dedicated to the IT department and the Help Desk. Therefore, in effect, the company is sponsoring the Help Desk and funding its operations. This is the simplest method for all involved as the budgeting is done in one central place and can be reviewed at that same level.

Chargebacks

Your business may want the Help Desk to be self-funding to some extent and derive its income from its own operation. This is commonly called a chargeback. A *chargeback* is a term that means that the cost to perform a service is funded by charging back the costs to the recipient of that service.

Before you pick a chargeback plan you need to make sure you understand yourself what you are trying to accomplish. Are you charging your customers for your services to merely recover costs or are you trying to influence their behavior? The answer to that question will go a long way in helping you pick a charging scheme. The major schemes to institute a chargeback plan are

- Bundled costs / fixed fees / subscriptions
- Unbundled costs / per user / per call
- Tiered support

Fixed Fees / Subscriptions / Bundled Costs

A *fixed fee plan* charges your customers a standard price each billing period for a set of products and services. It is good for the customer's budgeting needs, as they will always know what their Help Desk costs will be and can plan accordingly.

This fee can be determined in a couple of ways. One method is to include all costs that in any way are related to the Help Desk. This total coverage ensures that all expenses are accounted for in the chargeback. Another method is to include only those costs that are directly related to the operation of the Help Desk services. Where agent salaries, equipment, phone lines, etc. are included in both calculations, costs such as building rent, insurance, and magazine subscriptions would not be in the direct-relation fee calculation. It is recommended that someone in the finance or upper level IT management make the decision on the method used to determine the fixed fee.

Because you must take into account a large variety of situations, your cost should come out slightly higher on average than you actually spend. As customers realize that they may be paying for services they do not use or actually funding the costs of higher-use customers, they may demand a breakdown of costs. This is fine to do, but it will lead to the customers wanting to pick and choose their services in attempts to lower their costs. Therefore, it may be more advantageous to group the costs into general areas like administration, hardware, software, and salaries and display the information that way.

Per User / Per Call / Unbundled Costs

So we arrive at an *unbundled cost*. Unbundled means you have broken out all the components of your charges and effectively "menu-ized" them for your customers. While this will prove harder to plan for on the customer end, they are allowed to only pay for the services they actually use.

One problem you will run into under this charging plan is the costs of infrastructure changes or additions. If adding the *nth* user forces you to add another server or data line, who pays that bill? It is not fair for the last requestor to pay, nor will everyone else want to pay for a service that is not really on the list. In my ongoing restaurant scenario, you are okay paying for the food, but don't want to see the new stove cost on your bill! Hopefully, you planned ahead of time, knew you were close to new costs, and integrated the anticipated costs into your charges. However, if you did not, or the business grew faster than you could plan, there are a couple of things you can do. You might absorb the costs until the next billing review period and incorporate at that time. Another way is to assess your customer base a one-time fee to cover the costs. This will create much anxiety so go with the absorption and bill in the future.

Another issue around a *per call* fee is that you may force people who really need your help away from using your Help Desk because it is costly or unbudgeted. For organizations with an internal Help Desk, this is exactly what you do not want to happen. We created this Help Desk to allow your associates to do the job you pay them for and not fix the tools they use. Any plan that moves you away from that ideal is counterproductive and disruptive.

Tiered Support

You may find that you have very different levels of users with very different needs. You may have *power users* who demand much of the IT resources either by job title or importance to the organization or who just plain take up a lot of your time. Is it really fair for these users to be charged the same price when they consume more of your costs? If you have these types of users and they can be clearly defined, you should go to a tiered pricing structure.

Real-World Example

I have successfully dedicated Help Desk agents specifically to groups of these users. One example was committing a number of agents to our Distribution Centers that had recently automated their operations. We quickly found that these locations with radio frequency devices, bar coding, and scanners were much more complicated than our older Distribution Centers and required a higher level of support. As we were aligned well with the business we were able to show them how different they were and presented our plans to give them the service they needed. They agreed and, as such, also agreed to pay a different level of charges than the rest of the group.

Advantages of Chargebacks

There are many advantages to using a chargeback scheme for Help Desk services. Some of them are listed below.

- Allows expenses to be covered by customers
- Allows the development of business acumen
- Allows the Help Desk to make a profit if necessary
- Can have an impact on influencing customer's behavior
- Allows a comparison to other service providers

Allows Expenses to Be Covered by Customers   The entire idea of chargebacks is to cover the expenses the Help Desk incurs. Whether the charges cover the entire budgeted expense or only part of it, they do provide income to allow the Help Desk to keep operating. Chargebacks allow a direct correlation between what a Help Desk costs and the value it brings.

Allows Development of Business Acumen   Help Desk agents are not typically introduced to business rules and procedures as much as they are to technical issues and situations. In a chargeback environment, the Help Desk agents and its management team must think in business terms at the same time they are providing IT service and support. Each individual agent does not have be well versed in accounting rules, but he or she will need to understand the meaning of winning customers and showing value to the customer base.

When things come free, people can complain about the results, but only to a degree. When they are paying for that same result and are displeased, they are far more prone to express their dissatisfaction. The Help Desk staff must keep this in mind as it performs its duties. There must be a greater emphasis on the group to demonstrate its value in each of the things it does. Standards and rules that are forced on the customers must have a demonstrable value that the customer can see and understand. For dollars spent, value and effectiveness must be returned.

Business awareness is developed during this time as agents are hit with questions around costs of service. The agents must be well versed in the costing model that is imposed on the customers and be able to explain to the customer why things cost what they do. The agents must understand this to a level that they know the "whys" of the charges. Answering a question by reading from a script will not yield the same effect as an agent spouting off facts and figures backing up the charges.

Allows the Help Desk to Make a Profit if Necessary   There may be some instances where the business wants the Help Desk to show a profit, or at least have the opportunity to do so. Charging your customers for your services is a good way to go about this. The goal here is to make more money than you spend and this can get tricky in a Help Desk environment. True customer service will always present a challenge when it comes to containing costs and the proper balance must be maintained. For example, the adage, "I would do anything for a customer," needs to be reviewed because *anything* can get expensive if costs are ignored. Having the customer pay for this *anything* tells you how bad the customer really needs that service or product.

Can Have an Impact on Influencing Customer's Behavior   This leads directly to how chargebacks can influence the behavior of the customers. It is easy for a customer to demand a service to be performed or require certain deadlines or results when he does not have to pay for it. When an agent can respond with, "Okay, I will have it done. Your charge of $315 will show up on your next statement," the customer is presented with the fact that his request will cost him money. If the request is truly worth the cost, there should be no second thoughts. If the customer withdraws the request, the agent is able to see the value, or lack of value, the request would have generated.

Another way that chargebacks can influence behavior is their use of single points of contacts in their location or department. An agreement could be made between the Help Desk and its customers that Help Desk services would cost $100 per user per month. However, if the location had a dedicated, trained point of contact for the Help Desk, the monthly charge would be only $45. Now the business entity has an option. It could dedicate a resource for computer-related issues and reduce its fees or use its resources however it wanted and pay a higher fee.

The Help Desk gains on either option. If the business dedicates a contact, then the Help Desk achieves its goals of better-educated users and a reduction in call volume. If the business does not elect to have a single point of contact, their additional fees would cover the cost of the Help Desk employing more agents or other resources to overcome the volume. Work must be done to ensure that the cost structure makes sense and no one is being taken advantage of.

Allows a Comparison to Other Service Providers A complete income and expense budget for the Help Desk allows for a tighter comparison to other service providers. There may be times when the Help Desk needs to justify its existence or the value it brings to certain niches of the IT department. This can be done from a corporate overview but is harder to do from a customer's view unless they know what they are paying for the service.

Chargebacks allow a customer to directly compare the cost of doing business with your Help Desk against other similar providers they have run into. The business may not allow them to switch, but they could look anyway. This looking is not necessarily a bad thing. Wouldn't it be nice for a customer that is always complaining about your fees to find no one else in the city or area that could provide the same services for anywhere close to your costs? They may still grumble, but they now don't have other facts to back up their claims.

Disadvantages

Chargebacks overall also have some downsides. First is the overhead it creates. With this, you must now have an administrative piece that keeps up with the billing of your services. Add to that the inevitable requests of your users to want credits for downtime or for work not done satisfactorily, and so on. If this is your only option for income, it can be done; it just comes with a cost. If possible, tie any billing with a Service Level Agreement (SLA) where you and your constituents agree on what an expected level of service should be. We will cover SLAs later in the book.

External Customers *Income may be part of your business product if you are supporting external customers. Whereas chargebacks are an administrative way to recoup costs, business income from operations is totally separate. In these cases, SLAs are even more important, if not required.*

Chargeback Communication Planning

As with any new implementation, communication to all affected people is a requirement for success. With proper communication, problems can be resolved before they get too big, and plans can be made before work is disrupted. The three biggest pieces of communication needed in a chargeback scenario are

- Reasons for implementing the plan
- How the process itself works
- The advantages to the customer

Reasons for Implementing the Plan   Get ahead of the game and publish the reasons the Help Desk is operating under a chargeback cost structure before the questions start coming in. You know why you are doing it, don't you? If not, you need to step back, way back, and think of the reasons.

The thing you need to make certain the customers understand is that these charges are to cover costs and not to gouge them for services rendered. They are in a business world themselves, so the customers should understand that products and services have costs, and that the Help Desk works the same way. Perhaps without a chargeback plan some services would be eliminated. If so, include that in the communication.

How the Process Works   Document clearly the process and procedures from which the chargeback plan operates. Your customers need to understand what is expected of them as it relates to billing and payment and what is to be expected from the Help Desk in terms of services and administration. A formal document should be drafted that spells out everything the customer needs to know.

External Customers   *With external customers, you will need to get your legal department involved. Internal customers need to know the procedures, but in the end, everyone is on the same team. External customers will need to have a contract drawn up that spells out payment policies and terms, warranties, and other issues a business needs with its contracted customers.*

The document for the process can have many different options. Table 6-1 lists some common things to consider when you create your own.

Advantages to the Customer   We have spoken about the advantages of a chargeback plan as it applies to the Help Desk. In this piece of communication, you need to

General Area	Specific Issue
Services	List of services you can offer
	A clear definition of each service
Charges	Cost of each service offered
	When payments are due
	Where to send payments
	How credits are handled
	How late or nonpayments are handled
Changes	How to add services
	How to change or delete services
	How parties will be notified of changes

Table 6.1   Chargeback Plan Considerations

educate the customer on the advantages this plan will give them. Processes are far easier to sell to someone if they see that they get something out of it. If the customer does not feel that he is getting any benefit from this chargeback plan, he will fight you every step of the way trying to understand it. Three main advantages to communicate are

- A better budgetary process for Help Desk services
- Opportunities to pick and choose particular services
- The ability to exercise explicit customer rights

The first advantage for customers is a better process with which to prepare their own budget. As the services have been clearly defined with the appropriate pricing associated with them, the customer has a good idea of how to plan financially for computer services for the upcoming budget cycle. Unless the customer pays a flat fee or no fee at all for his services, he will not have adequate information to input into his budget. With the chargeback process in place, he can get a feel for what services he will be using and plug the resulting numbers into his planning numbers.

This leads us to the second advantage, which is the ability of the customer to control his own destiny. By having the ability to select the services he wants your Help Desk to provide, he can control the costs he will incur. If the customer has been using the Help Desk to procure computer equipment but his budget will not allow that for the coming year, he can simply not select those services next time. If the customer is interested in expanding his own capabilities but does not want to hire staff to do it, he can coordinate with the Help Desk to get that job done and pay the subsequent charges for the service.

You must be very careful with allowing the customers to pick and choose services whenever they want, however they want. If you ramped up staff for the anticipated year of services and all your customers dropped that from their plans, you would be overstaffed and will have incurred unnecessary costs. To prevent this, you need to set proper expectations up front on how and when a customer can select or deselect a service. Communicating to them why this is important should allow a fair and effective process to continue.

Last, an advantage a paying customer has is the ability to exercise true customer rights. While the word *customer* has been used throughout, it is natural for someone to expect a little more for something when it is paid for. For example, you can order a hamburger and a drink from a fast food place and expect the hamburger to be hot and the drink to be cold. Now what if the bag also had French fries in it that you did not order? If the fries were cold, could you go back to the counter and complain that they were not hot? You are the customer and have a right, don't you?

You do have rights, but they are enhanced when you pay directly for the product or service you were expecting. As a Help Desk professional, you will never express this to anyone, and you will always endeavor to treat all customers the same, but the paying ones tend to get more regardless. This does not apply only when you expressly state this fact to all customers from the beginning. If you have an agreement that allocates services and processes to be of higher priority when a customer pays for them, then obviously that should be followed.

Chargeback Implementation

The customers have heard about the approaching chargeback plan and understand why it is happening. It is now up to you to implement it. Attention needs to be paid to the timing around your startup. It is not a plan you institute overnight. Proper planning is important in a couple of areas:

Implementation must be planned so the customers can prepare their own budgets with this in mind. It is not fair for the customers to be hit with charges for services they have never seen or were not prepared to pay for. Just because you may have been working this plan for a long time does not mean they are ready for it financially. You must communicate the charges and what makes them up to all affected parties before they finalize their budgets.

External Customers *In the case of external customers, you may not be privy to their budget cycle, if they even have one. To institute a chargeback plan in this instance, it is only fair to inform them of the charges well in advance of the actual act. In the same ways you promote your Help Desk, you can inform them of the charges to come.*

Plan for a "pilot period" where the model can be tested and modified if needed. Despite your best efforts and late-night working parties, there will be a need to change the plan at some point. It is one thing to have your group think of all the possible scenarios. It is quite another thing to let the entire customer base loose on the plan to see what they come up with. For this reason, you should divide your implementation timelines into three parts:

- Internal testing
- Testing with a small group of customers
- Total customer base implementation

Internal testing basically means using this cost plan against real customer interactions but without their knowing about it. Applying the cost model towards the actual calls will show you potential issues you had not planned for. For example, you may have a model for charging customers for hardware installations that includes travel costs. You might not have planned for hardware install requests for customers in your same building, though. Is it fair that co-located customers are charged the same amount as customers miles away? Maybe so, but that needs to be part of the communication.

Once you feel comfortable that you have covered all the bases from your internal tests, it is time to move out to the real world. Don't feel too confident yet. Introduce the plan to a customer location that is representative of the overall customer base and is IT Help Desk–friendly. If one location is not a good sample of all your customers, implement to the smallest number that can adequately test the plan. The Help Desk–friendly customers will better understand what you are trying to do and should help you uncover problems without attacking you.

Aside from the advantage of learning more about your charges, the pilot period will also gain you some credibility in the field. If you are able to talk to new customers about how this was tested in other locations first, they may feel less threatened to come under the plan. What might have been a half-cocked IT plan to make money may now have alliances from those customers who helped you design it from the beginning.

With the pilot period over, it is finally time to implement everywhere. You will still run into new issues and problems no one thought of, but the total count of complaints will have been reduced by your careful introduction.

Chargeback Administration

We spoke earlier about chargebacks bringing a bit of the business into the Help Desk. If nothing else, the administration of the charges will require the Help Desk to understand charges and credits, invoices and statements. Look at this angle of the plan in its easiest form. Charges need to billed out and money needs to come in. It is likely that the Help Desk will not be the primary administrators of the billing of the services, but it is important that the Help Desk be familiar with its operation.

Charges need to come out of the Help Desk in some fashion. It may be as formal as an invoice detailing the services and subsequent charges. It may be a simple e-mail that lists the items and the charges are included in other internal mechanisms. In either case, the Help Desk must keep up with what is chargeable and include that on the document.

When the customer receives the charge, he must now pay for it. As with the invoice, it can arrive in multiple ways. The customer could send a check, pay off of a purchase order or credit card, or simply allow the internal mechanism to keep up with it. The fun part is when the charge is not paid or is disputed. How do you plan on handling refusal of payment or a customer wanting a credit for one of the line items?

These instances need to be completely planned for and spelled out before the first charge lands on a customer's desk. There needs to be a clear and firm rule for nonpayment and credit requests. Depending on the nature of your charges, the penalty could be handled through some form of compromise or it could be as tough as the Help Desk refusing to service the customer any longer. You could even bring in legal teams to help resolve the dispute. This part of the charging needs to be dealt with delicately as well. Years of strong relations with a customer may vanish in an instant over a minor dispute of charges for a service. Make sure you fully understand all the ramifications and benefits of the plan before you take action against a customer.

Professional Services

The Help Desk may generate some revenue under the auspices of professional services. Tied into the needs of your customers, professional services is a fancy way to track and charge customers for proactive work the Help Desk is in a good position to provide. Let's look at three potential services that could stand alone as professional services:

- Technology recommendations
- Procurement
- Hardware installation and repair

Technology Recommendations

The Help Desk will see almost every combination of people, hardware, and software that the customer could use to conduct business. They will become aware of what works, what could be improved, and what absolutely does not work. This information is valuable and could be applied to other customers who are looking at options of different things. An income potential is to sell this experience in the form of technology consulting.

Suppose a customer is adding a new location to his network and does not know how many devices he will need. He could contact some arm of the Help Desk organization to aid in the design of the computing within his building. The Help Desk cannot tell him how many people to hire or what products to sell, but it can help on the parts of the computer side. For example, the Help Desk can tell the customer what types of printers work best in a warehouse environment versus an office environment. The service could recommend cabling requirements or help on issues with integrating certain software applications together.

A professional services group must be close to the Help Desk but need not be a vital "on the phone" group of agents. You could rotate agents with the right skills in and out of the services group, but they cannot stay on the phone at the same time. To do this would cause lower service levels on supporting the customers and create distractions to the professional services group.

Procurement

Handling the procurement of equipment and software for your customers could be another source of income for the Help Desk. This is another example of where the Help Desk is not strictly a break/fix group but an organization that exists to serve the customers in their computing needs.

The Help Desk is in a good position to take on the requirements of the customer and match them to the right vendor or supplier. It is valuable to the customer because they can remain focused on their job at hand and not worry about getting the tools to do this job. The Help Desk benefits because it now knows what technology is being implemented in the field and can manage it through asset and change management. For a more complete account of ideas on how to implement a procurement organization within the Help Desk and a list of its benefits, refer to the "Procurement" section in Chapter 22.

Hardware Installation and Repair

Another service that could be billed out is hardware installation and repair. Continuing with the theme of keeping the customer focused on their own jobs, the Help Desk can sell its services to handle the connections of purchased hardware onto the network or other devices. Travel, hotels, meals, and so on could be involved so the costs would have to be covered somewhere. The customers could choose to do this themselves but may find it harder to do than they first expected and they may cause damage to existing equipment in the process. You would be offering them the help to do it from the Help Desk group or they could tackle it on their own.

Professional Services Caveat

The trouble with professional services arises when the customers begin asking why these services are not part of the standard Help Desk offering. "It's your computers, you come do it," is not what you want to be battling as you manage the Help Desk. This is why it is imperative that the services you provide as standard are clearly explained and agreed to by many people early in the process. Immediately following this is the clear and agreed-upon cost allocation plan you are implementing. If these are done well, the customers will not backlash against you when you present them with professional services. After all, they are not required to use them, are they?

Because they are not required to use you, it is important that you proactively communicate (market) your services and the value they bring to the customer. Before they have a chance to think, "Why would I use them for this project?" you can demonstrate to the customer how your service could reduce their own internal costs or increase the productivity of their people to do other things.

Cost or Expense Items

A Help Desk is like any other business entity. It needs money to operate. Hopefully, you will not have to sit down at your desk with a blank sheet of paper to start a budget. If the Help Desk existed in prior years, make sure you get a copy of that budget to build from. If this is the first year, try to get a budget copy of some other organization in the company to get you to a starting point. Below are some common expense items and how they fit in the budget.

Compensation

A budgetary item that may be completely out of your control is the salary levels allowed for your team. Help Desks began as an afterthought in many companies and therefore their salary levels were not given much consideration, especially when compared to programmers or systems administrators. Today, however, Help

Desk associates are recognized for the value they bring the IT department and their salaries are moving upward. Demonstrating this may take time and good measurements (like we will discuss in Chapter 13) will help but try for all you can at the beginning.

I am a firm believer in the "You get what you pay for" mind-set, and a successful startup needs more than clerical people. If the salary levels you are allowed are low against the market, try hard for other areas to help compensation. Make sure when you communicate salaries to recruits that you mention all the types of compensation you are providing.

Overtime

If your Help Desk agents are hourly, you will contend with overtime as part of their compensation. Overtime is the number of hours above 40 hours per week that an associate works. It is paid at a time and a half rate. So if the agent worked ten hours of overtime, he or she would earn 15 hours of salary. Overtime is obviously expensive and should be managed. The trick is managing it in a Help Desk environment.

Tight Management of Overtime   Agents whose overtime is managed very tightly will become very cognizant of the clock. The theory is that the minute the clock strikes the time agents are supposed to get off work, they are out the door. This is okay unless they were in the middle of working a problem with a customer at the time. A customer will not take too kindly being dumped just because someone has to go home.

Loose Management of Overtime   Conversely, if overtime is not managed, the cost to the business will rise and more scrutiny will be applied to the Help Desk and its management. Agents may work lower priority calls at the end of their shift just to accumulate the extra pay. You can't fault them for wanting to take care of open issues unless it is just to make more money.

Manage Overtime in the Middle   A balanced blend of overtime is the only solution. Educate your agents on the cost of overtime and its impact on the business and therefore the Help Desk. Acknowledge that some overtime will have to be incurred to take care of the customer, but reasonable efforts should be made to keep the times low. If you find overtime costs increasing, look into the reasons. It may be a particular agent working longer hours. If so, find out why. If all the agents on the team are contributing, research if the reasons are due to pure workload or other issues such as travel and training.

Pure workload could be a sign that the quantity of agents in the Help Desk is not sufficient. If your agents are well trained and focused on doing a good job, their hours may be out of necessity to serve the customer. Travel and training could come into play if the agents are paid when they travel. Now when they are on a plane travelling to a seminar, they are earning money. If this time is not offset at another time, your overtime costs will be harder to bring down. The important thing is to understand the real reasons you are racking up overtime dollars and see if there are opportunities to reduce it.

Other Perks

Remember compensation is more than a salary; it is also medical benefits, vacation, retirement plans, and additional career opportunities to name a few. Go beyond those normal, typical compensation items, though. How about offering a free membership to a local gym or sports club? Are there newspapers or other periodicals the associate would be interested in receiving? The paper does not even have to be directly related to the Help Desk. *The Wall Street Journal*, for example, is not a Help Desk paper, but it can have articles that apply to the business you are in or your customers are moving to. Maybe you don't subscribe to *ESPN Magazine* for each associate, but as long as they don't read it at their desks all day, why not? The cost does not amount to much at all, and it's a good way to compensate people for their work. Simple perks like these quickly add up to make the associate feel rewarded for the hard work and energy he puts into his job.

If you cannot think of good ways to compensate your agents outside of their salary, ask them. This method certainly takes the guesswork out of the process. Especially with your proven agents who you really value, inquire as to their wishes for additional methods of being compensated. Wouldn't it be nice to find out that buying someone some movie tickets every other month makes him feel rewarded and makes his family appreciate the company even more?

Salary Surveys

Be careful not to use salary surveys as gospel because for every high salary survey a Help Desk agent can find, a manager can find a low salary survey. The surveys are useful for directional use and noticing trends. Word always gets out among associates concerning compensation, so it is important that your basis is solid and you are heading in the right direction. Reviewing your Help Desk's salary compared to the rest of the IT department and your company's starting levels is a good place to begin. Look at outside surveys if only to gain an average perspective of the market rates. You may find that over time you are consistently paying over or under those rates and your methodology needs to be reviewed.

Dues

Dues and memberships to organizations should be budgeted for each year. Agents can learn many new ideas on resolving problems or implementing best practices by attending Help Desk meetings or seminars related to the IT profession. This gives them contact with the outside world and also serves as a break from the day-to-day routine of the phones ringing. Being recognized as a professional helps keep people motivated in their jobs, and being a member of a club or group helps lead to that. With that in mind, you can include certain dues and memberships in conversations when you speak with associates about their compensation. It is a cost that the company pays directly for an associate after all.

One opportunity to look for when planning memberships is to see if corporate memberships are available. Particularly if your Help Desk has many agents in it, you may find it more cost effective to acquire a corporate membership instead of accumulating individual ones. This helps your Help Desk be recognized as an entity onto itself, potentially gets more agents in the organization where they can benefit, and might be cheaper on the budget as well.

Facilities

Are you responsible for renting or leasing office space for your Help Desk? If so, don't forget to include these costs in your budget. The building may be free but any additional desks might cost you. Understand all these physical costs and how they will affect you. Include them in your budgeted headcount growth to come up with your total facility costs.

Maintenance

Maintenance items on the budget represent the costs involved with keeping things running. This is not related to electricity or gasoline. If your Help Desk has to budget for those things it would be in the Facilities column. Maintenance items include software and hardware maintenance contracts and services associated with keeping the systems up and functioning.

The best place to start putting this number together is by listing all the hardware and software you have implemented that you are fiscally responsible for. If you have an asset management system, that is the place to go. Once you have that list, begin gathering all the past year's invoices that were associated with the assets. Sort through the ones that are marked as support or maintenance and you have a starting number.

Next, look at the language of the contracts to see if any of the costs are going to rise (as warranties expire) or drop (as price discount levels are met). Factor that into your equation.

Last, find out as much as you can about coming initiatives that the IT department has planned. What hardware is planned to be installed and are there more software packages coming? Use your best judgment about what those maintenance costs may be and add them in. The resulting number is as good a maintenance budget as you can get. If a major initiative springs up that you had not heard of, the budget of that individual project should pick up the maintenance costs.

While we are on that topic, a value the Help Desk can bring to project planning is reminding everyone that there are costs involved in technology after it is acquired. Projects will probably include implementation and training costs, but project managers sometimes forget to budget for ongoing maintenance costs after all the fanfare dies down. These numbers can be as high as 15 to 20 percent of the acquisition cost so it is important enough to keep them in front of people. As the Help Desk lives every day in this world, they are a good source of information for the kind of support and maintenance agreements a project will need.

Office Equipment

Hardware costs can add up fast, so this category should get significant attention from you when building the budget. It is not just the price of a PC or server you need to consider. You also need to review the current state of your agent's hardware to determine if upgrades or replacements may be required. Review the overall IT budget to see what else may be coming. If the technology plan calls for significant increases in new technology for the customer base, you will need to increase your needs as well. Remember that the Help Desk needs access to the same hardware and software that its customers have.

A Quick, and Very Basic, Finance Lesson

When building the hardware budget, it is important to understand some financial considerations such as leasing, expensing versus capitalizing, and depreciation. This is important because depending on how your company finances this equipment, your budget line item will be affected. To see this impact, look at the acquisition of a $2,000 PC as shown in Table 6-2.

The monthly impact is a small difference for one PC, but know that the differences add up to when you are budgeting for many PCs and other pieces of hardware and software. This distinction is why you need to know the rules beforehand. If you want to cheat, just ask the finance group what you should budget for a $2,000 PC and plug in whatever they say.

Methodology	Monthly Impact	2 Year Impact
Company purchases and expenses these line items	$0	$2000
Company purchases, capitalizes, and depreciates over 2 years	$85	$2000
Company leases for 2 years at a .038 rate per month	$76	$1824 * but has no PC at the end

Table 6.2   Financing Method Demonstration

Office Supplies

Little things can keep people effective. Pens, notepads, folders, etc. are all items that will be needed over the course of a year so plan for them. Perhaps you provide all your agents with business cards. These can typically be done on a per person basis, so figure out how many agents you will have and multiply the costs.

Meals

Meals certainly sound easy to calculate and I agree. This category is really just how much money needs to be allocated to feeding your agents. I recommend that you add in some money for morale and recognition, too. It doesn't cost much to bring in a pizza every now and again to thank your agents for their help over the year. It's a fun, cheap way to bring your agents closer together. Closer? Sure, though it may just be physically as they wait in line for the pizza boxes!

Personal recognition can be given over a breakfast or lunch once in a while so put in some money to cover taking each agent out to eat once or twice a year. This gives them some one-on-one time with you or their manager to go over anything they want to. It also gives the manager that same opportunity to thank the agent for his effort or help him overcome challenges.

Outsourcing

Are there any partners helping you provide the services that you offer? Are there projects on the horizon that you feel the Help Desk is not qualified or resourced to handle? If either is true, you will need outsourcing dollars in the budget.

If you anticipate headcount troubles, provide outsourcing dollars as an alternative. The work ahead is real and someone has to handle the load. Whether it is agents on your staff or associates in another company, people are needed to perform the job. It may be helpful to include expected headcount increases AND outsourcing dollars in the budget. Then point out to the approving parties what you have done and have them choose which method they wish to spend their money on. Don't just enter the budget and walk away. You are responsible for helping them in the decision. It is just that doing it this way helps them see it in a financial setting.

Software Costs

Hardware doesn't do much good without software running on it. As you are calculating your hardware needs, work the software as well. The agents may need spreadsheets, word processing, or presentation software for the coming year. If you have plans to implement call management or phone system software, this is the place to record it.

Training

There are two methods I have used to determine my training budget. The first is on an agent by agent basis. I figure out what typical training classes or seminars cost, multiply that by how many outings I want to send agents to, and multiply that result by the number of agents I have. Don't forget those that you plan to hire over the year, too. While they may not have the same number of training events as existing staff, there may be opportunities, or needs, to send them off as well.

To put some numbers into that word equation, here is an example:

Cost of avg. class	# of events	# of agents	Total training costs
$1800	2	13	$46,800

Budgetary Estimates on Costs and Quantities

Have any idea on how much classes typically cost or how many events you should send agents to? Well, it certainly depends on the experience of your staff and the current workload of that staff. The more experienced your staff is the more training may not be required, but may be wished for. The desire for training does not decrease with experience. The effect here is on the cost of the class. Entry level classes and especially those on soft skills can be found anywhere from $600 to $2,000. As you get deeper into the skill set, the costs naturally increase. For these types of classes you should plan on a range from $1,500 to $4,000.

The workload of the agents will most definitely affect the quantity of classes they can attend. Absolute first rule here, though:

Do not sacrifice training because you are too busy!

If you use workload as the reason associates cannot get training, you are sentencing yourself and the Help Desk to an ever-increasing workload and a constantly high turnover rate. What you can do is review how many times they can go and for what periods of time. If you have a staff of one, it will be difficult to send that one agent to ten classes, each lasting a week. A good base to start from is having your agents attend two formal classes a year and allow that number to rise or fall based on the skill set of each agent.

The other method you can use is to budget your training efforts by the needs or categories you see coming. For example, if the future technology plan calls for installing a new ERP package or you plan to implement a new operating system across the company, a new skill set may be needed in the Help Desk. In that case, budget certain dollar amounts not to people, but to technologies. This method helps focus the training effort towards the direction you are headed. Individual agents are still encouraged to explore new areas to learn, but there is an overall expectation that it includes the technology plans that were laid out.

When calculating the training budget, take the opportunity to figure out the related travel and meals portion at the same time. A lot of training can involve travel and the agent has to eat, so this is a good place to get several pieces of the budget done simultaneously. If the budget is getting close to its ceiling and you have many more items to budget, you may want to research opportunities to bring training classes to your office instead of individual agents traveling to other sites. This is most effective where you have large staffs with similar skills because you can spread the cost of the training class over a larger number of agents. This reduces your training dollar per agent rate.

Travel

Travel costs can be incurred in a variety of ways—attending training, conducting training for your customers, or going to a remote site to resolve an issue. Travel can include airline tickets, car mileage, and hotels. The ways to calculate an accurate travel budget are many and can get confusing.

Take a systematic approach that apportions a like dollar amount for different categories of travel. Create a spreadsheet that has the components of travel in it and you can begin plugging in numbers until you reach a final figure you are comfortable with. Figure 6-2 is an example of this preparation.

Travel Budget Planning

Assumptions:

Airfare	500				
Hotel	125				
Rental Car	30				

Major Event:			**Minor Event:**		
Airfare	500		Airfare	0	
Hotel	500		Hotel	125	
Rental Car	120		Car	30	
Major total	1,120		Minor total	155	

Agents	# of majors	Major $	# of minors	Minor $	Total Travel
Jaylin	2	2,240	2	310	2,550
Caroline	2	2,240	2	310	2,550
Clark	1	1,120	2	310	1,430
Corrie	1	1,120	2	310	1,430
Customer Training	5	5,600	12	1,860	7,460
Total Travel					**$15,420**

Figure 6.2   Travel budget spreadsheet

This level of detail can work proactively and reactively. Proactively, you can play with individual trips and lengths so your total falls within the parameters you think will be required or allowed. Reactively, you will be able to add or delete items if the budgeting committee adjusts your total number any.

If you have travel related to onsite repair services, I suggest you keep this budgeted amount separate from the rest. I would do this for two reasons. First, you may not be able to control these costs as well as the other costs, and you don't want to lose training travel opportunities because your repair service travels ran higher than you expected.

Second, this service is a prime candidate to bill back to your customers, and this can be done best when you have good tracking data to begin with. Keeping this part of your budget set aside helps facilitate the process.

Getting Budgetary Approval

There are a few occasions where budgetary numbers are turned in and accepted without debate or even cuts. The following are three ways to help you get the numbers you want and need:

- Separating infrastructure from the proactive work
- Benefits cases
- Providing alternatives

Separating Infrastructure from the Proactive Work

The first recommendation is to divide your budget into an infrastructure piece and a proactive piece. The headings are not as important as what you put in them. The infrastructure section has all the costs needed to keep the Help Desk up and running. Existing salaries, hardware and software costs, facility costs if required, and so on would go here. Review industry standards around customers or devices per agent to help you in planning for new hires and include those costs here.

The proactive section is where you put costs of items you feel would help the process but are not necessarily required. These could include costs for a software package you do not have or larger monitors for your PCs. If you separate the two costs you will be a lot more successful in getting budgetary items approved when they are labeled as "infrastructure" versus something else. When the budgetary ax swings it will more likely spare the infrastructure and only cut into the proactive. That is okay because if you have a benefits case for the proactive items, you may get them approved in the end, anyway. Also, if these items are requested later, you can show your foresight in planning for them even though they were not approved. Hey, it doesn't hurt to self-promote every once in a while!

A great place to try this segregation is in the training portion of your budget. As discussed earlier, you can determine your training budget in a variety of ways. This approach is how you present the dollars you want. Look at two inserts of a training budget. Figure 6-3 is the most basic.

As one line item amidst all the others, Training tends to blend in. However, when budgets need to be cut and training is a large part of the cost, it may actually stand out and have more chance of being trimmed down. So, take it another level in detail and break it out by agent. This doesn't have to be done on your main budget sheet, but can be provided in an attachment as shown in Figure 6-4.

. . . .	
Dues	$1,000
Office equipment	$3,000
Training	**$28,000**
Travel	$16,000
. . . .	

Figure 6.3 Basic budget entry

This budget is clearer and shows the approving committee how you wish to spend the $28,000. It is up to them to decide if you keep the entire amount or lose some. They won't point out a particular agent to reduce, but will have you do that. Their wish is that the total comes out to whatever they request. Obviously, if your Help Desk has 600 agents, it is not prudent to list each one on a sheet. In this case, it is better to list the groups of agents (frontline, second-tier, etc.) instead.

What if you did the budget in yet a different method as shown in Figure 6-5?

Since you are part of the technology planning committee, you know of the IT department's intent to move into the areas listed in your training budget. To prepare for this implementation, you want to send your agents off for training on these specific areas. When the approving committee reviews the budget, they will be forced more into making a decision on where they would want cuts to come from. Instead of wondering if one agent versus another would lose training, now

. . . .	
Training	
Frontline agents	
Chris	$4,500
Tara	$4,500
Rich	$5,000
Rob	$2,000
Second-tier agents	
Schuyler	$6,000
Judy	$6,000
TOTAL	$28,000

Figure 6.4 Training budget by agent

```
. . . . . . . .
Training
        Windows 2000              $7,000
        PC repair                 $9,000
        Networking fundamentals  $12,000
Total training                   $28,000

. . . . . . . .
```

Figure 6.5   Training budget by topic

an entire technology would be at risk. This method does not guarantee total consent, but it does show your strategic thinking and focus on the future.

Benefits Case

Obviously, anytime you want funding for something, you need to convince the people with the money why they should give you some. Because "Trust me" seldom works, a business, or benefits, case is a good way to get what you need. A business case can be a complicated form detailing balance sheets, income statements, marketing plans, and competitive surveys. A benefits case is much shorter and shows a simple form of the costs and returns of the proposal. We will concentrate on the benefits case in this chapter.

Return on Investment

The most important section of a benefits case is the part where you inform the audience of the value and return on investment that their money will receive. Because it is their money, the emphasis should be on the benefits the audience themselves will receive and not just what you can gain. For example, say you need money for new PCs. Telling the reader that you need them because they are too slow for your agents or they cannot display the graphics you would like will only get you so far. However, explaining how these new PCs will give your agents better tools to serve your customers will work wonders.

Hiring more people is another area where putting things in the correct perspective will help. Saying you need another person because everyone else is overworked may be true but the executives will have a hard time seeing what return they will get. Saying the new person will decrease problem resolution times and the Help Desk can expand its operating hours should work better. More on headcounts in a moment.

Measurable

Just as you should focus your benefits towards the reader, you should also make the results as measurable as possible. As the prior example showed, expanded hours and a decrease in problem resolution times can be measured and therefore the return is more easily seen. Nothing breeds success like success, so the more you can show that your historical benefits case performs as advertised, the more your audience will take your future requests for more money seriously.

Costs

Ah, but there is a cost to most benefit cases and you would be wise to recognize them. The owner of the money you need obviously needs to know how much you want. If you need more people, there are compensation costs that include salary, benefits, and whatever tools you buy for your associates. For our previous new PCs example, the costs are definitely the price of however many PCs you need. Costs also may include cabling and software. Just as you did in the benefits section, the costing section needs to show the timing of the monetary needs. It may be an initial outlay of cash or it may be a leasing program that spreads the cost over three to four years.

Sample Benefits Case

A proper benefits case needs to demonstrate the positives as well as the costs. In both sections, you need to be realistic and accurate. Fudging statistics might gain you approval one time, but it will catch up to you quickly. Focus on how your needs match the wishes of the money owner, and you will have a good chance of success. A basic benefits case form could resemble the one shown in Figure 6-6.

Let's walk through the sections on the benefits case form as if we were planning to purchase a call management package for the Help Desk.

Benefits—Revenue   Installing a call management package will not generate any revenue for our initial purposes so that column is zero. (Separately, you should recognize this line item as a potential income stream if you later decide to sell its knowledge and use for external customers.)

Benefits—Productivity Increase   For this business case, the largest benefits will come from an increase in productivity. We are counting on our agents to be more efficient in their jobs and provide better and more timely customer service. Using the package's expert knowledge system, the agents should be able to answer questions more quickly and get the business people back to work faster. So in the benefits case we will put some money in the productivity column for two reasons.

```
┌─────────────────────────────────────────────────────────────────────┐
│                          BENEFITS CASE FOR                            │
│                          Year 1    Year 2                             │
│  Benefits:                                                            │
│        Revenue                                                        │
│        Productivity increase                                          │
│        Cost reduction                                                 │
│        Other                                                          │
│  Costs:                                                               │
│        Acquisition                                                    │
│        Associate time                                                 │
│        Outside services                                               │
│        Other                                                          │
│  Annual Return on Investment                                          │
│  Cumulative Return on Investment                                      │
└─────────────────────────────────────────────────────────────────────┘
```

Figure 6.6   Benefits case form

One will be the increase for the Help Desk agents and one will be for the customers of the Help Desk. Estimate the hourly rate of a representative associate in each group, multiply that by the hours saved using the package, and insert the extension into the business case.

Recognize this is a soft area of the form. If you have 100 agents making $15 an hour and the package will save them 200 hours a year, the resulting benefits come out to $300,000 per year. That is quite a high number and could probably justify the purchase all by itself. How accurate is it, though? Will the business make that much more money each year? Probably not. This number should be included in the business case, but you should acknowledge to your audience that it is only part of the total equation. If the benefits case is a formal part of your company's procedures, you should really emphasize the "soft factor" of your estimates. You do not want someone coming back to you later because the company did not see a $300,000 earnings gain on the income statement.

Benefits—Cost Reduction   There is a fuzzy distinction between increased productivity and cost reduction when it comes to the impact on associates' time. If the software package, in this example, allowed the agents to go home earlier, then the impact would be recorded in cost reduction. If it allowed them to have more time to do other work, then the amount would go in increased productivity.

In keeping with the call management package business case, the package will likely reduce costs in customers waiting on problem resolution if the package can provide the agents with better access to the answers. Again, though, does it therefore increase their effectiveness or reduce the cost of downtime?

Other proposals will have a clearer distinction. Maybe it is suggesting to switch service providers with a lower charge. The important part of cost reduction is following up after implementation to ensure the costs are actually being reduced.

Benefits—Other This section of the benefits case is for any other benefits that will be achieved. They may have a dollar impact or something less firm to measure. Examples of this could be goodwill or increased customer satisfaction. The section may be used as a less formal area to list other positive effects the proposed plan will produce.

Costs—Acquisition Acquisition cost is the cost of purchasing, hiring, leasing, or renting any asset to achieve the proposed item. In our example, it would include the cost of the package itself, any hardware needed, training, and upgrades to existing equipment if required.

In other circumstances, the cost could be the need to hire more Help Desk agents to achieve the goal. Acquisition certainly seems harsh when it refers to people, but it is really just a common area in which to keep the outlay of funds for assets together.

Costs—Associate Time Much as we calculated cost reduction or productivity increases, associate time costS is found by taking the number of people needed to implement the project, multiply by their rate, and multiply again by the amount of time needed to finish the project.

"FTEs" or full-time equivalents may be used here. This is saying that the costs may not be specific people at specific times. It is convenient to use when the project will require parts of many people's time. For example, the call package may need a LAN administrator, some PC installers, and a trainer. The project does not need the Help Desk to hire these people nor will they be on the project full time. Without using the FTE plan, the project costs may look like:

LAN installation	March 1–March 31
2 PC installers	March 15–May 30
Trainer	May 1–May 30

Only looking at times may cause the benefits case writer to calculate costs based on 18 weeks. This would not be accurate because the people are not working on this project full time. They are only needed at certain points throughout the project.

The FTE calculation could be done by:

LAN Administrator tasks	10 days
PC installation	20 days
Training	10 days

This total would equate to 40 FTE days and more accurately reflects the cost of the project that should be included on the benefits case. Be wary on always relying completely on FTE calculations, however. They help show a more accurate cost on a piece of paper, but when was the last time you actually *met* an FTE?

Note
These times are NOT reflective of a quality call management implementation. To do that right will require much more time and resources. Our FTE sample calculation is for illustrative purposes only.

Finally, when doing associate cost numbers, you should consider opportunity costs at the same time. Opportunity cost is the cost of not doing something else because time is being spent on the project at hand. For example, the time the agents are spending installing the call management package could be spent on cold calling prospective customers to use the Help Desk's services. You could figure some ratio of calls per successful customer signing and assign that lost revenue to the project. This is quite time consuming and highly subjective. It is not recommended unless you want the benefits case to show ALL costs or the audience requires rigid parameters.

Costs—Outside Services Outside services are costs incurred by bringing in outside partners to help you with the project. In this example, it could be hiring the management package vendor to install the package or train the agents on its use. Where associate time costs involved the people in your own company, this section deals with anyone else who may be involved.

Costs—Other Other costs include anything that does not fit nicely into the previous cost sections. Care should be taken to itemize the costs on the benefits case so the audience can best understand it. Projects have a much harder time getting approval with a large *Miscellaneous* line item included for them.

Annual Return on Investment The return on investment is simply the sum of the benefits minus the sum of the costs. Notice that the benefits form has two columns, one for Year One and another for Year Two. This is done because many times the benefits of a proposal will not be realized until it has had time to grow and spread through an organization. Costs as well may decrease over time, allowing later years to increase in return versus the first year. Depending on the financial requirements of your company, the finance committee may want to see even more years or just the first. In our call management example, the cost of buying the package will show up in the first year but will not appear after that. There are additional costs, such as maintenance and support, but they should be detailed separately.

Cumulative Return on Investment An important element of the benefits case is to point out exactly when you feel the proposal will begin making a positive return on the investment. Obviously, the sooner it makes money for the company, the better. Where the annual return column shows benefits and costs for *each* year, the cumulative column shows the net increase or decrease when the years are combined. This allows the reader to see easily the year in which the return is made. Take another step and highlight on the benefits case the year or time the return is positive. A completed example can be seen in Figure 6-7.

Provide Alternatives

To show the executives that you have thought through the process, you may want to provide alternatives. An example is budgeting to support a new software package. Instead of just applying some ratio and saying you need x more people, you could also include an alternative that asks for $x to have someone else support it. This way the executives can align your needs with the particular business climate at the time. Some budget years you may be faced with keeping headcount down but told to increase your support offering. You could show you would need more people or more dollars to outsource. When the executives see the dollar difference, they can choose where they want the dollars spent.

The time to do this is not during the final budget presentation but beforehand. You may put your plan together and meet with individual people who will be approving your budget to run your ideas by them. Let's look at another example where the alternatives are tied to a particular new initiative IT is planning.

BENEFITS CASE FOR FORMING A HARDWARE PROCUREMENT TEAM		
	Year 1	Year 2
Benefits:		
Revenue		
$15 per device with estimated 1000 first year and 3000 the next	$15,000	$45,000
Productivity increase		
Will save 30 minutes per purchase for $20/hour corporate staff	$10,000	$30,000
Cost reduction		
Discounts by providing forecasts to vendors and bulk buys	$10,000	$45,000
Other		
Tighter asset management, standards adherence		
Total Revenue:	**$35,000**	**$115,000**
Costs:		
Acquisitions		
1 Clerical associate	$25,000	$28,000
1 PC	$1,500	$0
Furniture	$5,000	$0
Associate time		
(covered in new hire)		
Outside services		
Consulting help on setting up effective procurement operations	$5,000	$0
Other		
Training	$2,000	$2,000
Total Costs:	**$38,500**	**$30,000**
Annual Return on Investment	**($3,500)**	**$85,000**
		Profitable
Cumulative Return on Investment	**($3,500)**	**$81,500**

Figure 6.7 Hardware procurement benefits case

Distributing Software Upgrades to PCs in the Field Offices

Scope: The 1,500 PCs in our 45 field offices are running the older version of our accounting software. We need to upgrade the software before we roll out the new financial planning initiative that was approved this year. We see the need for this to occur every 18 months.

Resources needed: The resources to perform this task are not currently available, so we will need to acquire them. I have presented three plans I feel comfortable with. Because the dollars affect different pieces of the budget and I know that our business climate sometimes calls for emphasis to be placed in certain areas, I am presenting them all for your input.

Plan A: Purchase an Electronic Software Distribution Package

There are many software packages on the market that can allow us to load software upgrades on a central server, which will then send the upgrades to each network PC that needs them. Our PCs are all managed remotely anyway so this can work in our current environment.

Plan B: Hire two Help Desk agents

The current staff cannot visit all the field offices and answer the volume of incoming calls they have. These two new agents can travel to the sites and, once done with the project, they can augment my existing staff in the Help Desk. As this finance plan is recurring, they will be available for each rollout in the future.

Plan C: Outsource the distribution

We can contract with a vendor partner to do the work for us. I have a partner in mind that has done some network installs for us in the past and also has the expertise to perform this type of upgrade. Their rates are pretty good.

Cost comparison:

Software tool	$175,000 implemented
2 agents	$74,000 per year (fully loaded)
Outsource	$200,000 including expenses

Recommendation: I feel confident that the Help Desk will continue to grow with the way the business is continuing to grow. Since the rollout is not beginning for four months and it does not have an extremely tight time schedule, I recommend that we hire the agents and have them install the upgrades. They will be needed in the future operations anyway.

This plan should impress the executives at many levels. It appears well thought out and shows you can think of many ways to get a job done. There is a recommendation at the end, which can guide them to some conclusion. It also shows that while you can think of multiple angles, you also possess the decision-making skills to come up with a decision. Last, you present clear options that can help the executives make a good financial decision.

People vs. Tools

Another factor in the budget process is deciding how much automation you want or can afford. The question is, do you want people to perform tasks and run processes or do you want to implement technology to resolve issues? The example in the "Provide Alternatives" section was a place where the business can help you decide where it would like certain expenses placed. Obviously, there are needs for both at times, but having an overall plan, in your mind at least, will help in future planning.

If looking strictly at costs, you will usually find that technology is more expensive at first but over time is cheaper. Sure, technology can have maintenance contracts and upgrade costs but people do as well. We just call them different things. People involve salaries, promotions, reviews, and training.

What if you look at personable customer service? No matter how much the technology vendors try, no tool can match the friendliness and "good feeling" a person can bring to a situation. There are many people who are far less friendly than a machine but we will not be hiring them into our Help Desk!

An example of where you could have a choice is in the most basic act of answering the phone. You might decide to have a call dispatcher who answers the phone and directs the caller to the most appropriate section of your Help Desk. The dispatcher can greet each caller with a message of your choice, make the caller feel important, and then pass the caller along. You could use technology to do this instead with an ACD (Automated Call Distribution) and auto attendant system. This system could greet the users, provide them options from which they can choose depending on their problems, ask them to hold for an available agent, and route them to the agent by the option they choose.

The next Real World Example is a good example of not meeting your customers' needs even though it was technically a sound idea. Giving the customers what they want instead of what you think they want is a constant issue to keep in front of you. Rest assured that if you don't, your customers will end up making sure that you do or that someone else will.

Real-World Example

When we moved into a new building for our Help Desk, I implemented an ACD system. I advertised its use and promoted the fact that callers would not receive busy signals anymore and would get a Help Desk agent who could best resolve their issues. I even took some steps to organize our staff around the ACD options. What worked great for my group began receiving negative feedback, however. Users who always complained about never getting us because of busy signals in the past were now complaining about the impersonal machine and not being able to figure out the choices the ACD system asked of them.

The feedback became so overwhelming we were forced to act. Instead of scrapping an expensive new technology, we hired a temporary resource and added an option to the phone system that allowed the caller to be directed to a call dispatcher instead of being put on hold or directed by an impersonal phone system. Immediately many callers chose this option. The dispatcher did nothing different from the phone system; she took messages and passed paper to the agents, but our customers felt better. Subsequent surveys showed half our callers preferred this new method of receiving calls because they could deliver their messages without fear of them being miscommunicated. Our feedback rating climbed back to normal levels and we hired the temporary full time.

Budgeting Is Not a One-Time Event

The budget process should last the whole year. If your Help Desk is large it may feel like it already does, but the act of preparing income and cost estimates is much easier if you keep up with it all along. Whenever you run across a new item or increase in dollars, make a note of it somewhere. Perhaps you keep a folder for any new budgetary item. You could upscale it a bit and keep the entries in a spreadsheet or database. All are fine as long as you do it. Meaning to write it down or "knowing you will remember it at budget time" will doom you to failure. Time will only bring you new projects and challenges and will make the odds of your remembering all items hard to do. It takes no time to copy the invoice and place it in a folder marked Next Year's Budget.

Finally, get others involved in the budget process if you can. Even if you have only one other person, it will be worth it to show them some of the budget world. There are many advantages to this, with small disadvantages, as Table 6-3 shows.

Advantages	Disadvantages
More people can bring ideas and help you remember existing ones.	More people can slow the process down if they are not managed correctly.
Helps the associate learn more about business.	They may be disheartened if their ideas do not make the cut.
Prepares them for the process further in their career.	If technical enough, they may feel worse to have to manage numbers versus playing with technology.
Getting them involved helps them assume some responsibility in the process.	
The process is a break from the phones and can help prevent burnout.	

Table 6.3   Advantages and Disadvantages to Budget Teams

As you can see, the advantages outnumber the disadvantages both in number and in quality. Pick your places, but find some way to get more people involved.

Quick Recap

- What is expected of you at budget time? Do you have input into the budget process or will it be completed without you? Even if the budget will be written and approved by others, make sure to provide some input or suggestions for them to consider.

- Where will your money come from? You have to make money to spend money and now is the time to learn how you will make it. Will the corporate budget cover your expenses or will you have to charge your customers for your services? Either party will want a return on their investment so you will need to produce.

- Do you understand all your costs for the coming year?

- Is your organization geared more towards people expenses or technology? How will this affect how you conduct your business?

- Do you have plans to make next year's budget even more accurate and effective?

CHAPTER 7

Organization Options

How you lay out your Help Desk is critical and must be thoroughly thought out. Many forces may affect your decision such as physical space, type of customers, or even what days and times you provide service. In this chapter, I will discuss several ways to organize the troops and why you may or may not want to choose them.

What to Look For

- There is no one determinant when planning the organizational layout of your Help Desk. The three most important factors you need to consider are the breadth of technologies you will be asked to support, the number of customers you will be supporting, and the number of agents you can have.

- In addition to these factors, you need to review other issues that will impact how you organize the Help Desk. The first is the use of management. This chapter will show you when and how to bring managers into the equation.

- The physical location of the agents will also play a part in your Help Desk's design. You need to know the impact of your agents located in one location versus multiple ones.

- You must be flexible in each decision you make. This includes the structure of your Help Desk.

- There are many options you need to review when you organize the Help Desk. Some of these include having a common pool of agents that do everything, or forming separate groups of agents based on specialized skills, the type of incoming media used, or time of day considerations.

- Mergers and acquisitions are a growing event in corporate America. As companies look to gain new markets or streamline their operations, the role of the Help Desk must not be ignored. This chapter will review some of the steps you should take during any merger or acquisition.

Organizational Chart Factors

There are many ways to organize the structure of a Help Desk. Some of these choices are yours to make with minimal outside influence, but three significant factors will determine how you organize your Help Desk:

- The breadth of technology you will be supporting
- The number of customers you will have
- The number of agents you can have

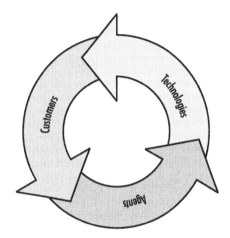

There is no exact sequence for bringing these factors to bear on the design. If you have more of one, it will affect the remaining two. The interviews you conducted in Chapter 4 with the executives and customers, along with the foundation you built in Chapter 5, will tell you what you will be supporting. Those surveys will also give you an idea of how many people you will be supporting. Both of these should, in turn, determine the number of agents you should hire and how you organize them. However, because your start-up budget may have a controlling hand in this process regardless of your technologies and customers, your decision process may not necessarily flow in that order.

Breadth of Technologies

Let's begin by looking at how many technologies you will be supporting. This list will have come from the As Is process covered in Chapter 4.

As you will see with customers, how you count the technologies depends on the definition of those technologies. Desktops, printers, and software may be one cut, and if so, you would say you support three technologies. Let's go a little deeper, though. If your desktops are made up of ASCII terminals and PCs, you should change that part of the count from one to two. If you have dot matrix and laser printers, make that multiple technologies as well. Finally, if your software is a mix of back-office packages and specialty applications, these counts could also be added.

Where do you stop? Stop just short of adding the different manufacturers to the count. At some point, the maker of the product may have some support quirks, but products are typically similar enough to not worry about for your overall Help Desk organizational design. For example, an HP Laserjet 4050N is not significantly different enough from an HP Laserjet IV to differentiate as separate technologies for Help Desk organization purposes. Crossing manufacturers from an HP PC to a Compaq should yield the same results.

Number of Customers

The second major factor in the organization of the Help Desk is the number of customers it will support. The number of customers using the Help Desk's services will affect the number of agents you employ, how you organize them, or both.

Customer counts are the numbers of different people who might call the Help Desk for support. For example, one customer can be a store or organization with 100 people in it. It is the entity that enlists the Help Desk for computing services. However, for this discussion, the customer count would be 100. Because the numbers and subsequent ratios of customers per Help Desk agent can drastically change over time, you can see why having points of contact within the customer organization can really help your operation.

You can determine your customer count by counting the number of people who work for your company or the number of people who sign up for your services. Understand how this count is aligned with the users of technologies. An employee count may reflect 300 people. In your company, 50 of these may be delivery people who do not use the technologies you support. Although they still may be able to call the Help Desk, you should use the 300 - 50 = 250 number for your customer count.

With this in mind, a small number of customers is anywhere from 2 to 500. If your customer count is in that range, you should not have to set up any elaborate Help Desk groups that are specialized or set apart in any way. Once you start getting above that number, you may find that some of the options discussed later in this chapter may provide some needed efficiencies.

Number of Agents in the Help Desk

Knowing how many agents you will have in your Help Desk is also a large part of designing the organization. The number should not be the exact number you begin your Help Desk with, but the number you can best estimate it to be for the next few years.

If you will have only one or two agents for the foreseeable future, you obviously do not have as many options to consider when you create your Help Desk's organizational chart. If the technologies you will support are narrow in focus—for example, if your Help Desk will support only Microsoft Office—the organization remains simple and your agents must specialize in that technology. However, the agents will have to be generalists (broad rather than deep in their skill sets) if they cover a wide range of technologies and services. Unless your customer base is also extremely small, it makes sense to combine your agents from a skill set perspective. If they specialize in their skills, you will not have coverage in those areas when one agent is out of the office for some reason.

The number of agents factor allows for more possibilities when the agent count reaches more than five or six. At that point, the options discussed throughout this chapter will come into play. Anywhere below that and you should organize your agents by grouping them all together and having them perform similar tasks. You could also put them all under one manager until the number of agents increases. After that, the flexibility of your organization extends to the flexibility of management as well. Management issues will be discussed in several places throughout this chapter.

Once you have this feel of technologies, customers, and agents, you can apply them as factors into your organization. The more technologies you have, the more you will need specialized groups of agents to adequately support them. The more similar the technologies are within your customer community, the more customers you can help with fewer resources. The more agents you can have, the more flexible you can be in how you organize them in the Help Desk.

In addition to technologies, customers, and agents, other factors will influence the organizational design of the Help Desk. These are not as critical to the way you organize, but will play a part and should be considered.

- The ability to have management layers
- The physical location of the Help Desk
- The need to remain flexible

Management Layers

A direct correlation between the number of agents you will employ and how you organize the Help Desk is the need for management. Obviously, the size of your staff will play a significant role in the makeup of your Help Desk. If you have a staff of five agents or more, I suggest you hire a manager specifically devoted to the Help Desk. In the world of troubleshooting, it is extremely easy for an agent to become so heads-down in any particular problem that she does not recognize how long it is taking to resolve. This may be measured in minutes or days. The feeling of "I almost have it" is consistent in good Help Desk agents and is hard to let go at times. A manager who is not constantly on the phone and has time to review an open call report can more easily see problems that need to be escalated to higher levels.

The ratio of managers to Help Desk agents is not set in stone. The more homogeneous the agents are in their responsibilities, the more they can be managed by a single manager. It is significantly easier to manage a group of ten agents doing the same job than it is to manage even half that number performing completely different functions. When we discuss different organizational options, it will be important to remember this. The more you group your agents into specialized segments, the more you will need management of some type to oversee them.

Working Managers

In small Help Desks, there may be a blur of agents and managers because the manager is also on the phone with the agents. A *working manager* is someone who is responsible for managing a group of people while at the same time performing many of the same duties as the people she manages. This arrangement can work, but it does need to be recognized. The working manager should be included when reviewing customer to agent ratios, but not as a full-time resource.

For example, if your Help Desk supports 100 customers and you have four full-time agents plus one working manager, it might appear as if you have a customer to agent ratio of 20 to 1 (100 divided by 5). However, it is strongly recommended that you calculate this as a ratio of 25 to 1 (100 divided by 4) because the working manager will have responsibilities other than full-time customer support.

There will be times when the manager will need to conduct associate reviews, meet with customers, or be involved in other administrative functions. The manager should be included in project meetings or other events where discussions of technologies to be deployed are taking place. For the sake of the agents and the manager, you should make it clear to the manager when you expect him to be directly involved in taking customer calls. It may be a permanent time slot when call volume is heaviest, or it may be full time, every day. On the other hand, your expectation may be that the manager uses his own discretion to jump into the fray when an agent is out or the workload is extremely heavy. With this discretion, remind him of the tendency to get bogged down in calls and not being able to realize that time has slipped by for other responsibilities.

Physical Location of the Help Desk

Does it matter if the Help Desk is on the first floor or the third? Not really. The influencing factor here is the location of all the agents in the Help Desk organization. A central Help Desk is located in the same building whereas decentralized Help Desks are located in more than one place. In fact, if your agents telecommute, there may be as many Help Desk "offices" as there are Help Desk agents! There are advantages to both the centralized and decentralized scenarios as shown here:

One Central Office	Multiple Offices
Easier to manage because agents can all be found in one place	Provides more coverage to customers during normal working hours because the agents can be in different time zones
Easier to communicate issues and conduct meetings	Provides better disaster recovery ability if something catastrophic impacts one Help Desk location
Easier to implement standards	Balances call volume by routing calls to the Help Desk with the lowest volume
Easier to cross-train agents	If multiple offices exist for telecommuters, the ability to attract and retain agents will be easier.
Team synergies can be gained by agents working closely together.	Your customers may speak different languages and local Help Desk agents can match that requirement.
Can leverage resources to better cover skill sets, vacation hours, and so on	Customers may need physical contact in short time periods (such as on-site repair).

Centralization makes it easier for you to manage your Help Desk because you can see and meet with groups of agents without as much planning. Decentralized Help Desks are needed when there is not enough room for a large number of agents in one area or when you are supporting multiple time zones and adopting a *follow the sun* approach. Follow the sun implies that the Help Desk location taking calls moves west as the time zones change. Basically, you can provide more coverage to customers but agents do not have to work longer hours or work in shifts. You may also have multiple data centers and need Help Desk associates physically located with the systems to perform operations and other batch-type jobs. Worldwide organizations may need multiple sites because of language differences, while companies that grow through acquisitions may have inherited separate sites.

You probably will not have a choice to centralize or not, but if you do, central facilities are always easiest. The ability to conduct management or training meetings, morale building events, and the like are much easier and more cost effective if the group is located together. This environment is also more conducive to cross-training and peer-to-peer learning. If you have common systems in different locations, you may also find that centralizing saves costs as well. Night operators or shifts can be consolidated and maintenance contracts combined.

Although a central place for the Help Desk is optimal, it is not required. The more specialized your organization, the less you'll need one common area for all. Teamwork and management are still done more easily together, but the other advantages to centralization are diminished.

Flexibility

Your Help Desk structure must be flexible as well. The business environment changes all the time. It may be due to external factors like the economy, politics, or natural disasters, or internal ones like new acquisitions, additional products, or shifts in the corporate structure itself. You know technology changes constantly. New communications or products can rapidly affect how your company and customers use the things you support. Your original layout may be absolutely perfect, but it may be absolutely ineffective if it remains static without review.

The organization needs to be flexible on a more daily basis also. Special projects may arise that require some of your agents to attend design meetings, or you may just need bodies to help run cable or connect systems. Particularly heavy call volumes may force you to move agents from one group to another just to answer the phones.

This ability to react to the needs of your customers is critical, but it will go mostly unnoticed by the customer base. They need help, your Help Desk is the place to call, and you need to do what it takes to provide that service.

Organizational Chart Options

So far this chapter has covered many things you need to consider when you put your team together. More of one factor combined with less of another can help you decide which factors are most important for the Help Desk to achieve its goals. Remembering the overall need to stay flexible and therefore recognizing that the organization may change over time, let's review some options to setting up shop:

- Create one common pool of agents
- Provide tiers of support
- Group agents by specialized skills, incoming call media, and time-of-day shifts
- Provide a quality control group

Create a Common Pool of Agents

The most basic organization design is to have one common pool of agents. All agents are equal in terms of job function, type of customers, and the technologies your Help Desk supports. These agents are called *generalists*, and they are expected to be able to resolve all incoming calls regardless of subject matter. This setup works best when your customer base has similar needs or uses narrowly focused technologies.

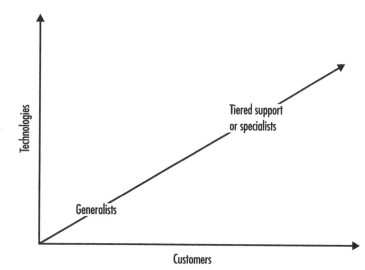

If you have only one or two agents, you will probably have no choice but to pool them together in their functions. Even as the agent count increases, this setup works perfectly fine. It is only when the customer needs or technology scope increase in breadth that you may find it necessary to move to a different organization.

An example of how this works outside the Help Desk world is in teaching. In the early grades, one teacher can teach multiple subjects to the class. As the class becomes more advanced, more teachers are needed because the level of detail is greater and one teacher cannot handle the entire load. The same applies to the Help Desk. As customers mature and use more technology, you need to bring in agents trained in particular topics to help support the customers.

Provide Tiers of Support

Another consideration is having *tiered support*. Tiered support is where one group of agents takes customer calls and a second or third group is available when the first group needs assistance. Again, depending on the size of your staff, you may want to have a *frontline* group and a *second-tier* group as shown in Figure 7-1. The front line performs triage and attempts to resolve as many problems as possible but in a short amount of time.

Once the front line identifies the problem and performs some troubleshooting, they pass it to another group of agents (a second tier). This is necessary when the act of answering the phones is important to your company and you cannot afford to have agents tied up on the phones resolving individual calls for long periods of time.

The second tier is usually made up of agents who are more experienced in the company or have more specialized skills than the average agent. Because they are more skilled, these second-tier agents can probably command higher salaries; therefore, you will probably have fewer of them than on the front line. The objective is to have the front line answer as many calls as they can and include the next tier only when the front line has run out of time or things to try. The second tier will also serve as a career step for the front line to move into.

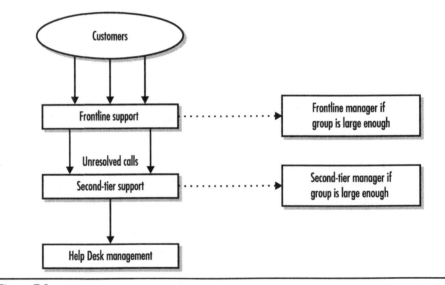

Figure 7.1 Tiers of support

Another goal is to continually train the front line to handle a wider variety of issues over time. This makes them feel better about themselves, and your customers get answers without being passed around.

Remember the Customer's Experience

Keep an eye on what you are putting the caller through, though. It is frustrating to have to explain your problem to one person, answer a lot of questions, and then be passed to someone else and have to go through it all again. A frontline agent should not just pass calls to the next agent in line, but should attempt to troubleshoot problems and then pass along as much information as possible to a second-tier agent. This strategy can fit easily in a Help Desk that supports users in both the same location and other locations. How do you support the caller who is literally a floor above you? Do you make him work through many troubleshooting steps when you could just as quickly walk up and do it yourself? If you do, fit it into this organizational model. Have your front line answer the initial call, but if a hands-on solution is needed, pass the call to the second tier to do the walking. Again, answering the phone is important and if there is no one there, you are missing that call.

Group Agents by Specialized Skills

Specialized skills may also factor in how you organize your Help Desk. Just as in our teaching example where higher grades require more teachers, more customers and technology may require specialized agents.

One group of agents who answered calls regardless of their nature staffed my first Help Desk. They would take a business software call one minute, then help a customer whose terminal was frozen, and the next minute troubleshoot a store whose phone line was down. Our call volume was low and our supporting staff of networking professionals and programmers could help us out if we needed it. As our customer count grew, we could not adequately learn all that was needed to even appear competent on the phone, so we specialized. The ramp-up time to train an agent to understand all that was necessary to support the customers had grown too long. We needed to specialize into groups so we could dedicate training for particular agents and make them more productive for the customers sooner.

You can specialize the Help Desk agents in two ways. One is by the technology they support and the other is by the type of customer they serve.

Specialize by Technology

One way to divide the agents when going to a specialized organization is by the technology they support. For example, you could organize your agents into a software applications support group and a hardware support group. Figure 7-2 shows how this can be done. The software staff could devote its training to learning the ins and outs of the application, while the hardware staff dives into details on the hardware your customers use. Cross-training is still a good idea when you split these groups. No doubt, the groups will have training unique to their areas, but some basic skill transfers will help each group recognize sources of problems better.

As the customer base or technologies grow, you can segment these groups even more. For example, you could divide hardware into networking, servers, and desktops. You could also support software with groups specific to back-office, sales, and manufacturing applications.

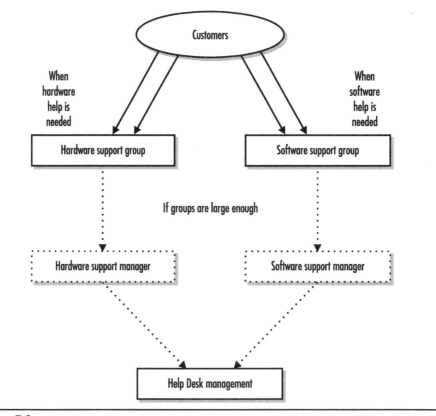

Figure 7.2 Specialize by technology

These specialized groups could require specialized management as they grow. You always need one overall manager of the Help Desk, but there is opportunity for mid-level managers to oversee each group you create. As with the other options, additional management level should be brought in when the staff count warrants it and not just because the group is separated.

Important to remember as you break out agents into groups is the impact this has on your customers. Customers have problems that need to be fixed and must understand where to go to get that help. You must be ready to educate them about whom to call and you must also instruct your agents to transfer errant calls professionally and efficiently.

Specialize by Business Unit

Just as you could organize your agents by the technology they support, you could also organize them by the business units that use the technology as shown in Figure 7-3.

If you support external customers as well as internal ones, you may find opportunities to segregate your groups by type of customer. This specialization does not have to be done as there are synergies you gain by maintaining a common pool of agents. If the products and services your customers use are different from the ones your internal customers use, this may be the way to go though.

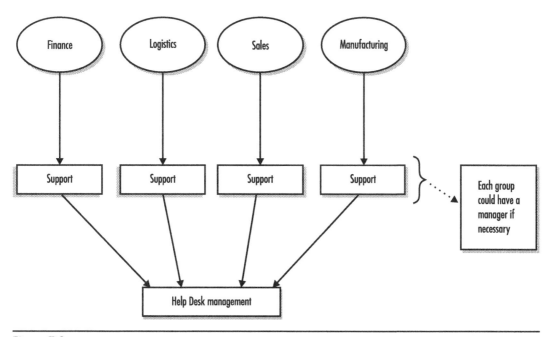

Figure 7.3   Specialize by business unit

You may find that individual units or departments within your organization require different skill sets to support them well. They may use different software applications, different types of hardware, or a combination of both. This could extend to support groups for internal associates versus external customers.

Individual business units may have the same technologies but possess a significantly different expectation of the services they require. Due to its importance, one or more business units may have needs that are tougher than other business units. Examples could be customers on an assembly line who cannot be interrupted for long periods of time or the whole plant becomes idle. When a computer issue arises in that section, it needs to reach an agent without a significant waiting period and it needs that agent to be very familiar with its operation. In this case, you could create a separate group within the Help Desk that is dedicated to the assembly line operation and is more heavily staffed than other ratios you have established.

I strongly recommend that you have a common management team not too far above these groups to utilize synergies where possible. Examples could be staffing help during peak times for one group, being able to see root causes of problems that are happening in the separate groups, and providing training to the agents that are needed regardless of the customer type supported.

Group Agents by Incoming Call Media

Yet another way to organize your agents is by the incoming call media. In this scenario, it does not matter who the customer is or why they are contacting you, but how. The more apparent divisions would be phone calls in one section, walk-ups in another, and e-mail, faxes, and Internet chats in another section (see Figure 7-4).

This separation technique combines similar skills and strategies to best help the customer. Answering the phone is a strategy all to itself with technologies, predictive patterns, and the like. The skill sets of the agents in this area need to be more concentrated on customer service attributes like strong communication and listening skills.

Walk-up traffic needs are a little different. The agent needs more interpersonal skills and must show noticeable attention to walk-up customers as they are standing right in front of him. An agent on the phone could have his feet on the desk and browsing a magazine during a conversation, but that won't work for walk-up traffic! Walk-up customers cannot be serviced with technology like the other media provide. Unless you have a system where a customer picks a ticket and waits for their number

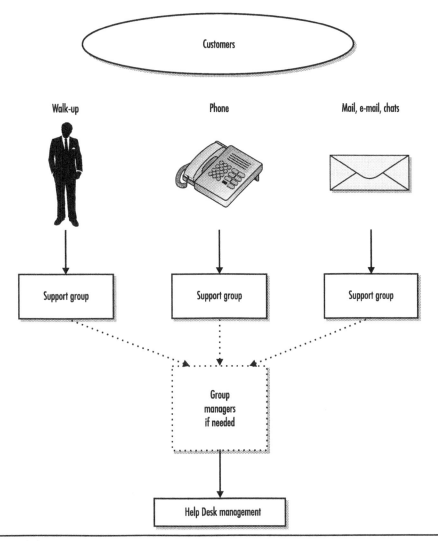

Figure 7.4 Organize by incoming call media

to be called, they will pretty much get an agent when they arrive. This makes prioritizing harder as every customer wants to be attended to.

Finally, e-mails, faxes, and chats involve even different issues. Answering e-mails and faxes can be performed at a different pace and can allow the answering agent to involve other parties for solutions that will not be as apparent to the customer. These agents need stronger writing skills than the other groups.

Although prewritten templates for certain responses may help the agents, they will definitely need to be more skilled at writing than verbal communication.

While this organization grouping is possible, it is not as effective unless your Help Desk is extremely large. Otherwise, your agents are spread across many groups and you might find one group continually busier than the others. In that case, you will have underutilized agents and lose a lot of efficiencies.

Group Agents by Time of Day

If your Help Desk is to be staffed *24x7* (24 hours every day of the week), *24x5* (24 hours a day, Monday through Friday), or at just more hours than a normal business day, you may consider organizing it by time of day instead of by function as in Figure 7-5.

You won't have much choice in this decision if the business requires immediate computer assistance all day long or really anything over ten hours. If this is the case, and you have all agents working the same time, you will quickly overwork

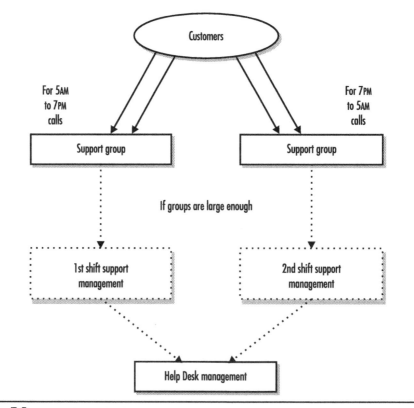

Figure 7.5 Organizing by time of day

the agents and burnout or turnover will result. By dividing the days into shifts, you can cover more customer office hours without working the agents too much each day.

For example, say you want to provide in-office hours from 7:00A.M. to 10:00P.M. with a workload estimated to require a staff of four. You could arrange the following schedule:

Agent	Beginning Time	End Time
Joe	7:00A.M.	10:00P.M.
Casey	7:00A.M.	10:00P.M.
Mikayla	7:00A.M.	10:00P.M.
Mike	7:00A.M.	10:00P.M.

You will have succeeded in being in the office for the hours you wanted, but you will probably not be able to hire a single person for the job. Fifteen-hour days are not a good selling point for the company!

As you have more planning ability than that, you could schedule the agents like this:

Agent	Beginning Time	End Time
Joe	7:00A.M.	5:00P.M.
Casey	7:00A.M.	5:00P.M.
Mikayla	12:00P.M.	10:00P.M.
Mike	12:00P.M.	10:00P.M.

Now you have good coverage that lasts through the necessary hours and each agent is working fewer hours. There is overlap from noon until 5:00P.M., which gives the groups time to update each other on events and problem statuses as well.

It is extremely hard to effect change or review the associates' performance if you do not work the same times they do. You cannot see how they handle pressure or what they do in their spare time. This cannot happen when there is physical separation either but the issues are different. When problems occur during the day, it is easy for a manager to see how everyone acts and responds to resolve it even if people are in different rooms or states. A suggestion for larger Help Desks is to have a management structure in place for agents working completely different shifts than others. If it occurs due to flex time that is okay; this is more about day shifts versus night shifts. One lone night guy monitoring the systems would not rate his own manager, but a team of five or more could.

Create a Quality Control Group

How about creating a separate group within the Help Desk that does follow up or quality checks? Maybe you rotate agents through it or keep it formally separate, but you could use this group for true customer service tasks that show the callers you care even after the call is over. Figure 7-6 shows what this might look like.

This group could be separated so that while the frontline Help Desk is helping customers who contact them, the Quality Control group can concentrate on other more proactive issues. These can include:

- Following up on random, or all, resolved calls
- Tracking and reporting metrics on the Help Desk and its calls
- Surveying customers on their experiences with the Help Desk
- Monitoring phone calls for quality

These are important features for a world class Help Desk to have. Remembering that we want the Help Desk to have a proactive mission as well as a reactive one, this quality control group can provide that service without harming the incoming calls.

Final Words on Organization Options

Table 7-1 summarizes the primary factors involved in each organizational structure we've reviewed so far. Each type works differently depending on the corporate environment you are in, but this can serve as a strong beginning point.

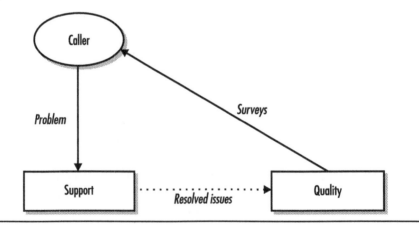

Figure 7.6 Quality control organization

Organizational Option	When Best Used
Common pool of agents	Small number of influencing factors (agents or customers or technologies)
Tiered support	High volume of calls where answering the customer's call is as important as solving open issues
Specialized skills	Expanded customer or technology usage when certain customer types demand a higher level of service than other groups
Incoming call media	Large Help Desks that have large amounts of incoming calls at all hours
Time of day	Customer needs cover many hours of the day and/or customers are in multiple time zones
Quality control groups	Customer service is paramount and attention to customer satisfaction is highly visible

Table 7.1 Summary of Organization Options

Remember, ultimately callers could care less how you are structured. They want their problems resolved. Regardless of how you are organized you must appear seamless to the caller. It must also be easy. You should not count on customers "figuring out" what to do when they need help. Having them call one phone number for a hardware problem, a separate number for software issues, and yet another number for miscellaneous problems will confuse and frustrate any caller. Providing options is good so customers can choose what works best for them. Just don't require the different options for those customers who only have a question they need answered.

Handling Mergers and Acquisitions

Many companies expand their operations, customer base, or resources by merging with or acquiring other companies. A *merger* is when two or more companies combine assets and begin operating as one larger company. An *acquisition* is when one company purchases the assets of one or more companies and begins operating as one larger company. Where acquisitions always have a dominant position, mergers may or may not depending on the situation. In this chapter, I will combine these two acts as each involves bringing two entities together. In addition, I will be focusing on your Help Desk being in the dominant company and assuming at least some of the new roles and functions.

Because people and organizations are part of the business, when mergers and acquisitions (M&A) occur, the departments that make up the company go along for the ride as well. This means IT, which means the Help Desk, so it is good if you know how to handle the situation if it arises. There are four main goals to strive for when you are put into this situation:

- Understand the business reasons for the M&A
- Create a plan to combine Help Desks under one reporting structure
- Communicate, communicate, communicate
- Combine resources where there is overlap

Understand the Business Reasons for the M&A

One of the goals of the Help Desk from the outset is to remain aligned with the company and its mission. In the M&A world, it should be no different. For the Help Desk to stay aligned with the business, it must understand why the business acts as it does and what it plans to do in the future. In M&A deals, it is not always the case that the IT departments combine, so therefore the impact on the Help Desk is limited. In other cases, the IT departments will completely combine, or one will take over the other, and the Help Desk is directly affected.

M&As occur for many reasons, but two of the reasons that affect the Help Desk's next steps the most are:

- Companies consolidate to gain synergies
- Companies combine at a high level but remaining independent operationally

Consolidation

In a consolidation mode, the two companies combine their resources to gain new synergies and leverage by acting as one. When this happens, IT resources are usually heavily involved because of the impact IT has on the rest of the company, and it is typically an expensive asset that needs to be handled effectively. Because the Help Desk is intimately associated with the customers and technologies of the IT department, it is natural that it plays a big part in any consolidation effort.

Consolidation strategies for M&A agreements create prime opportunities for cost-reduction planning. As the companies look for areas in which to reduce costs so should the Help Desk. This process should also happen sooner rather than later because the longer the parties wait, the more opportunities to cut costs slip by. Because the companies will want to move fast, the Help Desk should make attempts to participate early on. This chapter will discuss ways to do just that later on.

Independent Operations

Another reason for M&As is that companies can be run by the same entity but continue to operate as separate organizations. This kind of M&A can occur because the products or services these companies offer are significantly different or the geographic areas they do business in are unique from one another.

In this M&A strategy, IT departments and therefore Help Desks are usually not combined. The business or product lines have different relationships, and typically the computing systems that run the businesses are different as well. For this reason, when companies merge but decide to do business separately, the Help Desks of the respective companies will remain separate also.

Even in an environment such as this, do not rest completely idle. While your Help Desks may not become one entity, there are still opportunities to go after. Most notably, there is a good reason for the Help Desks to get together to share Best Practices. Your technologies and customers may be different, but the ways you conduct business could share many common processes. Take this opportunity to learn from each other and see what you can find to improve your own Help Desk.

When possible, get several key members of each team to meet regularly through the year to discuss past events and future plans. The Help Desk members can discuss how they process the work and what has worked best for their team. There will always be opportunities to learn and improve what you do by listening to others. Your Help Desk may have 300 agents compared to the other's 25, but that is no reason for the larger Help Desk to ignore the smaller one.

Create a Plan to Manage Help Desks Under One Reporting Structure

Devising a plan to combine the management of the two Help Desks is definitely one area you will not be able to control too much. It is doubtful the two companies got together just for the wonderful operations of the Help Desks at each company. Assuming that is true, there will be many considerations before the Help Desks' structure has been decided.

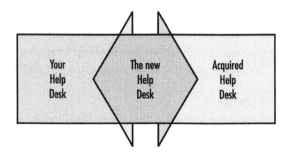

Unless the M&A has transpired with a dependent operation strategy, the Help Desks will ultimately be brought up for consideration. When this does happen, you clearly want to be seen as the leader. You want your agents and processes and customer satisfaction to be so outstanding that the businesses will naturally want you and your group to lead the combination efforts. This should be your goal for every day regardless of any situation, but you especially want this now. The team that can best help lead the combined companies to more productivity and better customer relations will be seen as the foundation, and all other groups will be brought into their processes (and management!).

Communicate, Communicate, Communicate

The word "communicate" is very important in the M&A process. While normal communications may allow the M&A process to proceed without a problem, the lack of communication can kill the process. Communication needs to flow in and out of the organizations. It needs to involve the agents and the customers on both sides. It needs to be consistent so rumors of hidden messages are kept to a minimum. Finally, the communications need to be started as early as possible in the process. There is a point that is too early, like before the deal is closed or before much of the details are known, but you need to talk to all parties as soon as you can.

With everyone you speak to, you need to discuss the process that is planned and the associated timelines. It is okay to tell people that a particular issue has not been decided, but it is important to follow up with them as soon as you know the decision. It is also okay to discuss changes to the timeline or the process. Be sure to also communicate why the changes were made so everyone understands the big picture.

Three main communication streams must be planned and implemented:

- The agents
- The As Is
- The customers

The Agents

For the Help Desk, there is nothing more important than establishing a communications process with Help Desk agents who may exist in the other company. They need to be involved as early as possible in this process. For certain agents, you may even bring them into your office to learn more about them and their processes. People get very anxious during M&As and a lack of communication will only add to that apprehension. Their careers, and therefore their livelihoods, are at stake and an information void is quickly filled with rumors and half-truths.

A first suggestion when designing a plan for the existing agents is to find out the skill sets and aptitudes of the staff. Communicate with the manager of their IT department to get this information, whether it is informal opinions or formal performance reviews. From there, you can divide the agents into three categories:

- Key associates
- Keepers
- The rest

Key Associates   Key associates are those agents whose skill sets, experience, and company knowledge are vital in keeping the Help Desk running. You need to identify and speak with these agents quickly. Their knowledge of the acquired Help Desk and its operations will be invaluable as you plan for future dealings or consolidations.

Keepers   Keepers are the agents you want to keep in the organization by all means. Note that key players and keepers can be in separate categories. Key players have knowledge that is important to understand and capture, but there may be other issues with key players that do not align with your Help Desk, including:

- Your staff already has the desired skill sets.
- The skill sets of the acquired key players are unique to their company.
- The acquired key players may have attitude or performance problems, or other team attributes that do not mesh well with your Help Desk.

These key players are still key to any transition, but they will not make your "keeper" list. The agents you want to keep may have unique technical knowledge, can fill voids in your Help Desk, or are quality associates who can be trained to fit into your plans. You need to communicate with these agents early on so they can recognize their status in your plans.

The Rest   The agents who are not specialized in their skill sets or have not been identified as coming into your own Help Desk make up the third category. There could be negative names used to categorize this group, but everyone is important at the beginning of an M&A and no one should be treated adversely. Now, after you have had time to learn what you need about the Help Desk there may be opportunities to gain efficiencies in the staff, but not at the beginning.

An Outsourced Help Desk   The acquired company may have outsourced its Help Desk to provide support. In that case, you should put that group in the key player category. Their knowledge is still important and must be understood. There may be a need to keep the arrangement for some time; you will need to find this out quickly.

The As Is

This piece of communication typically flows from the acquired company to the dominant company. It involves the dominant company learning everything it can about the computing environment of the other. The goal of this communication is to understand what is being inherited so you can plan how to accommodate these new elements or alter your organization to fit them in.

Depending on the technical nature of the IT staff at the acquired company, you may be able to send an inventory sheet for them to complete rather than visiting them on site. However, an advantage to going on site is that you will be able to meet their IT staff and get a feel for their skill sets at the same time you are getting an understanding of their computing infrastructure. This scenario plays out just as the original As Is assessment did at the beginning of your Help Desk's design. It just adds existing Help Desk agents to the items you need to learn more about.

The Customers

The customers of the acquired Help Desk definitely need to be included in the communication plan. As much as you try to incorporate new processes during an M&A implementation, the customers will notice an effect. Because of this, it is much better to inform them ahead of time of your plans and how those plans will impact them. Armed with this information, the customer can make any necessary arrangements and provide input as the proceedings develop.

| External Customers |

With external customers in the mix, it is imperative that you communicate with them. As part of the M&A discovery phase, you may find that external customers exist and perhaps even that service level agreements are in place. If so, you will need to find out all the details of the agreements and ensure they transfer completely into your Help Desk's operation. External customers will be especially leery with major changes an M&A can bring, so you need to interrupt their normal procedures in as few areas as possible.

Transferred customers will need to know your major plans as well as minor items that you may not initially think of. These items can include phone numbers to call when they need help, agents' names, and other logistical processes. Pull out all your Help Desk announcements and Day One plans, modify and update them as appropriate, and roll them out to the new customers as the time approaches.

Combine Resources Where There Is Overlap

The communication between Help Desks can still be an exchange of information even if the goal of the M&A is to maintain separate organizations. While there may be no immediate plan for the two Help Desks or IT departments to consolidate operations, there can still be advantages to the two getting together. Examples of possible overlaps can include the following:

- Job duplication
- Customers
- Vendors
- Facilities

Job Duplication

The two Help Desks may find that they perform similar functions in areas that are not deemed critical to the business. We are dealing with noncritical functions at this point because the companies may want the organizations to stay separate for some reason. Merging critical functions in the face of that edict from above is counterproductive.

Examples of job duplication may include procurement, asset management, and other administrative responsibilities. If there are jobs in both groups that basically procure the same grouping of products, it may be worthwhile to combine that area. What may have taken two agents in each Help Desk may be done with three agents in a combined operation.

$$2 + 2 = 3$$

Even further, you might be able to share recruiting efforts if both Help Desks are always looking for similar talent. While it may not be productive to compete for associates in the job market, there could be opportunities to combine efforts. Whether it be in common advertisements or sharing candidates that might not be right in one of the Help Desks, the HR function of the Help Desk should be examined.

Customers

Anytime you get involved in changing processes that directly affect the customer, you must be very careful. However, you may find that the two Help Desks share customers' needs. It may be computer support during multiple time zones or technologies that need to be supported. If one of the Help Desks is more familiar with a technology that is coming into play for the other Help Desk, the two should get together to share training efforts and Best Practices. They could also combine efforts when dealing with vendor partners or external support providers to ensure the best possible deal is being implemented for the companies.

Typically, the only way that two different Help Desks could share actual customers is if the customers are external. The customer may have large offices across the country, which use different Help Desks for different geographies, services, or technologies. You may find that the customer will be happy with any combination efforts on your part, as they should expect more coordinated support services and potentially better prices. You should expect more alignment with a greater degree of efficiency as well. In this case, it is a win-win effort for all parties.

Vendors

If the companies use the same technologies or vendors, there may be opportunities to leverage vendors because you can begin buying in a combined fashion and therefore ask for better discounts. Anytime you can buy more of a product or service, economies of scale should kick in and allow for better pricing. Even if the products are not bought at the same time, the Help Desks working together can forecast their plans to the vendors to gain some of the same deals.

Outside of pricing, common vendors can help both Help Desks in their own operations and planning. A common vendor can provide another set of eyes to notice similar or divergent trends between the two organizations. Then with political savvy, so as not to upset one or the other party, the vendor can make sure there are opportunities for each Help Desk to know the other's intention. This may save one Help Desk from buying products or services the other Help Desk already owns and can share, or can allow one Help Desk to educate the other on the benefits and concerns of an implementation plan the other Help Desk is about to undertake.

Facilities

Unless the Help Desks are close to consolidating or they are very large, there may not be too many opportunities to share facilities but it is worth checking into. If the Help Desks are expanding and looking to move into another building, there is a definitive advantage to the two groups working together. The ability to share common resources such as power, phones, heating, and air conditioning will save both companies a lot of money.

This sharing can occur if the Help Desks are interested in developing a disaster recovery site for their operations. Instead of the Help Desks leasing a building to move into in case their existing buildings are destroyed, the two can research ways to utilize space in the other's building. It might not be convenient if a disaster were to strike, but the cost savings for all those times between disasters could really add up.

Quick Recap

- The As Is process should have given you a wealth of information necessary to create a very effective Help Desk. Do you have all the information you need to make that happen?

- Will the mix of technologies, customer counts, and agents you are allowed to hire give you an opportunity to use any of the options we discussed? If so, which ones work best for you?

- Will your Help Desk be physically together or spread out? Do you have plans to manage it in either case?

- The organizational options presented in this chapter approach the customer service world from similar, but different, angles. Do you understand the benefits and costs of each in case your Help Desk changes over time?

- Mergers and acquisitions are happening all over the world at an increasing pace. Have you ever been through one? If so, can you apply what happened in your situation to the Help Desk industry? If you haven't, do you have a good sense of what is necessary if one occurs?

CHAPTER 8

Staffing Your Help Desk

There are many important items and issues you need to consider, plan for, review, and research as you build your Help Desk. Without a doubt, the most important issue of them all is the proper staffing of the Help Desk. No tool or process can overcome a poor team of agents. These associates are the link between the customer and the effective use of the technology in the company. You must take great care in hiring and caring for these associates. A world class Help Desk cannot exist without the staff in it being world class themselves.

What to Look For

- Just as the mission statement lays the foundation of the Help Desk and its services, job descriptions lay the groundwork for the staffing of the Help Desk. This chapter will detail many different items to think about when writing job descriptions.

- Your Help Desk agents need to have a wide variety of skill sets to make the Help Desk an effective and efficient organization. These skill sets will be listed here along with an explanation of their necessity and some hints on how to determine if potential agents have them.

- As your Help Desk expands, there will be a need for managers. While the skill sets of agents and managers are very similar, the attributes of a manager include several more skills. These skills will be listed and discussed in this chapter as well.

- There are several methods you can use to increase the staff headcount of your Help Desk. They range from basic reactive plans to others that involve estimating call volumes and agent skills.

- There are many ways to find agents. You can look within the company or outside it. Some sources can provide you quality permanent agents or temporary solutions to get you through high-volume times.

- Interviewing candidates for your Help Desk needs to be planned and thorough. Employing agents who are not a good fit will drain you of energy and time that could be better spent serving your customers. The interview process can be broken down into planning, the interview itself, and analyzing candidates after the interview is over.

Job Descriptions

A good place to begin with your staffing plan is to write job descriptions. You have your plan with services and standards documented. A mission statement exists to guide the overall vision of the organization. Now you need to draft some job descriptions for the people you will be hiring.

All you really need to do is make sure that every service you listed is written somewhere on a job description. Whether it is a frontline agent or a section manager, if a service is left out, no one will know who should be doing it.

Job descriptions come in many sizes and formats. However, they all must accomplish the same task of documenting what is expected of the associate who has that job title. It is important for both the associate and those people working with that associate to recognize roles and responsibilities. Job descriptions need to be clear and complete and easy to understand. Your interview candidates may ask to see one so they can know what they are getting into. Your boss will want to see it to understand why you want to pay agents all that money. Ultimately, you will find it helpful when the time comes for reviewing associates to determine if they have fulfilled what you expected of them.

Following is a list of components that should make up a job description. You can get the information from many sources to fill out these components. One source is this book itself—either from the examples included in the sample job descriptions or from the services and products we talk about throughout. You can also get information by looking at other companies or job advertisements in the papers. See what other Help Desks are looking for in agents and how that might fit into your group. Finally, and perhaps best, you can complete the forms based on the interviews you have done as we learned in Chapters 3 and 4. These interviews should have yielded extremely good information to incorporate into the job description. Remember Susan, the administrative assistant who knew everything about Microsoft Office? Learning from her side duties as the local "expert," you can determine what types of functions an agent performing those same tasks would do. Basically, you could insert her part of the interview right into the job description!

- Job title
- Reports to

- Primary responsibility
- Job duties
- Qualifications
- Objectives to achieve in this job
- Expected career length
- Possible career steps
- Salary range
- Physical requirements

I will discuss each of these components in the following sections. At the end, I will provide a sample job description for a Help Desk Dispatcher with these components gathered together.

Job Title

The title should start it off. Don't take this part lightly; MANY people care as much about their job title as they do about other pieces of compensation. It is a title that goes on business cards for others to see. It is what they tell their spouse, parents, and friends they are when asked. It also allows them to compare themselves with peers at work. This is all good as it is a form of pride in their job and what they do. Just as the term *Help Desk* has many varieties, so do the agents within it.

There can be many levels: Entry level, Trainee, Junior, Senior, Assistant, and Manager of. Adjectives can include Support, Technical, and Customer Service. Available nouns are Agent, Technician, Analyst, Representative, and Specialist. Mix and match any of these and build a career path from them. It does need to fit into the organizational model you have created. It should also be presented so that it helps agents understand career paths. In summation, make the job description meaningful and apply your job titles with pride.

Reports To

Hopefully, this is one of the easier components to know and fill out. All you need here is the job title that this job description reports to, not a person's name. This is done so that when a supervisor moves to another position, all the job descriptions that were distributed will not have to be changed. The change would only need to be made if the job moved to another position's purview.

Make this a required field to clearly show associates who is responsible for whom. There may be instances where an associate reports directly to another associate but is also under the guidance or direction of yet another person. This is referred to as a "dotted line" reporting structure, since this is how the organization would appear on a printed organization chart. Groups set up in matrix structures where people work more in teams than in formal organizations will commonly have this characteristic.

For purposes of the job description, this field should be the person formally charged with the pay, career growth, and management of this position. If others have influence on the performance of the position, you can list their names in subsequent fields.

Primary Responsibility

This is another required field and can be about one or two phrases. This is where you capture the essence of the job. Think of the primary responsibility as the answer to the question, "What do you do for a living?" If the responsibilities are very broad, you can certainly go into more detail here. There is not a mandatory limit on the length of this section. It should be used more in summary form, however, because the following component exists for a greater level of detail.

Job Duties

Job duties are the detail piece of the entire job description. Here each and every job duty the person has is listed. Bullet format works well here. This needs to be explicit for if it is too broad, associates may use it against you in their future actions. That leads me to the must have of all must haves on a job description….*And any other responsibility assigned by the manager.* This is your answer to anyone stating, "That's not my job." With a broad duty like *any other responsibility*, how can you miss? Truthfully, while the "not my job" line is real, this piece really serves to keep you from rewriting the description every time something new comes up.

Qualifications

Qualifications are the skill sets and experiences an agent must have to be assigned the job described. These can be formal and official or serve only as guidelines. It is good to express what level of experience is needed. Descriptors like required, preferred, helpful, beneficial, and requested usually do the trick.

This is really the section to list what you are looking for in a candidate. Education, work experience, specific training, and certifications are usually detailed here. Some jobs may require a college degree in a certain major, while others would be better filled by someone with a certain number of years of related work experience.

Objectives to Achieve in This Job

Another component on the job description is a listing of the objectives to achieve. Job duties list what the associate should do day to day while objectives list the goals the associate should achieve during his or her time on the job. These objectives will

- Show associates what is needed to move through the organization
- Help associates perform their jobs better
- Make associates more marketable, both inside and outside the company

Objectives range from types of training that need to be completed to work performance goals that can be achieved. They should serve to explain your wishes to the associate as well as inspire the associate to reach for more opportunities.

Expected Career Length

This component sets the expectation of how long an associate may be in this job. You want this in the job description to help you in career discussions moving forward. Some associates feel they are ready for each promotion that comes up regardless of their tenure on the job. This career length section will help them understand how you see tenure affecting other opportunities.

A clear expectation should be set with agents reading this part, however. It needs to be well understood that when the agent reaches this end time, it does not mean he or she is automatically promoted to the next level. Tenure all by itself should not be a reason an associate is promoted or moved to a different position. You need to be explicit about what goals need to be obtained along the way for promotions to occur. You can list these goals for the associate in the "Objectives to Achieve in This Job" component of the job description discussed earlier.

Possible Career Steps

"What is available to me after I do this job well" is answered in this section. Again, bullets work well to list potential job positions this particular job can lead to. Make sure you list the titles in the Help Desk career path as well as others that may be outside the Help Desk but are in related areas. It is good to consider all possibilities in this section, but be careful not to claim that wonderful opportunities exist everywhere. There won't be a time when an associate is denied a new job because it did not show up on the job description, but an associate reading a job posting may express interest in an opening based on what career steps it could lead to. Again, the objectives section can help show them what they need to do to move to the next level.

Salary Range

For internal purposes, you may want to document the salary range this job has available to it on the job description. Formalizing the salary structure for individual jobs beforehand will make any subsequent salary changes easier to get approved. Depending on the nature of your business, you may not want to make this available to the public. What a person makes is no one's business but their own, so publishing ranges without necessarily having the opportunity to discuss it with someone is dangerous. A potential candidate may not pursue a job because of the salary range shown on a job description posted on the bulletin board. What he might not know is that his own experience and performance may qualify him for a different range altogether. Some businesses publish this information openly in a manner that encourages associates to look at what other jobs pay as an incentive to reach for them. For the reasons listed above, however, I recommend keeping this section internal and letting it serve as a helpful reminder when you hire and promote associates.

Physical Requirements

For legal reasons you may need to detail the physical requirements of the Help Desk position. The laws surrounding discrimination are getting tougher and tougher and the job description is a good place to list the attributes necessary to perform the job. These could include manual dexterity for typing, ability to lift certain items such as PCs or printers, ability to sit for long periods of time, and so on.

Now that we've covered the components of a job description, we can see how they all add up for a Help Desk Dispatcher. See Appendix A for a sample job description with all the components in one place. In this appendix you will find other examples of job descriptions for different jobs in a Help Desk. You can use these as templates when designing your own descriptions. Remember, there are other places to find components and information such as your Human Resources department or even other jobs within the IT department. (Again, the four job descriptions are examples you can use as a template for your organization. The fourth description has more career and salary information on it that would perhaps be better used for internal and HR planning purposes. The information can certainly be shared with the agents but in a different format.)

| Note | *Not all the components listed earlier show up in the sample job descriptions in Appendix A. They can, however, provide more choices and options when you begin writing your own Help Desk job descriptions.* |

Skill Sets of Your Team

Okay, we have defined our customers and their needs. It is now time to define the skill sets of our Help Desk associates who will fulfill those needs. We will divide the skills between your Help Desk associates and the managers within your Help Desk. Although the skill sets of your managers may line up with the agents' skills, some distinctions will help you determine who is management material in this environment and who is not.

It is not always perfect to have a whole team of managers and "managers-in-training." I once started a Help Desk with only career-minded associates and ended up with closed-door sessions of people complaining every time there was a promotion and they did not receive it. These careerists also tend to have higher turnover. It is absolutely acceptable to have a solid foundation of Help Desk associates who come in each day, do their jobs, and leave at the end. These people are strong associates, and you will find them easier to manage. With that, let's look at common attributes of a good Help Desk staff.

Agent Skills

The agents who make up your Help Desk are the lifeblood of the organization. They are the primary interface between the customers and the IT department, so how they relate to the customers is very important. A good agent does not have to be the absolute best in each of the following skill sets, but he or she should be more than adequate in all of them.

- Strong communication skills
- Listening
- Empathy
- Self-motivated
- Energetic and enthusiastic
- Team player
- Ability to handle change
- Multitasking skills
- Ability to take on responsibility
- Logical thinking
- Composure
- General understanding of the product they will support

Strong Communication Skills

Communication is the most important attribute of a Help Desk agent. The agent must be able to express his ideas and thoughts in ways the caller can understand. Sometimes this means working with the caller at the most basic level, and sometimes working at a very detailed level. A strong skill for an agent is to determine quickly when to go deep and when to go slow. Asking a computer-illiterate person to reseat the memory chip will generate a bad experience because you will be talking over the customer's head. Equally bad is asking a computer-savvy person to "Depress the key labeled ALT, while at the same time, depressing the CTRL and DEL keys." This would be talking down to the customer and they will get frustrated quickly.

This can be especially hard when the communications are written. With the advent of e-mail and the Internet, written communications are more prevalent than ever. Through this media you lose tone of voice and cannot tell if the person on the other end is frustrated, joking, or merely calm. You cannot always know the caller personally, so agents must be able to work with all types of people.

A good communication skill is to ask intelligent and probing questions. By knowing what to ask a customer, an agent can more quickly determine the root cause of a problem and get the customer productive again. As we will discuss later, call management packages can provide standard questions that will help lead the agent towards the problem and its solution.

Listening Skills

Listening is the other half of the communication equation. Listening is a part of communication but its importance to the Help Desk agent calls for it to stand alone. A good agent needs to be able to listen to callers to root out why they are really calling. Callers may use terms that are ambiguous or flat out wrong, but the agent must get to their true meaning. The customers are not always right in the technical Help Desk world but they are still the customers. Rebooting the PC may solve their expressed problem of it being stuck, but hearing that they were in the middle of the payroll data process first and had not saved anything may save you from getting in hot water.

Empathy

Empathy should not be confused with sympathy. Empathy is the ability to relate to a person's situation and understand his feelings and what he is going through. Sympathy is more about having feelings for the person who is experiencing the problem. For example, if a PC crashes and the user loses all his data, an empathetic person can relate to this situation because he also has had PC problems and he's more inclined to dig in and show the user what options are available to recover the lost data. A sympathetic person, on the other hand, would feel horrible that the crash happened but might not even think about offering assistance except to console the user.

You want to make sure each caller feels their problem is important and will be given your complete attention and understanding. An agent may reset 15 passwords every day. The key is to not transfer that everyday, routine attitude to the caller. That caller cannot log on or access the information they need and they need your help.

Self-Motivated

Callers very seldom call to thank you for the system running all day long or because their accounting system added all the numbers correctly. They do call because they are down or something looks wrong. Help Desk agents need to be able to motivate themselves to do a good job without getting an "attaboy" each time they resolve an issue. Yes, the manager can help recognize good work but that will not be on a call-by-call basis. While no one deserves to be treated unprofessionally, many times the callers need you and they are under duress.

You may or may not get a thank you but you need to continue on without it all the same, while maintaining the same level of helpfulness and enthusiasm.

Energetic and Enthusiastic

Customers gain a large measure of satisfaction with their Help Desk experience from the attitude of the agent helping them. If they feel the agent is upbeat and hard at work on their problem, they will enjoy the experience more. An energetic agent turns an "I don't know" response into an "I don't know but I'll find the answer very soon" response. The customers will see this as positive and can have more confidence that their problems will be handled correctly. True, the overall goal is to resolve the issue at hand, but the attitude the agent employs in the interaction is crucial for a longer-term quality relationship with the customer. Interacting with anyone who is positive and personable will keep your customers coming back.

Team Player

There will be very few instances where Help Desk agents can continually perform their jobs solely by themselves. They typically will need help from programmers, business analysts, systems administrators, or vendors to research or resolve issues. Because of this dependency on others, the agent must be able to work in a team atmosphere. There will be times when a program bug creates havoc in the Help Desk, just as there will be times when an agent deletes an important file and needs help from someone to restore it. The ability to work with people and not work alone in a dark office somewhere is a must! Just because an agent has good phone skills does not automatically translate into interpersonal office skills.

I believe one of the most important objectives in hiring your Help Desk agents is to get them to feel and act as a team. This teamwork can be leveraged in problem solving and customer interaction to achieve many synergies. Every agent does not have to personally like every other agent. But with everyone working as a team while on the job, they can form a resource pool of knowledge that will make the Help Desk perform very effectively.

Ability to Handle Change

What is working today will be broken tomorrow and the technology that seems futuristic will be installed soon. A Help Desk agent needs to be very comfortable with change on a recurring basis. Standard procedures will change as the use of technology changes. Tasks and issues will change for agents. Customers will come and go, as will the staff around them. If a person struggles with a changing environment, a Help Desk career is not for them. Strong organizational skills are nice but if it means agents cannot adapt because it upsets their routine, those skills will only hurt them. Handling change is not enough; handling multiple changes at once is also required.

Multitasking Skills

Wouldn't it be nice if you received a problem over the phone and were allowed to ignore all other calls until you resolved that particular problem? Unless you are in a very unique (and quiet) Help Desk, this is highly improbable. Help Desks are busy places with new problems emerging, older ones reappearing, and some calls that are not problems after all. Add to this any special projects going on, and you will find a workplace that must be able to achieve multiple goals at once. Some issues must be worked in parallel instead of serially. This means that an agent cannot afford to work one problem, and only one problem, until it is resolved. While an agent is running a report to check out one issue, he can e-mail a customer for more information, and look through open call logs while waiting on even that response.

Your agents must be able to deal with multiple problems at one time and feel comfortable knowing there are open issues all the time. This multitasking ability may not be as common among people as you think. Many people absolutely cannot stand having anything unresolved before they go to lunch or leave at the end of the day. These same people may be driven crazy by a ringing phone that goes unanswered. While it would be wonderful to have all calls resolved by the end of the day, this is typically unrealistic. At the same time, the agents need to maintain the sense of urgency to complete as many calls as realistically possible. They should not let the little things slide because "I'll never get all of this done anyway."

Ability to Take on Responsibility

The Help Desk agents will have the operations of the computing system and customer interactions at their fingertips so they must be responsible people. They must recognize from the beginning that what they are doing is important, even though appreciation will not be overtly shown on a consistent basis. Nevertheless, the agent's role demands they carry out their responsibility at all times. Whether a company has $300,000 in revenue or $3 billion, it more than likely cannot survive without its computing system. As the Help Desk continually has its hand in these systems, its data, and the processes of its users, the agents that make up the Help Desk must understand how much impact they have.

A side demonstration of your agents' responsibility is their ability to accept blame when it is necessary and be up front in their actions. You cannot succeed if files are deleted or hardware broken and no one comes forward with an explanation.

| Note | *If you are the type of manager who publicly lambastes associates for mistakes, you will be fostering an environment in which associates hide their actions and cover up their mistakes.* |

You also want your agents to be up front in their explanations to customers. The answers "Sorry, that's company policy" or "I can't do that for you because it is not my job" are customer-service killers! If nothing else, don't verbalize those words and find someone who can make those decisions. Once the decision is approved or made, the agent can contact the customer with the necessary resolution.

Empowering your agents to take the necessary actions to achieve results is very effective. Let's look at an example of an assistant store manager wanting to purchase a PC over the phone. Company policy may require a written request, but the manager is on vacation and suddenly realized the new clerk starts the next week and will not have a PC otherwise. Technically, it is all right to turn down the request because of the policy. However, wouldn't it be nice if the agent recognized the situation practically? Knowing that one PC purchase would not be financially critical, the agent could take the request verbally and e-mail the chain of command himself of his action. This action will still allow everyone that needs to approve the purchase to be notified, and the harried manager on vacation would not mess up a new associate's first day.

It takes the right agent to earn this empowerment. Business or technical experience will help agents know when they can go an extra step or not. A PC purchase policy might be circumvented in the name of customer service, but changing passwords for senior executives without following certain guidelines may not be. Your guidance and consistency will help tremendously. Consistency is a must as the agents will get confused if an action is right one day and is viewed negatively the next day.

Logical Thinking

Help Desk agents need to be able to think logically. Typically their problems involve programming code or fixing technical devices and the resolution of their issues will usually not come artistically. Yes, you need to be creative at times but more often than not, you need to "think" through the problem and the course you need to take. Creatively leaping to conclusions will more than likely result in the creation of more problems rather than resolving the original one. Instead, an agent who can carefully work a problem in a step-by-step approach will be successful.

Composure

There will be frequent times when a caller reaches your Help Desk and will "express" his displeasure at whatever problem he is experiencing. A strong attribute of a Help Desk agent is to remain composed through these times and rise above the situation. The fact is that a problem has happened and needs to be resolved. The ability of an agent to work through an ugly, bad situation is necessary, unfortunately. No one should be subjected to a hostile workplace and abuse should not be tolerated. However, I doubt you can avoid bad language once in a while. Don't require your agent to sit through it if it can be helped, but also hope that it doesn't rattle the agent for hours or days afterwards.

General Understanding of the Product They Will Support

An untrained associate may not, and probably will not, know your products and services from the very beginning, but he does need to exhibit some aptitude for picking it up soon. Whether it is a background in business, logical thinking for reading program code, or technical experience to fix PCs, you need to get a good sense early on if the associate can thrive in your particular environment.

Deeper than just being able to answer a question, your agents will need to be sure enough of themselves to not let a customer take them down the wrong path. They need to apply their listening skills to hear the real problem that may lie underneath what the customer is explaining. Sometimes it is as easy as using the right semantics to resolve an issue. The user may not understand their technology but will guess what is wrong in an effort to help. "I keep saving to my hard drive but it isn't there when I go look for it" may take your agent down a certain resolution path. If the problem was really a floppy drive (the disks don't bend, so they must be hard), the agent, and the caller, will waste much unnecessary time.

An Outside Comparison

To apply all these principles, it might help to think of a good waiter. (In fact, these service providers can make excellent Help Desk staff!) Their effectiveness can mirror the process a Help Desk person goes through.

- Knows the menu and the food on it before called on
- Makes the customer feel comfortable in their environment and asks for their need

- Helps guide the customer through the decisions
- Recommends things to try
- Delivers the food in a timely manner
- Follows up to make sure the customer is satisfied
- Concludes with a nice attitude and welcomes the customer to visit again

To summarize, a good Help Desk agent will

- Know the product he is supporting and how it is used in the business
- Greet callers professionally and not intimidate them with technical terminology
- Listen to the customer's issue and ask questions to ensure they are on the same page
- Recommend solutions to the problem until it is resolved
- Deliver the solution to the customer
- Follow up at a later time to make sure the problem was indeed fixed and is stable
- Encourage callers to call back if they have any more problems

The skill sets needed in an agent are easy to list but are hard to find. Resumes and interviews will more than likely show all these attributes, so you will need to dig deeper to feel more comfortable that a potential agent truly possesses the desired skills. Some examples of things you can do and questions you can ask to determine these skills can be found in Table 8-1.

Skill Sets	How to Find Out About It
Strong communication skills	Conduct the interview over the phone so you can relate to how callers will interact with the agent.
Listening	Make sure they answer your questions directly.
Empathy	Have them name a time when they ran into a problem they could not relate to.
Self-motivated	"What motivates you?" or "What past recognition have you received that worked for you?"
Energetic and enthusiastic	Notice their tone of voice, their body posture, and whether they ask you questions to learn more themselves.

Table 8.1 How to Uncover a Candidate's Skill Set

Skill Sets	How to Find Out About It
Team player	"What do you do when you run into a problem you cannot solve?"
Ability to handle change	Ask for examples of changes that occurred in their previous jobs and how they dealt with them.
Multitasking skills	"How do you go about prioritizing a list of problems along with taking on new work?" or "Would you rather work on long projects or short issues and why?"
Ability to take on responsibility	Have them name a couple of examples in which they took on a new responsibility without being asked.
Logical thinking	"Tell me the steps you would go through to solve a problem like *xyz*?"
Composure	"What was your most stressful situation and how did you handle it?"
General understanding of the product they will support	"Tell me about your experience with *xyz* and how you have worked with it."

Table 8.1   How to Uncover a Candidate's Skill Set *(continued)*

Management Skills

Many of the skill sets that make a good Help Desk agent also are good for managers. In fact, in the Help Desk world it is strongly recommended that Help Desk managers have some experience in that environment themselves. So, as you begin to identify potential managers, review the list of skills from the agent's list and add the following skill sets as well.

- People skills
- Ability to see how the business uses the products supported
- Prioritization skills
- Decision-making skills
- Delegation skills
- Vision

People Skills

More than just communicating and working in a team atmosphere, the manager will need to work effectively with people at many levels. The manager will need to work with subordinates, customers, peers, and upper management to resolve issues and understand their needs.

Subordinates

Managers need to work with subordinates to challenge them to new levels of achievement in customer relations, technical proficiency, and career progression. The manager should be a motivator to keep the morale of the Help Desk strong and positive. The manager will need to be a coach who provides feedback to the associates and recognizes their good work. A good manager will also provide opportunities for associates to learn and grow into new areas that will help their professional careers.

Customers

Managers will not work with customers as directly as the agents, but there will be some interaction. During these times, the manager needs to understand where the customers are coming from on their issues and show empathy for their situation. He needs to be a good listener and follow up on any open or recurring problems that are brought his way. Last, the manager needs to exude confidence so customers feel their problems are being handled effectively and efficiently.

Peers

Managers will work with peers to get things done as well, especially when the Help Desk needs the skill sets of people in other departments or organizations. To this end, a good manager needs to understand the art of compromise, where sometimes you must give some ground to gain some. For example, the manager may provide some of the agents' time to help development finish a project in return for development's help in resolving an issue. This does not have to be formal, but both sides will sense when it's done correctly.

Upper Management

Finally, the Help Desk manager needs to work well with the people in the organization above. This is necessary when explaining how problems happened or how they were resolved, asking for additional resources and budget, or just expressing thoughts on growing the Help Desk department. Again, the Help Desk manager must show confidence so upper managers will feel comfortable that they do not have to get directly involved in each and every issue. The manager should not be afraid to give credit to others or to take blame for things he is responsible for.

Ability to See How the Business Uses the Products and Services You Support

Where the agent needs to know how the product works, the manager needs to understand its role in the business or how it relates to the customer. This is important in situations where workaround solutions must be implemented or more resources need to be applied to the issue. It is very helpful if a Help Desk manager can not only solve a problem but can also recommend other options on services or technologies as well. Remember that if you want the Help Desk to be proactive and to reach this level, you must know your customers and the technologies they use.

Prioritization Skills

A manager needs to know when to escalate a problem or when to assign additional resources to it. This cannot happen without the manager knowing the business, but the act of doing it and doing it right is a separate skill. There are many ways to prioritize a call, whether by the time of the call, how many people it impacts, or even the seniority of the person calling it in.

A manager is a keeper of a resource owned by the company. It is his responsibility to utilize these resources in the most effective way possible to achieve the goals and expectations of the company and its customers. Prioritizing the agents' work is very important to that process. Knowing when to dedicate more resources, be it people, time, or money, to one problem while others sit unattended, is a crucial skill of management and is vital to the success of the Help Desk.

Decision-Making Skills

A good manager by necessity must have good decision-making skills. It is not just a "brains" requirement, but the ability to know when and how to make them.

The ability to make a decision sounds easy enough—after all, people do it every single day. We decide to get out of bed, what to wear, and which way to drive to work. So with the large quantity of decisions that everyone makes every day, it would seem that everyone would be good at it. This may be the case in picking out clothes, but making decisions in business is different. A good decision in business may make a significant impact on revenue, the careers of others, or the completion of a major deal. A bad decision could bankrupt a company, cause people to lose their jobs, or end a long-lasting customer relationship. The weight of certain decisions can cause people to freeze or delay making a decision far longer than they should. A good manager will make business and associate decisions consistently, and must feel comfortable doing so. Likewise, you need to feel comfortable in your manager's ability to not only make decisions but to make decisions that best fit any situation. Because decision making is such an integral part of a Help Desk manager's success, we will spend some time on this topic.

Managers can use several decision-making styles. Depending on the situation, certain styles fit an organization or situation and some won't:

- Autocratic
- Bureaucratic
- Diplomatic
- Democratic

We will describe each decision style briefly in the sections that follow and will conclude with a summation of the issues surrounding these decision-making styles and when each style is best used (see Tables 8-2 and 8-3).

Style	When to Use It
Autocratic	When the decision needs to be made in a hurry When the decision maker is the only person with the knowledge to make the decision
Bureaucratic	When an approval process is required before the decision is finalized When an audit trail of the decision process is needed due to the importance of the outcome or for legal reasons
Diplomatic	When the decision maker is not the only one with knowledge on the decision topic When team "buy in" is important to the outcome
Democratic	When the decision maker has little or no knowledge on the topic When the outcome of the decision is not extremely important When the outcome of the decision is experimental

Table 8.2   When to Use a Certain Decision-Making Style

Style	Issues with Each Decision Style
Autocratic	Doesn't get an outside perspective Team doesn't feel a part of the process Doesn't provide opportunities to grow or see others in action
Bureaucratic	Very time consuming Very resource intensive
Diplomatic	Disheartening if consistently asked for ideas but the ideas are not used Assumes the right people are brought into the process
Democratic	Time consuming Resource intensive No real owner of the decision

Table 8.3 Issues with Decision-Making Styles

Autocratic An autocratic decision is made solely by the person making the decision. It can seem to "come down from above" or to be "made in a vacuum." The decision maker does not include others in the process although they may be directly impacted by the decision. There are times when this method is correct or even necessary, as we will discuss.

Bureaucratic Bureaucratic decisions imply decisions made with much red tape. It is typically a derogatory term that involves many people, issues, or paper. If a manager is felt to be bureaucratic in his decision-making ability, you need to understand its impact. Your company may require this type of thinking and that will work well. If your company does not require much formality in all its decisions, this manager will probably cause more problems than the number of benefits received.

Diplomatic A diplomatic decision is made in consultation with others. The decision maker will be ultimately responsible for the outcome, but others have had input into the process. The decision is diplomatic because other people had their chance to exert influence. If input is heard but consistently ignored, however, the diplomacy will be lost.

Democratic A democratic decision maker tosses ideas out on the table and allows others to vote on the result. This process rates high on the "team involvement" scale but low on "initiative" and "risk taking."

Table 8-4 shows you an example of these decisions styles in action. Take the act of picking a name for your Help Desk. Let's see how each type of decision maker would go about the decision.

The Decision Style...	...Will Drive How It Is Picked
Autocratic	"I decided on Support Center. Please make a note of it."
Bureaucratic	"After I send a request to Marketing for clearance, we can work on a name. I would like each of you to submit your suggestion in writing so we can tabulate the responses. I will then take the winner to Legal to ensure it is okay, and finally to the CEO for ultimate clearance."
Diplomatic	"I have several suggestions for our new name. I will list them here and you can add more if you want. Once we narrow that list down to three, I will pick our winner."
Democratic	"Here is the list we came up with. All in favor of..."

Table 8.4   An Example of Decision Making in Progress

Delegation Skills

Knowing when to delegate and whom to delegate to is a strong characteristic of an effective manager. It is different than being lazy and giving away work; it is actually getting as much work done as possible with the resources at hand. Depending on the situation, your manager should stay above the daily phone calls as much as possible. The more calls the manager directly takes, the more he will be immersed in them and the harder it will be to see what is happening across the whole environment. Taking calls has a longer lasting effect as well. Customers have a nasty habit of remembering names, and the next time they call, they may ask for the manager again. Agents answering the phone won't know if they should pass the call or if the customer just didn't know any other name.

Conversely, there are times when it may take longer to delegate a problem than resolving it on your own. In some instances, by the time you explain what is requested, provide helpful hints on how to do it, and then oversee the result, you will have wasted more time and energy than the effort deserved. However, be careful to moderate the thought, "If I want it done right, I *must* do it myself." This may indeed be accurate, but until you give others the chance to do it themselves, the thought *will* always be right. You must give others opportunities to learn and they will respect you for it. This will also benefit you as you can learn who in your group has the ability to step up to more responsibilities and who cannot.

Vision

Vision is a hot buzzword these days—in order to advance in a company you need to have vision. Vision equates to the lofty idea that you can see into the future and plan for trends and events that have not yet happened. This gets tricky because you may not be able to do anything about it, but you can predict it.

Vision is used here with a caveat. A manager who really acts as a supervisor to two associates should not be expected to have as much vision. Given his limited managerial role, he should be required to see only short periods of time ahead. It may be perfectly fine for his vision to extend through the week or month, enabling him to plan only for staffing levels and training needs. On the other hand, a Help Desk manager with a staff of thousands with locations across the world and a large budget needs vision that goes a lot farther. Your Help Desk manager must have the ability to see and plan for things coming their way.

Another Outside Comparison

Let's see if my waiter example from earlier can apply to the Help Desk manager. We will compare the Help Desk manager to the restaurant manager. A restaurant manager will

- Ensure the food is ready and the staff is prepared
- Take complaints from customers and reassign resources
- Understand peak periods of activity and staff accordingly
- Assume work responsibilities when workload demands it

To summarize: A Help Desk manager will

- Provide Help Desk agents the training they need to do their jobs and ensure that processes and tools are aligned with their needs
- Stay in touch with customers and managers to keep the agents and open calls in the correct priority order
- Understand the environment of the Help Desk so that it is staffed and resourced at the right times and on the right days
- Recognize when the workload is rising fast and will pitch in where possible to help out

In addition, your manager needs to know the product and how it is used in the business. Showing and feeling empathy for the problems of the customers goes a long way in maintaining loyalty and goodwill with your customer base. A career beginning in a Help Desk itself would certainly help.

Determining Headcount Strategies

There are many methods of determining headcount. You need to consider a couple of factors when you go through this process. Your organizational setup, described in Chapter 7, will go a long way in determining how you may want to determine headcount. External factors aside, the following are strategies you can use to add staff to your Help Desk:

- Add them one at a time
- Hiring for average load vs. peak loads
- Staffing on a N+1 basis

One at a Time

A starting point when addressing headcount is obviously how many people you should, or can, have. A common, and easy, way to build your staff is the "one at a time" method. To be sure, you have run across this in the past. This plan calls for you to hire a person, work him until he is truly overloaded, work him a little longer, and then hire the next person. This is quick to implement because you are not instituting a planned, formulaic methodology involving many facts and trends. Instead you are filling short-term needs in a reactionary mode.

While you will probably never be overloaded in staff headcount using this plan, you will not be creating good impressions with your customers or existing staff. The whole nature of this methodology is to wait until your surroundings and services are bad and then attempt to fix them. Your next hire will still need to be trained, which creates even more work for your staff, so the ramp-up time is quite long. Again, this is common, but I definitely do not recommend it as a standard practice.

There are a couple of instances when a "one at a time" plan works. The first is when you are proving the value of a new service. If you are not sure whether the technology or new idea will last long term, you may not want to hire additional agents just to support it. Using the "one at a time" strategy, you could hire/dedicate one agent to the new service at the beginning. As more and more customers use the service, you can watch its progress and workload. When it becomes apparent that the need for help is more than the one agent can provide, you can add more. At that point, the service will probably last, and the agents will not be wasted.

A slightly different scenario is a new technology that will be implemented in the customer base over a longer period of time. The prior example uses the "one at a time" plan when the success of the new service is not immediately known. In a long implementation plan, the success is a given; it will just take time to finish the rollout. Hiring agents as the rollout continues can defray personnel costs over the life of the project.

Averages vs. Spikes

A more planned staffing decision is to determine whether you want to be staffed for an average workday or you need staff to cover any possible spike in workload. The business your company or customers are in will influence this approach greatly, but you can also do either one regardless of the business.

At the beginning you could have estimated that your Help Desk would take 100 calls a day, with each agent capable of fielding 25 calls. With this thought, you would want four agents in the Help Desk. Determining the headcount in this manner is staffing for the average workload.

Now let's say you also know that on the last day of each month, your call volume will consistently be 150 calls. With an agent able to take 25 calls, you would need six agents instead of four. Planning this way is staffing for spikes in demand.

These spikes may take place within a day as shown in Figure 8-1 (calls are typically lower during lunch hours), or within a month (more at check printing or month-end batching), or within a year (fiscal closing or physical inventories).

In Figure 8-1, Thursday definitely stands out from the other days, just as June and December do in Figure 8-2.

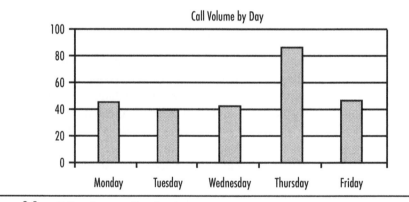

Figure 8.1 Call volume spikes by day

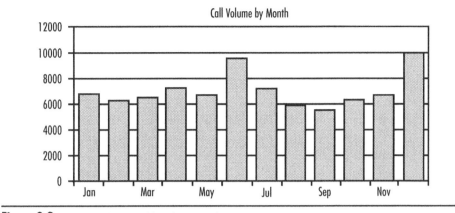

Figure 8.2   Call volume spikes by month

Budget may force your hand, as resourcing for spikes is more expensive than resourcing for averages. Staffing for calls that occur only occasionally requires more agents and related resources than staffing for the average volume and enduring the spikes when they happen.

Spike resourcing ensures that you do not fall behind when call volumes go up, but what do your associates do when the spikes go away? If you have a strong cross-training plan (and you should) or have several large-scale projects, it would be nice to staff for the spikes. This way you can have your staff work on side projects during the lag times and go back to problem solving when the volume goes back up. They can even spend time out with your customer base to get a clearer and more empathetic version of what your customers want or need.

The criticality of your Help Desk also may force you to spike resourcing. If the calls concern life or death situations or other time-sensitive situations, you may be required to staff for the most calls that could happen. A recurring theme throughout this book is that the customer does not care about your designs and plans as long as you are there for them when they need you. Staffing for spikes is the best way to cover those needs.

Most organizations do not have this strict requirement so it is recommended that you do not staff that high. There are other methods to help you in periods of spiked demand. If the spikes can be predicted, you can bring in temporaries, interns, or other part-time help to cover the periods of additional calls. If the spikes cannot be predicted yet occur frequently, you could use these part-time options to provide coverage but at a lower cost than full-time associates. Over time, the business will let you know if your average staffing plan is right or not.

Software applications to help you estimate staffing needs will be discussed in more detail in a later chapter.

N + 1

I do not advise staffing to cover the most calls you could take, but I also do not go as low as covering only for the averages. Instead, you can implement an N+1 staffing plan. At its simplest, this means take the staff count that a normal day would require (N) and increase it (+). The amount you increase it by is the typical number of associates you have out of the office because of vacation, sick leave, or training. This small increase gives you flexibility to cover the typical day even when one of your agents is out. Without this strategy, many managers face the "I cannot afford to send them to this or that seminar" dilemma because they do not have the headcount to do it.

An N+1 plan helps this occur without disrupting the business. It does not fix the times when multiple people are gone, but that is going back to spike resourcing, which is overkill in most organizations. Be careful if you explain your hiring needs this way to management. Your plan may sound excessive if you present it incorrectly. Don't hide the reasons behind the budgeted headcount; state you are keeping your resources at prime levels despite already approved times of leave.

Figure 8-3 depicts the four staffing strategies on a graph. The higher the strategy on the graph, the more expensive it is to staff. The farther right on the graph, the more likely you will gain increased customer satisfaction from the plan.

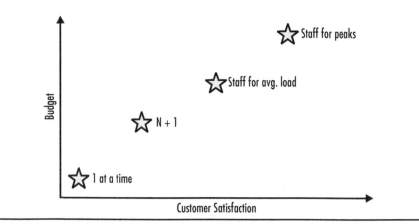

Figure 8.3   Staffing method impact graph

Methods to Find Agents

Now that we have identified what we are looking for in our associates, we have to go get them. As with our customer base, we can find these associates in two places—internally or externally. Either area brings with it pros and cons, but it is wise to look at both. Let's review the issues with each one.

Internal Searches

An internal search means that you will look within your own organization for candidates. This search is not confined to the IT department, either. The business or customers may have individuals who come in to the organization with one career in mind, only to find that the field of IT and the Help Desk has more appeal. This method brings many advantages. First, these people are already familiar with the company and can ramp up more quickly than someone from the outside. Internal candidates will already know the small things like corporate policies, human resource benefits, even where the bathroom is, and you can direct your time to other issues.

Hiring internally should also make a safer choice in that your reference checks are, or should be, more reliable. You get a firsthand look at how the candidate acts in your company's setting. An important skill set of your Help Desk associates is understanding the product or service they support, so if the associate once used the product in the business setting, he or she has a leg up on those who have not. On the other hand, hiring internally may mean you are not bringing in the technical skills you need. A balance among customer service, knowledge of the business, and technical know-how is important to achieve when building your team.

Even if you do not hire internally initially, it would be wise to keep it in mind for future hires. Many years after our Help Desk was in place we began an organized plan to run selected field associates through the Help Desk. The plan was to bring four associates from our stores into the Help Desk, train them, put them on the front line for 12 months, then send them back into the field. They would have been exposed to a much wider variety of branch functions and systems. By the end of the first nine months, two had jobs at other corporate departments and we kept the other two in the IS department. Their field knowledge had proven too valuable to the Help Desk and they are now fully functional Help Desk agents. The plan did not achieve our original goals, but its effectiveness did position this as a recommended practice for us.

Referrals

One step away from hiring internal associates is hiring someone based on a recommendation from an internal associate. Referrals are good ways to find candidates because you have at least someone who can vouch for the skills or strengths of the candidate. The candidate will also know more about your company or organization because he will have spoken about it with the person referring him to begin with.

Many companies offer compensation or rewards for existing associates when they refer a person who is ultimately hired into the company. This incentive encourages your associates to seek out others who would be a good fit in the company. So, in essence, you now have that many more "recruiters" looking for talent in the marketplace.

If you reward your associates for finding candidates, you may want to put some rules around it. For example, you may want to say they receive their reward after the hired person has worked for some period of time or passes a certain level of performance review. This helps prevent associates from recommending anyone they know who might cause more harm than good to the company.

External Searches

While you may be able to start your Help Desk using internal sources, it is highly unlikely you will be able to continually staff from within as the Help Desk gets larger. Your source then becomes the marketplace at large. Here you enter the world of unknown talent and attributes. Remember that you came from this world at one time and look how well you turned out. External hiring has its own advantages.

To begin with, the candidate pool is significantly larger outside your company. You have a better chance of landing someone with the specific skill sets you need and who is not set in the ways of the company.

External hiring is an effective way to bring fresh ideas into the organization. Although this book will give you all you need to launch and grow an effective Help Desk, these people can bring additional experiences to bear. Pull them in early in their careers, like the first week, and encourage them not to be shy with ideas and feedback on your operations. They need to understand that their ideas will not always be implemented but will not be discouraged, either. Some practices may not apply in your organization or may have been tried before with less than stellar results. However, even if one out of ten succeeds, you and your group gain. This practice also makes the new associate feel valued and part of the team.

Job Postings and Advertisements

Somehow you need to let the rest of the world know that you are in the need of hiring Help Desk agents. Unless you know the people you want and they, in turn, want what you are offering, you will need to advertise for your openings. The media you use may vary depending on where you are searching, but the content stays roughly the same. Overall the content should describe the job you have open and the skills applicants need to qualify for it.

The good thing is that you have this job posting already mostly written. Where? In the job descriptions you wrote earlier. For example, the job title will have the name of the job you are looking to fill and the qualifications section will list the skills you are looking for:

- College degree in computer-related field is beneficial

- Intermediate level working with computer hardware and software is required

- 1 to 2 years of IT experience is preferred

Job postings used to be limited to placing an advertisement in the newspaper and waiting for people to respond. You could widen your audience only by placing ads in more than one paper in whatever geographic area you wanted to target. With the amazing reach of the Internet today, job postings can be placed electronically and millions of people have access to it. There are Internet sites devoted to linking job seekers with job openings. Monster.com is one example. There an employer can post a job opening for anyone to see. At the same time, those people seeking jobs can post their resumes, and potential employers can look through the resumes proactively for candidates. This is a highly effective way to find many people to fill any number of positions.

Outsourcing

Another method for staffing is to outsource specific functions. Many companies offer complete Help Desk partnerships and are worth looking into. A safe way to explore outsourcing without total commitment is to use a partner to help in part of your support offering. Maybe you use them on a per-call basis to see how well they perform without turning your entire customer base over to them. Most companies that offer Help Desk services have different bundles you can choose from along with the complete package.

Working on the premise that you want your own Help Desk, we will continue to work on your own staff for the meantime. Additional issues and opportunities for outsourcing will be discussed later on in the book.

Staff Rotation

Many Help Desks begin staffing by other personnel rotating through the position on a part-time basis. For example, your programmers may take turns working the phones between projects. I do not recommend this solution long term. Typically this is seen as a chore and their work may not be at the levels you would like. There is also a constant pass-off of calls when one person's turn is over and someone else's begins. This solution is fine to start with, and can even lead to potential candidates doing this long term, but I would phase this out of your plans as soon as possible. For empathy's sake, let programmers or systems people work for a day or so in the Help Desk area, but only to learn the life of the support associate and not for a job.

Interviewing

You can find all kinds of books, Internet sites, and seminars devoted to interviewing, so we will not go into this topic in great depth here. However, some points are crucial to the process. As we continue to stress the importance of a good team of agents, it all begins with finding them, thus the interview. We will walk through items you need to consider before, during, and after the interview.

Planning for the Interview

Many people consider an interview process to be the point in time when the interviewer and the candidate are sitting in a room together. This is an accurate description of an interview but the process is begun well before the candidate first sits down to talk. Interviews are done to find the best person for the particular job opening you have. To find the best, you need to prepare properly by

- Including a good cross section of the staff you have
- Training your agents in the art of interviewing
- Analyzing resumes thoroughly
- Creating an interview form for your interviewers to fill out

Include a Good Cross Section of the Staff You Have

Building a team requires that peers work well together and getting them involved from the beginning helps. Hiring is not a democracy; you do have the final say and you should make this clear, but having the staff provide input makes them feel responsible for the decision. This also allows the candidate to meet the group with whom he or she will be working. If you have a large staff, try including more than one interviewer at a time. Be careful not to make it too large a group as you will intimidate the candidate and probably will not get the true picture. I recommend that you have no more than three people interviewing at the same time.

Train Your Agents in the Art of Interviewing

Imperative in this procedure is that your interviewing agents are trained in the art of interviewing. These interviews are the candidate's first real glimpse of your organization and they should be treated accordingly. The agents should understand what information you are interested in learning about the candidate and how to best get it.

Prepare a Strategy   The group conducting the interviews should know what is expected of them. Some agents may interview for team fit, interpersonal skills, and initiative. Others may be used for technical qualifiers where their goal is to understand the candidate's knowledge of the technologies and processes used within your customer base. There can be an overlap of questions that allows multiple people to get a feel for the candidate's answers, so you don't want to narrow their questions down too much. However, you don't want to finish the interviews only to realize later that no one questioned the candidate's stated skills from the resume. Each interviewer needs to recognize and understand their objective in the process.

To help train your agents, you may want to develop an interviewing packet that pulls together all necessary information for an interviewer. This packet could include qualifications you look for in a candidate, legal information, sample interview questions, and so on. A packet is especially useful if you will be growing a large staff and interviewing is a regular routine for the Help Desk.

Simulate an Interview   Interviews are important and should not be taken lightly. If you have staff that is not experienced in interviewing, it may be beneficial to conduct mock interviews before they actually conduct a real interview. A mock interview allows the interviewers to practice their questions and determine for themselves if the questions they want to ask flow as they expect. This practice also gives you a chance to see how they might act in a real interview and what type of questions they will ask. The interview is a stressful time for the candidate, so the interviewer needs to be calm and collected to help ease any possible tension.

Legal Considerations There are many legal issues around interviewing that must be taught beforehand. Questions such as "Are you married?" or "So where in Dallas do you live?" may seem like innocent and simple conversation pieces but it could make the candidate feel discriminated against because of his marital status or economic background. Where possible, let your Human Resources department question the candidate's personal attributes. Your group should concentrate on team fit, technical and service abilities, and other job-related activities. You can sit in on their initial interviews to get a feel for how they perform. Your presence will probably cause them some discomfort, but if you sit back and observe casually without scribbling notes at every opportunity they should be fine. The simulated interviews done beforehand will also give you time to unearth potentially harmful lines of questions.

Analyze the Resume Thoroughly

The resume should not be the sole reason to hire or not hire a person, but it will represent them initially and can give you strong clues as to how they will work out. Where you see possible issues, write them down somewhere so you can remember to ask about them. Warning signs are outlined in Table 8-5.

The items listed in Table 8-5 are not necessarily bad. Missing date ranges may mean the candidate was caring for a sick relative or got tired of working and just took time off. A degree in an unrelated field may have been what the candidate

Resume Warning	Possible Issue	How to Find Out
Vague or overgeneralized objective	Candidate not sure of what he wants in a career	"Can you give me more details on what you are looking for in a career?
Career objective that does not match what you are interviewing for	Candidate not sure of what she wants Resume is being sent to many openings and has not been customized	"Help me understand how your career objective matches the job we are discussing."
Jobs listed with no dates	Candidate did not stay long at those jobs	"Can you give me the months and years you were at each of these jobs?"
Date ranges not listed on the resume	What was the candidate doing during that time?	"I see your last job ended last June. What have you been doing since then?"
Many jobs in short time period	Not sure what they want in a career Job hop at the first sign of a better opportunity	"How can I feel comfortable that you will not leave us like you have these past few jobs?"
Education or experience not related to job opening	Not sure what they want in a career Trying to find a job in the latest "hot" market	"Explain to me how your French degree prepared you for a Help Desk career."

Table 8.5 Resume Warning Signs

wanted at the time, but has since learned of a different career interest. Several jobs may be due to business contracts ending beyond the candidate's control or family issues that caused them to move. There are many clues a resume can give; you should review it with some detail.

The appearance of the resume itself was something I used to analyze, too. I wanted the candidate to have taken pride in the presentation of his skills on paper as well as in person. In today's world of resumes being sent via the Internet and e-mail, though, resumes may lose their sharpness. Because of this, I have shifted completely away from judging the candidate by the appearance of his resume. (Misspellings still nag me, though!)

Create an Interview Review Form for the Interviewers to Fill Out

You have seen some of the attributes to go after and probably have more of your own to fit your environment. Capture these wishes on a form so the candidates can be graded. Putting this in writing forces some standards and allows the interviewers to compare candidates more easily. This by no means makes everyone ask the same question, but it does focus their time on the issues you want them to learn. How they go about finding it can be left up to them.

The Interview Itself

The interview is a time for you to learn everything relevant about the candidate as it relates to the position you are looking to fill. It can be done in person or on the phone or both. You can hold interviews by yourself or in front of a panel of interviewers. The interview can last ten minutes or over an hour. Whatever the method, the interview must achieve its primary goal of sharing information so both sides, the interviewer and the candidate, are prepared to make a decision on filling the position.

To reach this objective, the interview should include all or some of the following suggestions:

- Ask why
- Evaluate the candidate's phone skills
- Encourage the candidate to interview you as much as you interview him
- Interview the candidate; don't interrogate him
- Ask either/or questions with no wrong answer
- Discuss career goals
- Show the candidate the work environment

Ask Why

Lobbing softball questions is okay as long as you follow up with *Why?* Your candidate will have rehearsed his answers to all the popular questions and that is fine. Now you need to ask him why. For example, "I love working with people" sounds good and is something you want. "Because I broke up with my girlfriend and need company" is not. "I like working on multiple projects at one time" is a good answer, but "because I get bored working on anything over an hour" may not be. The point is you should make the candidate work some in the interview. Answers straight from the book could mislead you otherwise. In places go three deep. Ask the candidate why he answered your initial "why" question as in this example:

Interviewer	What interests you most about this job?
Candidate	The technology that I will get to support.
Interviewer	Why is that so interesting? (Why #1)
Candidate	Because of all the different types you have. It will be challenging to support them all.
Interviewer	Why will our breadth be challenging to you? Your resume shows them all in your experience. (Why #2)
Candidate	Uh, because I really have not supported so many at this level of detail. Our department used the equipment as much as I supported it.
Interviewer	So why did you list them so prominently? (Why #3 may be asked under your breath!)

Try this and you will see what I am referring to. You will probably get a surprised look like, "Do you really want me to answer that?" but it will be worth it. You want people of substance who know what they are talking about. This is one way to get at that.

Check Out the Candidate's Phone Skills

Assuming your Help Desk will be taking some calls on the phone, the candidate's phone presence is important. Can you understand him? Does he speak too low to be heard or does he mumble? I would even conduct an initial interview over the phone to truly understand this. Phone interviews are great anyway to save time on candidates who will not work out, and also give you the added benefit of hearing them across the phone instead of in person. Since many of your calls will be over the phone, take this time to listen to the candidate as if you were a customer and he was an agent. We used the following exercise over the phone to view their troubleshooting skills:

Phone Skills Interview Test

Have someone not involved in the interview draw a picture with geometric shapes of different sizes, numbers, and letters. Be creative. The number one could be *1*, or could be written out as *one*, or even as the Roman numeral *I*. Letters could be upper- or lower-case. For example, the drawing could look like

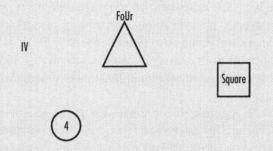

The interviewer takes the drawing without looking at it and gives it to the candidate. The interviewer has with him a blank sheet of paper.

The candidate is now asked to describe the picture without hand gestures or any other expression that could not be duplicated over the phone while the interviewer draws a new picture based on the candidate's instructions.

At the end, compare the two drawings and see how similar they are.

It is much harder to describe something to someone using only your voice. You will notice little clues about the person's ability to troubleshoot from this exercise. For example, the candidate will say, "Draw a square." The interviewer will perhaps draw a large square in the middle of the paper. If the candidate then says, "It is about 1/2 inch big and is in the top left corner," after you have already drawn it a different way, there will be a problem. Why is this important? Imagine that same person troubleshooting a PC problem with "Hit CTRL-ALT-DELETE," then continuing with "but you should save your work first!" The order in which you speak your thoughts to someone might save you from making a big problem much bigger.

Encourage the Candidate to Interview You

Another critical issue in the interview process is to remember it is a two-way process. Yes, you are interviewing the candidate and there is no doubt you will accomplish that task. In addition, some of your associates will interview the candidate. You must, however, allow the candidate the same opportunity. The candidate needs to know as much about your company, the position, and you as necessary to make a good decision. You want career seekers, not job hoppers. Many interviewers are tempted to make the job as attractive as possible and that is good. Stop short of making the job seem what it is not. If the person is required to carry a beeper, say so. If there is weekend work or travel required, say so up front.

Hiding these things is only postponing the inevitable. Soon the person will uncover these things and may decide the job is not right for him. If he decides to leave, you have lost time spent on training and must now invest in starting the interview process all over again. The training also took away resources that could have been spent doing other work in the Help Desk. Word of this "trickery" may spread through your area and this misconception could cost you good public relations. Poor public relations could then make hiring additional people even more difficult.

Now, what do you make of someone who has no questions to ask? If you are the fourth in line in a series of interviews, it may simply mean that the person has all the information he needs. If you are first, ask the candidate what he knows of your company to see if he has done much research and is comfortable with the situation. Without any prior knowledge, it would be curious for a candidate to not have *any* questions. Either you have done an outstanding job of telling him about the company and the job, or he has little interest in the job. Get someone else's opinion on the candidate to see if this lack of interest was caught by others and is a concern.

Interview; Don't Interrogate

No bright lights to see them sweat; see them naturally. Some people advocate "pressure interviews" to see how a candidate handles pressure. They make the candidate wait long periods before showing up, include many other people in the interview, and generally make the candidate feel uncomfortable. How a person handles stress is important in the Help Desk world, but the interview is not the time. Make the candidate demonstrate this attribute from previous experience and keep the interview courteous and professional.

Ask Either/Or Questions with No Wrong Answer

The purpose of this is to see what true tendencies the person has. For example, I always ask two questions geared towards finding out if the person is more technical in nature or more customer service oriented. I ask him, "Which is more important to customer service, accuracy or good follow-up?" I then ask, "How about speed or friendliness?" To almost a fault, my frontline software agents answer good follow-up and friendliness and my technical PC or systems candidates answer accuracy and speed. Remembering a rule we discussed earlier in the chapter, I always follow with why. By the way, you probably can guess why candidates choose accuracy as an answer. With a confident smile on their faces, they reply, "If you do it right the first time, there is no need to follow up." Only the most technically focused people cannot see that if the user does not know what CTRL-ALT-DELETE means, your potentially correct answer will not solve their problem. Last, I ask the candidate if he thinks he gave me the right answers, a test of confidence that has only once really amazed me. On about the fifth time I asked this question, the person said, "No." When I responded with why he did not, he just said he knew the answers were wrong. There is no wrong answer; it depends on your customer base, and the method will vary from user to user and situation to situation. Most people know there is no wrong answer, but that interview has kept me asking the question ever since.

Discuss Career Goals

This is a standard interview question any candidate should have a rehearsed answer for. Even then, I think it can lead to interesting information. Many people will come out and say they view this job as a foot in the door for other positions in either IS or the company overall. Don't take this personally and don't let this be the sole reason to not pursue the candidate. Instead find out how he feels the job he is interviewing for can help him reach those goals. If the reasons make sense, I think that is healthy. Career Help Desk associates are hard to find and your staff will never reach its correct level if you insist on hiring only them. You owe it to candidates, however, to inform them if their goals are not best served by taking your opening. Also keep in mind that actual work experience in your company may change their minds anyway.

I highly encourage you to set some expectations around time commitments to the person before offering him the job as well. You should inform new hires that you expect them to remain in their role for at least a year before they can begin to look elsewhere. This gives you time to train them and get some productivity out of them, and it is a short enough time period where they will not feel trapped forever in a job they don't aspire to long term.

Show the Candidate the Work Environment

After the interview, walk the candidate to where he will be sitting. Show him the data center and anywhere else he will work in on a typical day. If you have a fancy office environment with snazzy equipment everywhere, you will impress him and may win him over. If his work environment is a small cubicle with a lot of noise, show him still. Tricking someone into a job is a sure-fire way to lose an associate in a short time frame. You expect the candidate to be open with you; return the favor.

After the Interview

The candidate has left the office so the interview is over. Although the interview itself has been completed, you still have a few steps left to go in the process. Each individual who interviewed the candidate needs to gather his thoughts on what he heard, and get together to discuss them with the other interviewers. From there, you will have good information to make a solid decision as to whether to bring the candidate on to your team.

1. Fill out the review form.
2. Conduct a post-interview meeting with everyone who interviewed the candidate.
3. Check the candidate's references.

Fill Out the Review Form

You went to the trouble to create the form (didn't you?) so now is the time to use it. You want your interviewers to fill this form out pretty soon after their interview so the topics and points are fresh in their minds.

Conduct a Post-Interview Meeting

Have everyone bring their form to a group meeting to discuss what they found. Do not conduct this meeting in an open environment because it is unprofessional and improper to talk about people to others who were not involved. This meeting can bring out many good points that might not be found individually. For example, the candidate may have told one person one story but told someone else something different the next time around. Or one person may have gone into greater detail on an issue than someone else. It would be a shame for a candidate to be dismissed because interviewer A saw he had changed jobs too frequently. If this issue comes up, interviewer B may be able to add that he discussed it, and found out that family emergencies or other situations forced the issue and job hopping was not a problem.

Check References

This step is very important but is often overlooked in the hiring process. Sure you will get terrific responses from just about everyone (would you pick a reference that did not like you?), but sometimes you find out something. If the candidate was interviewing for a programming position and a Help Desk position, the reference may give you clues that were not intended. For example, if the reference thinks the candidate is applying for the programming position, he may tell you, "Sally is great on long projects. She likes being involved in something for weeks on end. I have always known her to prefer working alone without much interruption." That would contrast with your Help Desk environment, I am sure. The trick is uncovering the real attributes of the candidate.

Quick Recap

- Staffing your Help Desk will impact the success of your operation as much as any other decision. You must do everything you can to ensure that all the proper steps are taken to make this process work.

- Have you decided on the different job titles that will be used in your Help Desk? Once you have, you need to create job descriptions so everyone involved can fully understand their role.

- The alignment of the agents' skills with your customers' needs is critical. Do you have a good idea of the skills you think are most needed in your environment?

- Do you agree that your managers must have a foundation of the skills found in your agents? Don't forget that your managers also need attributes above and beyond these skills.

- How will you know to grow your Help Desk staff? Have you set an expectation with your senior managers so they will understand your plan?

- There are many ways to find the agents who will make up your Help Desk. Will you be able to find some internally? Will you have anyone to help you look outside the company to find agents?

- Once you find some candidates, you must interview them. This requires planning in addition to the actual interview. Is your team well versed in what you want to learn from the interview? Do you have a list of questions you will ask each and every candidate?

CHAPTER 9

Tools for Your Help Desk

Now that we have a staff, or at least we have start dates for them, what tools will they use to do their jobs? We will cover tools in three chapters. In this chapter, we will go over the tools needed for a start-up Help Desk by taking a figurative tour through a Help Desk area. As we "tour" the Help Desk, we will go over the tools we find in it.

Then in Chapters 15 and 23, we will go over tools to improve our operations. The philosophy is not to limit our staff's productivity, but typically start-up Help Desks are viewed as prototypes and their use must be proven. With that in mind, you want to keep expenses down as much as possible without hurting your associates or their chances for success. Conversely, you get what you pay for, so don't settle for low-quality tools. If you do, you will find the tools not being used or being replaced frequently because they break or need upgrading. This effort will cost you more money than you would have spent originally.

What to Look For

- The first tool you will encounter in the Help Desk tour is the actual work area in which the agents sit. The physical environment the agents work in can improve or reduce their productivity depending on how it is set up.

- Communication tools are next in line. The Help Desk exists completely to communicate solutions, processes, and ideas to the customers and associates around it and good communication tools are a necessity.

- When people first think of tools, they think of PCs, printers, and the like and these will indeed be discussed here.

- A common area available to the Help Desk agents is very beneficial. As you will learn, preventing burnout needs to be a major priority for a Help Desk manager, and providing an area away from the phones goes a long way towards achieving this goal.

- Finally, the culture of the company, the IT department, and the Help Desk itself will be discussed. Culture is a tool that can increase the morale and productivity of your agents and should not be taken lightly.

The Help Desk Work Area

The tour of tools you need to start your Help Desk begins with the actual area in which the agents will sit. Let's begin by opening the door to a well-lit, open area with cubicles throughout and a few offices on the outer edge. White boards are on the walls here and there with problem statuses and various other messages written on them. What you cannot see is that all the desks are protected against power flickers and outages.

Lighting

Good lighting is important for many reasons. For starters, proper lighting helps your agents perform better whether they need to read a manual or replace hard-to-reach memory boards. You should find the correct mix of bright lights versus regular room lights. For example, where your agents are performing detailed hardware work, you will need to provide brighter lights. If you can have the room also lit by sunlight, it will be even better. People like working where they can see outside so they do not feel as if they are stuck in a cave somewhere. Even if their desks are not directly by a window, people will like sunlight because it helps brighten their day. Many people suffer some form of eye strain from staring at a monitor all day, so wherever you can help them in other areas will be useful.

You need to also be mindful of the lighting at each desk. Some agents may want light in addition to the ceiling lights. If this is the case, you should make additional light available by installing a light underneath a shelf or allowing your agents to bring in a small lamp.

Offices Versus Cubicles

Many people want offices and feel the only way they can concentrate and get work done is to be in an office. For Help Desk associates, however, I feel this is ineffective. Cubicles in an open work area are more conducive to sharing problems and ideas. While noise from other conversations can be distracting if it is not handled properly, it can also allow agents to hear other people's calls that may help them. For example, if you are working on a down location in Dallas and you hear the agent next to you troubleshooting a store in Houston, it may be the same issue and you can save some steps in at least identifying your caller's problem.

If privacy for agents is an issue, your cubicles can have various wall heights to create some degree of privacy while still leaving an open path to the work area. Maybe you even have lower walls within each cubicle but higher walls on the outside to prevent walk-by traffic from interfering too much.

Cubicles also allow flexibility for any needed changes in the physical layout of the Help Desk. A pool of agents doing similar things may evolve into specialized groups that work independently of each other. A cubicle layout helps facilitate an easier reshuffling of desks, whereas offices are more permanent and harder to modify. Figure 9-1 shows a sample layout for a small Help Desk work area. Larger Help Desks can utilize the same principles with just more desks and offices.

Offices on the outer edge are for your managers. You could also use some of these outer edge offices as training rooms. Of course, the size of your department determines how many managers and offices you will need, but each of your managers should have an office if possible.

Managers should be close to the action to lend a hand or just hear what is happening, but some separation is good. If nothing else, they will need some privacy to conduct associate reviews or handle other personnel matters. A quiet place for the agents to train or be trained is also very nice. Agents can always sit at their desks, but the more they can concentrate on their learning materials the better.

White Boards

White boards are like chalkboards but use erasable markers instead of pieces of chalk. They can be very effective for drawing diagrams, posting messages for people to see, and training sessions. We have actually covered entire walls in a training room in white board material to allow large drawings and material to be written when smaller boards would not work as well.

White boards should also be placed in common areas where many people can see them easily. This is a simple and cheap communication tool you can use to display daily events, current statuses of problems, and even an in-office/out-of-office status for agents.

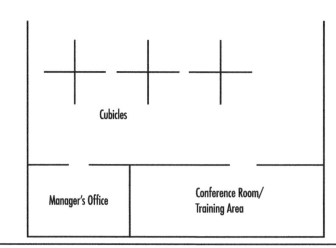

Figure 9.1   Sample Help Desk layout

Desks

Moving forward in our tour, we arrive at an agent's desk. It is nice and big enough to hold his equipment. Each agent has a phone, a PC, and other miscellaneous office equipment.

The desk is not an old doorframe on top of file cabinets (I have seen that once!), but an ergonomic desk with a comfortable chair and large enough workspace to easily view manuals, notes, and so on. The edges of the desk are rounded because sharp corners can lead to injuries over time by constantly pressing into your arms or legs. Your Help Desk associates will be spending a lot of time at their desks and the more these desks are geared towards an effective work area, the more productive your associates will be. Even if your Help Desk associates spend much of their time walking around the building fixing problems, it is still nice to have a home at the end of the journey. Make sure the desks are deep enough to hold a monitor and still leave room for the keyboard and manuals. Monitors are large today and take up a lot of room. Balancing a manual on your lap while typing on a keyboard is far from effective. For that matter, you can install keyboard trays that slide underneath the desks for convenient storage of the keyboard when it is not in use.

The desks should have shelves on top or close by for the various manuals, software packages, and hardware parts that typically accumulate on a Help Desk agent's desk. Remember you want to keep the desktop as clear as possible for effective use, and shelves are perfect for offloading some of the items that stack up over time.

Some associates want more file space because they are the kind who save every piece of paper they lay their hands on. Where possible and appropriate, try to accommodate these needs. It has proven very helpful on occasions for someone to be able to dig out an old memo or report that can help solve a complicated issue.

Depending on the area in which your Help Desk is located, you may want to invest a bit more in sound-absorbing walls. A Help Desk, by nature, is a loud environment and anything you can do to keep the noise down will be worth it in the long run. Other nice features for the walls are small corkboards for tacking up FAQs and notes.

Protection

The Help Desk needs to be up at all times, so power protection is strongly recommended. If your computer room is protected by an Uninterruptable Power Supply and/or generator, you should make sure your agents' desks are protected in the same manner.

Picture a mainframe data center in corporate HQ with a Help Desk next door supporting hundreds of stores across the country. A lightning strike takes out the power to the building and the lights go out. Your computer room is still well lit with the air-conditioning units running because the generator kicked in. Your stores continue running without realizing, or caring, that corporate has no power because the stores' computers still work. It would be very effective if the Help Desk was still up to help these customers when needed. It would disappoint and confuse your customers if you inform them you cannot help them because your computers are down and theirs are not. Stay proactive and available; protect your Help Desk from as many debilitating events as possible.

Protection should also include security. Help Desks typically have a lot of computer equipment around and the value of it all can add up very quickly. With the highest form of computer risk coming from within a company, a Help Desk area should be protected wherever possible. This could include a locked entrance to the area or even monitored cameras if the Help Desk is big enough to warrant them.

Closer in, the agents should be reminded to safeguard any important files or items that may interest a person with bad intentions. This safeguarding can come in the form of locking their desks and offices, powering off their desktops, and taking their laptops home or locking them in their desks when they leave. If there are customer reports or any other information lying around, these should be put away as well. You can also safeguard your Help Desk's security by making agents aware of what is going on around them. For example, you should educate your agents to look for suspicious people or activities that are not part of normal Help Desk work in your company. Someone who is unfamiliar to an agent should not be able to ask for entrance into the computer room or inquire about a password to the system.

A third form of protection is to tactfully remind your agents that most of the security problems in the IT world come from internal associates. You don't want to create a network of spies, but it is worth your time to make sure that everyone is aware of anything suspicious, even if it comes from within. Don't stress this too strongly for fear of destroying your team and making associates spend too much time watching each other, but it does not hurt for everyone to know how important this topic is.

Real-World Example

Each year, our entire company was audited by an accounting firm. Included in this overall audit was a review of the IT department for its security compliance. During one such audit, I was asked how protected our computer room was and who had access to it. All our agents and administrators had access to the computer room but were told not to allow anyone else in. However, I had never tested that policy and felt this would be a good time to do so. I persuaded the auditor to help me in testing the security-consciousness of the staff by asking selected individuals to let this "stranger" into the computer room.

Leading off with a "Can you let me in your computer room? I just want to look around a short while," the auditor first ran into a Help Desk agent. This agent paused a moment, then unlocked the door and let the auditor in. The agent's only extra effort was that he stood in the room while the auditor "looked around." The next "testee" was one of our LAN Administrators who had dozens of servers in the room. This person just plainly refused entrance to the auditor. I don't know whether it was because of security, laziness, or being too busy, but this associate passed the security test well. If only he had passed on the information that there was someone wandering around looking for computer room access, the associate would have made a perfect score!

Last, the auditor approached the systems administration group. These guys were always sticklers for security. In fact, their manager had been tabbed as our next Risk Manager. I thought it would be impossible for the auditor to pass this group, but I was sadly mistaken. The first one got up quickly, let the "stranger" in, and walked back out. That stranger could have taken or destroyed anything in the room and literally crippled the business. When the test was over, we had a good-natured but strong educational meeting for everyone reminding them why these policies were critical to the continued security of the Help Desk.

Help Desk Communication Devices

The first several chapters in this book discussed communication within and outside the Help Desk as a key ingredient to success. This cannot be stressed

enough. A Help Desk cannot be successful without a strong and effective communication plan and process. Much of this communication and notification requires tools of some
sort, including

- Telephones
- Voicemail
- Cell phones, beepers, and walkie-talkies
- Fax machines
- Call logs, e-mail, and collaborative packages

We will cover each of these tools in the following sections.

Telephones

First on the desk is a telephone. Unless all your customers are walk-ups, each associate must have a phone. If your associates will be on the phone for extended periods of time, you can provide headsets or shoulder rests. Do not make these required no matter how much value you think they have. Many people, women and men, work hard on their hair each morning and the headsets can do some damage. Be careful with the type that just goes over the ear because the sound quality is not as good as it is when you speak on a regular phone. Show you care but invest in headsets only if your agents request them.

Phone Call Routing

Allow me to stray a bit to discuss setting up your phones. It is easy enough to put a phone on each desk and wait for it to ring. The harder part is determining how you want your calls routed. It is important that you think through how you want incoming calls to work. There are several ways to do it.

Let's Go Solo   If your Help Desk is small, you could assign each agent his own phone number and publish it for your customers. In this way, the customers could contact a particular agent if they like him or have follow-up issues. On the negative side, you may find that certain agents are always called and others are sitting idle at their desks. Newer agents especially may not get called because no customer wants to suffer through the learning curve when they have a problem.

I always stay away from publishing an individual agent's number because I do not want to burn out my good agents and I also want to expose the newer agents to the real world of calls. As long as you resolve callers' issues in an efficient and professional manner, you do not need to distribute individual phone numbers.

The No Break   Another way to route calls is to assign an agent to be first in line, and his phone will ring first. If his phone is busy, then the next person in line gets the call. This method requires or "allows" the first agent to get all calls unless he is busy. I have seen this method employed in scenarios where a manager wants to expose new people to calls quickly in order to ramp them up to speed. This is a very stressful methodology because the first person seems to never have a break.

The Law of Averages   A more compassionate approach is configuring your phones to ring to the agent who has gone the longest without a call. Basically, the phone system helps spread the load among your agents equally. As long as your agents have similar skills to resolve problems, this method works well.

Group at a Time   This method of routing calls represents a blend of the previous two. Here you assign a group to always be first on call. They receive all calls unless everyone in the group is on the phone or away from the Help Desk. The call would then pass to a secondary group and roll through that group based on who took the last call. You do not burn out individuals because they belong to a group and you also protect other people by putting them in secondary or tertiary groups. This works well when you have tiered levels of support where one team supports the customers directly and another supports the frontline group itself.

A "Must Answer" Line   No matter how you route your phone calls, I highly recommend that you have a number set aside that is a "must answer" phone. We once put a bright red phone on the wall with the label "Bat Phone" above it. Everyone on the Help Desk was instructed to answer this phone at all costs. We did not publish this number to anyone other than internal IS associates so we were assured a line in. It came in very handy during crisis situations when the Help Desk phones were swamped and technical and escalation managers needed to speak to someone immediately.

You should install a telephone in the computer room if possible. If you have agents who do work in a computer room for batch processes, file saves, and the like, it can be very convenient to have a phone nearby. Otherwise, calls could be missed or the agents could waste time walking back and forth to their desks to handle the calls.

Voicemail

Voicemail is a common feature found in most businesses today. If you have not run across it, voicemail is the business equivalent to your answering machine at home. It presents the caller with a greeting, stores the caller's message, and allows the agent to hear the message whenever she returns to her desk. This is extremely valuable so customers can still leave their issues with the Help Desk even though they did not get to speak to an agent. The Help Desk can hear the message and route it internally to the correct resource.

Cell Phones, Beepers, and Walkie-Talkies

As we look closer at the agents, we notice a beeper or cell phone on their hips or a walkie-talkie in their hands. If your Help Desk provides services around the clock but your agents are not always in the office, they need cell phones or beepers. In today's world we use cell phones exclusively as they cost nearly the same as beepers and provide much faster response time. In either case you can also script your systems to beep or call you when defined parameters are reached such as downtime or operations nearing capacity.

Walkie-talkies can be used effectively if your customers are located in the same building or on the same campus as your Help Desk. This is a cheap solution to guiding your "roaming" agent from customer to customer so he does not have to come back to the Help Desk for his next assignment.

Cell phone and beeper numbers need to be communicated to all people who may need them. The circumstances under which the beeper or cell phone is used should be communicated as well. Emergencies can be defined in different ways by different people, but there are times when contacting a Help Desk agent at 2:00A.M. on a Sunday is not necessary. I recommend that you do more than just paste the number on a screen or documentation, though. We had a to-the-point message at the bottom of every user's screen that said, "Emergencies, call" and our phone number. Our person on call was awakened one night from a frantic branch associate. When he was asked the problem, the caller was confused. The caller answered, "The screen said there was an emergency, so I called you." I only hope the support associate was polite by not swearing at the caller and instead instructing him why the beeper number was there!

If you decide to provide your on-call agents with a cell phone, you will also need to effectively communicate your expectations about its use regarding personal calls. With many plans you buy a block of minutes so we always allow personal calls, but if the block of time is ever exceeded, the agent pays the difference. You should come up with a standard offering for a specific phone and service; if your agents want anything more, they can pay the difference in cost.

Fax Machines

A very simple and inexpensive tool for your Help Desk is a fax machine. For those agents supporting users in multiple locations, a fax machine can save valuable time and truly help to resolve problems. For example, if a user has a report with inaccurate information on it, a faxed copy sent to you can illustrate the problem much easier than discussing it over the phone. A fax machine allows the Help Desk agent to verify the "facts" before spending lots of time working on an issue. I have been in many situations where a report's information was in question but I was able to see a time/date stamp on the report that showed it was days old. Small things like this can add up in a typical day of the Help Desk agent.

If your budget can afford it, there are many faxing software packages available that allow you to fax documents from your desktop over the network. This is even better than a fax machine as your agents can stay at their desks and therefore be more available for incoming calls. With this in place, customers can even fax in their problems the same way they use e-mail.

Call Logs, E-mail, and Collaborative Packages

A call log of some type is a requirement for a Help Desk. A call log is some tool or plan for an agent to record information on incoming calls such as the customer's name, location, and problem details. This tool can be expensive software packages designed explicitly for Help Desks, a database or spreadsheet, or even a notepad. Your budget will determine what kind of call log you use. Call management packages (or customer relationship management), which can cost thousands and thousands of dollars, will be discussed in more detail in Chapters 15 and 23 as you move to later stages of the Help Desk's operation. At this stage you probably will not need the most sophisticated technology to log your calls, but you MUST have something planned.

Customers want to tell you their issue once and then they expect you to resolve it. Although most will not mind if you take their information and call them back with a resolution, they will not be receptive to your calling them back minutes, hours, or days later and asking them to repeat the problem.

Picture a waiter taking your dinner order. You provide all the details including the salad dressing, condiments on the potato, and how you want your steak cooked. After waiting a long time, the waiter returns with what you hope is your food.

Instead, he shrugs his shoulders and asks you to repeat your order because he forgot it. How would you feel? You may get mad and leave the restaurant. Your customers will feel the same way if your Help Desk agents do this, too. Ask your customers to repeat a problem several times, and they won't come to the Help Desk.

The Help Desk is successful because it is a common area of knowledge, both physically and figuratively. Walking to another agent's desk or yelling across the room are two ways to share information or ask questions, but they are not always the best. In today's world, e-mail is one of the more popular ways to communicate. With its ability to attach documents, e-mail can allow agents to help each other solve problems without making copies or mailing paper back and forth. E-mail is instantaneous and understood by most anyone technical. Customers can send an issue into the Help Desk, it gets passed around to others who can help resolve it, and then a reply or fixed document can be returned to the customer. This is invaluable.

Moving away from e-mail slightly, packages now offer calendaring and other collaborative tools to allow agents to work together more effectively. Calendaring (or scheduling) can be used to display important dates and times that may affect the Help Desk or its customers. Events like scheduled downtime for systems or monthly operational plans for the business can be put on the calendar for easy reference by agents. Collaboration tools can help agents interact for planning and management issues. Overall, these software options are designed for individuals to act as a team to achieve their goals. This is extremely beneficial in a Help Desk world.

Help Desk Equipment and Technologies

Desks and phones and software are important, but so is the hardware that goes with them. Some equipment is required, some is beneficial, but the more you can arm your agents with, the better. The Help Desk should supply this equipment. Some agents may want to bring in their own equipment for one reason or another but this should be discouraged. Just as you want your customers to be using standard technologies, so should your agents. This section will cover PCs, basic office supplies, printers, and customer-owned equipment.

A Personal Computer

A required tool on the desk is a PC. Help Desk associates need to be able to access many things at one time and a PC enables them to do this easily. I have endured environments where acquisition dollars were "saved" and multiple dumb terminals were placed on each desk, but this took up valuable desk real estate and still did not allow room for spreadsheets, word processors, and so on. PCs are cheap these days and without them your Help Desk will be viewed negatively by your customers. PCs or thin clients are also needed for Internet e-mail. This form of communication is so standard these days it has become a must-have instead of a nice-to-have. Increasingly, Help Desk tools are PC-based as well so this investment is worth its cost for the long run.

If part of your Help Desk service is to travel to customer sites or speak in remote locations, a laptop is a valuable tool. Each agent does not need one, but you could provide shared laptops for anyone who travels to use when needed.

Basic Office Supplies

No matter how technologically advanced your company or Help Desk is, there will still be a need for basic office supplies. These supplies include pens, notepads, staplers, tape, paper clips and a holder for them, an in/out box, a name plate, three ring binders, and scissors. Nothing magic here, but they represent the little things that will be needed throughout the day for any office worker. The workday will be hard and frantic at times in a Help Desk and where there are places you can remove simple frustrations, you should attempt to do so. A pen and some paper are examples of simple tools that should not be overlooked.

Printers

Moving back to technology, the Help Desk should have an ample supply of printers available. You don't need a printer for every agent, but there should be enough printers available to keep the agents productive. The printers should be placed in an area that is close to the agents so they aren't wasting time walking back and forth to get printouts. Conversely, the printers should be not so close to the agents that a long printout is disruptive to anyone on the phone or having a conversation. If the facility requires the printer to be close by, try to install a printer cover that will shield some of the noise or put the printer behind a wall that can divert the noise. Even better is the consistent use of laser jets due to their low cost and reliability. Laser jets are easy to maintain and do not generate much noise.

Any printer you get should be industrial grade as the Help Desk will be generating much paper. Running reports to reproduce what a customer is seeing or to help resolve a problem is commonplace in many Help Desks. If you cannot afford several printers for a large group of agents, at least try to get printers that are fast. A fast printer can overcome a lack of quantity most of the time.

Customer Owned Equipment

Customer owned equipment does not refer to forcing your customers to buy hardware for you. Instead, it means that you want to stock your Help Desk with each and every device you are responsible for supporting. For example, the Help Desk should have available each model terminal, printer, and phone that will be supported so agents can re-create problems when working with a user. Unless you have lucked out and hired geniuses who can memorize everything, it is very helpful for your agents to have the physical device in front of them when they troubleshoot problems. I am not saying you need to provide every model for every agent's desk, but you should make all models you support easily accessible. Perhaps each associate can have a model and it can be shared if needed.

This might prove impossible if you are supporting an external customer base where you cannot control their devices or software. In this case, track the devices where you can, and if you see a trend or large volume of a particular technology try to bring that in-house.

A Common Area for Help Desk Agents

Looking up from the agent's desk, you notice a common area within each group of desks. This area is not filled with people working at desks but is available for anyone who needs to get away from their desk for a break or project work. If your group consists of only one desk, it can still have an open area that is separate from the desk. The common area has tools that are not required for each individual but can be shared.

Training Material

This common area is an excellent place for agents to get away from their desks but still be productive. Fill the area with training materials such as manuals, CDs, books, and videos to give the associates a chance to increase their skills in a cost-effective manner. This kind of training can be started and paused throughout hours and days as needed by the agent. It is cost-effective because the agent does not have to travel to sites and can be brought back to the phones in case of a spike in call volume.

Do not provide training through books and manuals only in this common area, however. While it is obviously more convenient to train your agents here instead of sending them away for training, you are still sending someone away from his desk. Use the Internet and corporate intranet wherever possible for easy access to information right from the agent's desk. The common area is meant to be a break from the incoming calls as much as it is to be the preferred place to conduct training.

Reading Material

Making related reading material available to your agents helps them keep in touch with the IT industry and the issues occurring around them. This reading material can provide a break from the grind of customer calls yet still be work-related and beneficial to both the agent and the company. Many subscriptions are free or can be purchased at a very low cost. You may have to fill out surveys frequently to maintain this "free" subscription, but five minutes out of your day is worth it.

If your budget is so tight that even magazine subscriptions are scrutinized, do not try the "You read it and when you are done, give it to the next agent" methodology. Unless your Help Desk is very small, this is not worth it. I was part of a management team that was forced to go this route and it was laughable. One guy at the beginning would have about three months of issues before he finally passed them to the next person. By the time the last person got them, if at all, he was reading about the coming of Pentium PCs while we were setting our watches to read Internet e-mail. I exaggerate the example but hope you don't miss the point.

Culture

Let's back up and think about the person sitting at his desk. He is dressed much like you, not like the geeks you once imagined. He shows up at work around the same time you do, even earlier most of the time. By listening to his conversations, you can tell he knows what he is doing as well.

Is company culture a tool? Sure it is. You want to match the environment of your customers wherever possible. If your customers are office workers and wear shirts and ties or dresses, have your agents do the same. You want your Help Desk to be viewed as an ally to the business and looking like them is a good start. Upset customers who work until early evening only to see you leave at 4:30 hurts you and results in negative feedback. If a customer knows you are there with them, it helps as you work through any problems they have. Maybe it is a case of "misery loves company," but I recommend aligning yourself with your customer base in as many ways as you can.

With that said, if your customer base is widespread and varies in environments, fight for business casual attire and normal hours with all your might. This helps you recruit and retain agents and maintain productivity. The job is stressful enough with people yelling at you all day. If a polo shirt and slacks can help overcome some of that, it is a small victory.

Quick Recap

- Tools are the third part of the Help Desk environment along with the people and processes. Equipping your agents with the right tools to get the job done is important.

- How do you like the area where the agents will be working? Is it lit well with enough open space for people to not feel boxed in? Are the agents sitting close to each other where they can hear conversations about issues that may affect them?

- Communication is crucial to the survival of any organization. How will your agents communicate with their customers and with each other? Do you have a good process that allows for effective and easy-to-conduct communication?

- Having the right hardware to accomplish tasks is extremely necessary. Do your agents have all the hardware they need to perform their jobs? Do you have PCs and printers available to all who need them? Do you have some sample equipment around that your customers use regularly themselves?

- A common area is nice for agents to get away from their desks and ringing telephones. Is there some place available for this in your area? If not, can you create some version of it?

- What is the culture of your organization? Does it foster learning and teamwork? Do you feel comfortable that your agents are aligned with the company and customers in their own culture?

CHAPTER 10

Beginning Operations

For weeks, if not months, you have been preparing for the Help Desk's introduction into the business. You have interviewed many people at all levels of the organization, the customer base, and the vendor base. From that, you have formulated a plan you feel will satisfy and meet everyone's expectations. Well, now you have reached the time to actually put all these plans into action.

This chapter will focus on two beginnings: the beginning of an agent's career in the Help Desk and the beginning of the Help Desk itself. Earlier chapters described building plans and future chapters will describe running plans; this one concentrates on the introduction of the people and the organization.

What to Look For

- The first day on the job can be stressful for anyone. There are several key things you can do to help make your agents feel more comfortable and be more productive early on.

- This plan should extend beyond the first day. You can add a few programs to the plan for the agent to work towards.

- The Help Desk will also have a first day. This chapter will cover the extensive planning on how to make your Help Desk's first day successful.

- You can introduce your Help Desk to all customers at once or over a phased time period. You will need to decide which one is best for you.

- You can treat this implementation much like a project plan with milestones, resource planning, and issues tracking.

- Once you are ready, you will need to announce the existence of the Help Desk. There are some items you will need to remember for this to work best.

- The first call into the Help Desk can validate all your plans or it can begin the need to modify them extensively. This chapter will provide some helpful hints to make the validation easier to reach.

A New Person's First Day

Just as the interview is your first glimpse at the candidate, the first day on the job is the new hire's first real glimpse of your organization. The associate will have gotten some idea about his new company's environment from the interview process, but nothing will hit him like the first minutes of the first day. It is how you set up this initial moment that will last for quite a while. Take the time to do it right, improve the concept over time, and turn it into a regimented routine for all the analysts that come after him.

Prior to Day One

There is much to do to prepare for someone's first day on the job. Some things will take some time to design while other things will take time to arrive and setup. It can be hard to take the right amount of time to properly prepare for a new person, but it truly must be done. The better you have planned the event, the more quickly the new hire will be aligned and integrated into the Help Desk team. Invest the time beforehand; it will be worth the investment. A few issues that will be discussed here include

- Deciding where the agent will sit
- Making sure he has everything he will need to work
- Having a training plan prepared
- Preparing an agenda detailing his first few days' activities

Decide Where the Agent Will Sit

Logistically, you need to think about where the person will sit. Do you have any choice or do you have only one open space? If you have the choice, do you put him next to an experienced person or next to other trainees? Is he closer to the manager than he is to the rest of the group? The agents closest to him will teach him as much as anyone about your operations, so choose carefully. New people will emulate the ones around them and assume that their actions must be approved, if not recommended, by upper management. Putting a new person next to a slack agent who surfs the Internet during his spare time will send the wrong message. Allowing the new person to see an agent working on other agents' open work logs when they are through with theirs will show the motivation and teamwork you want him to adopt. It is far better for the new person to see this in action than to be told by a manager.

Make Sure the New Agent Has Everything He Will Need

You need to also ensure that your new agent has all the tools and equipment any other agent has. It is a sign of disorganization for a new person to sit at his desk and not be equipped with a phone or a PC or a pen. You also show the new agent his worth to you. If you do not think enough of him to be ready with tools to learn and do his job, he must wonder what you do think of him. Even worse would be his new-formed opinion of the rest of the organization. I haven't seen the request, approval, and hiring of an associate occur within so short of a timeframe that equipment could not be ordered. You know what your new agent will need, so order it.

Don't take too much pain to plan out an arrival time of equipment based on your plans for the new agent to use it. For example, it is not worth the savings to delay ordering a phone just because the new agent will not be taking calls for some number of days or weeks. The associate will probably want to tell his family or friends how to contact him, and giving out his new phone number will be hard to do without a telephone to answer it.

Have any necessary system logins and passwords set up as well. While the associate will want to change his password once he gets settled, this is yet another administrative item that can get the new person working faster, and it shows him how much planning you have done on his behalf.

Another nice item to have ready is a nameplate. There is a sense of pride when a new person is shown his new desk and it is "his" from the beginning. The quicker the associate can feel wanted and a part of the team, the quicker he will feel comfortable in his surroundings and become a contributor.

When I arrived at my first Help Desk job, I was given a desk that belonged to someone else. I was told to work around his stuff until he returned the next week to move out. Feeling quite uncomfortable, I did just that. When the "owner" returned he found out that it was not his desk anymore and had to move. This communication and lack of planning created far more havoc than there should have been. I managed to move past this, but you should learn from this experience and be better prepared for your new associates.

Have a Training Plan Prepared

A training plan is also necessary. We have discussed the many ways to train an associate. It is now your time to put that into a plan of action. You could use a mentor program to help the associate learn his new career. Maybe you will put him on the phones immediately to teach him under fire. What is important is that you know what you want and how you want to deliver it. The new associates will also want to know so they can plot their new path in the company.

Prepare an Agenda for the First Few Days

Finally, you need to script an agenda for the first several days. By scripting, I mean creating an actual document. Keeping it in your head won't help the others, and you will inevitably be brought into other issues during the opening days. The written agenda informs the associate what to expect and keeps your existing staff informed as well. A written document looks professional and brings a sense of organization and discipline to your Help Desk. It can also be used over time for other new people hired into the group. The agenda is different than the training plan because it lists what will happen during a particular period of time. The training plan is specific to their learning new skills and procedures.

The level of detail on the agenda should decrease as the time moves farther out. If you have staff dedicated to training and bringing on new people, this time can be pushed out even more. I typically scripted the first one or two days down to the hour. The agenda described what the new associate would be doing at 8:00 as well as what he would be doing at 2:30. It listed topics to cover more than it did time of day. Don't forget to get some form of this agenda to the associate *before* he arrives. If nothing else, he needs to know what time to show up for work, where to park, and where to enter the building! Figure 10-1 shows a sample agenda for the first three days for the DME Corporation. It details for the new associate what he will be doing, when, where, and with whom.

Just as the agenda is presented to the new associate for information, so should it be given to the other agents who will be involved. They need to be familiar with the proceedings in case there are time overlaps or shortages that may affect future events on the schedule.

Day One

The day has come for the person you recruited and interviewed to actually show up for work and become productive in the organization. You know what you are going to do as the agenda has been created for some time. It's just time to go do it.

You know best what training plan to implement so that will be left to you. There are some simple items you should include in the plan in any case, however:

- Introduce the new agent to the rest of the team
- Take care of the small things
- Take the new agent to lunch

Introduce the New Agent to the Rest of the Team

The interview process should have allowed the candidate and some members of your team to meet. Now is the time for the new associate to meet everyone else. Your Help Desk agents will be significantly more effective if they act as a team. Getting them to interact on a personal level early in the process is good to do.

DME Corporation
Hardware Support Agenda
Paul Allison

Day 1-11/27			Day 2-11/28		
8:00-9:30	Tour of Corporate Campus and Technology Center-Skip Brantley		8:15-10:00	Location:	IS Training Room
9:45-10:30	Location:	IS Training Room		Topic:	Call Logging-Jake Dowdy
	Topic:	Policies and Procedures-Skip Brantley	10:15-11:00	Location:	IS Training Room
10:45-11:15	Location:	cIS Training Room		Topic:	Networking Equipment-Jake Dowdy
	Topic:	Logging on the System-Skip Brantley	11:15-12:00	Location:	IS Training Room
11:30-12:00	Location:	Your Desk		Topic:	Networking Tools and Methods-Jake Dowdy
	Topic:	Phone and ACD-Skip Brantley	12:00-1:00	LUNCH	
12:00-1:00	LUNCH		1:15-2:00	Location:	IS Training Room
1:15-2:30	Location:	Your Desk		Topic:	System Overview-Skip Brantley
	Topic:	E-mail and Time Tracking	2:15-3:00	Location:	IS Training Room
2:30-3:00	Location:	IS Training Room		Topic:	Terminal Models-Jake Dowdy
	Topic:	Review of Procedures-Skip Brantley	3:15-4:00	Location:	IS Training Room
3:00-5:00	Shadow time with a hardware associate			Topic:	Terminal Tools and Methods-Jake Dowdy
			4:00-5:00	Time to complete exercises	

Day 3-11/29		
8:15-12:00	Location:	Conference Room 154
	Topic:	Benefits Meeting
12:00-1:00	LUNCH	
1:15-3:00	Location:	IS Training Room
	Topic:	Time to Work on Exercises
3:00-5:00	Shadow time with a hardware associate	

Figure 10.1   Sample first few days' agenda

Not all of your agents will be best friends and that is fine. There is no need for them to go have drinks together or share personal information. What is important is that while at work, they work well together and toward a common goal. The first day on the job is always on lists of top stress creators, so make the person feel comfortable as soon as possible.

The introductions should not stop at just the Help Desk members, though. Give the new person a tour of the building and introduce him to key people in other parts of the organization. The new associate will probably have no hope of remembering all the names and faces, but it is a welcoming process that gets everyone involved early. You can give the associate an organizational chart of the company as well that may help him remember certain departments or functions.

Take Care of the Small Things

Your agenda will no doubt include training plans, time schedules, and other noticeable important items. Just as important, and easy to do, is showing the new associate the little things he will need during the day. Where the bathroom is located is always a good start. Is there a cafeteria or break room where he can keep snacks or his lunch? Does he park his car in a different place than where he did on the first day? You also can introduce the new agent to others who can help him with administrative needs, such as getting office supplies or dialing out on the phones. Again, these are small items that are not directly related to the job the new associate was hired for. However, needing to use the bathroom in a hurry and not knowing where it is will be higher than any other priority if the need arises!

Take the New Agent to Lunch

A simple gesture is to take the new person to lunch. Maybe you can take another agent with you or go alone. It doesn't have to be the fanciest restaurant in town nor should it be a fast food place. The act will mean as much as anything else and it gives the associate some informal time to talk with you. I used this time to allow conversations to center more on personal matters than on business. It let me learn even more about the person, not the agent, and he could learn more about me. This start helped when the agent needed to ask me for help.

Be consistent in this lunch plan. Taking one person out, then skipping one, then taking the next person out will send the wrong message. The place won't matter but the act does. Although some people will question why one agent was taken to a more expensive place than another agent was, this is a small matter and is not worth keeping track of.

For Days to Come

The first day is over and you have taken care of your new associate. The key to success is when he returns for Day Two and all the days to come. I have had an associate resign after one day and that is a bad feeling. Not only does it feel bad, but you also have wasted a lot of time and energy preparing and handling the person. With preparation and the interaction of your team with your new associate though, he or she will return. There are some things you need to keep in front of you to keep those following days efficient, effective, and fun:

- Conduct orientation programs
- Get the new associate doing stuff close to his job
- Learn from experience for next time

Conduct Orientation Programs

You have introduced the new person to his teammates and shown him around the building. I recommend that you have a formal orientation program to follow this that shows the new associate even more about the department and company. This program, a meeting really, will introduce the associate to the rest of the department. It doesn't require a one-on-one handshake, but is more a presentation of the other groups in the IS department and what they do. Also included in this presentation would be a high-level overview of the company itself and its products and services. Describing the culture and its needs from the IS department helps the associate understand how he fits in with the rest of the company. The Help Desk is a team within a team, so get its associates involved from the very beginning.

The orientation program should also include a section on basic processes. These can include how to use the phone system, how to read e-mail, and how to log work hours if that is a requirement. If you have a policies and procedures manual, give it to your new associate so he can familiarize himself with it between agenda items. Even better is to include times on the agenda specifically for this reading and review.

The frequency of these orientation programs really depends on the frequency that you hire new agents into the Help Desk or the IS department itself. There is no reason why this program cannot be combined for the whole department. It will be difficult to set a fixed time, say every 90 days, for this program if you only bring in a person every 90 to 120 days. On the other hand, if you wait until there are enough new people to "qualify" for this meeting to occur, you may have an associate who has been in the department so long before he is orientated that he could conduct part of the meeting himself. I suggest a plan that presents the program every 60 to 90 days with a maximum of 90 regardless of the number of people to listen.

Get the New Associate Involved in His Job as Soon as Possible

You did a great job in recruiting this person into your organization. He is excited about his new career opportunities and ready to make a name for himself. Can you imagine his disappointment when he receives his agenda in the mail and sees that he won't start helping customers for six months or whatever your training plans call for? Some people, especially the more technical-savvy ones, don't want to wait long periods of time to practice their craft. There is a strong fear in the IT world of skills becoming obsolete, and not using them could be seen as negative. This is less of a problem for typical Help Desk associates but one you need to be aware of anyway.

To this end, I am not recommending that you scrap your training agenda and put the new associate immediately on the phones. I am, however, suggesting that you mix in some time throughout the training for the associate to get involved in some way. It may be by shadowing an agent on the phone or reviewing past calls to get a feel for what is out there. Perhaps he could even research open calls to actually feel productive without having to interact with a customer directly so early. Don't rush an agent to the customers if he is not prepared. A customer will remember a bad experience, and if they tie that experience to an agent's name it will follow the agent around for a while. It won't matter that it was the agent's first day on the phone; the customer still had a problem that needed to be resolved. Use of shadowing where an existing agent listens in on customer interactions with the new associate is a good way to begin this transition. The agent can prompt the new associate with questions or answers as they relate to the issue. This is similar to the new waiter who has an experienced waitress following him around until he becomes familiar with things. The patrons get their food, the new waiter gets experience, and the waitress gets some feel for how the new person will work out. (There are many good relationships between food service folks and Help Desk agents, aren't there?)

Learn From the Experience

As with any plan of action, you should always keep track of the things that worked and the things that did not. Review your training plan to see that it brought the right things at the right time to the associate. Interview the associate at a later date to get his feedback on how it went. Did he know where the bathroom was before he needed to use it? Were the trainers and other people helpful? What other items could be added to the checklist that would make the initial experience more effective and less stressful?

Once you have this valuable information, incorporate it into your future agendas and plans. It would be great if you could have a strong agenda template that only needed to have the names and dates changed when another associate starts. You will always need to review the plan every so often because of technology changes and other corporate or departmental issues, but the template should remain close to the same.

The Help Desk's First Day

You are getting close to opening shop. The people are in place with the tools they need to do their jobs. Some form of training has taken place so they can resolve calls. Now all you need is to make it happen. This will be broken down into three sections:

- Developing an implementation plan
- Announcing the Help Desk
- Taking the first call

Developing an Implementation Plan

Whereas the work to date has been planning what the Help Desk will do for its customers, this plan is designating how you will make the Help Desk available to those customers. Remembering the "first impressions" cliché, let's take the time to plan this right so the delivery of services makes sense from the beginning. The elements of this plan are listed in Table 10-1.

We will now discuss each of these in more detail in the following sections.

Big Bang Implementation or Phased Delivery

The question you need to answer early in the planning is whether you will begin taking calls on all services from all customers from the beginning or parts of them over time. *Big Bang* implies taking all you plan to provide right from the start. In essence, your Help Desk will go from a nonexistent entity to a complete, operating organization. The other method phases your services in over time; hence, a *phased delivery* approach. This states that instead of taking on responsibility for everything on Day One, you would support some services,

Item	Importance
Big Bang or phased delivery	How soon you take on all your customers will determine many other aspects of the plan.
Resources	Who your resources are and how many of them you have at the start will determine the number of services and customers you assume.
Customer criteria	The customers you take on first can help you prepare for the rest of the customer base.
Milestones	You need to have set points of time during the implementation where you check your progress compared to your goals.
Issues tracking	There needs to be a formal process that captures issues you have run into and their status.
Evaluation planning	You will need to make decisions to determine whether the implementation can continue, must be slowed down, or should be stopped.
Metrics	Measuring your work is important and can help gain new customers or keep existing ones.
Next phase planning	It is important that you have a plan in place so you can recognize when it is acceptable to advance to the next part of your implementation.

Table 10.1   Help Desk Planning Elements

learn from the experience, and then move on. Unless you only plan to support a few customers in a few areas when your Help Desk is complete, it is best to phase in your plans.

In Chapter 5, we discussed which services you could provide early, and which ones you could provide later in time. A related way to accomplish a phased implementation is to phase in the number of customers you take calls from as well. This theory states that you take on a certain number of customers, review your performance and processes, then take on more until you are ready to open the Help Desk to anyone needing help. This theory will be discussed in more detail shortly.

Goals of a Phased Delivery   There are two goals to aim for when implementing your Help Desk into the organization:

- Review processes and procedures
- Achieve victories

Reviewing your processes in a phased approach allows you to endure the trial and error of your plan with a limited number of customers in a limited number of areas. It is far better to discover that your phone system can only handle five incoming calls at a time when you have five customers than when you have 500 customers needing your help. It is also good to learn that your agents are having a hard time supporting a particular technology when the number of customers relying on you is small. The time spent in this review or trial period is extremely valuable and should not be skipped.

The second goal is to achieve victories. Note that this is not "victory" singular. The victories you are seeking can be small and will not only occur at the end. They are all about gaining momentum heading into a total Help Desk offering. Examples of the victories include

- The first call
- Successfully handling the first problem through resolution
- Transferring a problem from one agent to another without dropping it
- Receiving your first thank you
- Using any of the technologies you have installed with success
- Discovering a fatal flaw in a designed process

Again, these are not necessarily monumental, but are stepping stones to a Help Desk organization contributing value to the customers and the company overall. Don't waste these opportunities to celebrate either. Each one may not generate the need to stop everything and throw a party, but you could recap the victories at the end of each day for a while. You want the agents to feel a part of the team, and better, part of a winning team.

Did you notice the victory of finding a fatal flaw? This was not a mistake. Setbacks should be recognized, but with an attitude of "Whew, glad we found that one early on!" instead of beating yourself up over creating the problem to begin with. To repeat, phasing in the Help Desk allows mistakes to be made with much less of an impact to the company overall.

Resources

By now, you should know the exact resources that will be available to you on the first day. These resources include agents, tools, and any other partners who will help you achieve success in supporting your customers in the Help Desk. The number of resources will have a substantial effect on the phasing in of services to your customers as shown in Figure 10-2.

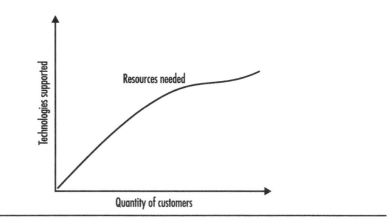

Figure 10.2   Resource needs with increased services

Obviously, the more customers you will support, the more resources you will need. Notice the resources needed in Figure 10-2 do not increase in a linear fashion, but in curves. This represents an efficient Help Desk and its ability to handle more work over time as it becomes more effective in its operation. This goal is reached by training, experience on the job, and formal processes and procedures being developed and improved.

As part of your resources plan, it is important to know when to expect additional resources. As you learn what an agent can handle in workload, you can plan when to introduce additional services and customers as you bring on more resources. A minor goal of yours may be to add more customers and services more quickly than you add agents. This will demonstrate your Help Desk's ability to leverage its strengths to provide more support for the company while keeping budget dollars under control.

Customer Criteria

Choosing your customers may only happen once, and that will be at the initial rollout of the Help Desk. After that, your customers may be added because of business growth or acquisition and you may not be asked. This choosing is really picking which customers you will support from Day One and subsequent implementations. The criteria for determining these customers include

- Your familiarity with the customers
- Their representation of the total customer base
- Their willingness to help you learn about your processes
- Their ability to withstand problems without harming their own effectiveness

Your Familiarity with the Customers   One suggestion to keep in mind while picking your test customers is to phase them in based on your relationship with them. Using this method, you may choose the rest of the IT department as your first customers so you can learn procedures while keeping them within the "family." Once you understand the process, you could move on to other departments or organizations that are physically next to the Help Desk. You still won't have an exact replica of all the expected customers, but you can certainly learn many things that can help you move forward.

If closeness breeds familiarity, picking a customer that is physically close by has its advantages. For example, if the support is falling apart at the seams and the customer cannot get any help, you could literally send an agent to the customer's site to provide support directly. This is the worst case, but better to plan for contingencies where possible.

Representation of Total Customer Base   You will learn many things when you begin supporting customers. Because this list of issues will be quite long at first, you want to ensure that the issues are closely aligned with how things will really be when you go live everywhere. For example, supporting customers who are very mobile will show you how to operate in that environment. However, if the majority of your customers are office workers, then you will want to introduce them into the phased approach earlier than the mobile ones. Eventually, you will want both, but begin with the customers who are most representative of the entire base.

Customers Need to Be Willing to Help You Learn...on Them   You should pick customers who will help you learn what works and what doesn't work in a positive atmosphere. It will be bad enough to find out that some of your best plans on paper do not hold up under customer interactions. Customers can help you learn by providing constructive criticism and not blasting you with complaints.

Some of your processes may become clunky and bureaucratic once you put them into action. The technologies you include at the beginning may have problems in their design or functionality. The customer may find this process hard to understand and think it's not worth the effort. Instead of the customer simply going in another direction, your pilot customers must be willing to work through the process and help show you ways to make it better.

It is important for the customer to give you feedback. Thank the customer for enduring the pain, but if they do not share the experience with you, you will not be able to fix it effectively for the next wave of customers. When the customer can document or list what happened and its impact, you will be able to analyze and review it more closely. If the customer can only sit back and try to remember everything, you will not get as much feedback as you need.

The best customers in this stage will be the ones you are familiar with or have met in your early interviews of defining drivers. Make them part of the team, show your appreciation of their efforts, and they should help make the Help Desk successful.

Customers Must Endure Problems Without Harming Their Own Effectiveness   It is nice if the customers who volunteer are friendly and perfectly willing to help in the process. Overriding this consideration is their ability to continue their own operations during this trial period. It will not do the company any good if part of its operations suffer to make another part of it succeed. For this reason, it is recommended that senior management help decide who should participate in the pilot and who should not.

This selection of customers does not necessarily mean the most profitable or highest revenue producing organizations; in fact, you don't want this to happen. Remembering that you need a strong representation of the whole customer base, it would not be wise to have only the best customers interact. Doing this may disguise weaknesses in the Help Desk due to the ability of the customer to overcome the issue themselves.

The preceding criteria do not contradict each other. Organizations can be strong operationally but not necessarily be the most profitable. At the same time, some customers may be very profitable, but lack good operations. This can happen in a strong location where the customer has a large market share. They may make money despite themselves. Anyone could pick the most profitable customers and include them in the test, but it will take regional or senior management to help you find those that are strong in operations too.

Milestones

Milestones are goals, objectives, or other places in time when events are scheduled to appear. You should establish milestones in your implementation planning to help track your progress. Then at any point along the way, you can chart where you are against the planned milestones as one measure of your achievements. Examples of milestones for your Help Desk implementation include hiring agents, adding customers, adding new services, or implementing different technologies.

Milestones can be days on a calendar. For example, you may plan that on November 14 you will add more agents to the Help Desk. Then when November approaches, you are reminded that it is time to start looking for people to fill those positions.

However, the milestones do not have to be arranged on a calendar. Instead they can just be placeholders for certain events. In Figure 10-3, you see that there are expected objectives to hire more agents, bring on more customers, and begin new services on a timeline but there are no dates associated with them. This is okay because it shows that before one particular goal can be met, other actions must happen first. So, before you bring on the Midwest regional customers, the Help Desk needs a second agent. Before the PC support can begin, a third agent should be added.

The benefit of using milestones without established dates throughout is that you can more easily adapt to changes in the schedule without having to redo all subsequent items on the plan. But what if our example had dates tied to each issue? It would look like Figure 10-4.

In this example, if the third agent was not found and hired until September, you would need to change the PC support and any item after that on the timeline to another date. This may not be a big deal, but if the timeline is very long it could involve many changes and recalculations. However, if there was not a set date tied to "Begin PC support," then nothing happens.

Depending on the items and the overall urgency of needing the Help Desk to be operational, you may have to establish dates at certain points in your planning. You could use these dates to announce coming events to customers or other parties, alert the Human Resources department to future staffing needs, or set firmer goals for your associates. It won't work to tell your next phase of customers that they can begin using the Help Desk for support "after we hire our third agent." In this case, it is better to set a date or a range of dates within which the customer can use the Help Desk. You need to be prepared to make the date, though, once you publish it. Expectations have been established and missing that date would not be a strong start! For this very reason, it is crucial that you set realistic and achievable dates from the beginning.

Figure 10.3   Events as milestones

Day One	Hire second agent	Add Midwest region customers	Hire third agent	Begin PC support
January 6	March 31	April 15	July 14	August 22

Figure 10.4   Dates as milestones

Issues Tracking

Issues tracking is the act of keeping pace with all events or items that crop up during the implementation so they can be followed until they are resolved. These events are not actual customer problems that have been called in, but instead are issues you have found in the operation of the Help Desk itself. A customer calling with a malfunctioning PC is tracked in your call log. The fact that the Help Desk PCs are not communicating with each other within your problem transfer process is tracked in the issue log. Other examples of issues could be procedural problems in your design, the use of technology in the Help Desk, or the skill sets of the agents. Another important issue might be that the agents were not trained in all the correct technologies your customers use. This is a crucial issue to resolve for your Help Desk to continue operating!

The best way to track issues in this part of the process is with an *issues log* (see Figure 10-5). An issues log provides a central place for all items to be

DME Help Desk Issues Log

Ref#	Item	Owner	Priority	Status
1	Voicemail only holds 10 messages	Casey	High	Open
2	No one is using the Internet chat option	Nigel	High	Open
3	Receiving many more calls earlier in the day than we expected	Dave	High	Resolved
4	Receiving printer calls on models that are not inventoried	Dan	Medium	Open
5	Senior management wants daily call volume reports	Rowman	High	Resolved

Figure 10.5   Sample issues log

recorded along with their status. This way you or others can see everything that needs work or attention quickly without walking around to everyone asking them what is going on.

It is beneficial to note a couple of the columns on this issues log. First, the reference number is there to help you more quickly identify issues. Without it, people will have to describe the issue to get a status, and over time the descriptions may become so similar that people will confuse the issues. Once this reference is used, don't change it. You have to be careful when inserting or deleting items that you don't resequence the reference numbers in the process.

Another item worth noting is the status column. At first glance, you may decide to just delete items off the log once they are resolved. However, there are reasons to keep them on the log or at least store them in a separate section. Keeping track of resolved issues will help you in any future undertakings that are similar in scope. You can review the old logs to see what someone encountered in previous implementations or who was involved.

There are several other items you can track for each issue on the log other than the ones listed in Figure 10-5. These items include

- Beginning date
- Person who originally turned in the issue
- Date the issue was resolved
- How the issue was resolved
- Person who resolved the issue
- Notes on the item
- Categories such as processes, technology, reports, and people
- Effects (allows the reader to see the impact of this issue on other things)

Tracking issues should not necessarily stop you from proceeding to the next steps in the implementation of your Help Desk. Just because the issues log contains 23 items does not prevent another milestone from being reached or another process from beginning. The priority of the items may factor into this, but there are no set rules for this to happen. The log exists to help you understand what is occurring in the Help Desk operations and to ensure that issues are recognized and worked on appropriately.

Evaluation Planning

The issues log you have been keeping might look like a lot of problems, but on closer examination there aren't many high priority ones. This is great and should help you feel comfortable as you continue implementing your services to new customers.

What if that is not the case, though? What if the issues log is full of high profile problems that are not being fixed in a timely fashion? If you find yourself in this situation, take a break. This break is not a five-minute coffee break, nor is it a two-week break. It is a time to get all informed parties together to fully understand what the issues are. These parties may be other Help Desk agents, senior management, or even customers. The point is to get everyone who can contribute to the high priority items on the issues log together to discuss them. It also gives you a chance to discover if all priority items are being worked on and given the attention they deserve.

Decide if Issues Are Really Necessary to the Help Desk   One decision these parties may make is that some of the high priority items are not really necessary to the Help Desk. What was once designed to be an integral piece of the operation may turn out to be not so important. An example of this could be the Internet chat communication piece shown earlier in Figure 10-5. You may have felt this media was very important to facilitate contact between customers and the Help Desk. So when it was not being used, you marked it as a high priority item on the issues log. After talking to many of the customers, you may find that it did not serve them as you both had anticipated, and they did not care to use it. What was once a high priority issue is now a low priority item, if anyone even cares about it at all.

The overall purpose of these meetings is to work the issues list aggressively and make sure that what you think is a potential showstopper is not. This is not about making excuses for problems and rationalizing them away, but if the issue truly is not as important as you thought it was, this is good to know.

If Severe Issues Remain, You Must Make Some Choices   Once you have determined from your meetings that the issues remaining on the list are critical to the success of the Help Desk, you must determine what your next steps will be once it is time to advance to the next phase. It will come down to one of three choices: you keep on going, you advance but at a reduced rate, or you stop completely until the issues are resolved.

The "keep on going" strategy is an aggressive approach that says you feel confident you can manage the impact of the high priority issues while still adding services and customers to the offering. You may not have a choice because of executive expectations or other commitments, but if this is not the case, a "keep on going" strategy is not recommended. New customers or services will surely bring with them a new set of issues. It will become increasingly hard for agents and managers to work on high priority items from prior stages while trying to keep up with the new requirements of the next wave of customers. Retain your focus on the issues to be resolved and work on them with concentrated passion until their severity is better under control.

Advancing at a reduced rate is related to the prior choice but is a little more cautious. It comes about from the desire to show progress but without the demands of a full continuation. It also still assumes you can fix whatever is broken without impacting new customers or services. What would work best is to advance in areas that would not be as directly affected by the high priority issues. Say you have issues with the staffing levels spread throughout the day. There is enough staff during the day but not when you cross multiple time zones. In this case, it may be okay to allow more customers in the time zone you occupy, but to restrict more customers in other time zones until you have your staffing levels better aligned.

The third approach is to stop completely until the issues are resolved to a more desirable level. You may be able to keep existing customers and services as part of your offerings, but you will not be taking on anything new. This approach may be necessary because of the severity of the issues or the demands of the customers and your management. It also assumes the expectation of your driving factors to be more willing to get it right than to make a previously established date. If you choose this strategy, you should work the issues at a feverish pace. Stopping the show is extremely visible and makes people wonder about the whole idea. This strategy is only recommended when the issues are horribly high and customer impact is intolerable.

It is a good idea at this point to bring senior management into the decision. This is important so they are kept in the loop and can interject other information that may affect the implementation. Make sure you take them your own plan along with the severe issues. They will appreciate that you have taken the time, and have the initiative, to come up with a suggestion instead of just presenting them with a problem. Overall, it will be better for you to bring them issues that ultimately get resolved than to allow them to think everything is going smoothly up to the point that the implementation fails.

Metrics

Metrics will be discussed in more detail in Chapter 13 because they are a critical process in the ongoing operation of the Help Desk. At this stage of a phased implementation of services, you will want to track some measurements so you can understand the impact of customers, technologies, and processes on the Help Desk. Because the Help Desk is in its first days, you may not have fancy tools to help you determine these metrics, so only go after the measurements that are important, and can be tracked with basic processes. For example, knowing how many times customers hang up the phone while waiting on an agent is important, but without phone system technologies it would be impossible for an agent to know such an event occurred. The important ideas to measure while you are rolling out your services are the ones related to volume, types, and duration.

Technology plays a big part in attaining certain measurements. Where you don't have the tools to automatically track events, try to come up with manual methods. If this is not possible because of the nature of the measurement, you should still note the measurement you want. Adding that this measurement will only become available with the purchase of a particular product may prompt management to let you obtain the tool. If the measurement is not that important to anyone, then there is no need for the tool at that time anyway.

Volume Metrics   *Volume metrics* are measurements that track the "how many" of things. "How many calls we are taking," "how many agents are working on that shift," and "how many customers we have" are examples of volume metrics you should record over time that are pretty easy to track. It is especially worthwhile if you have prepared some estimates beforehand and can monitor the actual measurements against your projections. Figure 10-6 is an example of a volume metrics chart.

By comparing your estimates against the real calls coming in, you can get a good feel on how things are going. In Figure 10-6, you can see that while you were

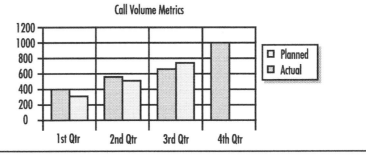

Figure 10.6   Volume metrics chart

better prepared during the first two quarters, the third quarter shows that you are taking more calls than you expected. If this trend continues, you may need to adjust the timelines of other events, such as hiring agents, or delay taking on more customers until you understand why the call volume increased.

Type Metrics   *Type metrics* are measurements around categories or classifications. Where volume measures "how many," type measures the "on what" or "by what." Examples here include "calls by agent," "customers by technology use," or "calls on selected topics." These metrics ensure that the volume of information is in the places you thought it would be. For example, look at Figure 10-7 on calls by category.

If you were planning to hire more software specialists than hardware agents, you may need to reconsider. Because of the customers using the Help Desk, a bad stretch of hardware issues, or some other factor, the agents you need should be more hardware focused. The time period for your measurements should be taken into account as well to allow for more accurate trend analysis. If the call volume was measured over a very short time, it may not be representative of what will happen in the long run.

Duration Metrics   Metrics that measure "how long" something took are called *duration metrics*. These are used to keep up with the length of time that selected actions and processes are taking. Comparing these against your plans will show you opportunities to conduct more training, streamline procedures, or just better educate everyone about what the expectations are. Figure 10-8 is an example of a duration metrics chart.

Because of the time it takes to resolve the different problems in the preceding figure, your agents need to spend more time on PC problems rather than other

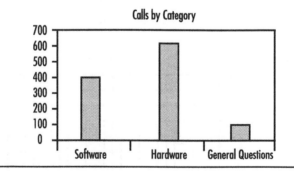

Figure 10.7   Type metrics chart

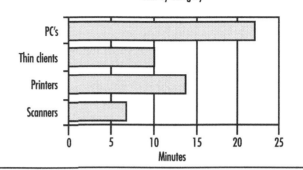

Figure 10.8   Duration metrics chart

hardware problems. If the company has plans to begin a corporate-wide PC implementation in the near future, you can have an idea on how your staffing levels will be affected.

The other way to view this is as a training metric. If you feel that PC problems should be resolved more quickly, you can institute a training plan for the agents to help make them more effective in PC resolution. Then, over time, you can measure the times and see if you find improvement.

Goals of These Metrics   Measuring your Help Desk is absolutely necessary in the beginning stages of offering service to your customers. This is THE time to learn about your plans and processes before the Help Desk is viewed as mission critical for all customers in all services. Metrics can provide staffing information such as quantity of agents, the hours they work, and the skill sets they possess. Early metrics can help you find holes in your processes such as where calls might get lost, find problems mishandled, or identify procedures that confuse the customer. Metrics can also show you technology issues such as what tools you will need to have in the Help Desk when the customer count gets real high or what technologies the customers have that you were not planning on.

Phased implementation metrics will evolve into routine operational metrics over time and will provide beneficial information about the performance of the Help Desk. Do not be embarrassed by the results of the metrics. It is a learning time for everyone and mistakes will happen. The victory you can achieve is to learn from the mistakes early to overcome them and prevent future mistakes from happening.

Next Phase Planning

The customers have been contacting the Help Desk for a period of time now and things are really happening. You are measuring the operations and getting some good feedback on how things are working. Milestones are approaching that call for the next wave of customers or technologies to be supported. It is time to answer, "How do I know if we should move to the next phase?" "Is 'good' good enough or is the issues log too full to continue?"

Prepare Your Decision Points at the Beginning   The trick to making this decision easier is to prepare the answers ahead of time. If the first time you ask yourself if you are ready to proceed is when it is actually time to make that decision, the decision will be difficult and you will feel pressured to make it. However, if all the critical decision points are prepared from the beginning, it will be much easier to make the call. If you put the decision factors off, there is a more likely chance that you cheat and massage data to make it fit. For example, a checklist of factors to be met for each milestone is good. Waiting until the end and deciding that "Perhaps taking a ton of calls each day is not that bad after all," is allowing a good metric, like call volume, to slip in importance and other factors to increase in importance. Flexibility is good and necessary, but only to a point. Don't ignore the facts of the operations in order to pursue or delay important goals and timelines.

Your Confidence Is Also Important   One factor in this decision that cannot directly be measured is your confidence in the ability of the Help Desk to proceed to the next phase. You were hired to make this Help Desk idea work and your intuition as to its state should not be dismissed. Pay attention to what you are seeing around you as much as what you are reading about it. Are your agents struggling to make good decisions and produce good metrics? Your customers are happy because they got their issues resolved, but could the Help Desk have done a better job? These types of questions are best answered subjectively and taken together will give you a better picture of the Help Desk than metrics can. Neither metrics nor your feelings should totally outvote the other; it is the balance that will lead you to make good decisions.

Don't exclude the input of the agents either. They are truly in the middle of it all and can add valuable input to the decision. They may not get to vote, but wouldn't you feel far more comfortable in deciding to proceed if all the agents are equally in agreement?

Announcing the Help Desk's Existence

Oh yes, let's get past that "it" exists and make sure you have a name for your Help Desk. I discussed the various names for Help Desks across the industry so that can be a starting place. You may want to add your company name somewhere in there to keep the idea that you are part of the whole team in front of everyone.

Tip	*You will want your company's name in the Help Desk name if you are supporting external customers. It not only helps them remember whom they are calling, it gives your company that much more publicity in the marketplace.*

Word of mouth will probably be your most effective method in the early stages. Whoever was called in the past can now pass the calls to your Help Desk. It would be best if you could script a short message for them so you can spread a consistent theme. If they are any good, they will want to say something more than "It's not my job," so the message is a win-win for both sides. "I can help you on this but want to let you know that we have a staff now devoted to this process for future calls," is a good way to help callers but start to guide them to the new Help Desk as well. If you can get executives to mention your Help Desk at annual or regional meetings, you gain a high level "endorsement" in front of a large group at once.

Educate your sales force about the operations of your Help Desk so they can spread the word as well. Support is almost mandatory these days with the sale of a product, so make sure the salespeople know important items to communicate when speaking with customers.

Word of mouth works best reactively. Once someone needs something, he or she is informed of the Help Desk and what it offers. You can implement some proactive methods as well. For example, if you can control what the screen says upon initial login, you can flash a message that has your Help Desk's name, your phone number, and so on. Do not keep this message on the screen for too long, however, as this screen space is valuable for delivering other messages, too. If your company has an intranet or a newsletter, getting space on that media is nice. If you can work with the suppliers of your products, get them to stick flyers in outgoing boxes with whatever announcement you want. Basically, get out in front wherever you can.

Taking the First Call

Much like preparing for an agent's first day on the job is the Help Desk taking its first call from a real customer. There will be anxiety and nervousness and hopefully excitement as the agents come into the office, sit down at their desks, and get to work. Here are four steps you can follow to make this first call, and the subsequent day, a success:

- Overcommit resources
- Dedicate an observer to watch the process
- Hold regular meetings
- Continually evaluate your methods

Overcommit Resources

The first step you want to take is to make sure you have enough resources to do the job you have laid out. Take this to the extreme of having more than what is necessary. You may not be able to do this with formal Help Desk agents, so jump into the fray yourself or have other related IT associates pitch in. As I have stated over and over, the Help Desk's first impression on your customers will happen only once, and it is important to get it right. While the results of the day may be somewhat affected by these extra resources, you can still get a good feel of what things worked and what things would not have without the additional resources. Don't keep these extra resources long—maybe only through the first day or until the true workload is understood.

Dedicate an Observer to Watch the Process

This observer is recommended to help keep an eye on things and to update the issues log as necessary. This observer can be you or anyone who is familiar enough with what you are trying to accomplish that they can recognize when it does or doesn't happen. If there is no one dedicated to this process, it will not yield good results. The agents can certainly provide input and ideas, but they will be so caught up in the actual job of being a Help Desk agent that they may not notice all the things swirling around them.

Hold Regular Meetings

In Chapter 5 I discussed holding regular meetings to keep the Help Desk agents informed of events. One choice was to have a daily meeting each morning or each evening. During the first days of your Help Desk, I recommend that you hold these meetings each morning AND each evening. Just as you should have extra resources to help with customers, it is okay to have an extra meeting each day for a while.

You should have this extra meeting to make doubly sure you are getting and giving all the information everyone needs to be at their best. Morning meetings can serve to remind the agents of upcoming issues or review processes, while the evening meetings can recap the events of the day and how they were handled. The issues log can be reviewed and updated here as well. These double meetings should be held until everyone feels comfortable with the way the Help Desk is operating.

Continually Evaluate Your Methods

Whether it is through measurements or meetings, the review and evaluation of your Help Desk's methods and processes must never stop. Your customers will never stop evaluating what you do, so try to stay ahead of them and find any weaknesses before they do. These weaknesses may not require major overhauls; they may only necessitate tweaks to parts of a process. Be careful that you are not changing processes without thinking the changes through, because these changes may have other effects you had not thought of. It doesn't do much good to fix one problem by creating another problem somewhere else.

With all that said, enjoy your success of building the Help Desk and watching it perform. Just don't sit idle for too long without a more objective perspective. The following chapters are devoted to helping you keep the Help Desk operation growing and even expanding it into new areas. If you pay attention to your processes and follow some of the suggestions in the following chapters, your Help Desk will be successful for a long time to come.

Quick Recap

- Do you have a complete plan for your new Help Desk agents? To make them feel they chose the right company and career, it is very important that you develop a strong, thorough plan.

- Do you have any ideas on how to get the agents to "see" their job before they actually begin working at it? Unless they are very experienced, agents will probably not take customer calls on their first day. If that is the case, how can they see what their new job will look like?

- Will you open up shop to all known customers (Big Bang) or phase them in? There are many risks in a Big Bang implementation, so try phasing it in first.

- Are all the resources available to make the first days of the Help Desk a success? This can involve not only people, but also the tools to make the agents productive and effective.

- Do you know which customers will be in the implementation first? Are they willing to work with you to make the Help Desk a valuable partner in the business?

- Milestones are good to help keep you on track. Do you have milestones listed that you can achieve over time?

- Tracking issues is also an invaluable tool to resolve problems as they arise. There are many items to consider when tracking these issues. Do you have an issues log developed and a plan to record and resolve items placed on it?

- What metrics will you be tracking during the first phases? Do the agents know not only what the metrics are, but how they should be gathered?

- Do your customers know that you exist or at least when you will? An effective announcement strategy will go a long way toward reaching the groups and individuals you need.

Action Plan Checklist

❑ Set up meetings with your senior management, IT department managers, vendors, and key customers to understand what they want and need from a Help Desk.

❑ Develop additional goals that you personally want to achieve through the Help Desk.

❑ Document your findings from the interviews to form the basis of the Help Desk of the future.

❑ Write a mission statement that clearly expresses your goals and objectives.

❑ Sit down with key associates to design the processes that will provide the services as defined during your interviews.

❑ Communicate to those around you the responsibilities the Help Desk will assume as well as those expected of the customers and IT department.

❑ Work with those responsible for budgets to calculate any income streams you will have.

❑ From that income stream and the processes you designed, detail all anticipated costs the Help Desk will incur the first year.

❑ Write down all known factors that will impact how you organize your Help Desk.

❑ Draw an organizational chart overview that will align your agents and their skill sets with the needs of the customers.

❑ Write job descriptions for each role you have created.

❑ Begin working with the Human Resources department to look for agents to staff the Help Desk.

❑ Prepare your interviewing strategy with those who will be involved in the process.

❑ Look around the physical layout of your Help Desk to make sure everything is there that you will need, in the way you will need it.

❑ Put together a list of what is missing and begin procuring it.

❑ Document a plan for opening your Help Desk including time lines, customer lists, and services.

❑ Take a deep, deep breath for the real fun is about to begin!

PART III

I Like My Help Desk.
How Can I Keep It Going?

CHAPTER 11

Preventing Burnout

Probably the biggest challenge you will face is keeping happy your most important asset—your agents. The Help Desk is notorious for high levels of burnout so you must take care to address its existence even before you actively see it. Retaining associates is significantly less expensive than recruiting and hiring new ones. Statistics have shown that bringing in new associates can cost as much as double the annual cost of retaining the ones you currently have. This chapter discusses many things you can do to keep turnover at a minimum. You will want to survey your associates as well to uncover their wishes and needs. Be careful with the survey, however; a well-intentioned survey can actually lower morale if you do nothing with the results. Just as you provide services for your customers, so must you provide incentives and rewards for your own staff.

What to Look For

- Burnout is one of the biggest threats to a Help Desk agent. Help Desk work is a constant stream of people complaining about their problems, and this takes a toll over time. Because your agents are the most valuable asset to your Help Desk, you must take measures to prevent burnout whenever possible.

- There are many signs to watch for when someone is burning out on his job. You need to be aware of them so you can recognize them if they appear.

- You can prevent burnout in many ways. Some are related to talking with the agents on a regular basis and recognizing their achievements.

- Creating a positive atmosphere on the job in addition to planning morale building events can also add enjoyment to the job and thus reduce burnout among associates.

- Some flexibility in your processes may also help agents last longer on the Help Desk. These include flexible work schedules as well as the option to work from home every so often.

- Trade fairs and organizations are also good ways to involve associates in the industry while getting them away from the phone calls. This is a win-win situation because agents get a break and you get more informed associates.

- Providing agents the tools they need to do their jobs is a proven method to keeping them happy and content. These tools and processes will also give your customers a more effective organization from which to get computer help.

- The end of it all is to show your agents that they matter. An ignored associate or someone who feels he is not valuable will quickly lose interest in his work. This is a basic fact that applies to anyone at any level in an organization.

Protect Your Help Desk from the Threat of Burnout

Burnout does not usually happen until the job has just drained the associate of a desire to even think about going to work. I say "usually" because burnout can happen early in your organization if the associate is already close to burning out from past experiences. Figure 11-1 shows the career life cycle of a Help Desk agent. We will cover this life cycle in more detail in Chapter 16, but I am bringing it up now so you can see where burnout comes into play for an agent.

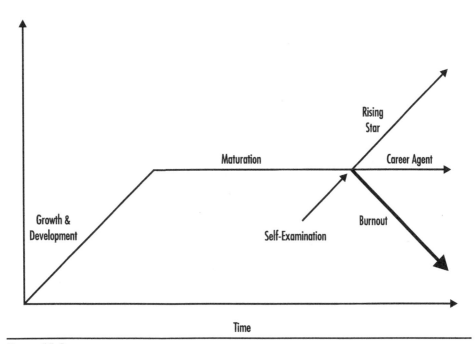

Figure 11.1 Help Desk agent career life cycle

An agent begins his career with a burst of energy and motivation to do a good job. Here he is growing and developing his skills, and his career is taking off. After a time of training and experience, the agent will mature in his career and perform his duties without much additional effort. At some point, he will go through a period of self-examination in which he questions his ability and desire to continue on this path. In this chapter, we will discuss agents who have burned out on their careers, and are beginning to slip in their effort and dedication.

An associate who has taken the downturn marked on the graph will require much time and work on your part to overcome. A burned-out associate is also harmful to the organization and should be identified as early as possible. It is widely known that retaining an associate is significantly cheaper than losing one and having to hire a replacement. For that reason, as soon as you see the potential for someone burning out, you should act.

Signs of Burnout

You can see many signs of burnout without conducting a survey asking people about their state of mind. Have you seen the following signs in your associates?

- Poor attitude towards others
- Consistently showing up late
- Taking an increased number of sick days
- Becoming more and more impatient with customers and co-workers
- Not attending group events
- Not caring for or showing an interest in training opportunities
- "It's not my job" expressions

If so, you may very well have an associate who is burned out or is close to burning out. You now need to begin the process of getting that associate back on the path to being productive and valuable to the Help Desk.

Ways to Reduce Burnout

Because every person is different, there is no one clear way to prevent someone from burning out on his job. However, you can do many things to create a positive environment for your associates that are not specific to any one person. Some agents may benefit from your ideas and others may not care about them. Your objective is to do what you can to provide a good workplace. Your agents will need to either fit into these plans or meet with you to go over other ideas to help them enjoy their jobs. Some common methods you can use to keep your agents from getting burned out are:

- Talk to them
- Recognize their achievements
- Create an open and fun environment
- Provide career advancement opportunities
- Hold morale building events
- Implement flex time options
- Implement a telecommuting plan
- Encourage them to attend trade fairs and seminars
- Enroll them in trade organizations
- Give them good tools
- Show the agents they matter

We will now look at each of these in more detail.

Talk to Your Agents

A simple way to keep your associates on the team is to have discussions with them over time. Some could be one minute long as you pass associates in the hallway. Others should be much longer where the topic can be anything from a current project underway, how the call volume is, or even last night's baseball game. These proactive conversations show your agents you have an interest in them, and this is helpful for someone questioning his reason for being at work.

These conversations will also give you invaluable insights into what your associates want. Ask them what they like about the job and what bothers them. If you have heard rumors that Chip is unhappy, go find out more. First, is he unhappy? Second, why? Dealing with any problems early in the process will give you a much better chance of turning them around in time.

Recognize Their Achievements

Another simple thing to suggest—recognize your associates and their work. A common theme or complaint among Help Desk associates is that their work is never appreciated. Compare them with the utility or phone company; you never notice their work unless it negatively affects you. Their good work needs to be acknowledged as well.

When was the last time you called your local phone company and thanked them for making your phone work? Well, the Help Desk is no different. Customers rarely call agents to thank them for their PCs turning on properly. Because customers are not doing it, you must.

Some Easy Ways to Show Recognition

Yes, *must* and not *should*. Do it regularly. It does not have to be much; in fact, your agents will notice even the smallest things. Walk by and tell them you appreciate their work. Forward e-mails from someone else who has recognized their work. These things don't cost much but would be worth many dollars anyway. Vary your actions, too. How would you feel if every good deed you did resulted in an "I congratulate you on your hard work" e-mail? Don't put it on your calendar or have your administrative assistant remind you, though. If it is not important to you, it will come across in your delivery.

Move to Bigger Things

Now that you are doing the little recognition things, expand to larger items. Have employee of the month awards. Whether it is a parking spot close to the building or a plaque on the wall, do things that reward your associates in places where others can see the reward. This expands their pride in receiving the recognition but can also provide another advantage. In one situation we gave out project badges that could be displayed to show others how many projects an agent had been involved in. People in other departments who see your management style of recognizing associates will find you and your group more desirable to work with. You might even find good candidates for future job openings.

Make Sure It Is Working

Now that you have been recognizing your agents in positive ways, have you looked back to see if it has been effective? Specifically, do you know if the things you have been doing to recognize your associates are aligned with the ways in which they want to be recognized? An example to prove the point might be giving out free movie tickets when someone does well. It sounds good because there are some good movie theaters in the area. However, what if the associate has two small children and no family close by? It might be very hard for them to see a movie with toddlers in tow. For years after my children were born, I didn't see a movie that wasn't rented. Although it is not impossible for the agent to use the tickets, it may be hard to arrange childcare, and he will actually have to pay more for a babysitter. What started out as a simple gesture remained simple and probably didn't get you the return you were looking for. In this case, you could either throw in some cash for a babysitter or provide some other type of reward.

You may have a group of agents who do not respond well to these types of rewards. Many people are motivated strictly by money or other compensation that will directly impact their own bottom line. While you may not have the budget or the desire to recognize your associates in this way, this issue needs to be identified so you can address it at some point. I am still a believer that hardly anyone turns down a free lunch or small token of recognition, so this effort is not wasted. It just may not give you the biggest return on your investment in these cases.

Create an Open and Fun Environment

The best way to keep people from hating their jobs is to make their work environment something they want to come to each day. Common sense? You would think so, but many people have a "It's only a job" mentality and don't attempt to make it any better than that. If these people are also managers, you have a problem because this thinking will permeate throughout an organization.

A Help Desk is a formal and professional organization and should perform that way. This does not mean that it must be strict and plain in all aspects. For example, allow agents to have pictures on their desks or other knickknacks that make their desks something personal to them. This gives them some comfort level in their environment even while they are busy on the phone. Keep an eye on this comfort level, however. Pictures of a girlfriend in her new bikini may make an agent happier, but it may cause others to be distracted, if not offended. Remember you are going for personal AND professional.

Make sure you are open in your dealings, too. You should not share salaries and performance reviews with everyone in the open, but make sure your agents feel they can trust you and can come to you if they need to discuss some issue. You want to be seen as an advocate who cares about his agents. While you do not have to be their best friend, you do need to be accessible whenever possible. Give them a venue to air out problems instead of keeping them bottled up inside until they explode.

Provide Career Advancement Opportunities

Another item mentioned frequently in agent exit interviews is a perceived lack of career movement. If an agent sees a future filled with answering callers' complaints for the rest of his career, he will no doubt begin looking for other opportunities. Where possible, create organizational levels within your Help Desk that recognize agents of high quality and skills. In some cases the title may be the only change; in others, the organizational change could come with a salary increase and more responsibilities.

In one organization, our Human Resources department would not allow us to create any more job titles officially so we did it internally. We had titles such as Support Specialist Trainee, Support Specialist Level 1, Senior Support Specialist, and so on, but these were only recognized in the HR department as Support Specialist. We did not treat these titles frivolously, however. There were tests to pass and skill sets to demonstrate over time before one was allowed to move up. We also laid out responsibilities that each title brought with it so the agents could know what was expected of them. Even in small Help Desks, I would recommend this. Even if your entire Help Desk staff is Senior in title, it still looks good to customers and distinguishes your staff from any new people starting in the group. The most important thing is that your associates see these opportunities and understand what is needed to obtain them. If they are not ready for a move, you owe them feedback on what they are lacking and how you can work together to overcome their issues.

Hold Morale Building Events

A common theme in this section of preventing burnout is to come up with ways to increase morale. One way is to hold special events that bring your team together for fun. You can always have a business theme, for example, leading off with plans for the coming months, but fun must be involved. These events can be small and inexpensive things like pizza lunches brought into the office or larger things such as field trips. I know you are conjuring up elementary trips to the zoo, but the idea still works. The key is to pick events the whole team can participate in. I always got recommendations for paintball "wars," but I never held them for fear of being the only one on the battlefield with paint hits from both sides of the war!

Your events do not have to be nearly this elaborate but do try to have something. I think you will be surprised how you and the company can get a win by just buying a pizza or making t-shirts with some logo on them for the associates. At times, try to include families and significant others in these outings. Families of Help Desk agents feel the stress and long hours, too, so recognizing this gains you morale points on multiple fronts. The purpose of your event should determine whether to include other people or not.

Real-World Example

We took our whole group, 20 at the time, to a Challenge Course in another part of the state. This course involved problem solving challenges that made us work as a team to overcome obstacles, like traversing mud flats by walking on cables strung between trees. Your teammates were on each side and could help you across in case you fell. The point was to show that others were around if you needed help. The course was led by instructors and safety helmets and harnesses were used when necessary, but there were definitely times when we felt a little unsafe. What we saw though was that the big guys could need help from anyone and even our smaller, older agents could do things on their own.

At the end of the day, we rented one large log cabin and everyone sat around a campfire and had pillow and food fights in the rooms. There were no business leaders making rules, but the natural leaders in the group took charge and were noticed by the managers. Pictures were taken and shared when we got back to work and the stories continued for literally months afterwards. Everyone agreed that we were riding as strong a team high as ever before.

Implement Flex Time Options

Another way to avoid burnout and retain associates is to allow flex time. Flex time is scheduling associates to less stringent start and stop times. Typically, you give them a quantity of hours or a range of times and the associates choose hours that fit within your guidelines. Flex time is a frequent request on associate surveys.

The closest I got to permitting flex time was when we went to 24-hour coverage and I let senior associates get first crack at what time shifts they wanted. They grabbed the ones they wanted and left the worst hours for the newer people. They, of course, revolted and adamantly didn't want to work then. I tried to let the team work it out, but was unsuccessful. We decided to implement a flex time policy if the team could agree on one, but because they could not, we abandoned the trial. Anytime this issue comes up now, we try to get the associates to create a flex time schedule everyone can agree on, but it dies a slow death.

The reason I never pushed the idea was that flex time works best in project work such as programming or documentation. Help Desks need agents available during a wide range of times and a manager needs to know exactly when the Desk will be staffed at certain levels. It is extremely hard to predict call volumes and spikes and you don't want to get caught in a low-staffed office schedule.

Insist on implementing a flex time process in your Help Desk? There are a couple of ways to do it and two criteria. First, you must always ensure adequate coverage during the hours you say you will be available to your customers. You must never forget this, no matter how much burnout and turnover you incur. Second, you should have a large staff to implement this type of plan. A large staff is necessary to make sure the Help Desk is covered at all times while agents are working flexible hours.

Two Plans to Implement a Flex Time Schedule

The first method is to allow flexibility in days of the week. Say you have your agents working five eight-hour days for a total of 40 hours per week. Instead, you could offer agents a four-day week, ten-hour day schedule as shown in Table 11-1.

Agent	Mon	Tues	Wed	Thur	Fri
Brent	X	X	X	X	
Kathryn	X	X	X	X	
Mark S.		X	X	X	X
Donna		X	X	X	X

Table 11.1   Work Schedule for Flexible Weekdays

This plan allows agents to work longer hours each day in order to gain a full day off work. You must plan this in advance so that each agent doesn't choose a Monday through Thursday shift and no one works on Fridays.

Another way to implement flex time is allowing your agents to choose the hours they come to work or leave work. Again, this plan must be coordinated carefully so that there is overlap during all necessary hours of the day. All agents cannot decide to come to work at any time—you might be completely without staff first thing in the morning or at the end of the day.

Implement a Telecommuting Plan

Telecommuting is a popular work term where associates work at offices away from the main place of business. These office areas can typically be in their own homes. It can be a full-time agreement or just a few hours a week. Telecommuting lets associates work in a more relaxed atmosphere, wear more casual clothes, and manage their own hours better. Offering telecommuting options can help reduce work-related stress among your associates.

Telecommuting is similar to flex time in that it functions more effectively in project work than in Help Desk activities. As with flex time, it is important to have your agents available to your customers, and this is hard to do while telecommuting without certain technologies in place. We will go over telecommuting implementation plans in more detail in Chapter 22.

Send Agents to Trade Fairs and Seminars

Other "out of the office" events that can also return valid business investments are trade shows and seminars. Send some associates to see new technologies or service companies. If you have formed work teams to review software packages, these shows can be very beneficial. Treat these outings as both rewards and training opportunities. Don't emphasize the training aspect too much, though; an associate will be far more interested in attending something if it's offered as a reward rather than a training exercise. Take this one step further by giving your group a list of all coming seminars in your area and letting them decide which ones to attend. Use judgment in not allowing just any seminar, but the "freer" you seem, the better.

If you attend fairs and seminars yourself, you can also reward your agents by bringing back goodies that may be offered while you are there. These trinkets are usually simple and covered in vendor logos so don't make the "gift" bigger than it is, but it does show the agents that you are thinking about them nonetheless. I used to get into contests with one of my agents over who could bring back the tackiest gift from any trip. Typically the winner spent the fewest dollars (or time!).

Enroll Agents in Trade Organizations

How about something with a longer life, such as becoming a member of a Help Desk association? There are a growing number of these out there, which is further proof that this profession has finally arrived. Typically trade organizations, such as the Help Desk Institute, Help Desk 2000, the Association of Support Professionals, or the Software Support Professionals Association, conduct annual meetings for high-level events and more frequent seminars for specialized topics. You could also sign up with an IT consulting organization like Gartner Group or Giga to learn more practices, trends, and coming events in the IT industry.

A real value is if the trade group offers local chapters. These chapters provide companies a way to network with other companies in their area on a regular basis. You can learn another company's Best Practices and see how their operations work in relation to yours. These chapters are low cost in money and time and are well worth it if you can join one. If there is not a local chapter in your area, start one yourself. This gives you exposure in the Help Desk world and still does not take too much of your time.

Give Them Tools to Do the Job

We mentioned early in this book that there are tools any Help Desk agent needs to be successful. Your agents will learn multiple ways to get the job done, perhaps even better than ones you could have come up with yourself. As their skills progress and the technologies they support expand, their need for more tools will also increase.

Your agents will become increasingly frustrated if you do not provide these tools. This frustration can even spill over to the agents' interaction with customers. "I would have fixed this for you three hours ago, but my manager won't let us have the software to do it. Instead we have to do it by hand and it takes much longer," is a comment that is inappropriate for customer conversation but could easily happen. The agent is fixing the problem, which is good, but he needs to complain to his manager, not to his customer. Complaining to the customer is a tricky ploy to try to get the tools, but it is a bad practice and should not be done.

An easy way to work towards letting tools help prevent burnout is to allow small purchases whenever possible. If an agent wants a device on his desk that holds folders, give it to him. If he wants a headset so he can work more efficiently while on the phone, give it to him. These are small dollar items that will return much more value in job satisfaction than the dollars spent. The bottom line in these tools is to show the investment you make in your associates and they will be more likely to provide you a positive return on that investment by their work. Be wary of the "keeping up with the Jones" mentality, though—if you buy a headset for one agent, you may easily have to buy 20 more for the others.

Show the Agents They Matter

Speaking of bottom lines, the one overriding thing you can do to prevent burnout in your people is to show them they matter. We have discussed many ways you can reduce burnout that involve spending money or spending time with your agents. You must carry these actions out in such a manner so agents feel you are not just going through the motions. Relate to them and their jobs and you will have strong agents who are willing to work hard for you.

Keep that positive work going by including your agents in more projects and thought-provoking work. Show them financial and operational reports from the business and how their work impacts the numbers. For example, you can demonstrate where the business is hiring people at a rate of 9 percent and the Help Desk is performing above average and growing at only 6 percent. You and the agents can be proud that they are delivering services without incurring a higher percentage of costs.

One final example of showing agents they matter involves your customers. One person I spoke with recently was in an organization that made hip and knee replacements. Their shop floor workers' only job was to assemble the various parts that made up the replacement joints. One day, the manager invited a recipient of a hip replacement to come onto the shop floor and speak to the assembly workers about how the new hip had saved his life from much discomfort and inconvenience. This 20-minute speech showed the workers that what they did mattered and they could take even more pride in the output of their work. If your Help Desk supports a business that can show something like this, please jump on the opportunity to try it.

Quick Recap

- Agents who are burning out show definite signs along the way. Do you recognize any of these signs in any of your Help Desk associates?

- If so, did you know about it before now? Do you have any plans on how to get them back on the team?

- When was the last time you sat down and spoke with your associates? The conversations don't have to be long, just enough to catch up on events in their jobs or lives.

- People around you are achieving their goals each day. When was the last time you recognized anyone for their work? Although they may not report to you, you can still recognize them so don't use that as an excuse.

- No foreseen career advancement is a leading cause of burnout. Do you have an organization chart that details the steps someone can take to move up the ladder? If so, have you shared it with anyone?

- You can buy a short-term lift in morale through pizza, taking people out for drinks after work, or taking everyone bowling. Do you have some ideas on what you can do in your Help Desk?

- Can flex time or telecommuting work for you? Are you informed enough to know the advantages and disadvantages to these plans?

- Does your Help Desk belong to any industry organization? Why not?

- If you ask your agents what they need to do their jobs, are there any tools they do not have? These tools, if indeed valuable, should be put on a list of things to purchase in the near future. Many people, including your customers, may benefit.

- Do your agents matter? Do you think you matter to your organization? They do, and you do, so at least make sure they know it.

CHAPTER 12

Implement Some
New Processes

Y ou have survived for some time on the processes you defined before you
started taking calls. If you got it all right from the start, and you haven't had
to make any changes, wow! You must have really received good feedback from
management and your customers. You now need to expand your processes in
certain areas. These will make your operations even better and more valuable to
your customers.

No one wins when an organization sits idle. As your Help Desk becomes more
comfortable and effective with its current processes, you should begin to look for
new processes and services the Help Desk can provide.

What to Look For

- Service level agreements are one of those processes you must implement.
  These agreements clearly define the expectations of the customers and the
  Help Desk to ensure that everyone is working towards the same goal.

- One new process is to simply increase the offerings you currently provide
  to your customers. Taken from your conversations with your customers,
  these ideas and needs add value to the organization from the Help Desk.

- Asset management is a process that can be very beneficial to a Help Desk.
  You can use this process to track details about the technologies deployed
  with the customers and to help troubleshoot problems when they arise.

- Determining and promoting standards within the company is also
  good. Standards allow a more efficient implementation of even newer
  technologies and can aid troubleshooting in many ways.

- No asset management is worth the time if there is not an effective
  change management process in place also. Change management
  provides a formal process to capture new products and services
  within the existing infrastructure.

- Training was discussed in earlier chapters, but is brought up here for more
  options. You should always be on the lookout for new, innovative, and
  effective ways to train your agents and your customers.

Service Level Agreements

A Help Desk can meet expectations with its customers by creating a service level
agreement with them. Service level agreements (SLA) are a formal way to set

expectations between your Help Desk and its constituents on what you will support and in what manner. The agreement must be a collaboration between the two parties to succeed. Once agreed upon, the SLA will give everyone a clearer understanding of what is expected when a problem is called in. There should be few ambiguities in this document so everyone fully knows what will happen from the customer and the Help Desk side.

Your agreement does not end with a typed piece of paper. Your SLA can be described as a "living document" for it will grow and change over time. It must be reviewed regularly with changes in business or the use of new technologies. Changes to the agreement should also occur as you listen to the needs of your customers. The document is only as good as the completeness of its descriptions and its ability to meet the customer's needs.

An SLA can sometimes be used to hide behind and that ruins its good intentions. Your goal is to help your customer as efficiently as possible and not to use the service agreement or contract as an excuse for not going above and beyond expectations. This chapter will discuss the creation and maintenance of an effective SLA.

Creating an Effective SLA

An effective and lasting SLA cannot be completed in one day as you sit at your desk. It is far more complicated than guessing what your customers want and writing it on a piece of paper. However, if you follow these steps, the resulting SLA will be completed more easily and with a much higher chance of success. The steps, in order, are

1. Identify all parties that will be affected by the SLA.
2. Determine if the SLA will be a contract or an agreement.
3. Create a template of the SLA for others to review.
4. Create a work team consisting of representatives from the identified parties.
5. Negotiate a final SLA from the template with the team members.

Identify All Affected Parties

The first step in creating an effective SLA is to identify all parties that will be affected or that will affect the issues within the SLA itself. Without this step, the SLA will ultimately fail. First, if the people who will be affected by the SLA are not identified, the SLA will not be able to adequately meet their needs because their needs will not be known. Remember, this is an agreement between multiple parties and if one side is not known, the agreement is more like an announcement of services instead of an agreement on them.

If you find that the affected parties have an extremely diverse set of needs, it is perfectly fine to create multiple service agreements. It will be difficult to create an effective agreement that is aligned with groups of customers who need completely different skill sets or hours of operations.

The second group of people who must be identified in the SLA are those who can affect the outcome of the SLA. These people have influence on the services described in the SLA and therefore their input is critical to the SLA's success. Picture yourself ordering a meal from a waiter. After you've ordered, you feel comfortable that he will bring you the food you wanted. However, if the cooks do not prepare the food you asked for, you will not get the services (the food) you wanted. Everyone who can have an effect on the SLA must be determined before you get too far in the process.

The groups that are typically involved in the SLA process are the customers, the Help Desk, other IT groups, vendors, and senior management. Table 12-1 lists some of the reasons certain groups should be involved in the SLA process. Your job is to uncover the particular people within each group who must be communicated with or brought into the design of the SLA so it can be best delivered.

Parties Involved	Impact on SLA
Customer	Primary party in the entire SLA process Receives the services and product described in the SLA Needs to understand how to ask for this service and how it will be delivered
Help Desk	Other primary party in the SLA process Delivers the commitments stated in the SLA Helps enforce the processes described in the SLA from both sides
Other IT groups	May be involved in delivering certain aspects of the SLA like uptime percentages and software bug resolutions
Vendors	May be involved in delivering services in the SLA like hardware field repair or installations May provide products in the SLA like hardware and software
Senior management	Provides the resources to uphold the commitments in the SLA Can be used as an arbitrator to resolve issues that arise in the implementation and upkeep of the SLA

Table 12.1   Groups Involved in the SLA Process

Determine if the SLA Will Be a Contract or an Agreement

The next phase of creating an SLA is to determine if it will be a contractually binding document or a "best effort" agreement between the parties. You cannot begin this phase until you have identified the parties because until you know who the document is for, you cannot know how binding the document will be. The identification process may be intuitive at this stage, but you must think it through beforehand.

An SLA that is contractual in nature will require many more details and processes than an agreement. While both should be well thought out and planned for, the contract version will be stricter in its enforcement. You will really need to have a complete understanding of the services expected when the contract is in place. Penalties for nonperformance, and even a definition of what nonperformance is, should be incorporated into a contract. Again, strive to work just as hard to fulfill an agreement document's expectations, but be more wary when the SLA is really a contract.

Create a Template of the SLA

The third step in the SLA process is to form a team of people to work through the issues of the SLA and what it will deliver. Before you do this, however, I suggest that you create a template of the SLA to serve as a foundation for the work coming up.

Proper preparation is a key to successful meetings and work groups. By having a template prepared of the SLA before everyone walks into a room, you are helping prevent too much time spent on topics for an SLA and not enough time spent on the content within those topics. You are not doing all the work yourself, and the template can certainly be modified if the group feels it necessary, but the beginning template can give the team a jump start on the work ahead. Your own jump start for the template came from the interviews you did long ago with the customers and senior management as well as from the experience you have gained up to this point.

Your SLA template should include the following sections:

- **Scope**   You should include a brief statement of what is covered in the SLA as well as a description of the SLA's overall intent.
- **Standard work schedules**   This section details what hours you are in the office, how you can be reached in any case, and the staffing levels. You may also list holidays and any important scheduled events like fiscal year ends or physical inventories.

- **Methods of contact**   In this section, you should describe the various ways a customer can contact the Help Desk. You should include names, addresses, and phone numbers if appropriate.

- **Severity levels**   Try to classify types of calls and your actions for each one. This should include when and who will communicate, an expected resolution time, and a clear escalation procedure if necessary.

- **Priority plans**   This section discusses how problems are prioritized.

- **Standards**   We discussed the advantages of standards earlier, so here you will want to list all the items you support. This way if a caller has something you have never seen before, he cannot hold you to resolution times you are not prepared for. It also gives users an idea of the equipment they should purchase if they want your help in supporting it. This works best in an attachment or appendix because of its length and tendency to change. You should also include any particular software versions or releases you feel are important.

- **Goals**   Here you will list what you will try to achieve and how you will know that you have done so. For example, you may say your goal is to resolve all problem calls within 24 hours 90 percent of the time. The point here is to acknowledge there may be times when you will take longer but it will be a clear exception. Please don't get too caught up in the percentages. We want to show the directions we are headed in as much as anything. Remember that this is a mutually advantageous document and it should not be used as a weapon against anyone. It is not worth the time for people to bicker over a call being answered in three rings instead of two when the point is to answer the phone as quickly as possible.

- **Penalties**   Which brings us to penalties. What's in it for the customer if you do not meet the goals stated in the SLA? You may agree they are just goals and nothing more. However, if your Help Desk is funded by external sources, you can bet that penalties may be in order if you fail to deliver upon your committments. You could set up a range of penalties like a free month of Help Desk service for each section disputed; you just need it all laid out in the beginning so each side knows what to expect. What about the other side of the agreement? Are you going to let the customer off the hook if they violate their end of the agreement? What if they bring in nonstandard equipment and expect you to enforce and/or support it? You see it is important for both sides to come to a consensus for service expectations. With this understood, the interaction between the customer and the Help Desk can be very effective.

- **A review period**   It is good to document when the SLA will be reviewed. Putting it in writing helps everyone feel more obligated to actually doing the work and following through on the commitments stated in the SLA.

- **A signature page**   The last page of the SLA should be for the team members to sign off on the document. This can seem trivial, but it is important. It can be very convenient for a team member to "not remember saying that" once the implementation has begun. At least his signature can remind him that he was there and had agreed to the plan at some point in time.

Again, as the design process begins to really uncover issues, you may find that some of these sections do not apply to your situation and additional ones do. That is perfectly fine. The template is only to provide a foundation for everyone else to build upon.

Create a Work Team to Design the SLA

As mentioned earlier, the next step is to create a work team to put the actual SLA on paper. An SLA cannot be created in a vacuum because it involves many people to work effectively. You don't want too many people involved in the design process, though. Instead, you want some representation from each of the groups that will be affected. From the first step, you will remember that these groups are the customers, the Help Desk, other IT groups, vendors, and senior management.

The work team needs to be large enough to cover all the affected parties and small enough to be able to work efficiently. Depending on the variety of customers you have, this work team could be made up of five to seven people. Many beyond that, and you will find yourself spending more time debating topics than documenting finalized solutions. If you feel strongly that you will need more people to achieve the best SLA, you may want to break out sections for different groups to work on. Once everyone is finished, they can all meet to review the assembled pieces. I advise against this if possible because the groups will not be as united in their work as when they were all together from the beginning.

The people you choose out of each group must be able to effectively represent their group in these discussions. This effectiveness comes from two angles. The first angle is that they must know enough about their own operations and needs that they can know what must be and not be included in the SLA. Without this knowledge, they are not needed in the meeting to begin with. The second angle is that they must be backed up by the higher levels of authority in their respective groups. They may be very knowledgeable, but if their results will then be debated and modified extensively, they are not the right choice either. Essentially, the members of this team need to be decision makers who can plan for the future interactions with the Help Desk.

Finally, these meetings need to be held regularly, but not all day every day. For one thing, the team members also have other jobs that cannot allow them to be away for too long. Also, because the SLA process can be very intense, the members could use breaks along the way to refresh their thoughts. Your goal should be to have meetings close enough together to maintain consistency and make progress, while not harming the operations of the groups around you in the process.

Negotiate a Final SLA From the Template

To date you have identified the affected parties, chosen people that can represent the groups, and created a work team to create the SLA. The only thing left is to draft the SLA. Note that this section is titled *negotiating* the SLA and not simply *creating* it. There is a specific reason for this.

The SLA design process will include people who see processes and procedures from many different angles. Customers will want to know how they can get services in the easiest and quickest possible way. Vendors and other IT groups will look to make sure they can provide these services in ways that fit their own comfort zones. Senior management will want to ensure that all defined processes make economic sense from a financial and customer relations view. Because your job is to combine all these views into one common vision, you will have to negotiate your way there rather than just arbitrarily create a document.

The best way to do this is to come into the process ready to ask "Why?" at every point of contention between the groups. If a customer demands to have the phones answered in one ring, ask them why that is important to them. If the Help Desk is saying it must have a minimum of three rings, ask them why. As the groups hear these answers, they can better understand each other's positions and will have a better chance to work towards a common solution.

If this common solution cannot be found, senior management will have to be brought in to arbitrate a solution. For example, let's say the team disagreed without a resolution on how much the systems must be running.

Customer view: "We have to have the systems up and running 100 percent of the time. Without this, we cannot guarantee the products can be shipped at our required rate."

Systems administrator view: "We do not have the budget to provide 100 percent uptime. We think that the current 97 percent uptime rate is reasonable. The business has obviously continued to grow at this rate. 100 percent is just not reasonable."

If the groups cannot or will not budge, senior management should be able to help. By looking over the forecasts of the shipping department and the technology requirements of the systems group, they can make decisions to accommodate one or both of the groups. In this case, the management team can grant more money for higher availability systems. At the same time, they can work with the shipping department to raise their comfort level that shipments can be made at an acceptable rate without 100 percent system uptime. Once the management team has made this decision, the team can get back on track designing the SLA with the newly approved issues understood.

Maintaining the SLA

Congratulations on finalizing your SLA! You can now sit back and concentrate on running the Help Desk, right? Almost. The SLA is a living document and must be reviewed over time. If it was written and then just put on a shelf, you will have wasted everyone's time. A proper SLA will live as long as the Help Desk does and will undergo each and every change the Help Desk sees. As customer needs change, so will the SLA. New technologies that are introduced into the field will inevitably require the SLA to recognize and accommodate them in new ways.

For example, as your organization does more and more business over the Internet, the availability of the system and your agents to help customers will need to increase. An SLA that calls for agents to be in the office from 8:00A.M. to 6:00P.M. may not suffice in the new electronic commerce world. As people can connect to your business without your store doors being open, they will run into issues that need resolution. Your Help Desk will need to modify its own operations to allow for this to happen. As this change develops, the SLA will have to be modified to document these modifications. If you are serious about the SLA (and you should be) you will need to formalize some processes around it. These include change management, regular reviews, and a reporting structure.

Change Management

As the preceding paragraphs described, it is important to keep up with change. A proper change management strategy needs to developed as it relates to the SLA. Basically, change management for an SLA calls for a process that recognizes any changes made in the customer, technology, or Help Desk environment that will cause the SLA to require modification. So when a new type of customer is brought in to your business, like e-commerce can do, your SLA should reflect the new customer's impact on your Help Desk and its operations. We will discuss change management in more detail later in this chapter.

Regular Check-Ins

One way to discover that the SLA needs modification is to formally review it every six months with the team who developed it. You can call the same team members back together for this, or pull in a completely different group of people. Either way, you want to review the SLA page by page and line by line to look for outdated processes that need to be changed. If your change management process works well, this list should be quite short. However, this regular review does not hurt.

One example of something that can be found during this review that change management will likely not uncover is the Help Desk's ability to reduce certain services. What may have seemed very important at the design stage may not have ever materialized during the actual operation of the Help Desk.

Communication frequency is an example. As the customers sat down to help you, they may have wanted updates on problem statuses every 30 minutes. This seemed logical as they could then better prepare workarounds for themselves, and could feel more comfortable that the Help Desk had not forgotten them. Yes, 30 minutes needed to be the minimum requirement!

One week later with ten open issues, each generating a phone call or e-mail every 30 minutes, the customers are getting swamped with communication. The Help Desk is certainly living up to its end of the agreement and is dutifully keeping the customers up to date. The problem is that the customers are spending more time reading e-mails than doing their jobs. More than likely, the Help Desk is spending as much time sending the e-mails as it is working on the problems, too!

Realizing that the SLA is a living document that serves the interests of all parties allows for changes to be made without a great deal of tension. SLAs are very important to have, but they will be closer to the real needs of people if everyone has some experience under their belt first.

Reporting

The third step in maintaining the SLA is the consistent reporting on its effectiveness. Major discrepancies in what is needed and what the SLA provides will be quite obvious to those involved. The smaller things that are not as easily noticed must be found through reporting. The Help Desk is responsible for initiating reports about the SLA.

As with any reporting we will discuss, you must be as objective as possible. This is not the time to promote your successes and hide your weaknesses. Live up to your part of the bargain and show the customers how the SLA is working. Are you answering the phones as promptly as you agreed to? Are you escalating problems in a correct and timely fashion? Your customers will know the answers to these questions intuitively; the reports will basically just confirm or repudiate their beliefs. You gain credibility by reporting bad numbers, which will help you when you report the good ones. If nothing else, this SLA may have legal ramifications that truly require you to report accurately. Without speaking of accuracy issues further, you do need to report regularly. Include the timing of the reports in the SLA itself if it helps everyone's expectations on what is needed.

Avoid Common Failures of SLA Attempts

Service level agreements can fail for many reasons. Improper design, lack of reviews, or just plain lack of caring will all cause an SLA to not meet the needs of those it was intended to help. Three factors can also cause an SLA to die a slow death:

- The parties hide behind the SLA
- The SLA is too complex
- The SLA set unrealistic expectations

Hiding Behind the SLA

A common mistake on the part of the participants of an SLA is to use it as a weapon or a shield. Typically, the customer uses it as a weapon and the Help Desk uses it as a shield, as shown in Table 12-2.

As Table 12-2 illustrates, the SLA can make it easy for one side or the other to make attacks or excuses during the course of business. This must be avoided wherever possible. The SLA must be an amicable agreement between both parties and should not be used at the expense of another person or party. If you find that your agents or your customers frequently invoke the "holy" name of the SLA to justify their actions, you need to sit everyone down and revisit the whole purpose of the SLA.

The SLA Is Too Complex

If the team sits down to plan for any and every contingency that may happen over time, the SLA will never get finished. Even if it were to be completed, the resulting document would be volumes of pages long. A document that big would be too cumbersome to use or too difficult to find anything in.

Group	Common Comments
The customer and its SLA weapon	• "You didn't answer the phone in two rings just now; therefore, I demand…" "The system just went down for the third time this month. The SLA calls for only two." "I beeped the agent on call and he did not respond in the required 15 minutes."
The Help Desk and its SLA shield	• "You didn't leave your full name and phone number in voice-mail; therefore, I could not call you back in time." "I still had four minutes before I was required to call you." "I sent your boss the status e-mail yesterday. I cannot help it if she did not tell you about it."

Table 12.2   An SLA used as a weapon and a shield

A service level agreement should be between four and ten pages long. It should highlight major courses of action that will occur within major sections of issues. Anything more than that will turn the SLA into a policies and procedures manual that is too much for its purpose. There are certainly opportunities for attachments or appendices, like listings of all supported software and hardware, but the SLA itself should be void of that much detail.

Likewise, the rules for notification and escalation should be made as easy to follow as possible. There are times when there must be qualifying rules around when actions are taken, but be careful on how complicated it gets. No one benefits from an SLA that calls for certain actions only when the time of day is aligned with the criticality of the issue that is aligned with the person calling in from a particular location. Believe me, SLAs can be written that allow actions to be taken based on an overview of general guidelines.

The SLA Set Unrealistic Expectations

The initial design meetings will bring out a wonderful world where all problems are resolved in five minutes with a full accounting of the resolution to everyone who could possibly care. Systems may go down, but the IT department fixes the problem while still maintaining enough resources to work on every other lower priority issue. Have you ever worked in such an environment? I have not. We can only dream of such a place, but do not allow that dream to carry over into your SLA. Most places are resource-driven and can only work on a certain number of top-level issues. Circumstances will arise in which a phone cannot be answered in the required time or a customer cannot be updated in a certain manner. These are all okay as long as a trend does not develop.

Recognize this when writing your SLA. It does no one any good if you promise things you cannot deliver. It is far better to get that out in the open from the beginning than to blindly hope things will materialize that you know cannot happen. If the group responsible for keeping the systems up is not in the design phase, it is not wise to make commitments on system uptimes. If your Help Desk does not have a controlling hand in that part of the process, you should not sign your name to a document implying that you can maintain a certain percentage of availability. If the customer requires this information, you need to get someone involved who can play a part in that particular piece.

Something else to watch for is including commitments you can control, but lacking the tools you need to show the results. For example, you may agree to answer the phone in under three rings 90 percent of the time. You can control this part of the agreement by putting agents in place to answer the phones when they ring. But do you have any tools to know that the phone only rang two times or that you answered it quickly 90 percent of the time? If not, you should not include this in the SLA. If you are forced to for some reason, you need to include a provision in the SLA that calls for tools to be purchased and implemented to track this metric. This could be a good time to bring senior management in to mediate.

Real-World Example

I once called the president of our service provider because their system kept going down. I pulled out our contractual SLA that called for 95 percent availability and monthly reporting of results. Since I had never seen these reports and wanted to see if my feelings were accurate, I called him to inquire about the reports. He informed me that they had no way to track availability so he could not give me the report. Astonished, I then asked him how he knew we were up 95 percent of the time. He responded back that he could not even know that. He followed by saying that they only included this line in the SLA because we asked for it. Our mistake was asking for something and being satisfied because we saw it in writing. We had no idea that it was merely words on paper with nothing behind it. To this day, we are working on finding another provider who can back up their words with actions.

When done correctly, an SLA is valuable at budget time. If your commitment level is unacceptable to the business section covered, then the business unit can battle with you for more resources to reach the service levels they require. It is much more effective for others to ask for money or people for you than just you by yourself. Beyond a nicety, SLAs are an absolute must if you bill out your services. Otherwise, you will spend far too much time negotiating rates and credits based entirely on the expectations of the customer. You can find a sample SLA in Appendix B.

Increase Your Support Offerings

While you and your agents are getting accustomed to the products and customers you support, it pays to revisit the original interviews and As Is documents you performed before the Help Desk existed. During those discussions, you ran across many needs of senior management and customers. There may have been instances where you had to postpone taking on the support of those needs in order to learn the basic support requirements of other products. Now may be a good time to look again at those products to see if your agents are able to take them on.

Aside from postponing product support, you may have established or continued outsourcing partnerships to provide the support that you were unable to offer during the initial setup. These are also good products to review on a regular basis to see if your Help Desk can provide the same services at a better price or level of operation.

For each product you agreed not to support when you began operations, you should review the reasons. It may have been due to a limited number of agents, the complexity of the technology, or just the sheer volume of products you were required to support. Your Help Desk may have grown in quantity or depth and breadth of skill set since then and you may find that those initial reasons do not apply any more. For all the reasons that a formal Help Desk brings value to a company, you need to expand your offerings when possible. If the reasons are still valid, that is fine, but do your homework to know that. After six months, review the products again in case anything has changed. This expansion will give your agents new technologies to learn and will give your customers a more centralized department to get help from.

Asset Management

For some time you have been logging calls and fixing problems and the Help Desk stays dutifully employed. Have you looked to see what you are supporting? The As Is process discussed in Chapter 4 gave you a good overview of the technologies and services you would be expected to support. As time has gone by, have other types of equipment magically appeared in the organization? *Asset management* is the process that tracks, records, and reports on the various assets and technologies in an organization.

Asset management is an important piece of any technology life cycle plan, but it is frequently overlooked. Many technology plans involve researching, designing, testing, implementing, and supporting technologies. Those are absolutely correct. However, an effective plan also needs a process that keeps up with the results of all that work. From there, future research and implementations can be best started and directed.

When you started you wanted to have a sample device of each type located in the Help Desk to help your agents troubleshoot problems. Have certain types of Equipment Been Failing More Often Than Others? Is It Due To Life Expectancy expiring or a manufacturer that was not quite up to your standards? These are questions that asset management can start to answer.

There are many tools in the marketplace to help you with asset management. Some are quite extensive, with the ability to reach out into your network and gather asset information; other tools are more data entry oriented with basic reporting capabilities. If possible, I recommend tying in your asset management system with your call management package. Now when you log calls about a device, you can pull up its information and history to help troubleshoot. Wouldn't it be nice to know the PC that is having trouble has been called in many times in the last week and maybe it has an underlying problem that needs to be resolved? How about if you could create reports that show that the new laser printers have been jamming three times more often than your old printer? This information could be used with your vendors to sort out problems and get them fixed across the enterprise instead of call by call.

Standards

An effective practice that makes Help Desk life easier is to have standards. These can be standard pieces of hardware, standard operating systems, or even standard processes and practices. The notion is the more you can standardize, the easier it will be to train agents to support and roll out new technologies. It eases procurement as the choices are more defined and will help with vendors because they can forecast your demand better knowing what you will typically buy.

Implement Standards Tactfully

You need to be careful when you introduce these standards to the business. Expect some resistance as others will debate your choice or show you why their needs do not fit within your guidelines. In some cases they will be right, so do not make your standards so rigid that you have to make many exceptions. The harder you try to enforce standards, the more exceptions you have to make because of politics or unique requirements, so that you end up with more exceptions than rules.

A good way to implement standards more quickly and effectively is to promote the advantages of standards to the organization. If they can realize that you are not creating standards because you are power hungry and just want to make rules, but because you are working in their best interest, they should be much more willing to work within your guidelines. If these standards get you better discounts, more focused training, or allow for a lower staff count, show these facts to your customers. Find ways to tie these trends to the standards so there is a direct correlation.

A subtle way to enforce standards is to be quicker in solving problems for those people using your standards. Whether this method is actually quicker or you are just prioritizing problems differently, you should work on standards and inform the nonstandards that they will have to wait until all your standard issues are resolved before you can help them. This is not a contrived act because you created standards to enhance and streamline efficiencies to begin with.

Inflexible standards also "force" those you support to seek out loopholes or workarounds. They will not inform you of these nonstandard maneuvers because they broke the rules, and you will find yourself with an environment of more technologies than you ever knew existed. I always felt that by promoting standards, discussing them with people, and allowing them to work within some guidelines I was better informed and the user community would ultimately come my way.

External Customers *You may find enforcing standards impossible for supporting external customers. You can suggest them and even offer price discounts on products and services if they are followed but you must be careful. You do not want to lose business and revenue by standing hard on software and hardware selection. Standards are very helpful to support so pick your battles wisely here.*

Standards are also useful for keeping up with version support. *Version support* is a term that relates to the practice of manufacturers and vendors to only provide support for current versions of their product. In order for the vendor to enhance their products without being forced to continually train their new staff on the older technologies, the vendor will inform their customers that they will not support their own product if the product is older than a certain date or revision number.

This practice can apply to your own Help Desk as well. If you are required to keep up with versions of software or hardware that are extremely old, your cost of support will rise. This is particularly the case with technologies that change constantly and can look completely different after a few years.

Change Management

So you are tracking assets and have good standards in place. That is an excellent service to provide to your company. What happens when something changes? Your hard-fought battle to identify and document assets and other items is suddenly out of date. Consequently, your database is now worse than it was before you started. Why is that? Doubt and uncertainty wreck confidence, and if you do not know if a certain piece of information is correct, how can you know if the next piece will be correct either? I am not suggesting you delete your files after the first change; I am suggesting you institute a strong change management plan that captures any changes to the items you are tracking. *Change management* is the process that tracks changes to the technologies, services, programs, or other items your Help Desk supports.

The Change Management Process

The process of change management is very simple in theory, but can be complicated in practice. The theory states that when something changes, someone makes a note of it and records the change in a database. Take it one step further, and have the change reviewed and approved before it is implemented in case there are issues to be addressed first. The trick is getting the change agents to tell you when they have done something. While tracking assets may be important to you, it is probably not that important to them. You need to continually communicate the value of this process to them. Your knowing what your customers have can help you support them better, provide them with updates as they come out, and even help prepare them for new releases if their version or model is not compatible.

The good news is that there are tools to help. If you are concerned with PCs and software applications, there is software to "poll" the network for their existence and configurations. There are also modules of software that can be added in asset management packages specifically devoted to tracking changes and keeping a history of them at your disposal.

Another way to reactively find out about changes is to review purchase orders and work orders to find work that has been done or assets purchased that you did not know about. Again, this is reactive and creates work, but unless the customers cooperate, you will have to be creative in how you find out what you need.

Note that tracking changes is not worthwhile unless you have a tracking system already in place. This could be your asset management system or documentation in a file cabinet. Change management will then be additional data that enhances and updates the existing information. The steps we will discuss in the change management process are

- Requesting a change
- Approving or denying the request
- Updating the change in a database
- Notifying the affected parties
- Auditing the database on a regular basis

Requesting a Change

The process begins with a person or group requesting a change. This might be the programming staff if you are tracking program releases of versions of software. If you track PCs deployed on the customer's site, the customer needs to tell you when they buy new ones, modify configurations to existing PCs, or dispose of them. The level of detail in your database drives how much information the customer needs to communicate to you. If you only know, and care to know, that there are four PCs in a store, it is not necessary for the customer to tell you if he adds 48 megabytes of memory.

The request can be handled in a variety of ways but it's best to create a standard method for people to request changes. The request can come via a document, an e-mail, or a Web page. The media does not matter as long as you receive all the information necessary to make an informed decision. This media also needs to be stored so that an audit trail is maintained in case someone needs to review the information after the change has been implemented. Figure 12-1 shows a sample change management document.

DME Corporation

Change Management Request Form

Requestor's Name: *Liz Saunders*   Request Date: *Sept. 14*

Date Needed: *Dec. 23*

Description of Change:

We need the night end process automated. The current program could be changed to run automatically unless specifically told otherwise. A file maintenance screen can be provided for the routine information that is input into the program.

Reason Needed:

The importance of the night end processing has grown significantly over the years. As our department has grown, there has been confusion over who is responsible for the process; subsequently it is forgotten much too often.

_____
Requestor Signaure

For internal purposes only

Resources Required:

Estimated Costs:

Estimated Timeline:

_____
Approval Signature

Figure 12.1   Sample change management document

Approving or Denying the Request

The approval process can be instituted in certain areas, but not others. It may be that your customers are just purchasing additional equipment and you need to know. Because they are paying for it, your knowledge of the change may be enough. In other circumstances where IT resources are involved to make the change, there needs to be an approval step. Examples of this include application adds and edits or new hardware systems and implementations. Be careful that the entity that approves or disapproves the request has the authority to do so. If you disapprove of the change but are not fully empowered to deny it, the requestor may proceed without your permission and the knowledge of the change will be lost.

Updating the Database

Finding about changes can be the hardest part of the entire process. Please don't waste that opportunity by not recording it properly. Whether your process is automated or manual, it is important that you keep all the changes, impacts, and resources in one place. If future changes need to be made or troubleshooting of the item is necessary, having all this information easy to find will help immensely.

Notifying the Affected Parties

A truly effective change management process will include the notification of affected parties within it. Informing those people who will be impacted by a change is important and will help the Help Desk keep calls to a minimum. This notification is done before the change is implemented and afterwards. It should include what the change is, what the expected impact on the customer will be, and what procedures to follow in case of a problem. Without this notification, customers will call the Help Desk once the change is implemented because they will be unfamiliar with what happened. There may not be a problem, but there will be something different from what they are accustomed to.

Conducting Regular Audits

I am sure you have a good plan in place and your constituents are updating you regularly. It doesn't hurt to check up every now and then, though. Depending on the size and scope of your database, I recommend an annual or semiannual audit of the assets. If you do not have an automated process, you can send out surveys to the customers and have them fill out the most basic of information. If you find discrepancies, you can then go back and inquire for more details.

For example, you may have a database of printers down to the year they were purchased, model numbers, and RAM installed. If you first survey for printer count and asset tags, you can find out if there are more or fewer printers on the site than you knew of. If it is the same count that you already have, you may let it go. This is a check-in audit and it passes the test most of the time. Now, if your database is small or you need exact information for reasons like lease terminations, you may go deeper. I think this high-level survey approach is proper because if you ask all the questions of everyone for everything, your response rate may be slow or nonexistent. Remember, this tracking is not in their day-to-day job function and it will be prioritized accordingly.

Change Management Is Continual

Change management is another process that does not end at a single point in time. As the audits indicate, if nothing else, there will always be work involved to keep your database up to date and accurate. This is a full-time process. The amount of technologies and processes you track will determine if change management needs a corresponding full-time person devoted to the process or just someone who is responsible but is not dedicated to it.

Intern Programs

A process to augment your staff is to establish an intern program. We did not mention this as a staffing solution earlier in the book because using interns to establish an organization is not recommended. However, once you are up and running and understand your operations, this can be a fine process. You can do this informally and use it every so often or establish a formal internship program.

Interns Can Fill Short-Term Needs

Informal internships come about when you need to fill a position quickly or have a project that needs additional resources to complete it. You can reach out to your local schools and see if anyone wants a part-time job. With schools, you will obviously have more luck in the summer and during other breaks. Interns can be hard to find quickly unless you have prior relationships with schools or other organizations. You may find that temporary services work better with this type of need.

Interns as a Part of the Organization

Formal internships take a bit longer to implement. I would recommend sitting down with a particular school or groups of schools and showing them your needs for the coming year along with the skill sets required. They can go back and work with the students who qualify and create a regular stream of resources as you need them. Many institutions offer credits for internships so the students will be eager to join. It also gives them invaluable resume material as they begin to look for long-term employment. You may also want to send some of your Help Desk agents to the school or organization to speak or conduct small seminars. This will go a long way to building and maintaining a positive relationship with that group over time.

In either case, there are several advantages to having an intern program in your Help Desk:

- **Staff augmentation**   Obviously, bringing on interns increases your staffing resources to enable you to do your job. In many cases, this type of position does not count in budgeted salary numbers but shows as an expense like in consulting or outsourcing services. In any case, this is a good way to add more headcount to the group.

- **Lower labor costs**   Typically, interns can be brought on much cheaper than full-time associates especially when costs like taxes, insurance, and so on are taken into account. Some interns will work just for the experience, but this practice is in decline.

- **Establishing relationships with the intern's organization**   I use the word "organization" here because interns do not have to come from schools. The advantage here is gaining exposure in the marketplace as a company that is in the business of IT. The organization providing you interns is getting good press for helping its constituents and they will likely speak highly of you for doing this.

- **Establishing possible long-term relations with the intern**   After the internship is over, you have a potential full-time associate for the future. Once this person is able to take on a full-time career, he or she may want to work for you without your incurring expensive recruiting costs. Once they come aboard, they should ramp up quickly as they are familiar with your operations and you can begin training them at a higher level.

Interns are part-time help and you need to realize the costs associated with that. You will spend some time ramping them up to your operations only to have them leave in some number of weeks or months. You will then need to start the process over again with the next intern or full timer taking his place. Interns are worth it, though, in the right areas. Whenever you have tasks that can be easily documented and don't require high levels of supervision, you have good work for interns. I would not recommend business-critical work where inexperience can inflict much pain on the business you are trying to support.

Training

We spoke earlier about training, but we now need to look at ways to further our associate's learning beyond their initial job training. Technical people are always concerned about their skills becoming stale, and if they do not see your organization providing them continual training you will lose them. A common fear among managers is that once their associates become trained in "hot skills" they will leave anyway for other jobs. While this can happen, I challenge you to think about what is happening if you do not continue to train them. Basically, your staff will be supporting technologies and operations using old methods and knowledge. Providing a good work environment with good communication aligned with continual training will do more to keep associates than anything else.

If you cannot get past spending training dollars and time to increase your agents' skills, have them sign a "train and stay" contract. This states that if they leave within a defined time period, they must repay you for any particular training you sent them to. For example, you send an up-and-coming associate to Oracle DBA training. This training is expensive but valuable. If the associate quits your company and takes his new skills elsewhere, he will be required to reimburse you for the expenses. It will not cover the time you invested but it will get real dollars back.

Unfortunately in today's job market this strategy is becoming more commonplace and necessary. It sends a message to the associates that you do not trust them long term. It also may not deter many people as they can just include this cost in a signing agreement with their new company. However, companies are spending more and more money on training only to see their newly trained associates taking that skill and going to another company.

If your training budget remains very tight, there are many ways to train agents other than sending them to a class somewhere. That type of training is the most expensive, anyway. It usually includes travel costs and meals and the agent is away from his desk for that entire period of time. A growing number of online training opportunities are available that can accomplish much of what classroom training can. Computer-based training allows the associate to learn new skills at his desk (or in the office anyway) at a rate he feels comfortable with.

If you have a large number of agents who need to receive training on a particular topic, look into having the class held on site at your company. Many times it works to your financial advantage to bring the instructor to your place of business instead of flying many agents to the training company. This strategy works best when your attendee count is high so that you can average the cost of the training across more people.

Cross Training

Previously, we spoke of training your agents in their existing skill sets. There are also opportunities to enhance the quality of your staff through cross training. Cross training is providing education on jobs and responsibilities not directly involved in their day-to-day jobs. This type of training has two advantages. First, it "grows" the associates and shows them you are still investing in them as associates and professionals. Second, your organization gets a win. Your win is that you now have multiple people who can perform any particular job function. This is especially advantageous in areas where you have limited staff. If one person were to abruptly leave the organization, you would be in bad shape. With an effective and targeted cross-training effort, you could pull others into the role for the short term until replacements could be found. You might even get lucky if one of the temporary replacements wants to take the new job. Mobility within your organization is good and sends positive signals to the rest of the group.

One warning is to ensure the cross training has some bearing on their current job. This is not a strict rule but if you allow anyone to train on anything, you will lose some synergies of the effort. You will also have a hard time denying anyone from learning job functions that you may not want them to go after.

Certifications

A debated topic these days centers on the value of certifications. By this I mean taking classes in particular technologies or manufacturing areas that result in titles or degrees. Vendors, government, or third-party organizations offer certification programs. Microsoft Certified Software Engineer (MCSE) and Cisco Certified Network Professional (CCNP) are examples of certifications that are popular in the marketplace today. Closer to the Help Desk profession itself are certifications specifically addressing the skills and needs of the Help Desk agent offered by organizations like the Help Desk Institute and Help Desk 2000. HDI offers training for its HD* line of certifications like Help Desk Analyst* and Help Desk Support Engineer*. Help Desk 2000 has Certified Help Desk Professional and Certified Help Desk Manager among its offerings.

Certifications may be required also. You may have a customer that says he can only have support from someone "officially trained" in a technology. A vendor may require it of your agents in order for your Help Desk to receive higher levels of support or maintenance discounts.

I am a big fan of training and the value it returns to the organization; individuals can use this to your disadvantage, however. Many people attach a price tag on the certification and demand higher compensation at hiring time or even after returning from the class. I encourage you to analyze the value the education itself brings instead of concentrating on the title. Book learning is good but experience is better. Not to say that some of the certifications are not taxing and do not require strong knowledge, but how to implement this learning into your environment is more important.

Especially before sending existing associates to these classes, it is crucial that you set correct expectations of what the certification will mean to you and to their careers. Be leery of someone who begins to reconsider going if you do not mention salary increases immediately afterwards. I would wonder about their true intentions if they do not recognize this as job training and see it as only as a way to improve their market value instead.

Another certification plan could be to offer internal certifications. Where the previous examples were external certifications offered by vendors and service providers, this plan could call for certifying your agents on internal processes to your company. In many cases internal training is a normal part of business. The associate sits with a trainer, goes over whatever the topic is, and goes back to his desk. Why not spice up the event more and develop your own certification plan that recognizes the completed training for the associate? This recognition could simply be pieces of paper or other tokens that are distributed upon completion of training. Many people like collecting certificates, pins, or badges that show others they have accomplished something. This training plan is also more aligned with your business and has definite value to all involved.

A slight variation of this internal certification is to offer it to your customers. We have spoken about training points of contact to empower the customer to better help themselves out of problems. You don't have to give the customer a piece of paper at the end, although you could. This plan more calls for the tracking of which customers have been trained on which topics. Maybe over time, you could offer incentives to customers who have completed certain levels of training. The more they know about troubleshooting and technology, the more your Help Desk can concentrate on larger issues that require a more technical skill set.

Soft Skills Training

It can be very easy to push technical training onto your agents to help them support the various technologies in your customer base. Do not forget that the other half of your Help Desk's goal is customer service. There are many attributes of a good customer service agent and there are many training classes and seminars to enhance these attributes in your agents.

A few examples of soft skills training opportunities include

- How to handle an angry customer
- Prioritization skills
- Management training
- How to build teams

These skills are as important to the success of a Help Desk agent as their knowledge of a technology. In fact, strong customer service skills can help overcome weaker technical knowledge. Soft skills training is usually cheaper than hard technical training and can be completed in a shorter amount of time. The return on the investment in the class can be huge, though. Whether it is to round out a strong personable person or to begin "converting" a techno-geek who would rather not work with people, soft skills training should be a part of any Help Desk training effort.

Quick Recap

- Do you have a service level agreement in place for your Help Desk and customers? Do you have plans to formalize it more and review its effectiveness on a regular basis?

- Were you able to provide the support services for all the products and technologies your customers initially wanted? If not, take some time to review what is still open to determine your ability to begin supporting them.

- Do you have asset management and change management procedures in place? If not, does another department in the company have this information? Understanding what your customers use in their business can go a long way to helping you help them when there are problems.

- Establishing standards is a good idea if you are able to implement them. Do you have standards already? If not, do you think you can communicate their value to the customers?

- Never stop looking for ways to train your agents and customers. The value that training brings will typically generate a greater return than the costs needed to obtain it. Do you think certifications can work well in your Help Desk? Do you have areas where you see cross training to be beneficial?

CHAPTER 13

Measuring Your Help Desk

We mentioned at the beginning of Part III that we liked the Help Desk and wanted to keep it going. How can we know how much we like it and how much value it adds unless we measure the people and processes that make up the Help Desk? Measurements are a critical piece of Help Desk life. They show you, the agents, customers, and management how well the Help Desk is performing and what areas may need improvement.

What to Look For

- There are several rules to remember when designing and tracking measurements. You need to always keep them in mind as you begin your own measurement strategy.

- Many measurements are quantitative in their results. These are more objective in nature and show numbers and times of actions. They are good for trend analysis and pointing to specific areas to continue or improve.

- Other measurements are qualitative. They are subjective and discover more about how well your agents and processes are doing. These types of measurements are just as important as the quantitative measurements because they can help you understand what is happening within the operations.

Rules of Help Desk Measurement

Certain rules must be understood when undertaking a measurement strategy. Measurements will show you things that must be fixed, things that are going well, and even make you think things are happening that may not be the case. Because of this, you must be very careful in setting up the measurements you wish to track. We'll discuss each of these rules, plus the different types of measurements and how to get them.

- Only measure what you will act on
- Measurements are only ONE thing to base your actions on
- Measurements drive behavior
- Always report your findings
- Report them in ways your audience can understand and appreciate

Only Measure What You Will Act On

Measurement for measurement's sake is a tremendous waste of time. Measuring because some book told you to is also a waste if you do nothing with the results. And don't think that displaying a graph on the board each month constitutes action. It is a start, but not the end.

A major reason to measure is to understand what is going on. Right in step with that is to see improvements or regressions from your operations. Based on the trends you find you will modify processes or behaviors. That is good stuff. What is not good is taking the time to capture measurements, maybe even write them down, but do nothing with them. You may not act on them because you don't know how to or because you don't care to. Either one is a waste of time and effort.

For example, let's say you start measuring the number of times a certain server goes down. Over time, you notice that it goes down frequently and at an increasing rate. This is good information to have. If you don't plan on doing anything with it, you are missing a great opportunity. You could have a chance to replace the server or some of its parts before it crashes beyond repair.

Lack of action sends a wrong message. First, it shows the person who gathered the metrics that his or her time is wasted performing that work. More important, it may appear that management is actually consenting to the inaction around resolving the issue. They will be confused as to why you would know of a problem and refuse to do anything about it. Customers know the server keeps going down, and they are impacted whether you measure it or not. They will notice the trends of problems as quickly as everyone else because their work lives are affected as much as everyone else's. Finally, management will be upset that the Help Desk has recognized a problem and nothing has been done about it.

Now, let's say the server was up a good amount of time consistently. There may be nothing to do then. That is not a contradiction to this rule. This rule says don't measure something you won't act on. If you take action on a troubled server, that is absolutely correct. Besides, knowing that a server is consistently up may provide valuable information for others when researching server vendors and configurations.

Use Measurements with Caution

You're convinced that measuring is good and you are ready to pounce on every opportunity to improve the events you measure. Great, just don't pounce before you look around. Diving in the water is fun. Diving in without knowing the depth of the water or the environment around you is dangerous.

Figure 13-1 shows the number of calls your Help Desk agents took in April.

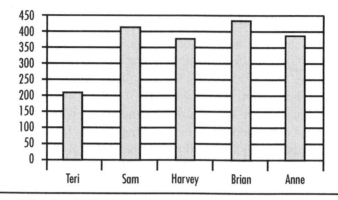

Figure 13.1   Calls taken by Help Desk agents

You review this metric to see the workload of your agents. You don't want anyone to be overloaded or avoiding work. With that in mind, Teri's call volume stands out. Diving in leads you to speak to her about her call volume and wonder what she does all day while everyone else is on the phone. Ten minutes later you stop lecturing and await her response. Looking shocked or mad or confused, she reminds you of the training class you sent her to for a week in April. Of course her calls are down; she wasn't in the office as much as her peers!

How about one more example? Figure 13-2 shows the uptime percentage of your servers in the computer room.

Your five boxes are divided between the NT and Unix operating systems. First glance shows you how much more stable the Unix boxes are. You know not to act quickly, so you watch these metrics over three months and notice they remain pretty much the same. Can you act now? Should you ditch all your NT boxes and move to

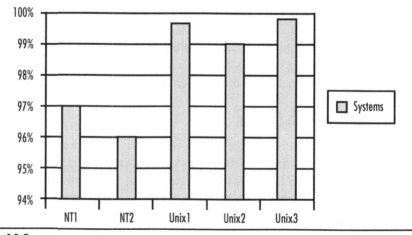

Figure 13.2   Server uptime

Unix? Some people would argue for such a move regardless of the graph, but that is the topic for another book. Shall we praise the Unix administrators for their ability to keep their boxes up and criticize the NT guys? Maybe. Or you could dig around and find out that the NT boxes are being rebooted each weekend for performance reasons, and the reboots are planned and understood by the customers. The graph alone shows you one view that is not complete.

These are simple examples to prove the point. Others can be more complicated or hidden. More graphs and numbers don't get you completely out of it either. They may corroborate each other and paint a richer picture, but you should still talk to the people who make up the statistics. If they have no reasons to contradict what you see, good or bad, then it may be time to act. Just remember: Don't dive in until you know the water you are diving into.

Use Measurements to Drive Behavior

Be forewarned about metrics and other measurements. Without a doubt what you measure will drive the actions of those you measure. An example is measuring and perhaps even evaluating agents on how many calls they take a day. Your thought is full of good intentions; the person with the most calls must be working harder than the others. While I am sure your agents are highly ethical and professional, some are not. If someone knows that taking a high volume of calls means rewards or good standing, he or she might be tempted to be short on the phone to get to the next call. This scenario results in bad customer service and the potential of return phone calls because the caller's problem is not properly addressed. What started as a simple measure begins to lower your customer's opinion of the Help Desk and harms the organization. Call volume is a good statistic to capture, however, and helps you make good decisions.

To overcome the tendency for some agents to perform directly toward metrics, use multiple measurements that will balance actions out. For example, measure call volume at the same time as you measure customer satisfaction. If an agent is rushing calls to reach a higher volume, the customer will surely notice. This action will show up on surveys because the customer will probably complain about the agent not taking the time to fully understand and resolve their problem.

Get your agents involved in the measurement process from the beginning. Make sure they understand that you are tracking different processes not to fire or criticize them, but to better understand the operations and what you can do to help. In the end, some might always try to "work the system," but well-informed associates will be less likely to go that far. Constantly remind them, and yourself, that overall quality is your goal and the measurements are just ways to keep track.

Always Report Your Findings

Okay, you now have a full array of measurements and you are in touch with the trends of the operation. But are you the only one who receives the metrics? If so, stop measuring because it is not worth all that work if you're doing it just for yourself. You need to share the results of your measurements with many groups of people no matter how good or bad the results are.

You can share this information by conducting metrics meetings and distributing the results through mail, e-mail, or the Internet or an intranet. Meetings may not be feasible depending on the quantities and types of people you will be sharing the information with. If the audience is geographically dispersed it is not feasible to hold a meeting to review your findings. Mail or intranet distributions also work better for audiences who will review the numbers more casually and for informational purposes, rather than to act on them.

Meetings do allow those people being measured to point out reasons for certain items or to answer questions about what is shown. A good idea if possible is to conduct a brief meeting to review the metrics internally before they are distributed to anyone outside the Help Desk. This gives you a chance to make side notes next to items you know will cause raised eyebrows from future readers. While many of the rules apply to any delivery system of measurements, we will assume the measurements are being presented or mailed to others from here on.

Report Findings to Multiple Groups

How about reporting to the agents themselves? Of course, it is important to share the outcomes with your associates so they can learn from them. You might even publish the measurements in a common area with everyone's results. This is not meant to punish the lowest marks but rather to reward the best ones and will also create some friendly competition among the group. I know if my scores were near the bottom I would do all I could to improve.

How about the customers? Don't they get to see how they are being treated or where their money is going? Sharing your findings with customers is beneficial and could be done with the same media you use to announce and continually promote the Help Desk.

An example could be reporting your call volumes while you are promoting the Help Desk's processes. So the message "DME's Help Desk can be contacted at the corporate office during normal office hours. Your phone call will be answered in the order it was received" could be turned into "DME's Help Desk can be contacted at the corporate office during normal office hours. Your phone call will be answered in the order it was received. Our agents take over 12,000 calls per month and we appreciate your patience if you do not get an agent immediately." This gets you a quick blurb on some statistics and also lets the customers know you are a busy operation. The numbers should not be an excuse for not answering the phone immediately, but should serve as general information.

If you are using service-level agreements, you must publish their resulting measurements. As we discussed in Chapter 12, these agreements should always have reporting capabilities built into them so all parties are informed of the results of the operation.

You should also publish your findings up the management chain as well. Although they may not get all the details, an executive summary would be good. This shows them how well the group is working and also shows you are on top of the situation. This summary would show statistics for the Help Desk groups versus the individual agents and could show uptime for the entire computing system versus individual servers. Have details ready, but don't overload the audience unless you are specifically asked for deep details.

Report the Good and the Bad

Remember, it is important to publish ALL the findings, both good and bad. If you were to publish only your high marks, the validity of your data, as well as your credibility, would come into question. It would be hard to believe that all your measurements returned such good results. Plus, if you published only the good scores, you may find yourself showing one type of statistic one month, only to not include it the next because the results were not good. The trends are where it's at, so overcome the bad marks with better ones in the future. The senior management team will be far more confident if you can show bad measurements but include a solid plan on how you will turn them around.

Report Measurements in Ways Your Audience Can Understand and Appreciate

There are four main themes to consider when displaying or presenting your measurements: know your audience, use terms the audience can understand, show how you calculated the results, and make the results visually stimulating.

Real-World Example

I once had a supervisor who asked all of his subordinates to list their accomplishments from the prior year. My peers rebelled at this, feeling that if he did not know already, then he was out of luck. I was amazed at their logic. Who would be hurt more if your best work was forgotten because of reasons beyond your control? You aren't bragging shamelessly because he asked for it to begin with. Bottom line: show your work and the work of your group.

Know Your Audience

This theme does not mean that you need to introduce yourself to everyone who will view your measurement results. It only means that you need to identify the people who will be seeing the results so you can ensure that what you are presenting will make sense to them.

Depending on the audience, you may use different terms. If it is the Help Desk agents themselves, you may use terms you both use routinely. The terms may not be industry recognizable, but the agents will know what you are talking about.

Knowing that senior management will see your measurements may guide you to summarize findings more than if you were to give the results to the IT department. Customers may want a lot of detail about their calls and problems, but not care about other stores as much. Senior management will be receiving many reports through the course of normal business and you don't want your reports to be lost in the shuffle. Making them easy to read with emphasis on the points that are important to the reader is one of the best ways to accomplish this.

Use Terms the Audience Can Understand

As with any presentation of information, your message is effective only if your audience can understand what you are talking about. For the most part, your Help Desk measurements will be shown to technical people like CIOs, Help Desk staff, or other IT associates, and to the business customers your Help Desk supports. The Help Desk works in a technical environment full of acronyms and names that are not well understood in the business world. Your measurements can be as technical as you need them to be, but the presentation of them needs to be "translated" to terms the business world can understand. Your audience may understand the literal words you use or the numbers you show, but if they cannot extrapolate your intent, you will have wasted your time.

For example, look at abandoned rate. You could show how the Help Desk's abandoned rate has dropped from 22 percent to 7 percent since your purchase and installation of a call routing software package. Your audience will probably be glad to see how the percentage has dropped but will not appreciate what impact that has on the business. If you can show them that this means 300 of their salespeople reach the Help Desk and get help for their problems on the first call, they may really appreciate it. With a high or increasing abandoned rate, the salespeople are spending more and more time with technology issues affecting their work instead of having their problems resolved. The business audience can now understand that your operations have made their sales staff more productive and able to work towards helping their own customers instead of waiting on your Help Desk.

Show How You Calculated the Results

The more detail you can provide initially on how your measurements were actually calculated, the more credibility your results will be given. This detail does not have to be presented with each reporting of the numbers, but it should be made available if the audience needs it. It may be wise to provide the background on the first report and then reference that it can be given again upon request.

How did you get this information? Only you know that answer. If you are reporting incoming call volume statistics, where did this number come from? Was it your phone system that tabulated the numbers or did you use your call logs? You do not need to inform the audience of the particular database query you ran or what software manufacturer you used, but you should note if the measurements were automatically captured or done manually.

The business audience will understand, and expect, that this calculating methodology is shared. Just as stockholders would not stand for a CEO to report "Profits this year feel a lot better than the year before," nor would your audience put much faith in "The Help Desk is open for customers all day long. At least it is dark when we come in and dark when we leave." Telling the audience, "Our call logs show a 34 percent increase in the number of printer calls this month. We would like some help from the training group to provide additional documentation on troubleshooting printers" would be received much better and your request would have a better chance of being approved.

Make the Results Visually Stimulating

The best and easiest way to accomplish this goal is through the use of graphs. Use large colorful graphs that grab the audience's attention. Presenting the findings of the past six months of call statistics using only words will be quite boring and hard to follow. Instead, you can use an appropriate graph to get your point across. What is appropriate? That depends on the metric and your intent. A good starting point is to use

- Pie charts to show proportions
- Bar charts to show comparisons
- Line charts for trends

Let's look at how we can display budgets, calls per agent, and call volume using these graphs. For the budget example, we want to show the executive management group how our budget is allocated. They have been complaining that we spend too much money on tools and not enough on the people. (What a nice problem to have!)

We could write how our tools are only 10 percent of the costs and that people costs are 65 percent of the budget, followed by facility costs at 25 percent. This shows that the weight is not on the tools, but your message would come across better in a graph like the one in Figure 13-3.

This graph makes it very clear that the people are a significant part of the budget and maybe you are not overspending in the "wrong areas" after all.

Next, we want to address an associate problem where Sam feels he is taking an inordinate number of calls versus the number of calls his peers are taking. He is complaining that he is doing all the work and everyone else is surfing the 'Net or goofing off. You could, and should, hear his issues and investigate his claims. If you find that his statements are not true, you could tell him he is wrong and that others are equal to his workload. Showing him this graphically, as in Figure 13-1, works well too.

From this chart, even Sam can tell that others are taking their share of the calls. You may have an issue with Teri, but many factors go into any measurement. Sam can still leave your office feeling overworked, but at least the numbers disprove that he is no more overworked than the majority of your staff.

For a last example, the CIO wants to see the impact of the new software that was released. He is hearing mixed results from the end users about its impact and he is confused. The programmers finished at the last minute, but the Applications Manager claimed the new software had no impact on the project. He has asked your opinion on how it went. What could a graph show? Figure 13-4 is an example.

What immediately stands out is that July calls into the Help Desk rose dramatically. If that is when the software was released, you can tell it had an impact all right. What you cannot see is the cause. Was the program full of bugs or

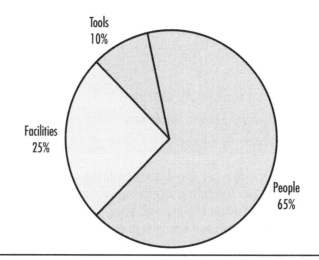

Figure 13.3 Budget breakdown

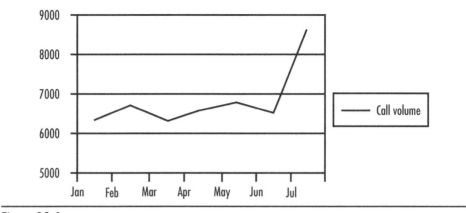

Figure 13.4   Calls per month

did the users just not know how to use it? Luckily, you are a manager of information and can also show results such as in Figure 13-5.

The vast majority of the calls were hardware related and not part of the software release. Of the calls that were part of the software release, though, most were training related. Your CIO can now go to the training group for more details. He may find that the late completion of the project gave them no time to prepare, or their materials just missed the boat. In either case, your measurements, and your Help Desk being the hub of information, point him to the heart of the issue.

Now that you understand the basic rules of measurements, let's look at examples of things to measure in a Help Desk world. There are many ways to measure performance that include quantitative and qualitative methods. Let's begin with some objective ideas.

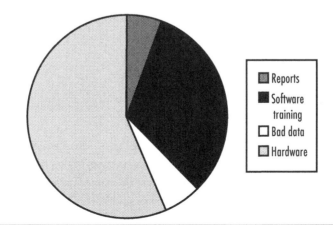

Figure 13.5   New software impact breakdown

Quantitative Measurements

Quantitative measurements look at the numbers and times involved in the Help Desk process flow. They measure number and length of calls, number of times your callers hang up before you answer, number of times your frontline associate solves the problem instead of passing it to someone else, and many other things. Your individual needs as well as the needs of your executives and even your associates will determine what you decide to measure. If there is no one who can take action on what you measure, there is really no need in doing the measuring in the first place.

The other driving factor that determines what you measure is the availability of tools to perform the work. Some measurements can be done manually, but others require a level of technology. Some measurements are best done using technology, but you need to take a hard look at these for their ultimate value. There is a low return on investment in measuring certain aspects of Help Desk activity if it takes a lot of time and effort for the agents to record those numbers.

I will go over some of the most popular quantitative measurements in this section. I will define each measurement, discuss ways to record it, and then offer some suggestions on what actions you should take for each measurement. The following list will definitely get you on your way to taking a good, hard look at your Help Desk. The list includes

- Call volume
- Calls per agent
- First call resolution
- Cost per call
- Abandoned rate
- Average talk time
- Average speed of answer
- Training-related calls
- System availability

Call Volume

The most basic of measurements, *call volume*, tracks the number of calls that come into your Help Desk. This measurement can help you determine staff size or the quality of programs introduced to your customer base. Depending on the technology your agents use, call volume can be broken down by time of day, method used such as phone or e-mail, or type of call such as hardware or software. This measurement can help you determine staffing levels and office hours.

Your call volume statistics can come from phone technologies, software for call logs, or any manual logs you keep. The amount of data segregation you can achieve will be determined by your technology choice. Phone call volume can help with time of day metrics but it won't help with problem classifications nor will it measure e-mails, Internet chats, and so on.

If you have a software package or a manual solution, you will still have more decisions to make. For example, do your agents log ALL calls? What if it is a personal call? What if it is a salesperson making a cold call? In some cases, you still want to include these calls in your measurements because they take up time; in other cases, you may not want to because you are trying to measure only your customer calls.

There is much discussion on logging all calls regardless of their purpose, or only logging calls that are pertinent to the Help Desk. If the phone is ringing, it needs to be answered. If the Help Desk agent cannot know who is on the other end of the line before answering, it will take her time to answer the phone. When calculating how many agents are needed to answer the phones, you might want to include all calls in the measurement. However, if you are after calls by customer type or technology, these calls are meaningless.

If you have an efficient tool to track calls, it is best to log all calls coming in. If there is an issue with categorization, you can create a *Miscellaneous* category and store all nonbusiness related calls in there. If you do not track all calls and use a mixture of phone technologies and software applications, keep in mind that the volumes reported will be different. Because phone technologies cannot know about e-mail messages or any other customer contact outside the phone system, they will obviously not report these interactions. On the other side, if your agents do not log *every* call taken, the phone system will report calls that your application does not show. These discrepancies are all right and should be expected as long as the difference is not too large.

Calls Per Help Desk Agent

Here is an easy one. Take the call volume in any given period, divide by the number of agents who took those calls, and you get *calls per agent*. This call volume can originate from your call logs or the phone system statistics. It doesn't matter that much because all by itself, it tells you very little. What it can be used for, though, is a comparison against the other agents.

The best way to use this measurement is to take the average calls per agent and then review where each of your agents stands against it. As with most metrics, do not rest on this number alone.

It might not be fair to think that Vicky taking 30 calls a day is working harder than Jess, who takes 18. Jess may be troubleshooting PC operating system problems whereas Vicky is resetting passwords. However, if they are in the same position, it may behoove you to look further into the discrepancy. Over time, you could use this metric to establish staffing guidelines at budget time. If you were getting good productivity and customer satisfaction when agents were taking 30 calls a day and now they are at 45, it may be a signal to get more associates on the Help Desk.

First Call Resolution

Now that you are tracking how many calls you take, you can look at first call resolution metrics. *First call resolution* tracks how many times the caller has her problem solved when she hangs up from the phone call. This is a bit harder to measure than pure call volume because it involves some subjectivity. For example, the caller may think the problem has gone away but what happens if it returns five minutes later? Is this a new problem or the original one? Without a call management package to help, this is also hard to track. If your agents track call volume by tick marks on a piece of paper, they now must keep a separate set of marks for resolved problems. Phone technologies won't help because they only record that you took the call and that you hung up. They cannot know if the problem reported *during* the call was resolved or not.

I believe this measurement is best used with a directionally correct mentality. Knowing you resolve 90 percent of your calls during the first conversation will not lead you to different actions even if that number is really 85 percent or 93 percent. Knowing that your resolution rate is 20 percent does point out major issues, though. Unless you organized your Help Desk using a dispatcher group that only records issue to be worked later, 20 percent is a terribly low resolution rate. It could point to your agents needing more training or more expertise closer to the front line. Remember your customers want answers and want them soon, so getting resolution as early in the process as possible is best.

Cost Per Call

Cost per call is a popular measurement that looks at your overall Help Desk more than at each associate. This measurement takes the cost of providing Help Desk services, divides it by the number of calls the Help Desk receives, and shows your cost of doing business per call taken. Although it would be nice to know how much your Help Desk costs and the benefits it produces, I have never been a strong advocate of this calculation because it can often be very difficult to get an accurate number. In the beginning of your operation, you have many issues to combat and easier measurements to track. As the Help Desk gets underway and becomes fully operational, you can begin to look towards this type of measurement. It gives you good data for trend analysis, helps justify the need for your Help Desk, and provides a cost basis if you use chargebacks.

Trend analyses of your cost per call can yield good information. A decline in the cost per call may show you your Help Desk agents are getting more efficient at their jobs and are helping customers better than in the past. It can also show you that any new processes or tools are taking effect and helping the agent do their jobs.

Increasing costs per call show different aspects. Are your agents being trained on any new implementations of technologies in the company? Is the call volume just so high that the agents cannot keep up and have to work less effectively to get the job done?

There can be many causes to changes in the cost per call over time. Significant trend changes should be further investigated to discover their cause and effect.

Cost per call analysis can also help you if your Help Desk comes under scrutiny. These numbers are useful if different areas of the operation are being reviewed for outsourcing or are being handled by a different organization. In Chapter 20, we will go over outsourcing protection in more detail. If your company measures its business associates for effectiveness, it would worthwhile to see how your Help Desk stacks up. The work may not be the same, but it gives you some idea of where you stand in relation to the rest of the company.

One practice that requires cost per call measurements is charging back costs to your customers on a per call or tiered basis. If you do not know how much it costs you to take certain types of calls or calls overall, how will you know how much to bill your customers? You are in for a losing fight, and business, if you charge less for your service than it costs you. Unless you are funded by additional sources at the same time, you cannot survive in a negative cash flow environment. Now, the subsequent charge to the customer may be higher than they are willing to pay and that will be a problem. In that case, you really need to take the time to understand what is making up the costs. Until you can reduce your costs, you will be working while in debt.

So if you want to use cost per call measurements, do it right. Take the time to acquire an accurate cost. You can calculate these measurements in two ways. One way is called *fully burdened* and includes any and all costs associated with the Help Desk. Remember, there are far more things involved than just salary multiplied by the number of agents you have. The agents' benefit packages, telephones, PC costs, and so on need to be added up. Basically, every cost that would go away if you disbanded your Help Desk should be accumulated and then divided by the number of calls you take.

The other way to measure your cost per call is to look at only the costs related to the call, rather than the Help Desk in its entirety. Therefore, use the agent's salary and any tools he uses but exclude costs such as facility costs. As an agent gets more training and learns his job, his costs will go down and that should be noted. The rent you pay for the building your agents work in has no bearing on their lowering costs per call.

Neither measurement is right or wrong. I would use one over the other depending on what I needed to show. If it was whether the Help Desk should continue to operate or not, the fully burdened cost should be used. If I wanted to see the effects of a new software package for the agents, I would use the related cost method. The key is to openly communicate how you are deriving your measurement so no one is misled.

Abandoned Rate

Abandoned rate is a measurement that shows you how many times someone called your Help Desk but hung up before reaching an agent. This metric is designed to show you staffing levels, that is, having enough people to answer the phones, but it can also show training challenges. If you have a high abandoned rate (over 10 percent is generally agreed to be high), either you do not have enough people available to take calls or they are staying on existing calls longer than the customer expected. Review what projects your agents are working on that take them away from the phones. If they are spending a lot of time walking to customers' desks, you may need to find other ways to provide that service while finding more time for the agents to answer the phones.

On the other hand, an extremely low abandoned rate may point out opportunities for improvement as well. Customers will certainly appreciate that every time they call the Help Desk they get an agent, and you cannot fault that. However, if you are able to maintain a very low abandoned rate during call volume spikes, you might have too many agents available for the phones. Either look for ways to slow down the growth rate of your staff or look for more proactive projects and work that can help the customers in other ways.

Abandoned rate is an important metric to track because it shows you the business you are missing. If this number remains high, customers will go elsewhere for their needs and that runs counterproductive to the Help Desk's mission.

If your agents do not get calls because the callers hang up, the agents will obviously not be able to count and track the calls. Abandoned rate can only be captured if your phone system can track it or you have an Automated Call Distribution (ACD) system that can do it. Therefore, this metric is more expensive to track than others but it is worth the investment. For world class Help Desks, it is a must.

Average Talk Time

A metric to help with your quantity of agents and their training levels is measuring the average length of time they are on the phone. *Average talk time* is the length of time your agents spend on the phone with your customers. This metric is best calculated with phone technologies. The other way to get this measurement is for your agents to watch the clock when they answer the phone and again when they hang up and record that result somewhere. This metric is good to have but is not usually worth capturing manually.

Before claiming that your times are good or bad, look for trends between agents in similar positions. If John averages five minutes a call and Kim averages fifteen, there may be reasons worth your review. Perhaps John knows more and can just solve problems easier and faster. On the other hand, maybe Kim is friendlier and takes the time to make sure the caller is satisfied.

To best understand these trends, make sure you are comparing apples to apples. Hardware calls may take longer than software calls. Down locations will take longer on average than down devices. Comparing agents will not be appropriate unless they are working on similar issues. Watching the tracking of this metric and exploring the reasons will help ensure your on-phone work is best utilized. The results may cause you to organize the Help Desk differently or route calls in a new manner.

Average Speed of Answer

So, you have the quantity of calls coming in and you know how many times people hang up. *Average speed of answer* is the other piece of the communication puzzle because it is the time that callers spend on hold waiting to be helped. This is another measurement that requires technologies like ACD systems to calculate. Without technology, it would be impossible to truly know how long a customer waited on hold. The closest you could get would be to survey them and get a sample figure, but that would be highly subjective. You would probably get as many "forevers" as you would accurate times.

The less time it takes an agent to answer a customer's call, the quicker the customer reaches an agent. If the times are low and the abandoned rate is low, your staff is doing a great job. If the times are high, look into alternative solutions. An easy way is to hire more people to answer the phones. Or, as customers wait on hold, maybe you can play different messages that provide answers to frequently asked questions or announce coming events. If your group's follow-up skills are good, you can urge callers to leave a message instead of holding and assure them you will return their call as soon as possible. There is no set good or bad speed to answer calls. Your customers will dictate what they expect and can tolerate more than an industry average.

Training-Related Calls

Training-related calls are calls from customers that are preventable by training. This measurement divides calls into necessary and unnecessary buckets. The unnecessary bucket tabulates calls to the Help Desk because someone other than an agent can resolve the problem, customers are not trained to resolve the problem, or customers are not aware of tools they can use to resolve the problem themselves. Necessary calls on the other hand, as they relate to this metric, are not preventable by training sessions with the customer. For example, a bad memory chip that causes a PC to stop working would require a call to the Help Desk. However, calling because the paper jammed in the printer or asking about a software question may be deemed training related because this does not *require* a Help Desk associate to fix it.

This measurement is not a reflection of your Help Desk but is very valuable to the organization. Imagine if the group responsible for training your users knew that 30 percent of the support calls could have been resolved by the users if they had been trained correctly. Now the training group has an area to focus their next training plan on. The ability for the Help Desk to notice trends in customer needs makes the Help Desk an important asset to the company.

This is a subjective categorization and should be used for noticing trends versus looking for exact numbers. It should not be used as a weapon *against* the customer, but as a tool *for* the customer. The customer may not know that training is available for their issue and would use it if they did. Monitoring the type of problems that training can prevent will make them more productive if you communicate your findings in a nonthreatening manner.

The only effective way to track this call type is by the agents taking the call. If you can add a training-related field to your call tracking software, you can have the agents select this field or not for each call they take. If you track your calls manually, you will need to educate your agents to mark this type of call.

System Availability

A very good measurement to track is system availability. *System availability* is the amount of time your customers' computing systems are available for use. This is separate from system uptime. The difference? A system that is *up* is a server or mainframe that is functioning correctly from a hardware, operating system, and applications view. An *available* system is when your user community can reach it. Having your data line connection cut between your building and the server would be an example of a system that is unavailable even though the systems are running fine. Shown another way, your car can be up because its engine is in working order but the car is unavailable to you if the doors are locked and you have no keys to get in.

Systems administrators are typically concerned with system uptime as that is their box being measured and they want it to look as good as possible. Help Desk agents who are aligned with the customer want to see system availability numbers because that is what concerns the customers in the end. Both numbers are very important to an IT department and the company, but the customer's need for an available system is most important.

The importance of tracking these separately is that the result will point you in different directions. Much downtime will lead you to the manufacturer or implementation partner for answers and help. Unavailable systems will lead you to a root cause elsewhere like networking issues or security problems.

Calculating System Availability

An issue when calculating system availability involves defining *who* is available in the calculation. In the following example, we will assume system uptime and availability numbers are the same.

For this example, let's say you have four machines running your stores. Each machine represents a geographic region, North, South, East, and West. The machines have a different number of stores on them.

North machine	10 stores	10 hours	100 available uptime hours
South machine	10 stores	10 hours	100 available uptime hours
East machine	5 stores	10 hours	50 available uptime hours
West machine	5 stores	10 hours	50 available uptime hours
Total	30 stores	40 hours	300 available uptime hours

If the North machine goes down all day, what is your uptime? If you treat each machine equally, North's 10 hours count as down and the remaining machines' 30 hours count as up. Therefore, take 30 divided by 40 for a 75 percent uptime.

What about the business entity running exclusively on that one system? They are down 100 percent of that day. Bragging to the executives about your 75 percent uptime will cause them to lose trust in you because they know full well they were not up that much time. What if you weighted the machines by the number of stores on them?

Now North has 100 hours of downtime to the other machines' 200 hours of uptime (South's 100 + East's 50 + West's 50). So, the North's machine going down for a full day equates to:

$$200 \div 300 = 66.7 \text{ percent uptime}$$

Your uptime percentage dropped even though the same machine was down for the same amount of time. The difference is the number of stores that were affected by the downtime. While a weighted measurement is more complicated to calculate, I believe it is much more representative of the situation.

These examples are shown because measuring availability is important and can lead to much time, energy, and dollars to correct. Knowing how much a business unit or enterprise is down will guide you in correct directions and allow you to deliver what is needed.

In keeping with one of our main themes, remember the end customer does not care for the definition of availability; he just wants access to the computer when he needs it. It is important, however, to fully understand the expectations of downtime from your customers because constant uptime is expensive. Being up 90 percent of a year sounds pretty good until you realize that is being down for over 36 days. Settling on 99 percent uptime then will get you only 3+ days of downtime. It is when you get to the 99.99 percent uptimes that you see downtimes in minutes per year.

Getting your systems to be available this much of the time will require expensive solutions, either in redundant equipment or high failover technologies. As mentioned before, align yourself with your customers on this. Systems in hospitals or emergency services would require this much attention, whereas back-office software may not need anything close to it.

Qualitative Measurements

Where quantitative measurements look at the how many and how much of something, qualitative measurements look at how well something or someone is performing. Thanks for knowing you took 125 calls this month, but how well did you serve your customers and how well did they like the experience? By its nature, qualitative results are subjective and interpretative. The same process involving the same associate may get good feedback one period and below average the next. Again, the trick is uncovering the trends and the reasons behind the feedback. From there, you can learn what to do to improve or what to leave alone becauseit is working well.

There are several ways to obtain qualitative measurements. Some are described in the following list.

- Surveys
- Regularly scheduled review meetings with your customers
- Process studies
- Consultants

Surveys

The most popular way to get qualitative feedback is to conduct surveys. It is also an extremely quick way to irritate people so you should pay strict attention to its implementation. You can obtain survey information in many different ways. For example, you could call your customers, e-mail them, send memos, or just have an Internet/intranet site available for them to use whenever they want. You can survey proactively or reactively. Reactive surveys could occur once a customer has used the Help Desk for its services. After the service has been performed, you could send a survey to the customer to gauge the quality and effectiveness of the Help Desk. There is nothing wrong with the good old suggestion box either, but there are so many more ways to get at more people these days. Here are some rules you should follow when conducting surveys:

- **Plan your surveys so they measure events you can do something about.** Asking how a user liked a new enhancement even though you did not design it or could not change it under any circumstances should be left to someone else. On the other hand, asking how quickly and effectively you resolved a recent problem of theirs works well.

- **Survey events or feelings that are very recent.** I would preferably ask about things that occurred no later than the day before. Anything beyond that will tend to cloud answers with other issues that are not part of the survey. Oftentimes, the person being surveyed may not even remember the event you are inquiring about!

- **Ask the questions that matter and no more.** I would keep the number of questions between 3 and 7. You won't get much information if your survey has fewer than three questions, and if you have more than seven questions, the survey becomes too burdensome to complete. Surveys have no value if they are not returned so your goal needs to be to make the survey easy to complete.

- **Use a mixture of numerical and open-ended questions.** Numerical questions with a range of 1 to 4 as answers allow one to more easily compare responses and prevent anyone from making inferences or drawing conclusions about the answers. I recommend using even numbers in your range, though. I see a lot of 1–5 questions and it is easy to grade people with 3s if you are ambivalent. Using even numbers forces the responder to pick a side. You are either over the halfway mark or under. Open-ended questions allow responders to express their thoughts without the bounds you place on them. You may pick up valuable input from this free-form entry that you were not thinking about.

- **Use clear and easy-to-understand language.**   Just as in the quantitative measurements, the presentation of your questions should be easy for readers to follow. Use terms and questions they will understand and can answer with the most accuracy. It does you no good if the customer responds to a question that was not what you intended for them to answer.

- **Carefully monitor the frequency with which you survey a particular individual.**   As with the quantity of questions, too many hits will only begin to bother the person and the answers may begin to turn against you.

- **Publish all your findings.**   It is very easy to promote your successes but it is equally important to demonstrate that you recognize your weaknesses. Your findings will increase in credibility if those viewing them see more than "Good job" and "Nothing is wrong."

- **It is imperative that you follow up with an action plan.**   I recommend combining the publishing from above with an action plan showing that the time the users gave to your survey was worthwhile. For example, you could say, "Many of you mentioned that you could never reach us after 6:00P.M. To that end, we have instituted work shifts that will extend our office coverage until 6:30." You cannot please everyone, though. You may need to say, "Many of you mentioned that you could never reach us after 6:00P.M. Due to budget restrictions in place, we cannot staff beyond 5:00. We have approval next month to hire additional staff and we will use this additional resource to extend our hours." Please communicate this message correctly. Making excuses that are never rectified does no one any good and makes you look ineffective. Acknowledge outside events that affect your environment but have a plan to combat them!

- **Follow up with shorter surveys to track your results.**   It is good that you published a plan but did it work? You won't know for sure unless you ask. I said earlier that you need to watch your frequency and this includes follow-up surveys. All you want to do is hit a sample of your customers to see how they reacted to your changes. This follow-up survey should be far enough into the future that your plan can take effect but close enough to the past that the old world is remembered. If you did a good job, this is just another way to get recognition. If you did not, you need to know so you can adjust your plans accordingly.

- **Track responses by customer types.** By classifying your responses you can determine if there are patterns in the feedback of the customers. If you combined all responses together you may find a mixed bag of positives and challenges. Upon further review, you may find that the negatives are centered on a particular type of customer. With this information you can investigate the issues and/or problems that are common to these customers and have a better chance at resolving them.

Regularly Scheduled Review Meetings with Customers

Surveys are good ways to gather feedback from your customers. An even better way is to schedule regular meetings with them to get this feedback. This is, of course, only better if you and the customer have time to do it. If your customers are widely dispersed, this process may be hard to pull off successfully. In that case, it may still be worth the time to meet with your largest customers or those who need the most attention for any reason.

These review meetings allow for more interaction between the reviewer and the person being reviewed. This increased interaction should lead to an increase in the alignment between the needs of the customer and the processes of the Help Desk. As with all surveys and information gathering processes, you must try hard to ask all the right questions and take appropriate action where necessary.

Process Studies

Performing process studies gives you the opportunity to watch the flow of your organization to reinforce strengths and resolve weaknesses. A good way to do this is to watch the actual life of a call from its inception to its completion. You can see a call come in, watch how your agents determine who answers it, how they work it, who they may pass it to, how they resolve it, and what they do once it is resolved. From this study you can see where a call may get bottlenecked or lost, where management gets involved, and what the customer goes through to get a question answered. While you could measure the time it took to perform the tasks, it is more important here to just view the process.

If you can afford it, have an outside party perform the process studies. They can watch with a more objective eye and see things you may have taken for granted or not paid much attention to. The outside resource can then present their findings and any recommended plans of action in a document for you to review.

Consultants

Another way to evaluate the effectiveness of your Help Desk is to bring in external experts. There are many consultants or other groups that will come in, analyze your Help Desk's activities, and then report back to you their findings. This can be very useful, as they should have a database of other Help Desks to compare you against. Outsiders can contrast you with other Help Desks and take a less biased view.

Before bringing in a consultant for this, you need to interview them carefully. Ask them how many data points they have relative to your industry. See examples of the reports and findings they will produce when they are done. Note how much time your staff will need to be involved to complete the review. If it is a lot, make sure you have the time to do it right. If it is very little, you may need to question how accurate the review will be if they do not need your associates involved.

Quick Recap

- Are you comfortable with the idea of measuring your Help Desk? This should not be seen as drudgery or work that has no value. It can reap significant gains for you if done correctly.

- Measurements will drive the behavior of those being measured. Have you thought through how the agents will see the measurements and what actions they may take in response?

- The audience of your findings is a big part of what and how you report the measurements. Do you have a plan for sharing the information with different segments of the business?

- Many graphs were shown in this chapter. Do you have the tools to present your measurements in a similar type of fashion? Do you have the tools to even capture the information to begin with? If not, what measurements do you see being able to track?

- It is a good idea to list all the items you want to track. It is also good to get a feel for additional things other people may want you to track. Do you know what these things are?

- How do you feel about sending surveys to your customers? Do you think they will take the opportunity to respond? Before you answer too negatively, give it a try.

- Having someone outside the Help Desk look at your processes can be very helpful. It can also cause anxiety for yourself and those being watched. Do you have a credible, objective resource you can use for this purpose?

CHAPTER 14

Promoting Your Help Desk

The word has been spread that your Help Desk exists and there are beginning to be signs that people actually like the services you are offering; good job! Now let's promote yourself even more, both to existing customers and to those who have not used your services. The methods you use to promote your Help Desk will greatly determine the continuing success of the operation.

What to Look For

- A promotional campaign is a valuable way to inform your customers and management on the existence and achievements of the Help Desk.

- Your customers are a primary audience for this promotion. It should be directed to those who use the Help Desk as well as those who do not even know it exists.

- Crafting your promotional campaign's message is a relatively easy task. Look to your early interviews, surveys of customers, and your own call logs for the foundation of the promotion.

- There are many ways to deliver your message. They can be as simple as publishing your mission statements and measurements or as complicated as holding technology fairs and designing graphics for screen savers and mouse pads.

- Designing and implementing a promotional campaign can take a lot of time. Using your agents as well as other resources can help spread this workload and generate more ideas.

The Promotional Campaign

You must take into account several considerations when beginning a promotional campaign. *Campaign* is used because this is not a one-time event that concludes after an initial e-mail or flyer. Your promotions must be a regular and long-lasting part of your plans. You should begin your campaign by asking the following five questions:

- What is the goal of your promotion?
- Who is your target audience?
- How do you develop your message?
- How will you reach your audience with that message?
- Who can help you make these promotional materials?

Establishing Some Goals

Any good plan needs to have a goal in mind so people will know if it has been successful or not. A promotional plan for your Help Desk is no different. Sit back and think what could be achieved if people knew of all the things your Help Desk was capable of accomplishing. Five goals that come to mind are

- Attract new customers or business
- Maintain existing customers
- Convert customers who have not been satisfied in the past
- Inform senior management on the achievements of the Help Desk
- Strive for accurate representation of your services

Attract New Customers or Business

A good promotional campaign will alert and attract new customers to the item being promoted. For the Help Desk, this means that more customers will know of the Help Desk and what it can offer. It doesn't necessarily mean that more customers will start calling you each and every day with problems. Remember that one of the goals when you built the Help Desk was to empower the users to do more things themselves? That is still a valid goal but does not mean that you should not promote yourself. Instead, this campaign can inform technology users that the Help Desk exists for them and that if they run into trouble they have some organization to help them.

If your Help Desk supports external customers and generates revenue from its services, then it is only good that you attract new customers. The more customers you have, the more revenue you can generate. This brings in more opportunities to increase resources and leverage them against the growing customer base.

By advertising what you offer, existing customers may learn of other services that they can benefit from. The customers may not know of all the things you provide and this promotion can help educate them further. This, in turn, helps the company because it enables the associates to be productive faster when they encounter technology issues.

Maintain Existing Customers

The second goal of a promotional campaign is to maintain existing customers. As I just mentioned, the Help Desk may have expanded its services over time and existing customers may not be aware of what you have done. Use this time to update everyone on what you offer and how it is best used in the organization.

Many studies show that it is significantly cheaper to retain an existing customer than to attract a new one. This applies to the Help Desk as much as it does to any sales organization. While you should have designed your processes with ease of use in mind, you still have to work to educate new customers on whom to call for what. If a customer stops using the Help Desk, two things will happen. First, the organization will have different groups seeking help in different places, which will cause inefficiencies. Second, the Help Desk will look bad to its remaining customers and will have to do reactive work to keep everyone else happy.

Convert Customers Who Were Not Satisfied in the Past

That leads to the third goal of the promotion, converting customers who are not satisfied. The Help Desk may have received a call one day from a customer needing help. Because of poor execution, bad timing, or any number of other reasons, the help the customer received may have taken too long or was incorrect. Now the customer doesn't want to call back again, and looks to other groups to help them next time. These groups may be internal associates or outside organizations. In either case, the synergy gained by having a formal Help Desk will have lost some advantage, at least with that customer.

A successful promotion should show customers that the Help Desk works hard to resolve their problems and has done so for many associates. Your promotion could include examples of past problems and actions the Help Desk took to correct them. Perhaps you could even ask those unhappy customers for help in detailing the bad experiences to get their input. Not sure how you will know who is happy or not? Believe me, you will know if you listen to your customers at all.

Promoting actions that help overcome historically bad problems shows unhappy customers that the Help Desk may have resolved the issues that caused them grief and it is okay for them to call the Help Desk again. This message also shows existing happy customers that the Help Desk is not sitting still and is continually working to improve its operation and services.

Inform Senior Management of Your Achievements

Some or all of the senior management team initially agreed to build the Help Desk. It is now your turn to proactively promote all the accomplishments and processes the Help Desk has achieved since its inception. Chances are that the most feedback the management team will receive otherwise will be negative feedback. This occurs because of the nature of Help Desk responsibilities. When problems happen, the Help Desk is called and many times upper management is alerted as well. The name of the Help Desk is linked with the problem and it is sometimes hard for people outside the issue to differentiate between the two.

Your job is to help people distinguish between the Help Desk and the problems it's expected to resolve and to show the management team all the positive things that are happening on top of handling the technology problems.

Here's a good example: If the network were to go down for an extended period of time, there would surely be calls into the higher ranks of management informing them of this large problem. When management asks the caller what is being done, the answer would be something like, "I called the Help Desk an hour ago but we are still down." With this type of reply, the Help Desk is now an owner of the problem that is impacting the entire organization. Problem status reports could update the management team on the progress and ultimate resolution, but taking more time to speak on the topic may be worthwhile. If you could publish later some findings that detailed how the problem was handled and any work done to help the down locations through the downtime, you could show more value. Perhaps you found ways to route their connections to a different path or even hand-delivered important reports that could not be printed remotely otherwise. These things show that the Help Desk is not just a call-taking entity, but a value-added organization as well.

Strive For Accurate Representation at All Times

An overall goal of your promotions is the absolute need for accuracy in the message being promoted. Claiming you offer a service that you don't or that you have resolved process problems that still exist is much worse than having done nothing at all. You will look either inept or like someone who twists the truth. If you promote a new service that is not ready, the customer may see you as someone who is not prepared and may wonder about other claims you make. Even worse, a false promotion may make a customer doubt your honesty and integrity. Neither of those situations is good and will cause much harm to the effectiveness and value of the Help Desk. Make sure you work hard to include accurate information in anything you publish.

You may not be the only one promoting your Help Desk if you support external customers. The sales force that works with customers in a business situation may also do some of the work informing customers of your offerings. This is good and can really help spread the word about the Help Desk, but it can also create a lot of unnecessary work if the message being spread runs counter to reality. A salesperson may "enhance" the abilities of the Help Desk if it will help bring more customers into the business. While the salesperson is surely acting in good faith with a "I thought the Help Desk had that already" or "Well, they used to do it that way," the bad feelings an erroneous message creates is not worth any price. The salesperson loses because he or she will be doubted on the next thing he or she tries to sell.

The Help Desk will look bad when the customer requests a service that might not exist. The customer also loses. The customer may have created or removed processes with the thought that the Help Desk can handle new things for them.

Targeting Your Audience

Defining the audience is important any time someone needs to deliver a message. Deciding whether to convey a point using pictures versus detailed formulas and analyses should only be done after determining who will be receiving the message. For that matter, understanding whether the audience even cares about your topic is critical to learn before resources and time are spent creating the message. Help Desk promotions should reach out to the same people who drove the design of the Help Desk. This group includes customers, management, and vendors.

Customers are necessary for all the reasons discussed in the "Establishing Some Goals" section earlier in this chapter. The Help Desk exists only for the needs of its customers, so the more the customer knows, the more the Help Desk benefits.

Management should be a recipient of the promotion campaign because it is the group that allows the Help Desk to exist and probably funds it as well. The promotion aimed at management will be different than the one aimed at customers, but it should include the same information. For example, customers may be given trinkets or small tokens that remind them of the Help Desk and its services. The message to management may be more directed towards the effectiveness of the Help Desk than how to use it. The message can also inform management of your promotional efforts towards the customers so management knows what you are doing.

Vendors or other outsourcing partners can also be an audience for your promotions. Informing them of your plans and services can help them understand more ways they can help you in your efforts. It will also help set the expectations you can have with them. If you aspire to do well in supporting your customers, you have to be able to obtain the same level of service from them.

A More Generic View

You just finished reading how the audience can be made up of customers, management, and vendors. Let's take a more generic look at potential audiences for your promotions as well. By doing this, you may get more ideas on where and to whom to send information. The general overview would include

- People who use your Help Desk
- People who have heard of someone who has used the Help Desk
- People who haven't even heard of the Help Desk or don't know what it does

Current Users of the Help Desk   Whether it is a customer, manager, or vendor, your audience should always include current users of the Help Desk. A stated goal of the promotion is to retain current customers, so don't leave them out. These customers are the easiest to find since someone on the Help Desk interacts with them at some intervals. Gaining their information from a database or from your call logs, you can send promotional material to them or make it available during the Help Desk interactions.

Potential Users of the Help Desk   Another good audience to tap into consists of people who have not used the Help Desk but know someone who has. You need to target these people for a couple of reasons. First, the information these nonusers may have about the Help Desk may not be all that good or accurate and you need a chance to correct it. Their sole opinion may have come from a lunch conversation where other pertinent information was left out. Second, the nonuser may have heard good things, but the topic may have been about a service this nonuser does not need. Your promotional campaign can show them all of the services you offer. Once you know more about this nonuser, you can demonstrate particular services to them while showing them how it will benefit their own situation.

People Who Haven't Heard of the Help Desk   The last broad potential audience consists of people who haven't even heard about you and your Help Desk. They go through their jobs and when they need technology help, they search for someone who can provide the answer. These people are definitely worth the time to find and educate about the Help Desk. If they are internal to the company, they are probably duplicating efforts or using someone's time that is best used elsewhere. If they are external to the company, this is a good opportunity to bring in more customers and all the benefits they provide, such as more revenue or exposure in the marketplace.

Developing Your Message

A good way to learn what message needs to be communicated is to review customer surveys. From these, you can get a feel for the things the customers enjoy (so promote this) and the things they wish you had. If you already have these services, definitely include that in the promotion. If you are close to implementing the services, you can include that in the promotion as well. Just make sure that the services will be real and delivered in some known time frame.

Another source of information is the interviews you conducted before you built the Help Desk. Your senior managers, customers, peers, and vendors all spoke of issues the Help Desk could address, so you will have a good foundation of the items they are interested in. Your promotional campaign can now serve as a communications mechanism to announce that those services are available and how they can be accessed.

A third source of information is your call logs. By reviewing the type and description of the calls that come into your Help Desk, you can get a feel for promotional information. An example could be in determining whom to notify of an upcoming software release. One audience could be the customers who have called your Help Desk in the past with related software issues. This should not be your only audience, but it can serve as a beginning point.

Getting the Message to Your Audience

There are many media that can be effectively used to reach your audience. These include paper, electronics, audio, video, and personal interactions. For our purposes, the delivery mechanisms will be broken down into "leave behind promotions" and "event promotions." After their brief introduction, we will align popular examples of these promotional types with your customer and management audiences.

Leave Behind Promotions

Leave behind promotions are promotional items that can stay with the audience. These can be memo pads, screen savers, mouse pads, pencils, coffee mugs, and stress balls with your Help Desk's name and number on it. If you have designed a logo for your Help Desk, put it on too! All you are trying to do is keep your name and number in front of people.

Event Promotions

Event promotions are promotions that happen at a point in time. They can happen at regular intervals but are not items that can sit on a desk. For example, you can conduct tech fairs, sponsor trivia contests, or speak at meetings or seminars with your customers or management present. Because they are more interactive than "leave behinds," events give you a chance to deliver a bigger message with more time to work with the audience on the issue.

Table 14-1 provides examples of when these promotional types are best used with particular audiences.

You will note that there are many similarities between the customers column and the management column. This reflects the fact that your management team is also your customer in many ways. They will use your service when necessary but they also need much of the same information that the customers do.

	Customers	**Management**
Leave behind promotions	Newsletters Job aids Distribute mission statements Distribute monthly and annual reports	Newsletters Distribute mission statements Distribute monthly and annual reports
Event promotions	Intranet and Internet Technology fairs Speaking at meetings Downtime communications Trivia contests Birthday or congratulation cards User group meetings	Intranet and Internet Technology fairs Speaking at meetings Downtime communications

Table 14.1   Promotional Examples and Target Audiences

This table gives you some ways to promote your Help Desk that you can then build on for even more opportunities. Although some of the examples are self-explanatory, let's look at others in more detail.

Newsletters   Whether you write your own articles or have them submitted on your behalf, use a newsletter to stay in front of your user base. You can write about your plans for future implementations, detail statistics about your call volume, or provide frequently asked questions and answers. I suggest making it informal (much like this book) so you don't bore your users with technical jargon they do not understand. Humor is good, but keep it professional at the same time.

Corporate Intranet or Internet   As with the newsletter, use the 'Net to get your message across. The Internet or an intranet is effective for the same reasons newsletters are, and you can use interactive features and updates more frequently. A hidden benefit of this media is that you can get your message out to MANY people at one time and it communicates passively. Proactive is good but passive is good also. Blaring out to people about how good you are can come across as self-serving. By simply displaying information for others to come to, you may get some good press without appearing selfish or annoying.

Technology Fairs   Though more expensive than the other examples mentioned, technology fairs can be a great way to show your customers the technologies and practices you support. Fairs allow the customers to "touch" the products and they can be shown how the products work and are used in a business setting.

Real-World Example

A successful fair we put on one year in our corporate headquarters was held in late November. We announced to the building that we would have PC experts in a room for certain hours and everyone was welcome to come by and discuss PC issues. It turned out to be a big hit, as everyone wanted to know about what PC or joystick or scanner to buy for a Christmas present. It has since become an annual event the associates look forward to. We were able to use something in their lives to help promote technology as well as our ability to help them.

Alhough you could hold a tech fair for external customers, you may find it more economical to get on the agenda at an established fair or show. Using their advertising, you could reach a wider audience and be seen in the light of other established service providers. Of course, now you can be compared and contrasted more easily. Put on your best show!

Speaking at Meetings   Another good way to spread the message is to get invited to speak at staff meetings or regional gatherings. Tailor your message to their situations so your talk will be as relevant as possible. If you have statistics, show how this group relates to the company as a whole. Show them where you think you can help them best and answer any questions they have. If you cannot answer them on the spot, show your strong follow-up skills and get back to them as soon as you can. Your presence in this type of environment will gradually allow them to see you as a person who knows his technical stuff but can speak their language as well. Becoming "one of them" makes you a strong ally moving forward.

Downtime and Problem Status Communications   Promote yourself while announcing bad news? That's not a contradiction. Your customers will certainly pay as much attention to these messages because they directly affect the customers and whatever system they use. With this "captive" audience, you gain opportunities to show them what you know and how you can help. Your message may be negative, but if the audience can see your confidence and knowledge of the impact, you and your Help Desk can rise above the bad situation, particularly if you resolve it quickly and correctly!

Birthday or Congratulation Cards   You can use birthday or congratulations cards to remind the receiver that the Help Desk exists. Notes of congratulations on a birthday or job promotion can make the recipient feel good. While downtime communications help get your message across during stressful times, congratulation messages get your message delivered while delivering good news. They don't take much time and give you a more positive return on the effort you invested.

User Groups   User groups are meetings the Help Desk can sponsor to answer questions about problems or upcoming events, or proactively reveal new technologies and their uses. These meetings are good because you can deliver your message to many people at one time and the attendees can hear about issues other people are having and learn how to resolve them.

User groups are also good times to focus on a particular product or service. Perhaps the service is new and needs to be taught. Or, the product may be creating many calls to the Help Desk and you can use the meeting to educate the users on the proper way to use the product.

Getting Help with Your Promotional Materials

A full-scale promotional campaign can take a lot of time to develop and implement. During all this time, you cannot forget you have customers who need help resolving problems and not just receiving material on your Help Desk. The scope of your promotion will show you how much time your agents can work on the project.

It is good to use your agents for this whenever possible. They are the ones most in touch with the customer and the details of the message so they are good contributors. Getting them involved also gives them a break from the incoming calls, which helps reduce burnout.

If you need more help than the agents can provide on their own, look to your company's marketing department for assistance. Designing promotions is their profession and they can be an invaluable source of materials and ideas.

If your company does not have a marketing group or they cannot provide all the help you need, look to the outside. Perhaps you can contract with an outsourcing group to develop the material for you or deliver the message to your audience.

Overall, the promotional campaign can be fun and educational for all involved. And it should not be limited to just your primary audience. You, your agents, and your managers will gain good information and insight into your customers and their processes. The everyday workload will make promotions hard to accomplish, but it will be worth your time in the long run. An educated customer base and management team can be strong allies in the ongoing operations of the Help Desk.

Quick Recap

- Do you have information you would like your customers and managers to know about? Did this come from your interviews before building the Help Desk or from more current conversations with them?

- Will your main audience be happy customers who need to learn more about the services you offer, or will they be unhappy customers who have had bad experiences with the Help Desk? Or will you concentrate your promotional efforts on those potential customers who have not used the Help Desk but could benefit from doing so?

- Do you have some good ideas on how you can deliver these messages? How many did you come up with that were not on the list?

- Do you have enough resources to help you with this in-house or will you have to go outside the company for assistance? In either case, keep some of your agents involved. This will help strengthen the content of your promotions as well as boost the morale of the agents.

CHAPTER 15

More Tools for Your Help Desk

If you built your Help Desk strictly from this book, you have a staff of agents sitting at a desk with a PC and a telephone. Let's give them more tools so they can take your organization to new levels of effectiveness and efficiency. The initial tools allowed you to open shop, but you must now move to increase their productivity and the value you bring to your customers. Providing your agents more tools also shows your commitment to their success because you are investing in their work. Your customers will feel better with an enabled Help Desk, especially if the additional tools are used effectively. Budget concerns, physical limitations, and size of staff all directly affect the availability of the following tools, but keeping them in mind as you progress will be important.

What to Look For

- A call management package is the first major tool you should acquire for your agents. The incoming problems are the heart of the Help Desk and they must be handled correctly and efficiently.

- Telephony tools are the next major resources to bring in for the agents and customers if telephones are a primary source of contact. These tools make your Help Desk look very professional and enable it to operate in the same way.

- A Web presence is another good way to share information among your agents and with your customers. It can reach a large audience quickly and can be updated easily.

- Electronic display boards, a computer lab, and documentation are other valuable tools to increase the effectiveness of your agents. They will make the agents learn more about their jobs, which, in turn, will help them deliver better service to your customers.

The tools discussed in this chapter can be broken down into a few categories. These categories are software for managing calls and problems, telephony tools for incoming phone calls, and more tools for the Help Desk area itself. As your Help Desk grows in size and importance, you must continue to invest in portions of each category to add value to your customers. The tools discussed here include

- Call management packages
- Telephony tools including ACD and IVR

- Electronic display boards
- Web pages
- A computer lab
- Additional knowledge management tools

Call Management Packages

The first major tool I would recommend you purchase for your Help Desk is a call management package. There are many kinds of software packages available in the market that can help you manage your calls, your customers, their problems, and their resolutions. Call management packages are similar to contact management packages in that they capture information from callers to help you work with the caller. The distinction is that call management packages take the information to work towards a resolution to a problem, while contact management uses the information to help you familiarize yourself with the caller and better process the call itself. This book will use the term *call management package* to relate the benefits of all the different types to the Help Desk.

What do your agents use now? Notepads, sticky notes, their hands? What happens to open problems when the agent working on it is out sick? Having a call management package resolves many of these problems by keeping calls in a central place. Their capabilities range from simple call tracking to sophisticated tracking, escalation and notification, and problem resolution. There are even packages that allow the agent to speak into them, and the call is logged verbally!

As with any major purchase, there are many steps to consider and plan. The major steps to help you implement a call management package in your Help Desk include

1. Requirements gathering
2. Software review
3. Vendor review
4. The "test drive"
5. Implementation

I highly recommend that you perform all of these steps during the process. Some may be done at varying levels, but all are necessary. These packages can be expensive in money and time and their value to the Help Desk can be high or low depending on your efforts.

Requirements Gathering

If you are forming an outline of the tasks necessary to buy a package, you need to go a deeper level in the requirements section. I suggest you have an effort that goes after the needs of the Help Desk, its agents, its managers, and senior executives and a separate effort that looks at budgetary limitations and possible system limitations.

If you are completely unfamiliar with any options a call management package can provide, I suggest you look into trade shows, support and services magazines, and the Internet for information. There are scores of packages in the market that can accommodate your smallest to your largest needs. Once you have a handle on what the basics are, you can begin the requirements gathering for your particular situation.

The Help Desk Agent's Needs

This is the part where you decide just what you need or expect from the call management package. Do you need just a method to count calls or do you need something that will record requests, transfer them to a particular group, and track the requests through completion? Does the call management package need to help you resolve the problem or just know about it? There are many things it can do and many will be described shortly. But before we get there, we have to gather all these needs.

A good suggestion is to form a work team to review the needs and wishes of the Help Desk. As We Mentioned In Chapter 11, This Project Will Make Your Associates feel part of the management process and will give them a break from the routine tasks of answering phones. Include veteran agents as well as newer ones on the team. I would also include a manager if possible to allow a different view of the Help Desk's needs and to potentially keep the group focused and controlled.

The work team should treat this effort as a project. There should be a project manager to run the team and ensure that it is making progress. This project manager does not have to be a professional project manager, but she does need to clearly understand the goal and the type of work that needs to be done. There needs to be timelines to measure the project against, and a deadline for all the team to work towards.

Once the list has been created, you should prioritize the items. It will be full of many great ideas, but there will probably be some items on the list that are more critical than others. Don't give up on any of them; just know which ones are requirements versus niceties. To get you started, here are some common offerings from most call management packages.

Call Entry   Entering calls into the package MUST be quick and easy. The package is only as good as the information put into it, so call entry must be streamlined towards your work. I have had the misfortune to spend some significant amount of money on a very nice package that failed because it asked too many questions at the beginning of the call. Our agents found it much simpler to write down the problem information with the intent of loading it in later. Of course, later never came and calls were missed. I proceeded to spend more time "encouraging" its use than the package could give back to us in benefits.

Open Issue Tracking   Inquiry screens and reports need to be available to present open issues in a variety of ways. Let's bring back our diagram, Figure 15-1, that distinguishes calls from problems to see what you may need.

A good call management package will distinguish between calls and problems. It will take call information like caller name, time of call, problem description, and category and record it for future reference. It will also keep data on the problem. What was it, how was it resolved, and by whom? Who took the call and who solved it will not always be the same.

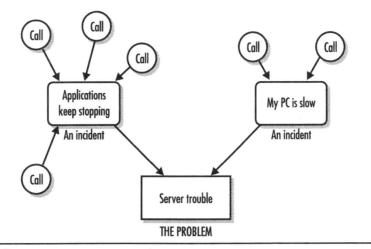

Figure 15.1   Calls, incidents, and problems

The package should be able to tie calls to problems. This helps in a couple of ways. First, it can show you how often customers call on one problem. This is helpful, for example, to show a programmer how one bug caused scores of calls into the Help Desk. Yes, she only messed up once, but the ripple effect was more costly.

These problems will remain in your database for historical reporting and trend analysis. A good feature of your package is its ability to relate subsequent calls to a previously entered problem. One problem may exist that causes many calls over the next days, months, or even years. It is helpful to be able to demonstrate to others that a single problem is the root cause of so many calls over time. This information may help you in prioritizing the resolution of the original problem.

Yet another relationship is tying calls to a location. A down data circuit can take a location down and all your customers in it. It is not uncommon to have many of those customers call your Help Desk to report the outage. Again, this is one problem causing multiple calls. The cost of the outage climbs as those customers are on the phone and taking up the resources of the Help Desk agents at the same time. It is a highly effective tool to track these instances and show management at some level how often this happens. When this happens, it forces you to staff more heavily than if one contact at the down location called the Help Desk to report the downtime. Part of your value is to expose inefficiencies in the whole organization and this example is a good one to use. Yes, your job is to take calls from any customer; this reporting just helps them realize that effect. The other customers in the location could be working other tasks, maybe long distance calls would be reduced, and more of your agents could be helping other customers.

Second, the call-to-problem relationship will help in future problem solving. Using Figure 15-1, a package's knowledge base can aid the agent in relating slow PCs to server problems. It will not always be the solution, but suggesting the agent look at the server may help him resolve the call without wasting much time on the PC itself.

With that distinction behind us, the inquiry screen for a call's view or for a problem should show data for multiple audiences. At the agent level it needs to show the information necessary to resolve the call. A manager may only want to see the quantity of calls by problem type or length of time. You may also adopt a policy where you give open ticket numbers to the caller if you cannot resolve the problem while on the phone. Most all call management packages use a call ID number upon entry of the call and you can in turn give this number to the caller. If callers call back for follow-up (shame on you for not beating them to it) they can reference this number so any agent can easily find it in the system through the inquiry screen.

Expert Systems   While some call management packages only allow you to log calls and change their status, others actually try to resolve the problem for you! This is done in a variety of ways and these paths get better and better each year. This piece is one of the most critical aspects of a call management package as it can really return much value for your investment. The most popular of these expert system technologies are

- Text search
- Decision trees
- Case-based reasoning
- Fuzzy logic

Text searches take key words from the problem entry screen and match them with key words already established in the database. It may analyze "My *printer* is *jammed* and will not come *on line*" and find all solutions entered that have *printer, jammed*, and *on line* in them to present back to the agent. The more information given to this expert system, the better chance it will have to find the resolution specific to that problem. Basically, it will have more words to compare against the database.

Decision trees are another expert system. A decision tree is a tool that guides you through questions and branches out to possible resolutions depending on how you answer the question. For example, you could use a decision tree to coach agents on answering a stopped printer call as follows:

Stopped printer — Are there any lights on the printer?

    Yes. Is the online light lit?

        Yes. Is the data cable plugged in?

        No. Hit the online button and try to print.

    No. Flip the power switch. Are there lights now?

        Yes. Does it print now?

        No. Is the power cable plugged in?

Of course, this looks better displayed in a flowchart diagram, but you can tell it allows all kinds of solutions based on the answers the caller gives. Great care needs to go into designing this resolution tool because your newer agents will use it without questioning its correctness. Even the order you display the questions and answers are important so you do not cause a new problem by trying to resolve the initial one.

Case-based reasoning is another tool offered by many packages. Case-based reasoning works very similarly to decision trees. The difference between case-based reasoning and decision trees is the order required of the questions and answers. In a decision tree it is imperative that each question is asked and answered in a specific sequence. Case-based reasoning allows the user to answer the questions in any order as he works his way towards a resolution. This is beneficial when there are questions a user does not understand or know the answer to.

Fuzzy logic is an extremely powerful expert system that "learns" answers to questions on its own. This is not space-age technology anymore; it is widely used. By relating past calls, problems, and answers, the fuzzy logic tool can begin to "understand" the strengths of certain situations as they relate to certain resolutions. The more it sees a type of hardware issue being resolved by an action, the more times it begins to recommend to the user that that action be taken the next time a similar problem is input. This system is nice because much of the knowledge creation that is typically done manually can be done automatically.

While an expert system can help you resolve problems, keep in mind that there is much effort needed to get it up and running and even more to *keep* it running. If you do not take the time to do this right from the beginning, you will have wasted a lot of money in this investment. Later in this chapter, we will go over some suggestions for implementing call packages.

Other Call Resolution Aids   There are many other ways a call management package can aid the agent in resolving problems. There can be actions in the package that point to segments of your database for frequently asked questions, common problems, or common error messages. Some have "flash updates" that serve to show current, hot issues that may be affecting the customers. This type of update is usually presented for the agent to see quickly and easily, as it may be the source of high call volumes.

Call Classifications   To best enable call resolution and to get more details for call statistics, the package should have several varieties of call types. Examples of call types can be the type of problem called in, the media used to place the call, and the severity of the call or issue.

One classification is defining the problem itself. For example, wouldn't it be nice to have your hardware calls separate from your software calls? Go deeper and break down the hardware between desktops and printers and deeper again by model or manufacturer. By doing this, agents, and the package, can find suggested answers more quickly because the historical database is broken down into parts. You can also report back to your executives and customers on the types of calls you take. If you can determine that a large percentage of your calls occur in a particular area, you can help your training or sales departments go after the root causes.

Another example of call classification is breaking down how your calls come in. Here you can have telephone, e-mail, walk-up, fax, and so on as choices to help you know where to dedicate resources. If a lot of calls come in as walk-ups you may staff differently than if they arrive via telephone.

An important call classification that should be in any package is severity. Severity is the importance of the call, which can help in gauging its priority. Severity levels can be numerical (1 to 10), or *high, medium,* and *low,* or *business critical, business interrupted,* and *normal request.* Most packages will allow you to provide the terms used in the different levels.

If you work under a service level agreement, it is nice if your package can automatically increase the severity of a problem under a set of rules you define. For example, you can tell the package that all calls rise one level in severity each day they remain open. That way, open problems can bubble up in importance under the appropriate circumstances.

These are just three examples where classifying calls can be used effectively. Ensure the software you are looking at has multiple ways to do this.

Call Transfers   More important when you have a tiered organization, the ability to transfer calls within the package is very nice. This allows the problem to be passed without the next agent in line having to ask the caller for all the information again. A recurring theme in this book is that callers do not care how you are organized as long as they are treated nicely, efficiently, and effectively. Having to describe symptoms of their problem over and over violates that rule. Call transfers also give the manager an opportunity to see who is transferring and what is transferred, which will help identify training opportunities.

Escalation Management   What happens in your Help Desk today if a problem goes unresolved for too long or your agent does not know how to fix it? Odds are he escalates it either to a manager or to someone who has a better chance of fixing it. Packages out today have features that aid in this process. You can assign "rules" to problem situations which, when invoked, cause an action, again which you can define. For example, you can create a rule that says any problem designated as System Down that is open for more than one hour should be reported to you via e-mail. Now you are automatically kept in the loop on those types of problems.

Customizable   No package can deliver exactly what you are looking for in the exact format you need, so if that was on your list of requirements I suggest you rewrite your list.

There are two levels of customization: modifying the source code and modifying screen layouts and operations. Modifying the source code is quite involved and will challenge you in the future if you were to take upgrades from the manufacturer on the software. Changing the screens and their operations, on the other hand, is easy to do and does not hurt you at upgrade time. Any package worth its salt will give you both abilities, but I strongly recommend using only the latter. If you find yourself in a situation where you must modify the source code, you must document it well or have the software company do it for you and document what they did. This will prove worthwhile in the long run. Going this route may provide you the best-tailored package for your operation in the short term, but long term there will be issues. Taking upgrades is one area, but getting support may cost you, too. Some companies will not support packages that have been modified extensively. You may also modify how your Help Desk operates over time and the package no longer quite fits. Now you will be stuck in a pattern of changing the code with every change in your process.

Overall, you should find the package that best fits your organization's needs out of the box. If the package is a market leader, it has been molded over time to fit strong Help Desk processes and yours may be no different. On the other hand, perhaps modifying your processes to match others may be worth it.

Ties into Other Software   Looking ahead, you may find yourself wanting your call management package tied into other packages that help you run your Help Desk. For example, if you have an asset management package (discussed later) you may want it linked to your call management package so that problems entered in your call management package automatically call up inventory details if equipment is involved. Or you may want it linked to your phone system so that when the phone rings, it identifies the caller from a phone list and brings up the caller's information in your call entry screen before you even say hello! If you receive many calls via e-mail, ties into your e-mail software are extremely helpful. Otherwise, your agents will read an e-mail message, have to type it into the package, and then await resolution. Clicking an integration icon or program can save keystrokes and time, both of which are crucial in a heavily loaded Help Desk environment.

Web Enabled   The Internet is the rage these days and the ability for your call management package to be used over the Internet is very valuable. You can use this feature if you have decentralized Help Desks but want them linked together. You might even want your customers to have a shot at resolving their own problems by entering their call into the package and seeing if it can resolve it for them.

If you do this, you really need to use the system for a while internally first. You want the package to work with as few problems as possible, so take the time to work them out before inflicting it on your customers. Be sure to work the package as objectively as you can. It is one thing for your agents to just know what buttons to press and in what order, but can your customers instinctively know this too? If not, you need to ensure they are well trained in how to use the package. The tool may be great, but if the customer is frustrated in using it, you will not get the benefits.

External Customers   *For external customers, strive to get at least some of your support services on the Web. The Web reaches a wide audience in a less expensive fashion than long distance or toll free calling. Do not restrict their contacting you to this medium, however, because there will be times when it is unavailable. You might have a down server, or their device to use the Web might be the device that is in need of the Help Desk.*

If you decide to provide this tool to your customers, see if the package can distinguish between public and private knowledge. Public knowledge is information anyone can see, while private knowledge is restricted to authorized users like your Help Desk agents. You may want to separate the two when resolutions require technical experience your customers do not have or if there are problems in the database specific to the internal operations of the system.

Limitation Requirements

A major requirement, and probably the most important one, is the budget you will be allowed to work with. All the features in the world can be requested, but if there is no money, there will be no package. You need to be able to justify why you need this expenditure and show the value it will bring to the Help Desk and the business at large. This will go a long way toward getting budgetary approval.

The budget needs of the package will come in two ways. First, there will be the initial capital outlay to purchase the software and any neccessary hardware. You may also need money to help install the package and train your agents on its use. This expense can equal or even exceed the cost of buying the package! Next will be the support and maintenance fees. Be prepared for all of these situations when seeking the money. The first two are up front; the third will be needed annually.

The other limitations you need to understand will be the system itself. You need to know the operating system it runs on and the hardware requirements. The software will probably need a server to run on and have certain minimum requirements for the PCs. Most of the major packages run under multiple operating systems so you should be covered. The PC minimums should be carefully reviewed, though. You may find yourself needing more initial capital than you thought because of the need to upgrade many of your PCs.

Review the Software

Once you have a general idea of your needs from a call management package, I would suggest you send out a Request for Information (RFI). An RFI is a document you can send to vendors to find out information about their packages. Because vendors will take some time to respond, get the RFI out early in the process while you are still working on the exact needs of the Help Desk. Then when it is returned by the vendor, you can know just what you are looking for.

Once all the RFIs arrive, you can begin the task of comparing your wish list to the offerings of the packages on the market. It is best if you can get a demonstration copy of the software. Words in a glossy document are nice; having the actual software to play with is definitely better. As soon as you can, narrow down your potential list of packages to two or three. If you keep more than this, you will spend a lot of time just comparing software and I always found it confusing to keep up with all the varieties. Narrowing it down to one package at this stage will restrict you too much and you lose possible negotiating leverage when it comes time to buy it.

While you work through the different packages, keep a running list of the good and bad things you find. A lot of the times you will find features you didn't know existed or that you can use. To keep track of all the features, create a report with columns that show the features you want, how the packages rate, and how the packages stack up.

For the issues where the package works in a way that does not fit your Help Desk's procedures create a "Gap list." Where the features report compares what you are looking for and how the packages rate, the Gap list details just the missing issues and what could be done to overcome them. This document provides a nice summary upon which to make final decisions because it shows the reader how much work must be done in order to implement that particular package. Figure 15-2 shows a sample Gap list.

Review the Vendor

From the same RFI, you can get good information on the vendor that makes and supports the software. Find out what staff they employ, both in numbers and in skill sets. This is important because you may need help implementing, customizing, and supporting the package from purchase time forward. If the vendor sells you the product and goes bankrupt a few months later, you will be in a bad situation. Look at prior-year fiscal reports to gain some understanding of their financial stability. Look at their customer list, not only from a reference view, but to see who else thought this package was worthwhile to buy.

The Test Drive

Reviewing the package for selection purposes is similar to looking at cars on the sales lot. You know generally what you want, but you need to see colors and features in person to feel even more comfortable. Once you narrow the list down to one car, you take it for a test drive. It looks good on the lot and the engine started nicely, but how does it run on the road? More important, does it run in the manner you want and need?

Ref#	Category	Gap	Prio	Workaround
1	Call entry	No field for job title	M	Can rename an unused field
2	Call resolution	Accessing expert system is cumbersome	H	Customized programming to make easier
3	Reports	Not many pre-programmed reports come with the package	L	Must spend significant time for us to develop what we need
4				

Figure 15.2   Sample Gap list

Arrange for the vendor to come on site for a demonstration. They can show you the features of the package and how it works. This will save you time in discovering all the neat tricks the package can do. Relate this scenario to the car salesperson showing you the engine, cup holders, and the various features of the seats and trunk arrangements. You may get a lot of information you don't think you need at the moment, but it may come in handy further down the road. The information may point out things you didn't even know you needed. I know I never knew I needed cup holders in the backseat.

During the test drive, install the demo package on an agent's desk and let her use it through the course of her day. Make her enter actual calls into it, resolve problems, and use any other feature you are interested in. What you are looking for here is to understand the flow of the package and its alignment with the flow of your Help Desk's operations. You may find that your standard procedures run counter to how the package was designed to be used. This is not a showstopper, but any items like this need to be thought through. It may be that you research to see if the vendor can change the package to fit your needs. It may be that the package designers had a pretty good idea and you want to modify how you process the work. Neither way is horribly wrong. If the gaps are ignored, however, your efficiency will suffer.

Implementation

Implementing a call management package correctly takes a good deal of time to design and prepare for its use. Because it is designed to help you resolve the problems entered into it, it must be well thought out. You will need to load in customers and their locations, you will have to set up categories of problems, and you will probably have to load in some rules for troubleshooting problems in your environment. Once that is done, it is extremely difficult to change major elements. Imagine having thousands of calls entered broken down by category and caller type only to find you left out a major part of your system. Do you take the time to reclassify the calls or do you leave them as is and start over? If you take the latter route you will have effectively lost the value of those initial calls.

To avoid these problems, you should have a *knowledge engineer* to create and maintain your package's contents. The size of your Help Desk and database will dictate whether this is a full-time position, but at the very least you should formalize it into agents' duties. They can prevent duplicated efforts as well as ensure uniform data layouts for ease of use. Again, this is a good opportunity to involve multiple people from your Help Desk. They live closest to the calls and can help you make decisions that will be as effective in practice as they look on paper.

While internal Help Desks can preload all their callers from the corporate roster, external Help Desks may not know all their potential callers. If you know the companies, at least you can load that and build the caller list once someone calls in. Or you may find that who the actual caller is does not matter as long as you capture equipment type or service needed. Think these decisions through as your initial design plan may force you down roads you don't wish to travel.

A good call management package will be one of your strongest tools for your agents. It is not something to pick up off a shelf, give to your agents, and then walk away from. It takes time and energy to pick the right one for your Help Desk. More time is needed to learn how to use it technically and within your processes. You will spend even more time keeping it up and running and aligned with your changing needs. All this work is still a positive investment to make. World class Help Desks do not exist without well-implemented systems to record, track, and monitor customer calls.

Phone Tools

For any Help Desk that receives a large number of its problems from phone calls, there is a significant gain from employing phone technologies. Basic technologies like voice mail, and increasingly complex yet beneficial tools like automated attendants and ACD systems can help field incoming calls. We will discuss some of the more complex tools in the following sections.

Automated Attendant

An automated attendant is software that front-ends your phone system for incoming calls. It allows you to have a message that informs callers of system events and prompts them for information before an agent answers the phone. If you organize your Help Desk into specialized groups, the automated attendant can ask callers for their problem type and route the call to the group most likely to resolve the issue. Think of this as using technology in place of an agent to answer every call with a standard message.

Automated Call Distribution System

An Automated Call Distribution (ACD) system is software that allows you to design and control the flow of your calls. The ACD can route the calls, provide queuing if agents are busy, and maintain statistics for incoming calls. ACD systems are expensive and can get even more expensive when you add more features to them. I recommend ACD systems in four instances:

- Reporting needs
- Large numbers
- Complexity
- Service level management

Reporting Needs

Throughout this book I discuss different measurements to use for a variety of situations and issues. Many of these can only be achieved if an ACD system is in place. To be truly effective, your Help Desk must know how well it is doing and where it can improve. A powerful tool to help with this is the ACD system.

Some helpful reporting capabilities you can use include measuring your call volume, the times you are called the most, how long you stay on calls, and how often people hang up before reaching an agent. Managers can use ACD statistics to keep up with how long agents are on the phone in case you want to give them other projects to combat phone fatigue. Real-time information can also be made available to show how many callers are waiting for an agent so you can redirect resources if necessary to handle the load. A manager can also see who is available to take calls and who has made themselves unavailable. This is good to monitor to ensure your agents are handling their share of the load.

Large Numbers

As your Help Desk customer count grows, you may need help managing incoming phone calls. Your Help Desk may also have grown in agent headcount and configuring your call routing to this number is beyond your abilities. If this is the case, ACD systems should make it into your plans. Its very name, Automated Call Distribution, equates to handling calls in an efficient manner. The larger your Help Desk becomes, ACD systems become more and more valuable.

Complexity

Whether it is due to a varied technology mix, a customer base that is broad in its needs, or the organization structure you created, ACD systems dramatically increase your ability to survive. If you divide your Help Desk into specialty groups based on technology, it would not work well to have a customer call and get just anyone who answers the phone. If that agent is not familiar with the customer's problem, the customer will get bounced around until the correct resource is found. Integrated with an auto attendant, an ACD can provide routing options to the caller and point the call to the correct set of agents.

If your Help Desk is organized centrally but your customers are divided into certain categories, the same principle applies. Customers can be alerted to use certain choices when they need support from the Help Desk.

Service Level Management

Some Help Desks will be required to have this tool to keep up with service level agreements or other commitments to the business and its customers. There is no easy way to track average talk time or average queue time without an ACD system. There is no way to keep up with abandoned rates without this system. If any of these measurements are part of your service level agreement, you need to invest in an ACD system. Other Help Desks will need it to track and review key metrics in the Help Desk environment. All in all, the numbers an ACD system provides are extremely valuable and should be sought after if measurements are wanted.

Implementing an ACD System

An ACD system will be a customer's first impression of your Help Desk, so you need to design it carefully. You should take quite some time to sit down and carefully plan exactly how you want it to work. If you have no experience with this process, you should hire a consultant to help you with it. More than likely, the ACD vendor offers this service and can be very helpful to you. They will have implemented their system in many places and can suggest ways to implement the system in your organization.

When you do go live with the system, stay very alert to the operations for a while. If you notice that the Help Desk is not getting any calls, don't assume no one is calling. Perhaps the system is not allowing them in! Test the system thoroughly and run through every possible menu choice. Make sure you can stay on hold if needed. Run reports early in the process to see if the database is being updated as you thought it would. These reports will become a major factor in future organization efforts and staffing levels. If they are wrong, you may be making decisions that run completely counter to what is actually happening.

Interactive Voice Response

Interactive Voice Response (IVR) is a system that allows a caller to type information into their touchtone phone and the computer will return information or perform actions as designated. Resetting devices and passwords are two very popular examples of using IVRs in Help Desk situations. This technology empowers customers to achieve results on their own without Help Desk agent intervention. It also allows the agents to concentrate on resolving more difficult technological issues that need their expertise and experience.

Electronic Display Boards

Display boards are electronic devices that allow you to scroll messages and statistics for your staff to see. You can get them in multiple colors with multiple lines displaying a variety of messages. If you get an ACD system, you should get a display board tied in to it. From there, you can show total calls taken, how many people are waiting in queue, or how long they have been waiting. Basically, any statistic captured in your ACD system can be transferred and presented on an electronic board. Messages can flash in colors when they cross certain thresholds to alert others to adjust their work.

The boards can be large for many people to see across a large room. They can be small enough to fit on top of your PC so no one can claim a blocked view. In fact, some companies have installed display boards on top of the users' desktops along with the agents' so important messages can be delivered to the correct audience very quickly. If your Help Desk covers a large physical area or is organized into different groups, you may find it beneficial to have multiple boards that can be better targeted to the particular groups. These boards are relatively cheap, making them affordable for even small Help Desks.

Be careful in managing the messages displayed on the boards. Some Help Desks keep their messages directly related to the business at hand. While it is nice to announce someone's birthday or anniversary, you don't want a critical message to go unseen because your agents are so used to the board showing miscellaneous things. They need to know that when something scrolls across or flashes at them, they need to take immediate notice. Other Help Desks display messages related to the more personal side of the Help Desk. The boards are used to congratulate agents on achieving training or certifications. The boards can even display game scores or news events. These types of messages may generate more interest from the agents than the other news. If this is the case, the softer messages will get them used to looking at the boards and business information will have a better chance of being read.

A blend of the two is probably best. Perhaps you can differentiate the message types by color with Help Desk–related news in one color and miscellaneous messages in another. If the board is large enough, you could devote the top rows to one type and the bottom to the other.

Web Page

A Web page on the Internet or intranet is a fantastic tool to service your customers. It is available day or night and can reach all your customers equipped with a simple browser. There are three categories of service that a web page can offer:

- Sharing of information
- Gather feedback
- Interactive processes

Sharing of Information

A Web page is best used to share information with its viewers. Remember one of the goals from the beginning was to become the hub of information. Web pages can be easily updated, visually appealing, and rich in content. The information can be seen on the screen or printed out for future reference. In fact, the ability to distribute information without having to print, make copies, and mail to everyone is one of the Web's biggest advantages. Below are some common items you can put on your Help Desk's Web page.

Troubleshooting Guides

Part of the effort to empower your customers and reduce incoming calls to the Help Desk is to provide troubleshooting guides to your users. For example, the basic steps to connect a PC to the network or fix a jammed printer can be documented and put on the Web. Then, customers can access this information when they need to resolve their own issues. Furthermore, they can print out the troubleshooting guide and put it next to the printer. Now, it is available at the point of the problem. Don't promote this printing too much though, as it takes away the benefit of updating the documents as new features or issues arise.

Frequently Asked Questions

Frequently Asked Questions (FAQs) are related to troubleshooting guides. You can create FAQs by assimilating the most common calls your Help Desk receives and publishing them in one document. As opposed to a troubleshooting guide, which walks through all possibilities of a topic, FAQs combine the results with the highest impact. Sample FAQs for Microsoft Word, for example, could include

- How can I save my work?
- How can I change the size of my characters?
- How can I print a single page of my document?

You would probably not include deeper topics like macros, bookmarks, or hyperlinks unless they were widely used in your course of business.

Calendar of Events

A calendar of upcoming events is another nice feature on the Web. It doesn't necessarily have to be a true calendar, but it does show what things are happening when. These could include planned system downtimes, next releases or upgrades of software, or even the Help Desk's hours of operations. Your customers can use this information to better plan their own events. It would be highly unproductive for a customer's site to plan a work weekend to catch up on work and that be the same weekend you are taking the system down for maintenance. This calendar can make them aware and able to plan their operations within your plans.

Whom to Call for What

As your Help Desk gets bigger or more specialized, there will be more questions from the customer base on whom to call for what. If I have a follow-up question, do I always call the central number or do I call someone else? You may also find this if you are getting calls for issues that are not related to the Help Desk. If you find this happening, it may be worth your while to publish outside items in this section. Your overriding goal is to serve your customers, and if you can point them in the right direction for any of their needs, you are doing well.

Metrics

We spent a chapter discussing metrics and measurements and whom to give them to. Why not make them available on the Web page? This is a fine way to show your constituents how your operations and agents perform. Obviously your metrics are constantly changing, but the Web page is easy to update and can handle this type of work. You can also get a bit more fancy displaying measurements on a Web page rather than on a piece of paper. Viewers can expand, shrink, or drill down for more information if you set it up that way. This makes the measurements even more powerful as the viewer can see them from a multitude of angles.

Service Level Agreements

Your service level agreements are worthless if your customers are not aware of them. They also will not have the correct expectations around service if they don't know how you are set up to operate. Providing the service level agreement and current performance against that agreement on the Web is another way to easily keep your customers informed and up to date.

Status of Issues

For projects that last a long time, you can provide statuses on the Help Desk page. You could start with a list and allow the viewer to drill down for more specifics. The project's description, its intended benefits, timelines, and even related training material can all be linked from this spot.

Statuses of hot issues can also appear on the Web page. If customers can become used to looking on the Web page for the status of open issues, it can help reduce incoming calls to the Help Desk and reserve more of the agent's time for resolving problems.

Online Presentations

If speakers at annual meetings, regional presentations, etc., save their presentations, you can put their slide shows on the Web page. With this tool, all others in the organization can see what information is being disseminated even if they were unable to attend. This helps everyone feel a part of the team and helps keep alignment of the associates from the highest person to those lower on the organization chart.

These are just a few examples of the types of information you can share on a Help Desk Web page. You can get even more information and ideas by reviewing your incoming calls. Look at common themes from the callers and post them on the Web, too. This is a win-win proposition. Your customers get the information they are seeking, your call volume goes down, and you can expose the customers to other topics as they look for what they want.

Gather Feedback

The Web page can also be used to gather feedback from your customers. It can be as easy as a "click here to send a message" or a survey that prompts the viewer for answers to your questions. You can have it anonymous, ask the viewers for their names and phone numbers but not require it, or require them to complete that information. If your network is configured for it, you can even capture the network address of the responder and find out who it was. This can come in handy for verifying that the responders are who they say they are. You could use it to identify the anonymous person as well, but that would be cheating.

The Web page is for sharing information as we discussed, so use this opportunity to share the results of the feedback with the users. All the input you receive may not be appropriate for publication, but most of it should be. If others can see that you are not afraid to share responses and are willing to learn from them, they will be more willing to provide yet more feedback or even assume more patience while you work through the issues. Don't forget the positive feedback that can show readers you are doing things well also!

Interactive Processes

The third benefit of a Help Desk Web page is its ability to interact with the person accessing it. You can design the page to do more than display information or ask for feedback. The page can also perform actions depending on the viewer's request. Below are some examples of its interaction.

A Media to Contact Help Desk Agents

The Web page may bring to light questions for the people using it or they may go to the page specifically to ask a question. The Web is good for this. A simple and cost-attractive option is to have the viewer ask a question and the system send an agent an e-mail message with the question in it. The agent can then find the answer and contact the viewer with the answer. Another way is to tie the page into your phone system. In this case, the viewer clicks on an agent or group's name and the system automatically calls the appropriate party. This is cool stuff but is more expensive than a regular e-mail system.

Close to that and far more inexpensive is chat. *Chat* is a medium similar to e-mail but is more interactive. Think of it as a combination of e-mail and phone conversations. When you call someone on the phone you contact them once, and then have a conversation with that person until you end the connection. E-mail prompts you for an address each time it is sent. Chat combines the two by contacting the receiver once (phone) but the conversation occurs by typing (e-mail). Chat is a very effective tool to communicate short messages without having to search people down or wait on hold.

Training

My systems training group implemented a Web-based learning set of classes off our Help Desk page. It listed the classes offered, so the viewers could access the particular class they wanted. The page then asked them to log in and proceeded to display training information on the topic. Mixed within was a series of questions that tested the users on the information that had been presented. Their answers were stored (using the login data they provided) and graded. At the end, if a person had a passing grade, he was informed and could move on. If a person had a failing grade, he was also notified and was advised to review the documentation at a later date. This information could be e-mailed to his supervisor as was warranted.

Procurement

Chapter 22 will go over procurement services your Help Desk can offer, but remember that a Web page is a great place to start it. In fact, this is a form of e-commerce that is the buzz these days! The good thing about offering purchasing options from your Web page is that you also get a chance to display any standards, best practices, and troubleshooting guides along with the purchasing section. This can also tie in nicely to your asset management and change management processes. What better way to know of equipment or software coming into the organization than with the very purchase of it!

Some organizations use this opportunity to get the vendors to help fund the page and its upkeep. This can be done by displaying the vendor's logo next to the items to be purchased, like a billboard, or by the mere fact that that particular vendor is the only one listed for that product or service. The vendor will probably want to see the number of times the page is accessed on a regular basis to help them justify their "advertising" on your page. This type of reporting is easy to do and there are many packages that can help you perform this task.

An even better use of resources is to get the vendor to set it up for you and provide a link from your own page to theirs. This can serve as your own private portal into the vendor. If he is set up for it, the vendor can easily maintain his own product catalog from his site, which will pass easily into your system. This gives the user a consistently updated program and the vendor has something that can best tie into his own system.

Web Page Design

The task of designing a Web presence can be quite daunting. It is a constant interface with your customers and how it looks and operates will make a direct impression (much like an ACD system) on your customers. With that kind of weight to carry around, you want to get it right.

The best way to do that is to treat this as if you were starting your Help Desk all over again. Don't reread this whole book, but you should bring back the same process you used for the building of the Help Desk. Only this time, create a work team of agents to help you do it.

Again, the work team should repeat many of the same steps you used for the Help Desk. It should interview customers and existing associates to see what they need. It should also determine what skill sets the customers have so you can measure their ability to even use the Web page for the things identified. If the customers are not strong technically, they may have a harder time using the services from the Web page. The work team also has the benefit of reviewing current processes and procedures from the Help Desk to see what actions and questions can be utilized through the Web.

Once the work team has a good list of ideas, it needs to organize them in ways that will make sense to the future user of the Web page. In just a moment, we will go over some recommendations for organizing your page. Don't just sit down and begin coding the pages from the list of ideas, though. It would pay off to sketch out these ideas on paper to ensure the flow of information works well. Once the design is done, it will be much easier to code from that instead of coding from a list of ideas that people thought of.

Finally, once all that is done, you need to announce and promote the Web presence just as you did the Help Desk. Show the customers and agents the benefits of using the Web and encourage them to use it wherever possible. Listen to their feedback and be willing to adapt your ideas towards their suggestions.

Once the Web page is in full production mode, you can disassemble the work team. You should not, however, leave the Web page on its own from now on. If a lot of people are using your Web pages or are accessing them for information on important processes, you may look into devoting someone full time to the maintenance and support of the pages. Your company may have Webmasters already, but if your volume can justify it, find out if you can have your own. The Web can be a contact medium just as your phones and e-mail are, and you have agents devoted to that. You will know from reports and customer feedback if the Web pages are worth this resource. If done right, it may be an easy decision for anyone to make.

Many books and seminars are devoted to Web page design, and I recommend that you pursue them as your Help Desk's page gets larger and is more heavily used. Until then, here are three simple guidelines to keep in mind:

- Ensure the information is easy to find
- Display the pages efficiently
- Design the pages so you can track their usage

Easy to Find Information

The first guideline is to keep the information easy to find. The rule of thumb is to keep all information within three clicks. This means that viewers should only have to click on links or pages three times before they reach their desired place.

This can be hard to do, and although it's not required, you should think about it after you come up with your Web page's initial design.

One easy way to help in this effort is to keep the most important information closer to the top of the page or make it easily accessible from the home page. This goes for information that is most frequently requested. People don't want to waste a lot of time looking for something they need. Because you want your Web page to be an effective tool for your agents and your customers, keep the "good stuff" available and easy to find.

You may want to include a "How to use this Web page" section on your home page. It can actually be on the home page or you can provide a link to it on another page, but this information can show the user what is contained in the Web pages and the general format of it. Much like a table of contents and chapter summaries in a book, a how-to section on the Web will make the experience for first-time users more enjoyable and productive.

Efficient Display Criteria

Another related guideline is to keep your page efficient in its display. Snazzy graphics that flash and scroll across the screen look pretty but can get in the way. They take up valuable bandwidth, which can cause other problems for your system. The user ultimately wants the answer to a question and does not want to wait for pretty pictures to pop up. The pages do not have to be Spartan, but keep the graphics in check.

If you use your Web page to attract new customers, you may need to use the snazzy graphics and display options more generously than if your customers are already locked in. Sometimes the presentation wins the initial round and can give your Help Desk a shot at business. You still will need to deliver the goods at the end, but every little bit helps in attracting business.

Track Usage

You really need to track how your page is used. This is a good metric to add to your list discussed earlier. Who hits it is important, but what is hit is even more beneficial. A page with an inordinate amount of hits compared to the others should be recognized. You will need to pay attention to its design so that it is efficient. You should also review what is on it and how it works to see if there are items you can carry over to lesser-used pages.

For pages that are not hit much, if at all, you also need to pay attention. Why isn't anyone going to them? Are they so hard to find that no one even knows they are there? Maybe the information on these pages is out of date or irrelevant to the needs of your customers. This is good to know so you can update the pages or kill them altogether.

Computer Lab

A working computer lab is another tremendously valuable tool for your Help Desk. While physical limits may determine its feasibility, a lab allows your agents to "see" a problem with their own eyes and allows troubleshooting to occur without tying up a user on the phone while you guess (though as an expert, of course) your way to a solution. A lab also allows you to experiment with new functionality without affecting the production environment.

Stock the lab well. Include as many of the technologies as you can that your customers use. We have spoken in previous chapters about providing your agents with the same hardware and software your customers use, and a computer lab is a perfect place to store them. A lab is also a good place to keep technologies your research departments are beginning to look at. Why wait until your customers are already using a product before your agents get to see and use it?

If budget allows, build your lab with proper planning from the beginning. Give yourself plenty of storage cabinets, drawers, and bins. Keep some of them locked so items that always seem to disappear can stay around longer. Make your desk space really deep to accommodate large monitors with tools in front of it. Run a power strip and network connections all the way around your lab so agents can plug in anywhere without searching for an outlet. At one company, we built the lab as an extension of our computer room so it had air conditioning, raised floors, and was power protected with an Uninterruptable Power Supply and diesel generator. This is overkill for a lab but it came in handy on several occasions.

Even if you have lockable cabinets, I strongly recommend you lock the doors to the lab when agents are not in. A working lab is typically full of equipment and it may take a while to notice a laptop or monitor missing. Tools and peripherals like modems or NIC cards are frequently taken from a lab with best intentions to be returned, but are quickly forgotten when the next fire needs to be put out.

Additional Knowledge Management

Earlier, we discussed expert systems within call management packages. This expertise was really the information your agents and others put into the database. Nowadays this is referred to as "knowledge" and the value of capturing it electronically is gaining acceptance. There are ways to manage this knowledge and distribute it to others, such as fax backs and documentation.

Fax Back

Fax back is a customer self-service tool that allows a customer to receive documentation of information without having to talk to an agent and it is available any time day or night. Fax back is a technology that walks a caller through a menu of options and automatically faxes the caller with the chosen document. It is a great way to give access to standards and policies and troubleshooting guides without human interference. This tool can be replaced by the Internet or intranet, but is nice for those customers without that type of access. Visually it could work like this when a customer calls this system:

From a touchtone phone
Press 1 for documents on PC Best Practices
Press 2 for information on troubleshooting printers
Press 3 for a DME Help Desk agent listing
......
Press 1 to return fax to the line you called from
Press 2 to enter a different fax line
......
Thank you for calling DME's fax back system

Documentation

A call management package can create much efficiency in your process, but sometimes you can't beat good old documentation. The call package is only good when you are with a device capable of running it; what about when you are away from your desk and need help? Documentation of wiring diagrams or network layouts may be needed while sitting next to a router or phone closet, for example. Aside from technical specifications, one document that is extremely beneficial to a Help Desk is one that describes policies and procedures and Best Practices.

Whereas a call package gives you answers, a policy manual helps define what is expected of your Help Desk in the implementation of those answers. It could describe hours of operation, the timing of monthly batch runs, or proper escalation and reporting procedures. You could present the policy manual as a rules and regulations document, but it will be perceived much better if it is offered as a guideline to help those who need it.

Best Practices documentation can be your policies and procedures document for your customers. It shows them how your support offering can best be used in the workplace. For example, you can request users to power down their PCs at night, save their data every so often, or use spreadsheets versus heavy databases. When mixed in with a service level agreement, Best Practices are even more effective because they help align what you expect the user to do along with the operations of your Help Desk.

Documentation is a wonderful tool for agents to resolve problems. Having an area where manuals and documentation can be centrally stored is very helpful to a Help Desk. It can also include trade magazines and training brochures (maybe even this book!) for work-related reading. Increasingly, corporate intranets or CDs are replacing library needs but there are times when nothing can beat grabbing the book and digging into a problem.

| Note | *No one ever really claims to read the manual; it is an affront to one's purported expertise. Put PCs in the library for Internet research to expand your agents' readings even further. Do this and you can call it a media resource center for an even fancier name!* |

Quick Recap

- What tools in this chapter do you already have in your Help Desk? Are they providing you the return on the investment you anticipated? They should, but if they are not, have someone help you review their implementation.

- Whether you refer to it as call management, problem management, or contact management, you need software to help you manage the interaction between your customers and the Help Desk. How do you perform this function now? Does it offer the same services that were listed in this chapter?

- Telephony tools provide a professional and effective front end to your customers. Can your phone system handle the tools discussed? Is your Help Desk organized to facilitate a phone system that helps you route calls better?

- A Web page is another professional front end for your customers. Do you have an intranet within which your Help Desk can build a Web page? Do you have the skill set in the Help Desk or IT department to publish this work?

- Knowledge management is a valuable process to undertake. How would you be affected if your most senior agent were to leave? How about if something were to happen to you? Have you taken the time to share with others the processes you work through to get work done?

CHAPTER 16

Developing Your People

So far, we have covered implementing new processes and acquiring more tools to help get the job done more efficiently for your customers. The growth and existence of your Help Desk cannot be maintained, however, without the constant nurturing and development of the people who staff the Help Desk. Without your people, your tools will sit unused and your best processes cannot be carried out. As someone responsible for building and managing a Help Desk, you must pay attention to your associates and their needs. They can take you and the operation to greater heights than any tool or process can hope to.

Developing your associates will be one of the most important responsibilities you will undertake in your career. This chapter is devoted to processes and ideas to help you achieve this goal.

What to Look For

- A Help Desk agent's career life cycle is depicted graphically in this chapter. This life cycle has several phases that mark the progress of the agent's career over time. I will describe each of these phases in detail and provide hints on how you can recognize them. I will also discuss the responsibilities you have as a manager when those phases are reached.

- Providing feedback to your agents is probably the most important thing you can do to help them succeed. A very powerful tool to do this is an associate review. Time should be taken to make the review process a learning experience for the associate and the reviewer. From this interaction, the associates will learn what they are doing right and what issues they have to improve upon.

- Teamwork is a foundation from which Help Desks can grow and succeed. While you might have a functioning Help Desk without its members acting as a team, the Help Desk will be significantly enhanced in its productivity and efficiency if the agents all act as a team.

- People and teams need managers at one level or another. This chapter will walk you through ideas on identifying future managers and ways you can incorporate them into your organization.

Agent Career Life Cycle

The Agent Career Life Cycle, shown in Figure 16-1, is a graphical depiction of the career advancement Help Desk agents will find themselves in over the course

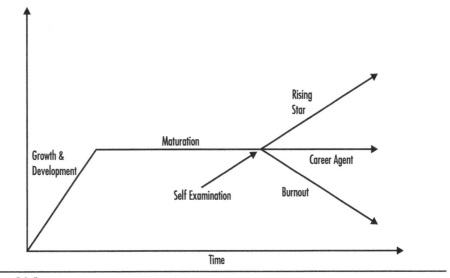

Figure 16.1   Agent Career Life Cycle

of time. Along the way, several events will guide the agents from one milestone to the next. These milestones are not formal objectives everyone speaks about over lunch, but they represent the issues and challenges all agents will face at one point or another.

The vertical axis shows the advancement of an agent's career as seen from an organizational chart or responsibilities viewpoint. The horizontal axis is the time that passes as the agent's career continues. This time is not a standard measurement because it differs from one agent to the next. One agent may reach the maturation stage in a matter of weeks because of his past experience and skill sets. For another agent, this stage may take months or even years to reach. How fast an agent reaches each stage is not the point of this graph, although it may affect the agent in terms of compensation and promotion opportunities. Instead, the timing of the graph should help you and the agent understand common issues you both will face at that particular stage. Let's walk through each stage and discuss the things you as a manager should be aware of.

Growth and Development Stage

This stage of an agent's career represents the beginning of his career. The agent has just been brought on board and should be energetic, motivated, and willing to learn everything it takes to be successful.

Even if the associate has prior work experience in the Help Desk environment, he still has much to learn. Your company will probably have different procedures and your customers will behave differently. The technologies you support may be the same, but your customers may use them for varying applications and business situations. The point is that even the most experienced agent starting on your Help Desk is not beyond this growth and development stage. He may not stay in it as long as other agents, but there are always opportunities to learn and grow.

Manager's Responsibilities During Growth and Development

The stage of growth and development explicitly implies that the agent will be learning new things at the beginning of his new career in your Help Desk. The manager's job is to make sure the environment surrounding the agent is conducive to learning. The manager should look for ways to motivate the new agent and help guide him through the intricacies of the Help Desk or your company. Putting some of your best existing agents alongside the newer agents will help them learn what works and what does not in your particular environment. Encouragement should be more visible at this stage than during other stages to keep the upward drive of the agent intact. Also, opportunities to attend training classes or get involved in multiple projects should be made available. The agent is as willing to accumulate knowledge now as he ever will be so take advantage of a receptive audience.

Maturation

After the agent has grasped the job, he begins the stage of his career called maturation. The agent reaches this stage when he understands the job requirements and the expectations that come with them. He has received formal training and experienced many of the events and issues that can come an agent's way. Although issues may arise to challenge him and make him think, the agent is basically in cruise control.

This stage will typically last longer than the other stages. This is not a bad place for an agent to be either. Help Desks need quality agents who understand what is expected of them and are comfortable with it. Agents are still learning and should still gain new skills, but the core aptitude of the job is in their grasp.

Manager's Responsibilities

A manager should begin to concentrate more on understanding the career direction of the agent during this stage. Time should be taken to meet with the agent and learn what he likes and dislikes about the job. His input is valuable to make the job better for other agents and for the individual associate. The manager should be a good coach and give good feedback for work done well and accomplishments reached. Where the agent's performance is not up to standard, the manager should let him know so the situation can be improved. This feedback is very beneficial to the agent in the maturation stage.

Self Examination

An important point of an agent's career is self examination. Neither the agent nor the manager will know when this exact point in time has been reached, but it definitely marks a potential turning point in the rest of the agent's career. From this point, there are three paths the agent can take:

- Rising star
- Career agent
- Burnout

The agent will not declare any of these verbatim, but his actions and feelings toward the job will be in one of these directions. Here, the agent has begun to look around and wonder if this career is right for him. He will review the past, anticipate future possibilities, and ponder what it might take to get there.

Manager's Responsibilities

The manager's view is very similar. She has reviewed the agent's career and his achievements, compared his skill set to those of the other agents, and begun to plan what the next opportunities may be for that agent. Depending on this view, the manager may plan additional or different training, begin discussions with the agent about his own wishes and career objectives, and try to match those wishes with other job opportunities that will be available. Table 16-1 shows how the views of the agent and manager can be seen from different angles.

Consistent reviews and communications will show the manager and associate if their respective views are aligned or not. Later in this chapter, we will go over associate reviews and methods you can use to get the most out of the interaction. If the views are out of alignment and there is disagreement over the potential advancement of the agent, neither party should ignore it. The agent particularly won't ignore it because his career and livelihood are at stake. The manager should not ignore it either because the sooner problems can be addressed, the less negative impact they will have on the rest of the organization.

Career Path	Agent View	Manager View
Rising Star	Agent has mastered the skill sets needed for the current job.	Agent has mastered the job and demonstrated traits needed for the next level of responsibility.
Career Agent	Agent has a full understanding of the current job and really likes it. Job's hours, expectations, and recognition align well with the agent's own goals.	Agent has done well in the job but does not show enough of right traits to move to the next level.
Burnout	Job has worn agent down. Agent cannot handle customers' constant problems with minimal appreciation from them.	Agent's job performance is slipping. Agent doesn't work with the team. Agent treats customers with no compassion or professionalism.

Table 16.1   Two Views of an Agent's Career

Rising Star

A rising star is an agent who realizes he is good at this job and is looking for more opportunities. From the manager's perspective, the rising star could be someone with great potential even though he has not expressed it yet. In either case, this person is someone you want to take care of. If you do not begin managing this associate's career, frustration may set in and the associate will begin looking elsewhere for more opportunities.

Many people have talked about not wanting to have too many rising stars on their team because there would be too much competition for open positions and the rising stars would be harder to manage. While I agree that you probably don't want every one of your agents to be a rising star, you sure want a majority of them to be. Look at it selfishly. If you have no one who is ready or willing to step up to the next level and you are up for a promotion, do you think the company would promote you without anyone in line to replace you? Maybe, but maybe not.

Your challenge with many rising stars will be finding increasing levels of responsibility for them. Some of these may be formal promotions within the organization, but they can also be lateral moves that expose the associate to new and different job functions. The agents have proven they can handle the current load you have given them; now give them even more. Even if there are not any open positions to move your rising star into, there will always be other responsibilities within the Help Desk they can learn.

Just as the growth and development stage showed an associate moving up in skills and responsibilities, the agent in the rising star phase will also be moving up. If you don't have any formal duties available, give him some of your own to see how well he performs. This is great training ground for him to learn new skills, and it also gives you an opportunity to see him in action. Don't let the fear that you cannot keep rising stars happy prevent you from growing agents into that role. There is always plenty of work on a Help Desk to keep many people happy and contributing.

Career Agent

A career agent is someone who seems to be content with carrying the maturation phase out indefinitely. Career agents understand their role and are perfectly happy staying in it for the foreseeable future. Because of family commitments or other contingencies that may be outside the professional atmosphere, these associates enjoy knowing their hours each day and what the work will typically be like from day to day. When we spoke of having many rising stars in your organization, the only other career path you want is the career agent.

Career agents will form the foundation of your Help Desk and will allow it to run solidly over time. Rising stars will grow the Help Desk as well but they will then move to other opportunities up or outside the Help Desk path. Career agents are extremely valuable associates and you need to recognize them as early as possible. If you don't, you risk giving them too much responsibility, and they will lose interest in the job altogether and this can lead to burnout.

It may seem obvious that everyone wants more responsibility and opportunities to move up the corporate ladder. If you believe that, you may think you are rewarding career agents by increasing their duties or promoting them into management positions. However, what you will have done by accident is move these agents into positions they do not want and this will make them feel anxious and nervous. Their well-known day will be disrupted and things they never had to worry about before may become a normal part of their day. If this goes on unchecked, you will soon lose those career associates.

Ignoring career agents completely is less of a problem, but it still needs to be addressed. Career agents are indeed happy with their spot in their job but would probably not turn down attention and recognition. Moderate increases in compensation, training, and responsibilities will never be turned down and will serve to keep them comfortable.

All this is not to portray career agents as simpletons who have no ambition or possess minor skills. They are hard working agents who provide quality customer service and help keep the Help Desk alive. They are just even-keeled and don't need major changes to keep them motivated. For whatever reason, the Help Desk provides them the challenge and satisfaction they need in a job. Don't label them poorly or downgrade them in your mind; use them to the advantage of the Help Desk and its customers.

Burnout

Chapter 11 was devoted to the burnout phase of an agent's career so we will not spend much time on it here. Burnout can happen at any point but can be easily prevented by staying in touch with your associates and understanding what they need from the job to keep them happy and challenged. Your rising stars may become burned out if they don't see any movement or promotional opportunities available for them anytime soon. Career agents may get burned out if they are pressured to do more than they are comfortable with or are not appreciated or compensated at all for their work.

Some people will just burn out from the pressure of the Help Desk job itself. It cannot be emphasized enough that the Help Desk agent gets significantly more complaints from customers than calls of appreciation. On really bad days when the system keeps crashing or the latest technology has been implemented incorrectly, an agent will experience as low a job satisfaction day as any other profession. The goal is to balance those awful days with other times of high satisfaction and opportunities. Most people only need to know that there is light at the end of the tunnel, even though they cannot see it for themselves yet.

Associate Reviews

An important factor in keeping associates happy and on track is to give them feedback. While this should occur throughout the year informally, you should have a formal time set aside each year to sit down with your associates and review their performance. From this discussion, the associates will learn how they are doing in the job and what things they can improve. To help you with this effort, this section will discuss aspects of performance reviews, the review process overall, and the review form itself. Yes, a written form that captures the topics and issues you want covered.

The Process

The review process should be a formal event that is planned ahead of time so all parties can be prepared. Managers need to know what this time period is because they are the ones actually conducting the review. The associates being reviewed should know this time as well, so they can come prepared with any issues or questions they would like to discuss.

Avoid Surprises in the Review

This preparation period brings up one rule that you should strive to always follow—the review's content should never surprise the associate. The associate may not be able to predict each and every comment you put on the form, but he should not be blown away by anything either. For an associate to not know he is being graded poorly or superbly means the manager and the associate have not communicated well between the reviews. All through the year the manager should be working with the associates on their performance and discussing how things could improve or stay the same. The perfect review conversation is one in which these issues are reinforced or commended and the associate only learns more about the impact of the issues. So make a note: reviews should be boring with regard to surprises.

Frequency of Reviews

How frequently you conduct reviews depends to a certain extent on the rest of the company. Your formal review communications should never be less frequent than the rest of the company's. In fact, if there is an opportunity to have more interactions, you should do so. Because you are constantly communicating with the associates, though, you do not need to have more than two formal sessions a year. This may be hard to do if your staff is very large, because writing and giving a review that is truly valuable for the associate takes time and effort on your part. However, associates will always take feedback, and keeping them aligned with the company and your own goals may make multiple reviews a year necessary.

Time with Pay Adjustments

Regardless of the frequency of the review, you should try to have the review occur close to the same time as any annual increases or bonuses. Written reviews are nice and can really impact how associates act or perform, but typically nothing gets their attention or affects their performance more than money.

A review saying "Your performance was lackluster this year and you really need to improve," is certainly backed up if you also follow it with "So therefore your raise this year will be substantially less than last year's." However, a review saying "Your attitude continues to be superb and the customers really like dealing with you" is nice, but if you follow with "and I would like to give you 10 percent more than the company average for this work," your message will really be received well!

If the reviews cannot be given at the same time as any pay adjustments, it is still important to refer back to the review when you give or don't give pay increases. The connection will not be there from a time standpoint, so you will need to make that connection in the conversation.

The Review Itself

Review time can be a stressful period for associates. Despite all the feedback you have provided along the way, the agent will still be nervous about what will be said in the review. How can they know what you really think until you communicate it during this formal occasion? This seems like a rhetorical question, but it is true for most people. An agent can certainly think he is doing a good job each day, but sometimes it is just hard to tell what a manager will say. Unfortunately, an associate with extended tenure has probably had at least one "surprise" review from a prior manager, so until you can prove that you work differently, he will probably be expecting the same from you.

Face-to-Face

The review should be face-to-face if at all possible. Mailing a review form for someone to read or calling them on the phone cannot equate to the interpersonal qualities a face-to-face conversation can have. E-mails and phone calls don't allow for body language or facial expression, and e-mails don't even allow for tone of voice, all of which are vital to effective communication. Meeting directly with the associate removes those barriers.

Honest and Candid

We have spoken about the uncertainties the review can bring, but the uncertainties must end before the review is over. The conversation must be honest and candid and should provide the associate a full recap of the past year, month, or whatever time period your review covers. Some people suggest that reviews should be only good or only bad. This is puzzling because it forces the reviewer down a path that might not fit the associate being reviewed.

Saying only good things when there are issues to be dealt with is hiding important information from the associates. Issues will not magically go away if associates do not know about them. Aside from ignoring problems, you may also run into trouble if the problems do not go away and an associate needs to be terminated. There might be legal issues if you need to fire someone but he can show that his last several review forms were all glowing and complimentary.

Noting only bad things on a review is not much better. While you may have passed the message about an associate's issues and shortcomings, you have not given him anything to build upon. In this case, the associate leaves the conversation feeling like a complete failure and questions whether this career is right for him.

Without a doubt the best possible review is one in which both the positives and the negatives of an associate's performance are brought out and discussed. You can show him where he needs to improve, point out the areas in which he is succeeding, and share any other information pertinent to the Help Desk.

Give Specific Examples

Honesty and candor should be a goal for all reviews. To give your comments even more meaning for the associate, you should provide specific examples to back up your comments wherever possible. "You really need to be more courteous when you speak with customers" is much more effective if you can also say, "Last week when you were helping the Greenville store manager, you upset him when you worked on his printing problem." With this additional information, the associate can relate what you are saying to an event and should be able to see your point easier. Without these examples, it is up to the associate to align what you are saying with his actions.

Giving specific examples also allows the associate to explain his actions. There may have been extenuating circumstances you are not aware of that could redeem the agent in your eyes. Be careful that the associate does not spend a lot of time defending each and every point you make. At some point, the principle behind the examples is more important than knowing there was a reason driving every problem you bring up.

Show Impact on Company's Goal

Along with examples, it is beneficial if you can show the associate how his actions impact the company and its goals. It may be very hard to directly tie an agent's actions to the profitability of the company at large, but the more you can show how he is directionally aligned the better. You want your agents to work hard for themselves and their careers and you also want them to work hard for the company and its customers. To continue to work hard, they need to see how they are related to the company. Reviews can serve to tie their performance to their career and future as well as to the benefit of the company.

Linking the Help Desk's work to company goals may be found in customer surveys or from other forms of customer feedback such as, "The report you created last week for Bryan in San Diego ended up being shown at the annual sales convention. It is being used as an example of how salesman can use information to land new sales accounts in declining markets." This is a fantastic statement you can pass along to an agent that will make him feel proud that his work matters and is contributing to the rest of the company.

The Actual Review Form

Now that you have an idea of how you want the review process to transpire, you need to take some time to formulate the review form itself. Remember that this process is formal and should be documented. There should be much conversation during the review, but the written form should always be included.

Your company may completely control the actual review form so there may not be much leeway in its format. If there is a chance for you to have your own review form, please seize that opportunity. If there is not and you must use the standard company template, you will need to do that. I recommend that you add more information either to the form, through an addendum, or worst case, incorporate it into your conversation. For the purposes of this book, I will assume you can have a hand in shaping your own form.

Numbers Versus Comments

There are several varieties of reviews and most are effective. Some use a rating scheme of numbers to grade an associate. An example of this can be grading someone on a scale of one to five for each category:

	Poor		Average		Excellent
Customer satisfaction	1	2	3	4	(5)
Works well with team	1	2	3	(4)	5

Other reviews use comments where the reviewer writes notes and thoughts for each category as in this example:

Customer satisfaction

Brantlee continues to receive excellent feedback from the customers she serves. I have never received a complaint about her work. She is one of the best Help Desk agents we have on the team.

Yet even other reviews use a combination of the two, rating the associate with numbers and comments. This combination is the best method. Reviewing someone with a numbered scale by itself certainly allows for easy comparison from agent to agent or year to year, but it does not tell the agent much more than that. Comments alone are more descriptive, but their subjectivity does not allow for good comparison between agents or even between the reviewers.

The combination of numbers and comments gives you the best of both worlds. The associate can quickly see their rating by reviewing the numbers and can read your comments to understand the numbers better. Of course, neither of these should replace the conversation, but it will allow the associate to leave with something tangible to go over afterward.

Sections

It is good to have two separate sections on the review form. One is standard and crosses all job titles. The other is more flexible and is used to review the performance of a particular job title or associate.

The standard section is used for all associates. It includes categories and topics associated with everyone on the team. These are typically soft skills such as teamwork, customer service, responsibility, prioritization, and showing initiative. The goal of this section is to grade the associate on items that are important to his job, but are more general in nature.

The second section serves to give the reviewer more leeway in grading the associate both for his particular job responsibilities and his position in the company. These items may include management skills or technical aptitude that will not apply to every Help Desk agent, although they are very relevant to any managers or more specialized members of the team. Without this section, you would need to leave certain items blank for many Help Desk members or be so general that it would be hard to complete reviews in a standard way for everyone.

A good place to develop the actual items and topics that make up these sections is the job description. The job description will show the qualifications someone needs to perform the job as well as objectives he or she needs to achieve while in the job. You will need to do some work to translate the job description into a reviewable format, but this will get you started on the form.

Career Interests

At the end of the review, you should include a section showing the associate his future in the company. This is where you can get and set expectations for actual jobs or job responsibilities that you and the agent are interested in pursuing. The agent can add his own remarks and wishes along with those of the reviewer.

The important part of this section is to make sure the expectations are properly set. Just tossing out that someone might reach a certain job is wrong and unproductive. Showing an agent what it will take to get that job or achieve other goals is the purpose of this part of the review.

Figure 16-2 is an example review given to a rising star agent.

Developing Teams

Here is a test for the mathematicians reading this book. When is the following formula true?

$$1 + 1 + 1 + 1 = 5$$

It is true when you are counting the effectiveness of four agents that work in a Help Desk that operates as a team. It is an old adage that says the whole is greater than the sum of its parts, and this cannot be more true than in a strong Help Desk team. The ability to get your agents to work together in such a strong fashion that they truly consider themselves part of a team should be a primary and continual goal of any Help Desk manager or leader.

Why Teams Are Important

Teamwork in a Help Desk is one of the more important keys to achieving customer satisfaction. Customers like to be treated nicely and professionally, and they want their issues heard. If agents can act together to respond to a ringing phone or an unread list of e-mails, customers will get their chance to be heard. However, if your agents work individually and have an attitude of "That's not my problem; my work is caught up" or "It is time for me to leave no matter how busy the next guy is," then you have a long way to go toward being a team. The team players will answer any phone because it is best for the customers and the customers' perception of the Help Desk.

Teamwork comes in handy during spikes in call volume as well. Your Help Desk may be organized into separate groups that handle a particular technology or customer type. This is fine and appropriate in many instances.

Now let's say you divide your Help Desk agents into internal and external customer support and the systems for the internal customers crashed. Phones will be ringing off the hook and people may be standing in line at your desk to get attention. On the external side, all is well and many of your agents are reading training material for future releases. Wouldn't it be nice if some of the

DME Corporation

Associate Evaluation

Associate's Name: <u>Brantlee Lemmink</u>   Position: <u>Senior Help Desk Analyst</u>
Review Date: _____   Date of Last Review: <u>5/6/99</u>
Supervisor: JASON CAMPBELL   <u>HQ Info Sys</u>

Please rate the associate on each characteristic using both the numerical ratings and comment lines. The numerical ratings range from 1 for poor performance to 6 for completely exceeding expectations.

1. Self-motivation, initiative   1   2   3   4   5   6

<u>Brantlee has strong and positive motivation attributes and practices. She never hesitates to jump into areas that are in need of help.</u>
<u>A good example is last month's audit period where Brantlee worked extra long hours to resolve several printing problems they were having.</u>

2. Skill, competency in the position   1   2   3   4   5   6

<u>As a leader of a widely diverse group, Brantlee has to understand many skills and areas of competence. Her main skill is to recognize</u>
<u>situations and bring the appropriate resources to bear. I consider her my most skilled analyst in this role.</u>

3. Customer service   1   2   3   4   5   6

<u>A consistent strength of Brantlee's is the care of her customers. I look for her to raise the level of her team as well. She tends to take</u>
<u>many of the harder issues on herself and needs to let her team have a chance to prove themselves as well. There are never complaints</u>
<u>from the customers, however.</u>

4. Team player   1   2   3   4   5   6

<u>Brantlee is the consummate team player. She helps out anyone without a complaint. Again in a positive way I hope she lets</u>
<u>others get opportunities to reach her level.</u>

5. Communication skills   1   2   3   4   5   6

<u>Brantlee's role involves the notification of events as well as the setting of expectations of the customers and she does this well. Her e-mails</u>
<u>are descriptive and easy to understand. She is extremely proactive to the issues that need to be communicated.</u>

6. Ability to handle change   1   2   3   4   5   6

<u>No problems here. Brantlee's world changes from a variety of angles. She has increased her responsibilities, the techologies she</u>
<u>supports, and the projects that come her way. All this happens without negative comments from her.</u>

7. Shares ideas and best practices   1   2   3   4   5   6

<u>Brantlee is full of good ideas and she understands how to best mix technology and DME business. Her documents on PC Best</u>
<u>Practices were included in the Help Desk Organization's seminar series for its world class topics!</u>

8. Overall   1   2   3   4   5   6

<u>Brantlee's group is one of the largest in the department and she leads it well. It is important that she passes her strong skill set to those</u>
<u>associates on her team so they all can continue to excel. I see her next big step in the creation of the external customer support group.</u>
<u>She is a true leader and has had an excellent year. I look forward to her having an even more productive and valuable year coming.</u>

Career Development Objectives
<u>Create the external customer support group</u>
<u>Manage the entire Help Desk organization</u>
<u>Learn whatever technical competencies she has interest in</u>

Figure 16.2   Sample review form

Associate's Comments

_____

_____

_____

_____

_____   _____
Associate's Signature/Date   Supervisor's Signature/Date

Figure 16.2   Sample review form *(continued)*

external support agents could field some calls just long enough to get through the system crash notification? As a manager, you can certainly walk out and make some agents answer the phone, but it would sure be nicer if they recognized the situation themselves and helped out the others. This shows teamwork, and the calling customers will certainly appreciate it. There must be criteria when this can happen because you don't want to hurt the external customers by helping the internal ones, but this can be easily communicated and understood.

While customers want good treatment, they also want their issues resolved. When your agents are working as a team, they can help each other resolve open issues even though their own call logs are empty. Sammy may have a full log of high priority issues that customers are impatiently waiting on while Robert has just a couple of low priority items. If Sammy and Robert worked together as a team, they could ask each other for help and get the highest priority items resolved before the lower ones were worked on. Again, the manager could make this happen by constantly reviewing open call logs and sorting out the highest ones, but this will get increasingly harder as the size of the Help Desk grows. For members of the team to do this automatically would be much more effective and would contribute to a high degree of customer satisfaction.

Teams Can Be Formal or Informal

These teams I speak of do not have to be formal entities that march around in the same colored outfits. In fact, the examples given earlier can occur very informally and are more in the spirit of teamwork than happening within a formal team. In this spirit, cliques are not teams even though the people who are in cliques will probably work well together. You want your team players to feel a part of something as much as you make them a part of it. Ways to facilitate this will be discussed shortly.

Help Desks work best when people *act* as a team. The only team may be the Help Desk itself, or teams may be formal groups within the Help Desk. You may form teams by the support function they perform such as the internal and external support groups. The team may be formed by the time of day the agents work or the physical location of the Help Desk agents. You could have a day shift and night shift team or a United States team and a European team. Teams may be formal, though short in duration, such as those formed to work on special projects for finding a call management package or implementing some new technologies.

When you have formal teams within the Help Desk, you must maintain the overall objectives of the Help Desk's mission. Denise may be part of the Metro support team and does well there, but, more important, she must always know that she is also part of the Help Desk team.

This multi-teamed atmosphere is not hard to maintain—examples of it exist all around us. In football you have teams, be it the Redskins or Dolphins or Vikings. But within those teams, you also have the offense, defense, special teams, and practice squads. There may be players who participate in multiple places but they are always part of the entire football operation. There is no reason your Help Desk cannot work in the same manner.

How Teams Can Be Developed

The best way to get someone to do something is not to make him do it, but to get him to feel as if it was his idea in the first place. My wife doesn't make me do chores around the house, but finds ways to show me the benefits of my doing them. You can try to make your agents work as a team although you will be more successful if you create an environment where teamwork is beneficial and the agents will want to join up.

There are many ways to facilitate teamwork in the Help Desk. The first is by dealing with the agents in combined ways even though you do not mention the word *team* during the process. Having the agents all sit in the same area is a good start. The examples of agents helping each other on their own can be achieved much more simply if the agents are close enough to hear the challenges of their peers. It works much better for an agent to lean back and ask others for help than if she has to get up and walk over to someone else.

This book has brought up measurements many times and these can get people to act in certain ways. You can measure how well Tom and Frank and Allie do on their customer service surveys to reward their work. If you measure and report the three agents together, however, they will start to care more about the performance of the others. I know if I am graded or compensated in part by how my peers are doing, I will take some time to help them when they are having problems. I will also be more inclined to ask for their help when I need it. Call volumes, abandoned rates, and customer satisfaction are all good metrics to use in group measurements.

You can also do more obvious things to create teams and teamwork. The job titles of senior agents can be a starting point. Instead of having a *Senior Analyst* that coordinates the work of others, call that person a *Team Leader*. You have to hope that if someone is a team leader, there is an actual team of agents to lead.

If you have several groups of agents in an area, you could hang signs from the ceiling that specify the teams that work in that particular section. This can help walk-up traffic identify where certain groups are if they need help, but this will also help those agents sitting under the signs feel a part of something unique.

Finally, you can have the agents participate in team building events. Whether it is just a pizza party every month at lunch, drinks on a Friday evening, or a corporate-sponsored seminar that speaks directly to building and maintaining teams, the agents will see their peers in a slightly different light and perhaps can relate to them as people instead of some guy who sits next to them.

Developing Managers

The beginning of this chapter focused on developing the associates in the Help Desk. These individuals are vital to your success and great care needs to be taken so they continue to feel valuable. From there, these associates can form teams to get even more work done as a group. A next round of development is to grow certain individuals into managers. This process, which is continual and ever-changing, can be broken down into three broad categories:

- Identifying those associates who can be managers
- Offering the opportunity to those individuals
- Growing them further in the role

Identifying Associates Who Can Be Managers

First, let's begin with the fact that not all people are management material, nor do all people want to become managers. One of the most frustrating things you can take on is trying to make a person something he is not, so don't do it. Doing so will make the person miserable because you will be giving him responsibilities he does not want. You will be miserable because he will pass many of his problems on to you for advice or resolution. Most important, the people under the manager will be miserable because they will be managed by someone who does not have his heart in it. Managing people is an extremely difficult task that can take a lot of time and energy from you. This extra burden can be dealt with if the manager enjoys the work overall. All jobs have good and bad sides, and management is no different. There are not many more gratifying roles than watching the growth of an associate professionally and personally. This is made even more special by your having played a part in it.

By listening to their career plans and watching their work, you can decipher who can take on more responsibilities. These "potential managers" will typically come from the rising-star phase of the agent life cycle. Career agents do not want the extra work, and you certainly do not want to prevent burnout in people by promoting them into a position over others.

Don't let seniority be the main factor in picking managers either. Tenure may give an agent more experience in the daily happenings in your environment but it does not magically give him the qualifications to be a good manager. Many, many people will have problems with someone becoming a manager when they have been with the organization longer, and you must address this concern by meeting with the tenured person and explaining why he was not chosen. He may not agree but he can at least have some input to build from for the next opportunity.

As we discussed in the "Management Skills" section of Chapter 8, managers need to be good with people and good with processes. On the people side, they must be able to get quality work from their subordinates, deal with any professional or personal issues that affect the work environment, and deal with those outside the Help Desk to resolve escalated issues or questions. They need to learn when to delegate issues and when to keep control themselves.

On the process side, they need to be able to see across the whole organization to help determine priorities and workflow as well as align the right person with the right problem. They must be patient and understand the root cause of issues to best resolve them. Hastily making changes or snap decisions will many times cause more problems or lead to the loss of respect from your associates.

Offering Management Opportunities to Those Individuals

If you are unsure of an associate's ability to manage, but you need someone to step up, go informal for a while. Instead of making the desired associate a formal manager and moving people under him, make him a team leader at first. This person can "manage" the daily tasks of the group but does not have to deal with HR issues like compensation and career growth. This interim step will allow you to see the interaction of the group from both the up-and-coming manager's view and the view of the soon-to-be subordinates. If all works as you hoped, it is a minor step to bump the team leader to a more formal manager of the organization. If it does not, you can move him to another position with little fanfare. By that time, there may be a clear-cut candidate who can move in and take over formally.

The test of the success of the manager-in-training should not result by a vote of his subordinates. It is not proper to survey the people under the manager to find out how he did and if the "experiment" should continue. There may be opportunities to informally inquire of certain individuals you have a good history with and trust, but overall you should judge the effectiveness of the manager by the results he or she achieves. You should also be able to get a good sense whether the people respond well to the manager without having to flat out ask them.

Putting someone in a managerial role for the first time can be intimidating. Good managers will feel the pressure to perform well themselves as well as the pressure for those under them to perform. For this reason, start the responsibilities of the managers at a low level and increase the functions over time as they become more comfortable with the role. You can have your managers strive to create the most effective and efficient processes they can while you take on the burden of costs and budgeting. This keeps them focused on taking care of the end customer. If they are always looking over their shoulders at funding problems, good ideas may be stifled or bad ones created because money took over. Budgets and cost control are important, but let them run in the idea stage. This is not saying that every idea they come up with will be funded and implemented, so you need to help them understand the impact of their ideas. As you move to develop their careers even further, bring them in at budget time so they can see the processes involved.

Growing Them Further in the Role

The most important thing you can do once you put new people in a management role is to back them up. They need to feel they are truly in this position and have your belief and trust in their ability to do the job. Beyond their feelings, this backing needs to be real. The associates who will report to a new manager need to fully understand what the role of the manager is and how the reporting structure works. If the associates sense that the new manager is not fully empowered in certain areas, they will come to you when they disagree with decisions the manager makes. This should not be allowed to happen. This is not to say that everything the manager does and thinks will be right. However, it does mean that you should allow some mistakes to happen and see how they are corrected. If you see a mistake in the works and need to prevent it from happening, make sure you do it with the manager and without the associates. They need to see the manager in a positive light and without your influence at every step.

Soft skills training is another way to grow your managers. Trial by fire will certainly teach them many lessons but some of those lessons will come at a large cost. Spend that cost in a more enlightening manner and provide managerial training to your managers. Classes and workshops are offered in many places and you can find good, fundamental training that lasts for a day with an inexpensive price tag. These classes can give the new manager good ideas that can help the manager in do a better job.

Another good way to grow managers is to invite them to an off-site seminar that you conduct. Don't just stand in front and lecture. Instead give them real-life scenarios they must come up with solutions for. This way you can see how they would act in certain situations. Have them present their plan in front of the others. Now, the other attendees can hear how others think and learn from them. Once they have finished presenting, go over the pros and cons of their plan. Debate is good; there will be few times when there is a clear-cut correct answer, and all can benefit.

Quick Recap

- An agent's career phases can be seen in the Career Life Cycle graph. Are you able to identify where your agents are in relation to that graph? Can you tell where YOU are in that life cycle?

- Does your company do performance reviews? Do you already have a process in place for sharing the strengths and weaknesses of your agents?

- Whether you have two agents or 200, the Help Desk needs to work as a team. Do you feel comfortable that you have created an atmosphere that will allow teams to form and work effectively?

- How is the management structure working in your Help Desk? Have you identified associates who can take on more responsibilities even though it may not be as a formal manager? If your Help Desk has more than ten people, you may have good opportunities to implement some management training programs to grow your people into these roles.

CHAPTER 17

The Business of a Help Desk

Help Desks exist to support technology and the users of the technology. For this reason, Help Desks are generally made up of technical associates who understand how to resolve technology issues.

Help Desks are part of a business, however, and therefore must operate with business considerations. Just as budgets, income streams, and expenses were discussed in earlier chapters, the Help Desk is really surrounded by business rules and processes. You need to understand some of these processes to operate the Help Desk itself. This chapter will go over some of the ways that business influences a Help Desk organization.

What To Look For

- Total cost of ownership is a model for showing that there are far more costs involved in a technology than just the acquisition price. Understanding the implications of these costs will go a long way in helping your company receive the return on the investment it needs. Your Help Desk can influence these costs in several ways.

- Contracts also influence how a Help Desk operates and serves its customers. Software maintenance can be a big factor. There are several items to look for when reviewing and signing a software maintenance deal.

- Implementation and services contracts are other documents that can impact the Help Desk. Getting the right terms and issues on these contracts is worth your time. Many of these items will be described in this chapter.

Total Cost of Ownership

Total cost of ownership (TCO) is the measurement of the complete cost of a product, technology, or service. This much-used principle attempts to educate people that the cost of buying something is only part of the total equation. Although TCO is used extensively in technology decisions, it is not confined to it. For example, if you are car shopping, you may find two similar cars with a similar sticker price. That sticker price is the price you would pay to purchase the vehicle. As you know, there are other costs involved in owning a car. Insurance, gasoline, and general maintenance are all added costs that must be incurred to own a car. Combining all those costs is a step towards understanding the total cost of owning your new car. This section will help you learn more about TCO and how it relates to your Help Desk. Throughout much of the section, we will concentrate on PC issues within TCO as that is a common consideration for businesses today. Overall, we will look at four areas:

- Breaking out the elements of TCO
- How the Help Desk can influence TCO
- Recommendations for managing TCO in your organization
- Caveats of TCO

Elements of TCO

TCO is important in the technology world because it can help you make better, long-term purchasing or upgrade decisions with the technology you own or are looking into. If you were to concentrate merely on the acquisition price of a product, you would probably never buy anything new. What you currently have is paid for and any purchase will cost you more money. TCO can show you that staying with old technologies incurs a cost that may far outweigh the price of an upgrade or new purchase. TCO is made up of four general areas defined in Table 17-1.

Capital Costs

Capital cost is the cost of the product or service you are buying. This line item within TCO is the one cost everyone recognizes when looking to purchase

TCO Area	Definition	Examples
Capital	The cost involved in acquiring the product or service	The price paid to buy a PC or software Leasing fees incurred to lease hardware
Technical support	The costs to support the product from an IT or Help Desk perspective	Salaries of the Help Desk agents Training for the agents Time spent developing standards with vendors
User support	The costs spent by the end user to use the product	Training for the user Time spent "playing" with the product
Administration	The costs incurred by the company to handle the administration of the product	Time spent tracking and auditing the product Dollars spent procuring and installing the product

Table 17.1 TCO Elements

something. It is the cost of the PC or the price the store charges you for software. It also can include any upgrades you make to these technologies over time. So when you buy more memory for a PC, this cost goes into the capital cost category. Some models take this section even deeper and include the cost of money or tax credits. For your purposes, this is going very deep and I suggest you stick with the price paid for the product when calculating capital costs.

Technical Support Costs

Technical support costs include all the activities a Help Desk provides in relation to technologies. It is the agents' salaries, training dollars, and any outsourcing help that is used to support the customers. Time that the Help Desk and the IT department spend on developing standards, working on configurations, and planning for new implementations is included as well. Also, any work done to create user groups or newsletters for your customers can be put into this category.

Whereas capital costs are pretty easy to see and calculate, technical support costs are much harder. We have discussed that a Help Desk life is fast and filled with multiple projects and issues occurring simultaneously. In the middle of all that, it is difficult to remember how much time is spent on "training" a customer versus "supporting" a customer. To get a complete TCO cost for technical support you will need to know how much time the R&D group is spending on experimenting with new technologies or developing standards. Is anyone measuring the amount of time that systems administrators spend reviewing capacity planning and server utilization graphs? To fully understand your TCO, someone needs to be.

Because this is one of the hardest categories to measure, it is probably the least understood by those outside the IT department. Because it is the least understood, odds are that it is the hardest to get additional funding and resources for technical support. The customers only know that when something breaks they call the Help Desk and it is fixed. That people are spending time making the product more stable and efficient is difficult to see. Promoting the activities of the Help Desk as discussed in Chapter 14 remains an important part of a Help Desk's plan.

End User Support Costs

As technical support costs are hard to calculate, so are end user support costs. The benefit you will have on the technical side is that at least it is your department you are measuring. In this category, it is all the users of the technology that you need to understand. For the devout customer service readers, we are using the word *user* here in positive terms. They are still your customers, but they also use the technology.

Typical costs in this category include the time the user spends on developing documents and spreadsheets, learning how the technology works, asking or answering their co-workers' questions, and dealing with the "futz factor." The futz factor is time spent by the user on low-value added tasks such as adding screen savers, arranging icons on the desktop, or changing fonts and colors in a document.

Administration Costs

The administrative costs within the TCO model are easier to see than the two support pieces; however, they are typically ignored when looking at the price of a technology. Without these costs and resources, the technology will be poorly used and maintained.

Some examples of administrative costs are audits, legal work done around contracts and licensing, enforcing policies and procedures, asset management, purchasing, and installation. Much of this work is obviously necessary but is not easily thought of when someone goes to buy a product. Your challenge will be to uncover who is doing this work, the user or the technical group, and then investigate and track the related costs.

How Your Help Desk Can Influence TCO

With that introduction to the elements of the TCO model, you can begin to see that there are many costs and much time and resources spent on each and every technology deployed within the customer base. Just as there are examples of many elements within a technology's total cost, there are several ways your Help Desk can initially influence these costs and make an impact on them as shown in Table 17-2.

TCO Category	Ways to Impact Cost
Capital	Centralized procurement can bundle purchases and gain volume discounts.
Technical Support	Implement remote desktop management tools. The formal existence of your Help Desk alone will help lower this cost. By concentrating on the process of support, synergies can be achieved.
End User Support	Provide online training guides. Establish standards. Provide FAQs to help users help themselves more quickly. Provide tips and tricks to get more out of the technology.
Administration	Implementing asset management can ensure all technologies are being used and not stored somewhere. Review contracts to find better purchasing and support terms.

Table 17.2   Help Desks Can Impact TCO

Recommendations for Managing TCO

Whether you choose to track TCO for all your products and services, or only some of them, or you have no plans at all, it is worth calculating the TCO for your major technologies at least once. After that is done and you see the results, you can then continue the practice or stop it altogether. If you do embark on this calculation, I recommend that you do so in four steps:

1. Put together your own numbers for the technology you are measuring.
2. Look for good opportunities to impact your TCO.
3. Monitor trends over time.
4. Communicate the importance of tracking TCO to others.

Put Together Your Own Numbers

Many organizations (Gartner Group, Help Desk Institute, and Help Desk 2000 are good ones) can show you their estimates for the TCO of given technologies. Some consulting groups call TCO by different names, but their intent is again to show there is more than the purchase price to consider for technology use. Because each company uses technologies differently, you should calculate your own TCO. You can certainly use their estimates as a starting point, but you will need to insert your own assumptions and thoughts into the categories as you go along.

Make sure your assumptions are quickly and definitively used instead of exact facts. This entire process is intended to give you a basis for making decisions, not to make exact financial decisions down to the penny. So much of this calculation is based on assumptions and averages that it is foolish to think you can get it exactly correct. Give it a good effort and try your best to not leave out any factors, but do not lose sleep over the numbers. Know that someone else could go through the same process, come up with different numbers than you did, and you both would be right. As with many measurements, the trends of the numbers are as important as the numbers themselves.

You will need to involve others in this process. It can be informally asking your agents about the time they spend on certain items, or more formal interviews with customers inquiring about their habits. As mentioned earlier, you are looking for general times and dollars from the people you speak with. If they give ranges, that is okay. Split the differences and input a good average of what you find. So if the people you speak with say the costs are anywhere from $1000 to $5000, use $3000 and keep moving. You may get answers related to time, such as "a full day a month" or "two hours a week." If so, get with your HR department to find a generic average hourly rate for the associates, and apply that number to the times indicated.

The best way to perform the actual calculation of TCO is within a spreadsheet. Down the left side will be the four categories—capital, technical support, end user support, and administration. Indented under each category will be the line items you wish to track such as Help Desk agents, purchase price, training, and asset management. The next column will be a representative hourly rate of the typical person performing that task. Yes it can vary greatly, but remember this is an estimate used for trends and comparisons.

The next column will be the time spent for *each* of the devices you are measuring. So if you have 1000 PCs, this is not the total time spent on the 1000, but rather the average time spent in a year for one of the PCs.

Multiply the hourly rate times the average time spent and you will have the extension for that particular line item. Add all the lines together and you will have the TCO for that technology over whatever time period you choose. For a good analysis, include several time periods to see if the technology is expected to increase or decrease over time. An example where the TCO could decrease over time is end user support. Once users become more familiar with the technology, they should have fewer questions about its use. An example can be seen in Figure 17-1.

Look for Good Opportunities to Impact Your TCO

A world class Help Desk does not sit by the phones waiting for them to ring. It also looks proactively for ways it can enhance the efficiency and effectiveness of its customers and the company. Reducing the TCO of your technologies is one good way to accomplish that goal.

As discussed in prioritization skills, what you go after first can be determined by any number of factors. For TCO impact, you should look first for easy opportunities and then those that are large in scope.

The reason easy solutions are picked first is because of the inexactness of TCO. Unless you are certain that your calculations are just right, it will be hard for you to know if any changes you make affect the lowering of your TCO. So, it makes sense to look for easy ways to lower the costs because you will not have wasted as much time and energy if the changes do not take hold.

DME Corporation
Total Cost of Ownership for a PC

Category	Rate	Year 1 Hours	Extension
Capital			
Hardware			1500
Software			400
Total Capital			$1,900
Technical Support			
Help Desk	$16	3.0	$48
Configuration	$18	0.5	$9
Standards	$18	1.0	$18
Training	$16	2.0	$32
Newsletters	$16	0.2	$3
Planning	$18	0.3	$5
Total Technical Support			$115
End User Support			
Training	$14	40.0	$560
Peer to Peer Support	$28	5.0	$140
Futz Factor	$14	50.0	$700
Total End User Support			$1,400
Administration			
Asset management	$18	1.0	$18
Audits	$18	0.5	$9
Purchasing	$18	1.0	$18
Installations	$18	1.0	$18
Total Administration			$63
Total TCO (First Year)			$3,478

Figure 17.1   Sample TCO calculation

Once you can see a cause-and-effect relationship in your actions with TCO, it certainly pays to go after larger wins. It is obvious that the more you can take out cost from owning and operating a product without affecting the satisfaction of those using it, the better the company will be for it. Look to the examples given earlier for ways your Help Desk may affect the TCO of a product or service. There are definitely many ways to lower costs of doing business, so you should be able to find processes in your operations that can be fine-tuned. Just remember that taking costs out that in turn negatively affect your customer is a terribly bad thing and will hurt you more than the incremental cost savings would have helped. Some people get so caught up in reducing cost that they lose sight of this important aspect of customer service.

Monitor Trends Over Time

I believe the most important objective in measuring TCO in your business is watching the trends over time. If the Gartner Group says that a PC's TCO is $5000 and your calculations say yours is $3000, this does not necessarily mean that your way of doing business is $2000 per desktop more efficient. What is more important is that your $3000 in the first year is $2750 six months later and on down to $2000 as shown in Figure 17-2.

If you are using the same assumptions to figure these costs, you have been making an impact on the bottom line of your company. Conversely, if recent upgrades or purchases cause your number to rise to $3500, there is a problem that must be discovered and resolved.

The trends should be reviewed both over time and when major changes occur in the business. You may monitor TCO calculations every six months for a check in. However, if the IT department introduces new radio frequency devices in place of wired desktops, that is a significant enough change to warrant a new look at your TCO.

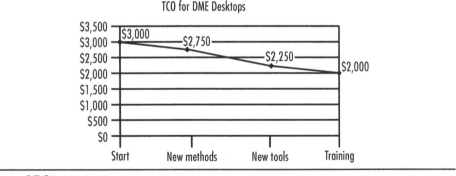

Figure 17.2   Declining TCO

Communicate the Importance of Tracking TCO to Others

You may be able to sleep better at night knowing you are doing a good job at managing TCO, but don't keep it to yourself. Let others know what is happening. This helps in a couple of ways. First, it shows your customers and senior management that your group is being proactive and finding ways to help the business. They can appreciate your efforts and perhaps find more resources to allow you to make even more advances.

Second, this information can educate others about the advantages of managing TCO and they can work on their own initiatives to lower TCO in the company. Now that you have established the groundwork, the rest of the company can think of new ways to affect TCO and get more return on their technology investment. Your leadership and business savvy can be seen by many people and can only help your career as well as the company's budget!

Many of these efforts will take time to really lower costs. For example, instituting a user training program will incur costs up front but should return benefits for the long term. Your Help Desk is another primary way to affect TCO. You need to communicate that the Help Desk and other strategic plans are an investment and that over time this investment will pay dividends. If plans and actions are changed frequently because reductions are not immediately seen, the costs of the process will outweigh the benefits. If the ideas are solid and you monitor the trends carefully, the results will prove themselves out.

Caveats Concerning TCO

There is a lot of good stuff that tracking and managing TCO can do for your company. Being aware of it can produce good ideas and actions even if you never measure the first cost or benefit. So why isn't everyone on this TCO train and riding it to greater efficiencies? There are two big issues that come to mind:

- The accuracy of your estimate
- Relying too much on TCO in making decisions

The Accuracy of Your Estimate

I have mentioned several times that TCO should consist of estimates based on your best assumptions. With all this vagueness, how accurate can the TCO calculation really be? You need to fully understand the operations of the technology from both your Help Desk's view as well as your users' view. You need to look for hidden costs that may be a significant factor in TCO but are hard to find. The costs around user experimentation and peer support are good examples. Can you really know how much time someone plays with his new screen saver or asks for help from the person sitting next to him?

As you plan actions to lower the TCO, you may very well be shifting costs from one group to another. An example may be in training. Let's say you declare that the Help Desk will facilitate all training sessions on a technology and that the users should come to your group to arrange the proper training. Using this scenario, you may change your TCO estimates by reducing end user training to zero and modifying technical training to the actual costs incurred by your Help Desk. This assumption makes sense but is it really happening that way? Will users tell you they are not following your plan and are getting training on the side anyway? Without knowing this, you will be promoting a possible TCO reduction that never materialized.

Relying Too Much on TCO in Making Decisions

Close to the accuracy of your estimate question is the issue around the TCO calculation altogether. The issue is the effectiveness of comparing the TCO of one product to the TCO of another in making a technology decision. To best see this, let's compare the cost of owning a typewriter to owning a PC.

If you used TCO as your sole decision criteria, the typewriter would win everyday. Its acquisition price is lower than a PC's, and the cost for technical support is cheaper for a typewriter as is the cost for end user support. Finally, the administrative costs of maintaining a typewriter fall below the PC as well. If someone were to investigate upgrading all the typewriters in the building to PCs and used TCO as their decision criteria, there would be no PCs purchased. The typewriter TCO is simply lower across the board than its PC counterpart.

Now, no one would debate the benefits that come with a PC over a typewriter. PCs can save documents, simplify editing, and add pictures and graphics. So holistically the TCO model has challenges when it ignores the benefits side of a technology. Keep this in mind as you promote its virtues through the organization. Sometimes people can latch onto an idea and attach more importance to it than you initially wanted. TCO is a good tool…when used correctly.

Software Maintenance Contracts

While we have spoken some about different software packages, we have not discussed the buying of the package; specifically the licenses and maintenance contract.

There are several things to keep in mind when buying software such as call management packages, ACD systems, etc. A few items are:

- **Look at recurring costs as much as acquisition costs.**   Many people concentrate on the asking price of a product and feel comfortable once that has been negotiated. I would encourage you to negotiate the annual maintenance costs as well. Most maintenance contracts begin at around 15 percent of the list price of the product. Therefore, no matter how much you actually pay for a product, the maintenance cost will be based on the product's list price. Maintenance costs can also go up over time as the price of the package goes up. Don't let that happen to you. First, get the annual fee down to between 8 and 10 percent and base it on the actual sales price instead of the list price. Ask for the first year to be free, after which the fee can go up. Put a cap on the amount the maintenance can increase. These things may seem small at first, but over time you will be reducing the total cost of owning the software.

- **Look at how many upgrades and releases go out each year.**   If the vendor sends out many releases and fixes each year, it may be worth your while to get the maintenance. If you plan on taking the code and revising it a lot, you may forgo the maintenance, as it may not apply to your code anymore.

- **What is maintenance anyway?**   I have mentioned it in each section above but it is not defined. Will you get on site help if there are problems? Can you call anytime day or night or only during the workweek? Is there a charge per call or by person? There are no right or wrong instances; you just need to know what you are paying for and if it is aligned with the criticality the software requires.

- **Buy in quantity when possible.**   Negotiating a large sale is easier than negotiating a smaller one. If you can afford it, look into the near future for license requirements and purchase in advance to allow the price to be discounted further.

- **Understand when the vendor's fiscal periods end.**   In order to meet budgeted sales quotas, you will quite often find better discounts when a vendor's fiscal period is coming to an end. If you can time it near their fiscal year end, even better!

- **Let vendors know you are looking at their competition.**   No one wants to lose a sale over minor discrepancies, but they especially do not want to lose a sale with a competitor looming close by. I personally don't recommend going back and forth between vendors to drive the price down. While you may gain a good price in the end, it tends to create ill professional feelings and you never know when you might need the "losing" party again.

- **Understand the definition of user.**   Two common ways to define users are named and concurrent. *Named* users require you to "assign" each software license to a particular user. If you have 200 people using a package, you would need to buy 200 licenses. *Concurrent* users require you to buy the number of licenses equal to the maximum number of users using it at any one time. Therefore, if you have 200 potential users of the package but only foresee 50 using it at a time, you would only need to buy 50 licenses.

Obviously, concurrent licenses are easier to manage because you don't have to keep up with each individual user and they are cheaper to acquire. On the other hand, you need to fully understand the consequences of going over the limit. Some software licenses are user-friendly and nothing happens. The software vendor counts on your professionalism and ethics to purchase more licenses when your concurrent user count exceeds what you initially bought. Other vendors are very strict and deny users access to the software if you go over the limit. This could hurt if the software is in production and your business associates are prevented from working because you saved some money at acquisition time. It may be as simple as a phone call to get more licenses, or worse, you may have to sign more legal documents to add more licenses. All that being said, I would ask for concurrent users every time possible when buying software. The ease of administration is higher and total costs to the company are typically much lower.

- **Understand who has the right to use the licenses.**   It is pretty straightforward that your company has the right to use the software you purchase. What about a sister company of yours or any company you acquire? Will they have rights to the software? What if you use particular software for your external customers to access or use your system? Will it be legal to do that? You may not have much luck in the customer scenario but if you are an acquiring company or have other partnerships, you will want to explore your rights to use the package.

Implementation and Services Contracts

As you begin using external resources to help you run your operations or even to install products, you will begin signing contracts for these services and implementations. Just as we discussed some things to watch out for with software licenses, let's also go over some issues with implementation and services contracts.

- **Understand when the vendor's fiscal periods end.**   Just as with most purchases, better deals come timed with vendor fiscal periods.
- **Let vendors know you are looking at their competition.**   Again, for the same reason as software licenses, healthy competition does not hurt the process.
- **Incorporate milestones into your payment schedule.**   Many projects take weeks or even years to finish, so paying for everything up front hurts the return on your investment because you bought a service or product but cannot get maximum use from it until it is completely installed. Adding milestones to the implementation path provides incentives for your implementation partners to stay on schedule as they want their income stream to be regular and on schedule.
- **Bundle services where possible but unbundle costs.**   You will typically find advantages pricewise if you use the same vendor to design, sell, and

implement the service. Basically, you are giving them more room to add margin in the sale. Although I encourage using the same vendor for this reason, you must require them to list their costs of each service separately. By doing this you may find individual areas where they are putting in high margins to overcome other areas where they were forced to be more competitive. If they refuse to do this, you should wonder what they are hiding. I address this issue merely from a fiscal standpoint. If the partner excels in product design but has high prices and no implementation plan, it will probably not be worth the project pain to save a few bucks.

- **Understand all costs involved.**   In addition to product and service prices, it is imperative that you understand miscellaneous costs like travel time, meals, and after-hours' expenses. I would discourage paying for travel time or, at the very least, you should closely monitor it. If your partner likes to fly their implementation team home every four days, this will get expensive and will make your project costs climb higher than you originally figured.

- **Put the nonsolicitation of associates in the contract.**   Your partner will no doubt have a paragraph in their contract that says you cannot hire their associates during or after the project; make sure the language is reciprocated. Fair is fair, right?

Quick Recap

- Did you learn of new costs that impact the total cost of a product or service you support? Do you think others in your organization understood these costs as well?

- Your Help Desk can play an integral part in reducing these costs. What plans do you have to get your agents to pursue this goal?

- Have you ever done a TCO calculation for a technology? Take it easy, don't worry about being exact, and see what kinds of numbers you come up with.

- Do you get involved in contract reviews? It is important that you play some role in this responsibility because contract reviews can help or hinder the effectiveness of your Help Desk in the organization.

Action Plan Checklist

❑   Begin to gather information necessary to create a service-level agreement with your customers.

❑   Review your support offerings to see if there are opportunities to take on new work and processes.

❑   Begin to accumulate and publish a wide variety of measurements of your Help Desk and the agents.

❑   Begin some work to promote the Help Desk.

❑   Meet with your agents to determine what tools they need to perform their jobs more effectively.

❑   Meet with those in control of the budget to see what funds are available for these tools.

❑   If a review process is not already in place, create one. All associates should be scheduled for a review within the next six months.

❑   Calculate the total cost of ownership for one of your most widely implemented technologies to see what the truer cost really is.

PART IV

I Hate My Help Desk. Fix It!

CHAPTER 18

Identify Perceived Issues

So far, this book has taken the positive spin and worked with you on developing and maintaining a world class Help Desk. For those of you who manage, know of, or work in a bad Help Desk, now is the time to see what you can do to fix it. For those involved in a well-run Help Desk, it still may be worthwhile to read through this chapter in case you recognize pieces of your organization that can be upgraded.

I use the word "perceived" in the title of this chapter on purpose because some people may have problems that look one way but are actually based somewhere else. In the customer service world the adage "perception is reality" is strong, so the issues cannot be ignored. You have gotten this impression somehow, so it probably came from one of two sources: people expressing their dissatisfaction or your own review of metrics. No matter where it originated, I recommend going after both sources of input. There is no particular order in which this must be done because either source may confirm or contradict the other. Of course, the level of dissatisfaction will drive the extent of these actions. Going on a witch hunt every time someone complains will not lead to a high-morale work environment. Conversely, refusing to investigate customer complaints will not lead to a quality work environment for yourself and your career!

What to Look For

- There are two ways you will find problems with your Help Desk. The first is by the customer or affected party contacting you with the issue. The second is by your own review of metrics and process analysis. Both ways of discovery will be discussed in this chapter.

- Most complaints can be broken down into four root causes: bad customer service, bad processes, bad product, or bad people. Determining which is the real problem will take some work on your part but is time well spent. You need to look at the big picture when doing this work because what seems to be the problem may just be a symptom of something larger.

Interview Stakeholders

"Interview stakeholders" sounds really pretentious. Since I committed to writing this book in conversational tone, I should have titled this section, "Talk to People." *Stakeholders* is more specific than *people* because it implies the people who specifically have a stake in the well-being of your Help Desk. These people can include your customers, executive management, and the agents themselves. *Interview* implies a bit more formal conversation than *talk* because you really need to have a specific purpose during this conversation. While I am sure you have been doing proactive surveys in the past, you now need to go after the people who are complaining about your Help Desk. Remember, you might be the problem yourself, so be sure to make the interviewees feel confident that you welcome their thoughts regardless of where the problem lies. Next remind yourself that you need to get this input even if it hurts your feelings. Better to find out now than on a performance review or, worse yet, an exit interview!

There are some subtle differences between a routine survey and this conversation:

- **Your questions are very specific and detailed.**   Where your surveys were general to solicit any kind of information, this talk is specific. The person has expressed disappointment in the Help Desk's performance for some reason; you need to find out why. Keep it nice but make sure they explicitly explain their gripe.

- **This one is interactive.**   As the first difference implies, here you will be speaking with your audience and not just having them fill out answers to questions. You may need to follow up in areas to get more information. The main goal is to understand their problem.

- **Don't debate their input!**   Don't forget; you are just trying to understand why they are complaining. Don't debate or try to justify what happened unless it is clearly, unmistakably an error. Your part of the conversation should be mainly questions; only use statements to restate points. If their point does not seem to be worthy of whatever mess they have gotten you in, make them go deeper. Hopefully, they get to a point where they realize it is not all that bad and life can resume.

External Customers   *It may be hard to have this type conversation with external customers. You probably cannot just walk down the hall and begin talking. There still may be ways to get this information, though, by engaging someone else in the company to meet with the customer. This could be a salesperson who does business with the customer outside the realm of Help Desk operations. The point is to go after every opportunity to improve and understand the real issues and examples. Don't be satisfied to hear a complaint and move on. Don't pester the complainer but definitely try to get them to explain their position.*

Review Metrics

Hopefully, the Help Desk has some historical data you can dig into to see trends or problem areas. Reviewing metrics may allow you to find problem areas before your customer base does. This is a good thing. Complaining customers tend to spread bad words to others, which can leave a negative impression of your Help Desk with those who have not dealt with it directly.

When doing this, it is important to work the trends and not one or two bad periods. Decreasing call resolution times or rising abandoned rates for one month may be accurate but may not be a true reflection of the Help Desk's operations. If they continue over time, that is when you should begin to worry.

You should also take the time to correlate how factors that influence your business also influence your Help Desk. Air-conditioning companies probably have higher sales in hot months, which in turn may increase your call volume due to higher use of the system. Even over two to three months, it would not be right to call this a trend and blame your agents for not maintaining their call resolution times. If you had data from last year, however, you could know this was coming and prepare for it beforehand. The problem during that time period is real, but not representative of the long-term workings of the group.

Common Causes of Complaints

Whether your customers are complaining or you are, this section is assuming there is something wrong in Help Desk land. Having been to this land, I can divide the potential issues into four categories:

- Bad customer service
- Bad product
- Bad processes
- Bad people

You will need technology to help you for much of this. Technology will help provide you measurements to validate or dispute the issues brought up by your customers. If you do not have the technology needed to capture the measurements that follow, you may want to share with your managers the value the technology can bring. Without the technology, you will be forced to trust the opinions of the customer more and that will make proving things difficult. Let's now look at each complaint category.

Bad Customer Service

Okay, no excuses if this is the reason for complaints. Your sole mission on the Help Desk is to serve the customer, and providing this service in a professional and friendly manner is so easy to do. I am not claiming that maintaining your composure in the face of a yelling, red-faced executive is simple, but that person is beyond recognizing customer service, anyway. Empathizing with your callers, answering the phone politely, and calling them back with statuses are all good marks towards customer service, and if you achieve them, well over half the battle is won. Most of the time, strong communication with a caller is as important, if not more so, than the final act of resolving the issue. (Author's note: This is hard for my personality type to recommend but years of experience and customer feedback prove the case over and over.) Let's look at six leading areas where customer service is viewed poorly.

- "I can never reach anyone."
- "I reach them, but they don't know the answer."
- "I reach them, but they give me the wrong answer."
- "They think they fixed the problem, but they didn't."
- "They may know the answer, but they don't respond."
- "I reach them and they resolve my problem, but they are rude."

These complaints are generalized, but that is realistically how they come in. It is much easier to complain about something in general terms than with specific details. If the feelings are strong, a complaining customer will also use words like "never" and "always" to make their point come across stronger. They may be right, but typically their message should be used to direct you somewhere versus acting on the initial exclamation. It is up to you to drill down with the customer to best understand the exact nature of their concerns.

I Can Never Reach Anyone
An extremely common complaint of customers is that they cannot reach a Help Desk agent when they need one. "Never" is a strong word, but that is how it is

expressed. Let's pull out our metrics and see how we can validate their claim or find the problem. For this purpose we will use the following metrics:

- Calls by media used
- Calls per time of day
- Number of agents available for calls by time of day
- Average speed of answer
- Abandoned rate
- Average talk time

Calls by Media Used   We will review each of these in the following sections to illustrate how they can be used to validate the customer's issue. Figure 18-1 begins by showing a graph of calls by the media used by the customer. Right off, this tells you that while the complaining customer cannot reach you, many people can. At least you know the phone works! I start off with this to see where the agents get their work. It can also give you a suggestion for other ways for the complaining customer to contact you. For this complaint, we will work with the incoming phones as our area for review.

Calls by Time of Day   Next, you want to see how the incoming calls are spread throughout the day and compare them with the corresponding staffing levels. You can pick a representative day or average them out; the trends are what matters here. Look at Figure 18-2.

This is a basic Help Desk chart showing when your calls are received. This is a common and fundamental report that ACD systems can provide.

Number of Agents Available by Time of Day   Figure 18-3 shows the number of agents you have in the office during these times.

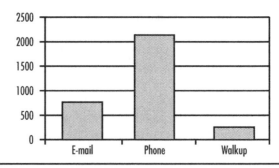

Figure 18.1   Calls by incoming media

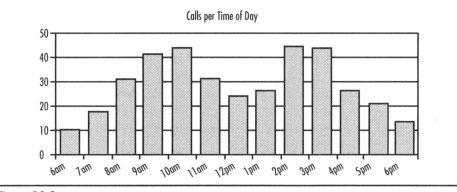

Figure 18.2   Calls per time of day

The first graph shows your calls ramping up around 9:00A.M., falling off at lunch, then spiking back for two hours at 2:00P.M. Your staff ramps up well in the morning, but departs too early. The graphs would suggest you keep some more agents to cover the 2:00–4:00P.M. call spikes. Another option if you can work it is to allow flex time, where some of your agents take a longer lunch break and work longer in the day. You can afford the lesser quantity during lunch as your call volume drops significantly. If your complaining caller usually calls between 2:00 and 4:00, you may have found part of the problem.

Average Speed of Answer and Abandoned Rate   I doubt that you will always be able to tie in "you never answer the phone" to a time of day. Another issue to review is the patience level of your callers. How? You could ask them but we will try another way. First, measure the average speed of answer. This is defined as the length of time a person is on hold while waiting for an agent to answer. For an example, let's say that your average time to answer the phone is 30 seconds. Now

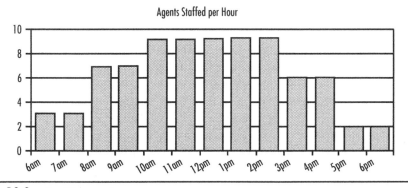

Figure 18.3   Staffing per hour

look at your abandoned rate. You will recall this is the percentage of time a caller hangs up before an agent picks up the phone. I have seen ranges from 5 percent to 10 percent as good goals. What if your abandoned rate is 26 percent? That means that over a quarter of your callers hang up after 30 seconds of waiting. They are pretty impatient. Perhaps you could have some music or news events playing on the phone while they are on hold to keep them entertained. You might even put messages about upcoming events on the phone system so the caller can be updated while waiting.

Average Talk Time   Expand this measurement to include average length of time your agents are on the phone. For this example, let's say that is three minutes. You now have a situation where each call takes you an average of three minutes to resolve but your callers on hold are hanging up after 30 seconds. With that disparity, complainers are right that they don't get through. They abandon ship before you are ready to board passengers. There is not much you can do here except communicate the circumstances to the customers. They need to understand that the staff is there and willing to help; in fact, they are helping others at the time.

If the issue persists, you need to make sure your agents are productive the whole time they are on the phone. If you have a recommended "Get to know the customer first" plan that encourages your agents to make small talk at the beginning of calls, you may want to scrap it. If the problem gets big, you may need to segregate your incoming calls into categories that allow customers with quick, easy requests to be routed to different agents than those who take a lot of phone time. Of course, you could always hire more agents to be available for the incoming calls. This sounds easy enough but it is obviously expensive and might be beyond the capabilities of many Help Desks.

I Reach Them, but They Don't Know the Answer

Now we are at the meat and bones of Help Desk responsibilities—fixing the problem. You must treat the customer professionally but somehow you have to resolve their issue and to do that you must know what the customer is talking about. The Day in the Life of training is very helpful here. You will recall this training is having the agent experience the day-to-day work of his customers so he can best understand how their work is affected by the technologies your Help Desk supports. You can know technical details about problems but if you cannot relate them to how the customer uses the product, you are in trouble.

You may not have to take a PC apart or edit massive lines of source code, but you at least need to know enough to get the call to the person who can do those things. I'll make it even simpler; you must appear to know that much in the face of the customer. It's only fair that if you can be judged poorly by someone else's perception, you should also be able to look good in that same light. You shouldn't try to slip by issues using the latest computer lingo, but you can appear knowledgeable about items without knowing the greatest detail. Make sure you capture as much of the caller's details as you can and then let them know you will look into it and call them back as soon as possible. (And you had better!) Take the details to your resident expert and get the answer. Also important is to learn *how* they came up with the answer at the same time; then perhaps you can apply that logic yourself next time.

It is good that we agree that your agents need to know how to fix the problem. How can we go after this issue if our customers tell us we are failing? You could use surveys to uncover the feelings of the customers on this issue. Find out why they feel like they do and how often it happens. It may be confined to a single agent, a group of agents, or a certain technology. Knowing this can help point you in a certain direction. It is subjective, though, so let's dig in to our metrics and look for clues. Here we will use

- First call resolution
- Transferred calls report
- Escalated calls report

First Call Resolution   First call resolution rates is a fine place to begin reviewing. You will remember that first call resolution is the percentage of time that the caller's problem is resolved during their initial call into the Help Desk. The theory should hold that if your agents are solving problems while the caller is still on the phone, they must be fairly knowledgeable on the topic. If you find that the resolution rate is high, say over 75 percent, you may go to the call duration measurement. This measurement works well when combined with first call resolution. This combination could show you that you are solving calls well but it is taking you a long time to do it. The skill set of the agents may be lower than once thought because they are putting the caller on hold while they run around the Help Desk finding someone who can help. The customer may get their issue resolved while holding, but the duration was unacceptable. Looking only at call resolution rates would distort this fact. If the first call resolution is low, then this metric probably justifies the customer's complaints and you need to look elsewhere for the cause.

Transferred Calls   The next place to look is at your transferred calls report. This measurement shows you where calls or problems were sent for resolution and how frequently. This number does not have to be low to be bad. Your organizational setup will determine this level as much as anything. If you have a frontline group that is really designed to field high-level calls and pass them to more specialized groups, your transfer numbers will be high. The key is to understand ahead of time what transfer levels are acceptable to you and what levels are high. Whether high or low, the transfer rate measurement can give you good information.

A transfer rate that is higher than your expectation means your Help Desk does not know the answers you feel they should. It could also mean they do not have the time to resolve the problem for some reason, but that would bring up other process issues you should already know about and have incorporated into your expectations. If you find this number high, you may need to train the agents more. Discover what type of calls they handle and which ones they pass and concentrate your training efforts there. If the problems are beyond the scope for that group, you may need to set up a different organization model. Over time, new technologies may have been implemented in the company that are beyond what you originally wanted that Help Desk group to handle. It may be time to revisit the model and put more appropriate agents in line for those calls.

Transfer rates that are lower than you expected may also be a root cause of this type of complaint. Agents that hold on to problems for too long before taking them to someone else will cause a problem. A low transfer rate could show you that the agent does not feel anyone else needs to work the issue and that given enough time, he will be able to fix it. This may be true and the agent just needs more time to work on it. It could be false, though, and the agent won't get it no matter how long he works on it. If you find certain agents or groups who are not transferring problems with extended open times, you will need to get more involved.

Escalated Calls   Another measurement to review when confronted with "You never know the answer" is the number of calls escalated by your Help Desk agents. This is not a measurement I normally track, but it will be needed if this problem hangs over you. The purpose of a calls escalated report is to show you how many calls reach a point where the agent feels someone else should get involved. The escalation does not have to pass the ownership of the issue. It may just mean that the problem has been open long enough for more senior managers to know of it. It could also be such a high-priority problem that it automatically triggers an escalation. The key is the priority. Good agents know and appreciate the importance of prioritizing issues. A lack of escalation runs counter to this and many times does not leave the customer with a good experience.

I Reach Them, but They Give Me the Wrong Answer

A worse problem than not knowing the answer is giving an incorrect one. If someone tells me that they do not know what the resolution is, I at least know where I stand. However, if they give me an answer, I may proceed not knowing that I have incorrect data or am working with hardware that is going to fail again. Incorrect answers hurt the Help Desk–customer interaction as much as anything. It ruins the credibility of the agent and the Help Desk, takes up more valuable time of the customer to work through the problem with someone again, and may cause business problems.

Consider a credit manager who needs an accounts receivable report that shows customers who are delinquent in their payments. If the Help Desk agent provides them with this document but has used an incorrect formula or other criteria, the manager may take strong actions against a very good customer. The situation will become embarrassing to the business and potentially harmful to the long-term relationship with the customer.

So what can you do to validate this possible complaint? Primarily, you will find this out through your interactions with the customers. Whether it's through surveys or other forms of feedback, the information will come to you from disgruntled customers who keep calling back to the Help Desk to get their problem resolved.

The closest you may come to uncovering this problem through quantitative measurements is through your call logs. If you can run a report that shows caller name and category of problem called in, you may see a trend of the same caller contacting the Help Desk for the same type of problem in a short period of time. By going deeper into the details, you may just find that the calls are for the exact same problem, not just the same type. This measurement needs your review before you assume this is due to bad problem resolutions. The caller may be the location's single point of contact and is merely funneling calls to the Help Desk on the behalf of others. The report will show you possible leads to this problem; it will be up to you to research more to see the reason behind the numbers.

They Think They Fixed the Problem, but They Didn't

Very close to the complaint that your Help Desk gives wrong answers is the complaint that the Help Desk concluded the contact with the customer believing the problem resolved, but it was not. The slight difference here is that the agent may have resolved the symptom of the problem (the incident) but did not completely fix the root cause (the actual problem). An extremely common example of this is when an agent has the customer reboot their PC to overcome errors or unlock the PC. Sure, the PC may reboot fine and the customer resumes working, but the locking may have been caused by two applications interfering with each other. As soon as the customer brings up those particular applications, the fixed PC may break again. What was counted as a resolved problem at the Help Desk end, will now resurface as another incoming call from the customer.

Other potential causes of this complaint are the agents working too fast and being careless or just not testing their work. The "need for speed" can cause more trouble for a Help Desk's perception than the value it brings. Speedy responses will cause agents to overlook clues to the root cause or cause them to make mistakes in their work that create yet even more problems. This is important to remember when you set up incentives for your agents. If you reward agents with high call volumes, you may actually be encouraging them to hurry their interactions with customers to move to the next call. What started as a motivational system may turn into a process that promotes poor customer service.

As has been stated many times, customer perception is critical to the success of your Help Desk. Giving wrong answers or answers that only serve to end a call more quickly will destroy customers' perceptions of your Help Desk's effectiveness. Agents must feel confident in their responses to issues no matter how trivial the problem appears to be. Small problems can turn into big problems quickly, so encourage your agents to make a quality effort in each interaction with the customer. If that means having someone else review their suggested resolutions to complicated problems, so be it.

They May Know the Answer, but They Don't Respond

As I mentioned earlier, responding to the customer is paramount and doing so in a timely fashion is just as crucial. It all starts with answering the phone or reading the e-mail or looking up at your walk-up customer. First impressions are lasting ones and this is where it all begins. A calm caller can start to lose his cool if he has to wait 15 minutes for someone to answer the phone. E-mails unanswered for days create an atmosphere that puts the Help Desk on the defensive before they even hear of the issue. Just short of hanging up on existing callers, please answer the phone or respond to e-mails as quickly as possible! Even if you have to say you are tied up and ask if you can call them right back, it will still help the situation.

Great that you answered the phone and are looking into their issue, but does the caller know what is happening? You could be working hard and involving technology experts all over but if the caller is still unaware of this, you may as well have been on vacation and forgotten all about the call. Following up on the issue, either while it is being worked or after you think it is resolved, exhibits strong customer service traits and is always appreciated by customers.

As with many other types of complaints, customer surveys are best to validate this problem. They will quickly tell you that your follow-up skills are lacking and that they feel abandoned by the original agent. If you have the ability to create categories in your call management package for type of call, you may create a category for "customer call back." This flag can be used to show how many times someone calls in to the Help Desk for a follow-up issue and not to initiate a problem ticket. This flag can then be reported easily to see how often the customer contacts your Help Desk for a second or third interaction.

Poor Attitude or Rudeness

"Yeah, what's your problem?" would never make anyone's list of recommended ways to answer the phone, yet Help Desk agents can give this impression without saying those exact words. Whether they hate their job or just woke up on the wrong side of the bed, the attitude of the agent will inevitably spill over into their job performance. Left untended, the attitude could spill over to the agents around them as well. This can happen either directly from the bad agent or from the perception that management is not doing anything about it. Reread Chapter 11 if you are wondering how to overcome the job-hating part. And since their job's focus is to help the customer, their attitude must be positive. The easiest way to teach this to your agents is to help them remember their own experiences as a customer who felt poorly treated. Perhaps it was at a restaurant where their order took forever or maybe a car garage that took several trips to fix a simple problem. We are all customers at some point each day, so it should be easy to recognize the importance of bringing a good attitude to the job at hand.

Rudeness is an extremely subjective complaint, yet very real. Measuring it typically involves surveying the customer base to uncover its true relationship to your Help Desk. There is one thing you can measure, though, that may be a leading indicator of a bad attitude and that would be the number of calls taken per agent. If one agent is consistently logging more calls than the rest, it could be creating an atmosphere of overload for that agent. I am not saying it should, but rather that it could. You could see that someone who is constantly working harder than normal could be more prone to adopting a bad attitude towards that which is creating the heavy workload.

Conversely, the agent with the lowest calls logged may be a source of the problem. This could happen because the caller hangs up the phone or asks for someone else when that particular agent answers. This can happen quite frequently to new people. Your customers will quickly identify who is good and who is not, and they will tend to request the good agents to help them. For this reason, do not treat an agent with a low call volume as a definite source of attitude complaints.

Bad Product

Even the most successful Help Desks take perception hits when the product or service they are supporting is bad. Because your group answers the phone for problems, callers naturally take their frustration out on the person answering. That agent probably didn't design the product, make the product, or test it, but since the Help Desk is the place to call, that agent is to blame. When reviewing complaints about the Help Desk, try to get to the root cause of the feedback. A caller being upset about a product always breaking does not give you much room to fix any aspect of the Help Desk. Your best chance is to effectively communicate the passion of the calls to the appropriate party within the organization.

This is a great opportunity for the Help Desk to help the bottom line of the organization. Great customer service cannot fix a bad product but it can help soothe the customer's bad feelings. If your group can do that long enough for the sales force or any other department to get involved, you will have made great strides towards being recognized as a highly valued member of the team!

Remember that graphs and numbers have more impact on the receiving party than just thoughts and intuition. Showing them the product's impact on the Help Desk as opposed to other events can have a strong effect. For example, look at the calls in Figure 18-4.

It would be a very valuable tool to be able to show the programming staff that the accounting module was creating significantly more calls than any of the others. They could then focus their attention on the cause of these bugs. Not only will the customers have better software, the Help Desk call volume will be reduced.

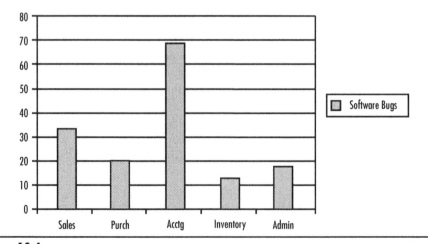

Figure 18.4   Call by problem type

If you have implemented an asset management process, it would be a good source for information on your technologies. You can see what models have been upgraded recently or have been completely replaced because of prior problems. Your inventory can also show you if the products are within the standards that were set for everyone. If you find many products that are not standard vendors, models, or versions, it may be worthwhile to develop a plan to work them out of production and insert standard technologies in their place.

Your vendor should want this information, too. If you are able to identify a recurring problem in their product, it is in their best interest to resolve it before many more customers find it and complain. You may not be able to get their full, immediate attention (especially if they are a big company), but it is valuable information for them to know about. Hopefully, someone will see your findings and resolve them in a timely fashion!

Bad Product Use

There will be times when the product is fine, but the environment is the problem. This environment can be the actual physical environment or the manner in which the product is used. The feedback you get from the customer may be centered on the product, so you need to look deeper to discover if there is more to it.

A common example is a company saving money by purchasing PCs intended for home use instead of commercial use. PCs intended for commercial use are typically more "ruggedized." This implies that they are built to withstand more constant use and dirtier environments. Because of this, there is a higher cost for the product. If you put a product designed for a cleaner, "nicer" environment into an office setting, there may be problems in the long term. So the PC is performing as it was intended, but the user of it has problems.

You can uncover this potential by asking follow-up questions when problems are reported. Slowness issues are good candidates for bad usage resolutions. A location that is constantly slow may have people downloading large files across the network throughout the day. The Internet is an example of the product in this case. The Internet is a good "product" for achieving many things but it can cause problems if used incorrectly. It seems very logical that if the location is slow each time the controller downloads files, the resolution should be to either perform these downloads at a different time or expand the bandwidth available for this function. Again, no one is doing anything wrong, but the way the product is being used needs to be modified.

Bad Processes

You could have the best people in the world supporting a strong product but if the processes they work under are broken, they will not succeed. These processes are typically created by management and may be easy to notice or hidden deep down. In either case, don't neglect to investigate your processes when rooting out problems. This may be hard, especially if you created the processes! Some common areas of problem processes include the following:

- Poor allocation of resources
- Not understanding whom to call for what
- Poor prioritization methods
- Poor escalation procedures
- Calls transferred inefficiently
- Poor tools or poor use of tools

Poor Allocation of Resources

The resources that will most impact the success or failure of your Help Desk are your agents. Having too few agents or too many will generate complaints from your customers. We spent a lot of time in Chapter 7 discussing organizational options for deploying your agents but if you don't keep track of how well they are working, the option you chose may be adversely affecting the customer service you provide.

Not having enough agents to answer the incoming calls or to work the problems being reported will certainly cause customers to complain. The pure volume of calls that cannot be addressed is exactly tied to customers needing help but not receiving it. Over time, an understaffed Help Desk will begin to wear down the agents and the dreaded burnout symptoms will appear.

Can *too many* agents cause complaints? Have you ever complained because the grocery store has too many cashiers and bag boys? Probably not, unless you understand that the costs of employing all those extra people are affecting the cost you pay for your service or product. If your Help Desk does not institute a chargeback for its services, your customers will probably not care about an extra number of agents available. In fact, they will like it because agents will always be around to answer the phones or work on their problems. However, if the customer is paying directly for these agents, they will want to have a say in the extra costs they have to bear for that service.

You may have the right number of agents but they are not organized in the right areas. You may find the Help Desk balanced by the org chart, but looking deeper may reveal that some agents are far more talented in areas other than the ones they are in. For example, if you are divided between hardware and software you may discover that some of your software agents really like or know hardware better and work only on those types of calls. Even simpler is when the balance you created is not aligned with the volume of calls you receive. While the call volume per agent does not have to be equal, you need to feel comfortable with how it is truly allocated.

There are many ways to validate complaints about problems in your allocation of resources. From the customers, it will be constant busy signals or the phone ringing forever before someone answers it. Phone reports will show you a high level of abandoned calls because customers got tired of waiting for help. A call transfer report may show a high number of calls between certain groups because the agents in one group are not equipped with the right number of agents or the right skills to handle the calls they receive. Finally, the agents themselves will be a good source of input on the process. They can notice as well as anyone that their organization is not aligned with the incoming needs of the customers.

Not Understanding Whom to Call for What

You may have created the best organizational layout for your Help Desk with all the resources perfectly allocated, but if the customer does not know whom to call for a particular problem, you will take a perception hit. Take walking into a library as an example. No doubt it is laid out nicely with all the books properly organized and divided into logical sections. The librarian can find any book or topic with ease, and there are helpful card catalogs, computers, and signs all over to help people out. However, if the public cannot find the book they are looking for, the library will have missed its goals. Although everything appears to make sense to you, make sure it also makes sense to the customers you support.

If your customers know about the Help Desk, you should only run into the problem of not knowing whom to call when you have segregated your Help Desk agents into separate functions. Obviously, if all your agents perform the same support functions, the customers should not have a problem understanding whom to call. It is when certain agents perform certain things that customers begin to get confused.

The best way to find out if this is a problem in your Help Desk is to get feedback from the customers and agents. It will be hard to determine this type of problem with quantitative measurements. Perhaps the best quantitative measurement to use would be a transferred calls report that could show a high volume of calls being passed from one group of agents to another. By investigating further, you may find that it was not due to the agent's lack of skill, but that the problem should have started in a different group to begin with.

Conversations with your agents can help you solve this problem. The question to them is simply, "How often do you get calls that should have gone to a different person or group?" If this is a low number, then your customers overall do not have a problem and you can address the complaint with the particular person calling in. However, if your agents report this happening frequently, you need to dive in to find a resolution. Your first place to look is at the common point where the decision of whom to call is made. Two examples of this decision point could be your overall organizational setup or within your ACD system where callers pick a menu item based on their problem.

Organizationally, you may have segregated your agents in a very technical, seemingly logical way. As a technology-savvy manager, you may have realized the skill sets needed to resolve issues and have divided your agents into groups based on those skills. Again, this makes sense from a Help Desk view, but how about from a customer's view? Should they know that their PC problem is based on the operating system versus the hardware? If so, a technical organization will make sense to them. If not, they will be guessing between your organizational groups when their PCs break. You need to be careful that your groups are divided in ways the end user of the technology can understand.

Another prime example in which a Help Desk's process can confuse customers is within their ACD system. Remember that this phone service greets callers with a message and allows them to choose from a menu of options to reach someone. Just like the examples on your organizational setup, your phone options must make sense as well. In fact, if your Help Desk is large enough to have agents grouped in very detailed areas, it may take multiple questions to route the caller to the correct group. Remember that the customer must feel comfortable dealing with the Help Desk and a "helpful" phone system will cause more problems than benefits if it cannot be understood.

So if your agents agree that they receive numerous calls that should have been directed to another group, a report from the ACD system showing transferred calls could be helpful. Use this report as well as your conversations with key customers, though, to get a good overall view. You may find that customers just choose any option to get out of the phone system and to a person. From there they can ask for the best person for their problem. I have even heard customers claim to choose their options not on who is best able to help, but on who is best at answering the phone at all! Their actual comment went something like, "I know to choose option 1 for hardware but that line is always busy. Therefore, I choose option 3 for applications because that line is never busy. They just pass me over to the right group once they answer the phone." If you have anything close to this example, you shouldn't spend too much time modifying your menu choices because that will not fix the problem.

Finally, you will need to take a close look at the practices of your agents when they receive a call that was designed to go to someone else. The easiest way out for the agent is to put the caller on hold, transfer to the correct agent or group, and hang up. Due punishment for the caller, the agent thinks. Your customers are your lifeblood, though, and punishment is the absolute wrong way to think of things. Instead, you need to decide if you want agents to take a crack at resolving questions even though they are in a different group. The plus is that the customer is not passed around and could be helped without multiple people being involved. The negative is that you divided your agents for a reason and it probably is related to their ability to effectively help in that technology. Having that agent help in matters he is not skilled at will harm the customer more than a passed phone call. You know your agents best and can decide on the best course of action for your own Help Desk.

Poor Prioritization Methods

You may be receiving the calls appropriately but your agents are working on the wrong ones first. Top paying customers may expect their calls to be worked first, but your agents may be working the calls in the order they are received. Should users unable to do their jobs be given priority over senior-level executives? These types of questions need to be clearly communicated to your agents as well as to your customer base. It is not enough for you to understand what is a high priority and what is not. The agents who are handling calls every hour of every day must understand this. Unless you have the time to micromanage the agents for each open call, they must be able to work this out on their own.

You will probably realize there is a problem in prioritization due to the incoming complaints from customers that come directly to you. Because the problem has probably reached a high sense of urgency at the customer's end, the complaints will more than likely come from a higher level of management than normal complaints. This escalation from the customer makes prioritizing problems correctly a very important skill of the Help Desk.

Discovering prioritization problems proactively will be difficult. Customer surveys will not give you this information because each customer will believe their problem is the most important. Therefore, each customer who complains about a lack of attention to their problem will not easily translate to a priority issue. However, if you begin to see a trend in complaints about timeliness from management, use your call management package for information. If you attach a severity level to each incoming call in your database, you can run a report of call resolution times by severity level. If you see that higher ranked calls are taking longer than lower ones, you may have found the validation you needed. It may be that the higher ranked calls are harder to resolve and are not being ignored, but this information will back up what the customers are telling you. You can now either devote more resources to resolving the hot issues or communicate to the customers about these findings and work towards setting new expectations.

Poor Escalation Procedures

What do you do with calls that have been open for certain periods of time? A common complaint from customers is that a frontline agent holds a problem too long and doesn't get help. This customer expectation may occur from a "hurry up and solve my problem" view or from the stance that they want managers higher up in the company to know that it is happening. As with prioritization, knowing when to get others involved is critical to Help Desk agents providing acceptable service to your customers. Working a problem night and day may show work ethic and determination in an associate, but that must be balanced with the needs of the caller in getting the problem fixed.

From a high-level view, it will be very difficult to distinguish escalation issues from priority issues. They look the same from a "just get it fixed" view, although there is a subtle difference. Priorities tell the agent *which* problem to work on, while escalations tell the agent *when* and *to whom* the problem needs to go. From a reporting need, see if you can get data on how long a problem is worked by an agent. Balancing that by your expectations on the length of time that is allowed before a problem is escalated, you can begin to see if you have problems with your agents not escalating properly. Software packages can also help this by performing specific actions as defined by you when a problem reaches a certain "age." Now the software is escalating problems for the agent in case they can't see the need.

Calls Transferred Inefficiently

Another source of customer complaints can come from an inefficient call transfer process. To the customer this inefficiency is noticed by long periods of time before problems are resolved, finding out that no one is working on the problem, or frustration at no one knowing the status of a problem because it has been passed around so much.

Resolutions that take too long to develop have been discussed many times in this chapter. While you are investigating the cause of this, look to transfers as a possible problem. The worst thing is for the problem to have slipped between the cracks and no one "owns" the problem to resolve. The initial agent may have worked the problem and passed it to the next tier of support, but if that tier does not know it was passed, the problem will sit around until it is noticed. This notification may be in the form of the customer complaining and that will look very bad.

If the customer calls in for a status of their problem and no agent knows what the status is, there will be multiple repercussions. First, the customer will have a hard time learning what is happening with their issue. Next, the Help Desk's organization will come into question. The Help Desk should be acting as one team, but if agents don't appear to be in synch, there will be doubt cast on other parts of the Help Desk as a result. This doubt may not be founded, but the perception that the agents cannot communicate well together will exist.

A third result of this poor process is that the customer will have a difficult time learning from the resolution. If the resolution is properly handled, the agent can show the customer how to solve the problem. This education is nice because the customer can possibly resolve the problem the next time it occurs based on this information. However, when a problem is passed so many times that the final agent solving the problem cannot piece together all the work that has been done, the customer will only learn part of the process. The end solution is good; communicating the path followed to reach the solution is even better.

Much like you have reviewed how long calls stay open for earlier complaints, poor transfer processes can be uncovered the same way. You should be able to take a sample problem and discuss the timing of it with the agents involved. If you detect that there was a long time between agents working the problem actively, you will begin to see that your process needs work. Another report that could help would be to see how many times a problem is transferred from one person to another. Knowing that the more people who are involved invites more opportunity for mishandling, you can begin to see organizational and training opportunities if you have a high number of three and four people touching individual problems.

Poor Tools or Poor Use of Tools

What happened to the recommendation to bring tools in for the Help Desk? Nothing. Just make sure they are the right tools and are implemented correctly. From ACD systems to call management packages, tools can be extremely effective in providing world class Help Desk services.

A first hint that something may be wrong with the tools or the way you are using them can come up in a conversation with a customer. If you are getting poor feedback about your performance and the customer refers at all to any tool you are using to provide service, you need to pay attention. The customer should not care *how* you solve their problem, but only *that* you solve it. For the customer to relay information about the tools means the tools are probably adversely affecting their interaction with the Help Desk. The agent is probably either blaming the tool directly or it comes up innocently in conversation. A statement like, "Hang on a minute while this software finishes up. It always takes a long time in the morning" can be part of a normal conversation between an agent and a customer. More than likely the agent is filling in time with light conversation instead of just sitting there in silence, but the message came out. Now when your customer complains to you about how long things take when they call, the customer can point to the software as part of the problem.

Review Your Use of the Tools   Take, for example, a call management package. To get its maximum benefit you may decree that ALL calls are entered before taking the next call. This makes sense because you need correct statistics for volume and call type. You also are smart and have all kinds of questions loaded into the call entry screen with required answers so calls are categorized for many purposes. What you have also done is added overhead to some simple tasks. Now when someone calls only to ask for someone else, that call is entered. The minutes or moments that the agents record low-value added information is preventing them from answering the next ringing phone. What may seem to be a poor allocation of resources is actually a potentially poor use of tools. This information might still be valuable to you; my point is to ensure that it is.

I suggest measuring the use of the tools where possible. Some usage may be obvious and not need a formal measurement. An ACD system, for example, gets used every time the customer calls the Help Desk. Other tools may require a more active review. Let's look at how we can measure the real effectiveness of a call management package.

Your benefits case for purchasing a call management package probably included how the software would help track calls through the Help Desk, provide reporting capabilities on the types of calls received, and aid the Help Desk agent in resolving problems. It's this third item, aiding the agents in resolving problems, that needs to be measured for its actual benefit. You can do this quite effectively by looking at the number of calls the software resolved and determining which expert system functionality was used.

Measuring the Number of Problems Solved by an Expert System   Several packages record whether an expert system was used in the closing of a problem through the software. If the agent just typed in an answer, that fact was recorded also. Obviously, the more times the agents use the expert system, the more effective the software is in helping the agents, as shown in Figure 18-5.

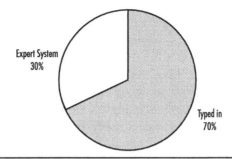

Figure 18.5   Method of problem resolution

From this example, you can see that the majority of problems were resolved by the agent typing in the answer. Looking back on your initial expectations of the value of the call management package, you can determine whether this is an acceptable ratio. I would suggest that unless the technology is *highly* unique, a 70 to 30 ratio is too low. The expert system is not being used as effectively as it could be. I would hope for a 75 to 80 percent usage of the package's features.

To get more into the details of what is happening, you can cut the data in two more slices. First, you could report on what type of calls are being resolved without the expert system to see if there is a common theme that can be addressed. Figure 18-6 shows what that may look like.

The areas that do not use the expert systems are within your production software and reports categories. This makes sense due to the nature of the other categories. Typically, there are more prepackaged answers available in hardware and off-the-shelf back-office applications. This is not to say that you cannot create more knowledge within the other categories, but that requires more effort and focus. It is now up to you to determine if that is effort and focus you are ready to take on.

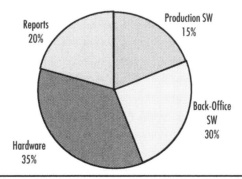

Figure 18.6   Problem types using expert system

The other angle to view this potential problem is viewing the breakdown of expert systems used when they are engaged. Figure 18-7 shows this example.

Here it is clear that the fuzzy logic and decision trees are used much less frequently than the case-based reasoning functionality. Again, you know your own system best, so you would review possible causes of this. This may not be a problem but can help you know which areas of your knowledge base need more work. Perhaps it is as easy as the fact that you have not provided the system with much knowledge in those areas. If you have concentrated in all areas with the same effort and do not feel comfortable with how the breakdown is split, you need to move to the next steps.

Review the Tool Itself The tool or technology itself may be the cause of your problems. Like fitting a square peg in a round hole, trying to make technology work in places where it does not fit will only lead to frustration and a waste of time. From magazines to the Internet to salespeople, many places advertise a perfect tool for any situation. This is very rarely true in practice, however. Every Help Desk and every agent is different, so the technologies that are used in those cases must be judged for their alignment with the particular situation. If there were an exact technology or practice that applied to every situation, this book would be easier to write, as it would just list all those rules. Because Help Desks are implemented differently for different reasons, even a Help Desk book must be flexible and cognizant of multiple environments. The same applies to the tools.

If you find yourself struggling with your agents or customers not using tools as you feel they should, it may be beneficial to step back and review the tool itself. The tool may not have been implemented in the fashion that best accommodates the needs of your Help Desk. It may be running in an environment that is not conducive to achieving its maximum benefits. Be careful if you feel yourself

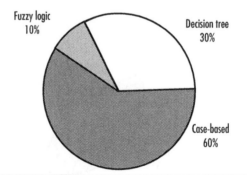

Figure 18.7 Expert system functionality used

requiring everyone to adapt to your tools and technologies. You may be right and they need to be convinced, but over the long haul they will know how it works the best and if it is suitable to their needs.

Bad People

I saved people issues to the end because the people part of the Help Desk equation crosses all the other areas. Sometimes, there is nothing left to review when validating customer complaints but the agents themselves. Think about it. People provide the customer service, people execute the processes, and people use the tools. The common denominator in all three is the human element. Some managers go directly to the people when looking for causes and that is not always right. Other managers seem to be blinded to the individual's impact and spend all their time looking at the other factors. Neither approach will always work.

To break down this element further, let's divide the people aspect into two categories: good person in a bad situation and a bad person regardless of situation. Please remember that the *good* and *bad* used here are not describing an individual's moral or ethical attributes but are directed towards their actions and skills within the workplace.

Good Person in a Bad Situation

There will be times when you have an associate who is liked personally but is failing in his job. He may be getting poor customer reviews or is struggling to do his job well despite his winning personality and general good nature. These problems usually last a long time because his personality makes it hard for managers to be critical. Agents, such as the one I've just described, tend to get more chances to improve themselves than those who have bad attitudes towards everything. This may be correct, but acting sooner can prevent future problems from arising. Situations that can make the nicest people look poor to the customers include

- Having them in the wrong role
- Being involved in the wrong environment
- Working in the wrong career

The Wrong Role   Sometimes your Help Desk has good people who are failing because they are not in the correct role in the organization. Despite your best efforts to identify those who are management material, perhaps one of your managers is not suited for that position. What was once a good agent is now a bad manager. This situation especially needs to be addressed quickly because a manager can depress morale quickly for those under him.

Another role that may create a bad situation is having an agent supporting a technology he is not qualified or interested in. This condition will probably be seen by negative remarks from the customers on the service they receive from this person. If the agent is not qualified, either he will be unable to solve the problem or, worse, he will create even more problems in his attempts to fix it. If the agent is not interested in the technology, he will be slack in his training efforts and not put forth much effort to tackle the hard-to-solve issues that arise.

Be sensitive to your agents' feedback when they speak about their roles, especially if this is a new position for them. You should know your people better than anyone and be able to distinguish the chronic complainers from those who have valid issues. Once you understand that an agent is truly not right for the role he is in, you must act. You can begin by training him or giving him a mentor to see if you can work him into the role better. Don't keep this up forever, though. Some situations are not meant to be, no matter how well they seem to fit in your opinion. If the person and the role are not good for each other, make a change.

The Wrong Environment   Another situation that can make good people look bad is to have them in the wrong environment. A Help Desk environment is a very distinct workplace and some people perform terrifically in it while others struggle. Aside from that, the work environment you and your company provide to your associates will also impact the quality of work you receive.

The nature of the interaction between your agents and their customers can work against the strengths of an agent. Some customer service associates are extremely people-oriented and need face-to-face contact to really show their skills. If your interface with the customers is 100 percent over the phones and through e-mail, those agents' skills may not show through, and over time the agents may become dissatisfied with their jobs. The root cause is not the job itself, but the manner in which they are able, or unable, to work with their customers.

The culture of your company may also dampen the enthusiasm of certain people. If your office environment is pretty formal and agents must wear shirt and ties or dresses, the rigors of everyday Help Desk life may begin to show more quickly than in environments where a more casual approach is allowed. Conversely, some people like a formal, organized workplace and would feel somewhat out of place sitting in an office where Frisbees fly across once in a while and agents hold loud conversations across common areas.

The best time and place to uncover this problem is during the interview stage. Remember that an interview should be a two-way conversation. If you set the stage at that point, you will see problems in the long term that may take a while to attribute to the work environment.

The Wrong Career   An extremely fundamental problem that an agent could discover is that a Help Desk career is not for him. The agent may know this on his very first day or it may take years to realize it. It may be that something just doesn't feel right but the agent attributes it to other factors. Externally, the signs may look just like those of burnout, wrong roles, and certainly a wrong environment, but knowing that the Help Desk career is the problem will be hard to determine from the outside. The agent's behavior could be seen by showing up late for work, taking extralong lunch breaks, and a general unwillingness to put in any extra effort.

Factors that may turn an associate against the profession are very core to a Help Desk. The requirements of ongoing customer service may not be right for everyone. Combine that with a normal feeling of not being appreciated by the customer and the impact is increased. For this reason, if nothing else, it is important that you recognize your agents all the time. Finally, most of the Help Desk work is short in duration. Unlike applications development that may involve months and years of constant project work, Help Desk work is short and quick and moves from one topic to another in a second. For those people who want to be absorbed into a project, this is not the life for them.

Bad Person Regardless of Situation

Having taken on the positive approach for recognizing people problems and relating them to the surroundings, we now turn to the more negative. There will be many cases where the person is the problem and that is all there is to it. Try as you may to say they are not positioned just right, or they need some training, there will be times when an associate is problematic and needs to be removed from the Help Desk, if not the company altogether.

Again, I am not talking about *bad* in relation to criminals or unethical people. I am, however, using this word as it relates to rudeness and not caring about others. People in the "bad person regardless of situation" category don't try to improve and seem content to stir up trouble around them and avoid anything positive. You know you are in this situation when you provide them feedback and they reply with strong denials, returned accusations, and poor excuses.

You can certainly be proactive and try to "fix" these people, but you are probably wasting your time and theirs. If you cannot even have a civil conversation about open issues, imagine what your customers must be going through. A bad person will reflect badly on your Help Desk and your management if not dealt with properly. If you are one of those people who can "work with anyone" and you feel like you failed if you cannot turn them around, take this view. You may be doing them a favor by removing them from the Help Desk and allowing them to pursue other opportunities to better fit their needs. Their acting out against you and the customer should be a clear sign that this is not the job for them and they need to go somewhere else.

Quick Recap

- Receiving complaints can be difficult as that means other people are criticizing your work. Do you feel comfortable that you can talk to those who are complaining in a way to best understand their concerns without coming across as defensive or insensitive?

- An effective way to find problems in your organization that doesn't involve anyone yelling at you is to review your own measurements. Have you begun measuring your Help Desk and the agents? Do you review it regularly to look for trends or problem areas?

- Complaints generally fall into four areas: customer service, product, process, or people. Are you seeing that your issues are concentrated in one area over another? Do you have a good plan to validate those issues and develop ways to overcome them?

CHAPTER 19

Move Forward

Chapter 18 discussed the common causes of customer complaints about Help Desks. It showed you how to recognize and validate them. This chapter covers the actions necessary to resolve lingering or chronic customer issues. Although it is impossible to go over every possible cause of customer dissatisfaction, this chapter will go over the primary factors that influence a customer's feelings about a Help Desk.

What to Look For

- The first thing you should do before jumping in to fix problems called in by customers is to watch what is happening. Get a good feel for the current environment so that you do not fix something that was not broken in the first place.

- Your next overall strategy should be to build upon your strengths. Take a positive approach to any situation when looking into its issues. The expression "Don't throw the baby out with the bath water" applies here. It means do not destroy the good things you have going in the Help Desk in an effort to fix the bad things.

- This is not to say that you cannot fix what is broken. Decisive action is necessary to overcome the weaknesses of a situation. Your customers and the organization need to know that you can recognize a problem and take the steps to resolve it.

- As you review your organization, build on its strengths, and overcome its weaknesses, you should also communicate your actions to others. This will give those around you the confidence that you are in charge and will do the right thing as needed.

Watch What Is Happening

Okay, you have gathered the data, both subjective and objective. Now what should you do? First, I recommend watching. Complicated, huh? Before you take any drastic action, observe the actual operations of the Help Desk. You should have enough information to know what to look for. Now you have the advantage of seeing things you might have seen every day but with the additional views of others' opinions or your own data analysis. I have also found that experiencing a problem yourself helps bring about the right amount of compassion and understanding. It's one thing to hear your agents are slow to respond to down systems; it is another to be down yourself and not get help.

If you have to confront an agent or group of agents, it will be much better to have your own examples to make your points. While they may be able to argue that someone else misread a situation, they will have less of a chance to pull that off with you. You will also be able to show them how a situation looked to the customer even though it seemed right to the agent.

Keep in mind that the more formal your observations are, the more you will be affecting the environment. It makes sense that an agent will be extracourteous on the phone with her manager standing nearby than if there were no one looking. More than likely there will be less idle chatter between agents and breaks will be more prompt. Unless you have some serious problems to resolve, addressing issues with the aid of casual observances should do the trick.

Build upon Your Strengths

It may surprise you that the first recommendation is not to go after the problem, but to recognize the danger in jumping right in and "fixing" things. Primarily, you run the risk of "fixing" things that are not broken. I bet somewhere down the line

Real-World Example

We had a serious problem with our PC support group in one Help Desk so I challenged my Technical Customer Services Manager to get involved and resolve the problems. All we knew for sure was that customers were complaining about everything in general. My manager began the process by watching what happened on sample calls and followed the technicians around for a couple of days. The agents were certainly anxious about this close scrutiny but the manager explained her reasons. This was not an exercise to catch anyone doing something wrong, but was intended to have an objective eye watch things to see what stood out.

After experiencing the process up close, she was able to determine several areas that needed help. These ranged anywhere from the moment a call was received, to the time the agent was dispatched to the user, all the way through following up on the call after it was resolved. If she had tried to fix things by looking through policy manuals or interviewing agents in her office, she would have never found the issues she did. It was only by living the same life of the agent and customer that she was able to uncover the majority of the problems.

your Help Desk is doing some things right. Take the "glass is half full" approach and build upon the things that are working correctly.

A simple example may be in working with an agent who exhibits poor customer service skills. A straight approach is to say, "You seem rude to customers when you speak above their head and use technical terms. You need to slow down and be nicer." Wouldn't it be better to say, "Rich, I heard you the other day working on Sarah's PC. I was impressed with how quickly you were able to solve it." As Rich nods his head in agreement continue with, "Sarah seemed confused by your description, though. You may want to go slower with her and others until they catch on." Words of encouragement certainly vary from person to person but anytime you can build from a positive, it helps keep the recipient from getting defensive too fast.

I would go so far as watching your overall speech patterns with people. Practice speaking about the positives in a situation first and addressing the negatives later. Your audience may feel as though "there is always a *but* coming" so be aware of this in your talks. However, people who are positive thinkers are strong motivators, and it is in your best interests to be one of those people.

As you are discovering your strengths, also look to your mission statement for help. This document was intended to describe your core competencies and goals as an organization. If these items listed are not among your strengths, you have some serious work ahead of you. These core competencies should be held onto closely and protected from distractions. Part V of this book will talk about new processes and tools that can further help your Help Desk, but they can also pull you away from your main work if you are not careful. If you find that you are unable to concentrate on your core competencies or are unable to perform them well, look at all the other processes you are working. Those processes that are risky or have just started may be good candidates to be reduced or eliminated if they are not contributing value to the customer and organization.

Overcome Your Weaknesses

I must have been reading some serious journals when I came up with these headings. *Overcome your weaknesses* is really *Fix the problems*. Listening, surveying, and analyzing all need to lead to accurately recognizing the problem and fixing it. Let's go back through some of the examples and see what we can do.

Overcoming Bad Customer Service

Table 19-1 captures all the bad customer service complaints discussed in Chapter 18 and provides some suggestions on how you can work to overcome them.

Although some of these suggestions modify the experience from the customer's side, most involve working directly with your Help Desk agents to overcome their weaknesses and improve their skills. For example, training is mentioned several times, but note that it is concentrating on an increase in *focused* training, not on additional training. This training effort is meant to narrow the scope of the information to deal with the specific areas needing work.

Complaint	Suggested Resolutions
"I can never reach anyone."	Offer alternate methods for the customer to reach the Help Desk (e-mails, faxing, Internet chats). Provide more ways to empower customers to resolve their own issues. Provide a voice-mail option, which is checked constantly by an agent. Provide a call dispatcher function.
"I reach them, but they don't know the answer."	Increase your focus on agent training. Provide each agent with a mentor to help him during calls. Implement tiers of support so calls can be transferred to higher levels of agents.
"I reach them, but they give me the wrong answer."	Increase your focus on agent training. Provide each agent with a mentor to help her during calls. Have someone follow up with the customer on calls to ensure their resolution.
"They think they fixed the problem but they didn't."	Have someone follow up with the customer on calls to ensure their resolution. Increase your focus on agent training. Implement a testing process that can validate answers to complicated questions.
"They may know the answer, but they don't respond."	Provide each agent with a mentor. Monitor call resolution time trends.
"They have a bad attitude and are rude."	Provide each agent with a mentor. Monitor phone conversations to help guide agents to better customer interaction.

Table 19.1   Customer Service Complaints and Solutions

Mentoring also appears several times. Mentoring is usually done early in the agent's career to help build positive best practices and start the agent off on the right foot. There is no need to limit this to an agent's first days, though. You can associate a mentor with an agent anytime there is a need for that type of help. It can be very effective to take one of your best customer service agents and sit him next to or near a problem agent. The mentor can better understand what is happening and work toward a solution if he sits with the agent on a regular basis. If you as a manager try to fix it by just dropping in and out, you will have a harder time getting to the root cause of the problem.

Developing follow-up processes is another leading suggestion in Table 19-1. You can establish rules if necessary to eliminate confusion among your agents. Perhaps you can require that all open calls over seven days require the agent to check in with the customer and inform them of the status. It can be a simple e-mail or a phone call, but the point is to let the customer know they are not forgotten. A simple note to this effect can go a long way toward maintaining good customer relationships.

The important thing in all of this is to demonstrate to the agents that you care about this aspect of Help Desk life. They need to see you act and react to high standards of customer service before they will expend great energy providing the service themselves. "Do as I say, not as I do" is not an effective strategy for a manager to take. The agents may work that way for a while, but it will not last and the customer will be adversely impacted. It is much easier to fix tangible things rather than intangible ones, so remain attentive to the art of customer service, practice it yourself, and your agents will follow.

Overcoming a Bad Product

A bad product can be a very difficult thing to overcome because in most cases you do not own all the resources necessary to incorporate a fix. With bad agents on the Help Desk, you own the right to transfer or fire them. With bad processes you can reorganize or redesign them into something better. Unless you manufacture the product, though, fixing it will require the assistance of others. Here are four ideas that will help you in this endeavor:

- Involve the vendor or manufacturer wherever possible
- Communicate your findings to others for more information
- Routinely involve competing vendors for demonstrations and training
- Create and publish Best Practices

Involve the Vendor or Manufacturer

Whether it is a PC model that fails more often than others or a piece of software with bugs, you need to find a way to get the originator of the product involved. You and your agents are the ones catching the heat and you are the ones best suited to catch the data. Gathering statistics on product failure complete with other details, such as the environment in which the product failure happens, can help the developer research the problem.

If the situation is right, you might also be able to arrange for the user to contact the developer directly. "Hey, programmer (I recommend using their name), can I have Donna call you with the details? She has very serious examples that I am having trouble following and reporting back to you." If the link is made, Donna can bring her examples and whatever other feelings to bear on the call. Don't shirk responsibility for future calls, but this can be useful for recurring, hard-to-find product problems.

Communicate Your Findings to Others

Turning around and publishing this data back out to the customer base can also be good. For one, it shows them that you are indeed aware of the problem. You might also get some "misery loves company" reprieves when the customer realizes that he is not the only one with the issue. Careful here, though. Without fixes in sight, you may also receive feedback like, "If so many people have this problem, why don't you fix it?" You don't want to appear to be passing the buck by saying, "The programmers have it" or "We'll just pass it to them…again," but the callers do need to know where the root cause lies. Become their advocate instead of their sounding board and they will come over to your side.

Involve Competing Vendors

It can take a lot of time if you find yourself forced to replace the bad product altogether. To help reduce that transition time, it is nice if you can work with competing vendors to use a demonstration model of theirs within the Help Desk. For example, if you currently use Hewlett Packard PCs, you could have Compaq loan you one of their PCs to use and test. If the HP model were to begin having many problems, you would be familiar with the Compaq model and could potentially switch more easily. This tactic would be expensive if you were forced to purchase competing models, so I recommend this only for mission-critical products or those that you can obtain for heavily discounted prices.

Be upfront with both vendors during this process. The current vendor should be given every opportunity to resolve their issues before you yank out their product. Constant replacing gets very resource intensive in time, people, and money.

However, the original vendor does need to know you are serious about using a quality product and will move forward if necessary. For the vendor providing a demo unit, be upfront with them as well. They will be expending time to help you with the demo as well as absorbing the cost of the unit they are giving you. You need to tell them your plans and how serious you are about evaluating their product. I found it very successful to work honestly with all vendors and they worked with me in the same fashion in return.

Create and Publish Best Practices

A good way to overcome bad usage of a product is to create and publish a Best Practices document. This document can describe everything from how the product works to how to maintain it.

The "how the product works" section should inform the reader on the proper use of the product. This information lets the reader know that the product was designed for certain functions and that other uses might lead to unexpected results. A laser scanner connected to a printer can certainly serve as a copier but that is not its designated function. Using the scanner in this way will probably cause it to break down more frequently or at least more quickly than you would have hoped.

The product maintenance information is something you see all the time and perhaps don't think about. Aren't you used to seeing, "Only store between temperatures 40 to 80 degrees" or "Do not store in a dusty or dirty place"? These are guidelines that suggest for you to take care of the product so that it will return the value you purchased it for.

Overcoming Not Knowing Whom to Call

One of the most frustrating issues I've received was the complaint, "I don't know whom to call about this problem." The problem was real but I felt I had done so many things to help educate the callers on this. There are a couple of ways to address this issue in both a proactive and reactive manner.

Proactively, you need to publish the names of the groups or individuals who should be contacted with all types of problems. Include their names, phone numbers, e-mail addresses, fax numbers, and any medium that allows the interaction between customer and Help Desk agent. Make sure you use terms that are user-friendly and not too technical. One reason for the frustration could be that you are publishing all this information but the customer cannot interpret it. Even when compatible terms are used, the customer may not know what their problem really is. They know what it looks like but not necessarily why it exists. For this very reason, it is wise to promote the groups or agents by how a problem *looks* to the customer instead of *what* it may be.

Reactively, you need to have your agents educate the callers at the time of a wrong contact. For example, if a customer calls your database group but they really need to be directed to your general software agents, don't just transfer the call. Inform the customer, "This problem will be best solved by the general software Help Desk; I will transfer you there now if you like." This polite message tells the customer that they are about to be transferred, but it also conveys the message that if this type of problem were to happen again, the customer should contact a different group for help.

Use this time to also ask the customer why they chose the path they did. If it was out of misinformation, the education mentioned previously will work. You may find out something entirely different, however. As mentioned in Chapter 18, the customer may intentionally choose the wrong Help Desk section just to get through to any agent. From there, they can ask for the correct person as if they had innocently chosen the wrong group.

Overcoming Bad Priorities

Service level agreements, when done correctly, should resolve priority and escalation alignment problems. Both the Help Desk and the customers have a general sense of when things should be handled. I assume by having problems here either you don't have an SLA or it is not working.

If your agents are not prioritizing well, I recommend first developing your own list of factors to be considered. Get them right in your mind and then go sit with the agents and find out how they prioritize. When they vary from your list, ask them why they chose what they did. They may be working from an old memo or thought they heard a manager explain it that way. You may also find that the callers themselves are setting the priority by invoking rules that fit their own, and only their own, needs.

Then show the agents your list and why you chose it. You can leave the list with them but be sure to explain that there will always be exceptions to the list. If any factor on the list is unclear, the agents can always check with you or other managers who are in tune with the factors. Remember your agents' strengths. They are indeed solving problems and probably even communicating well. They now just need to work on the right problem at the right time.

Overcoming Bad Tool Use

"I hate calling the Help Desk" is an awful attack and is exactly counter to your existence so you need to go after the underlying reasons with zeal. It may be one of a thousand reasons but it could be as basic as the phone system customers call in to.

Improper tools or tool usage can extend almost anywhere, but it will probably be the larger tools that cause your larger problems. Not only a phone system like the one described in the example, but also call tracking packages, Web tools, and other points of interaction between the customers and the Help Desk must be carefully monitored for their continued effectiveness.

Real-World Example

I was involved in setting up a new ACD system once and it was going to be the end-all to our problems. We were always getting complaints about busy signals and this system was going to solve it by queuing callers until we got off the existing call. Several Help Desk managers and I literally spent days designing this system to answer calls for us and route the callers to certain groups. We decided on length of hold times between "We are still busy; please keep holding" messages. We had many debates on what that message itself should say as well. The end result was a perfectly designed system that worked just as we needed it to. Unfortunately, our customers could not make it work. They chose the wrong group from the menu to be routed. They got tired of, "Your call is important to us. Please remain holding until an agent can assist you" every 30 seconds. (Seriously, try holding on the phone for 5 minutes with that coming at you every 30 seconds.) They were tired of a machine and wanted a human. We did not get complaints about busy signals any more...we certainly fixed that. Now we got, "We never get a person. The old system always got us to a person." Yeah, but you had to call us five times to get us! Luckily, I practiced my own "Don't debate the feedback" most of the time.

The tool was our problem and it needed to be fixed. We were adamant that it was the right solution; we just needed to fit it in better. So we wrote down all the complaints, solicited even more, and asked the callers how they would change it. Since we got several conflicting answers, we published our findings and went with the best we could. After implementing them, we had a tool that served our needs and helped our customers at the same time. I knew I had it as good as I could when the worst complaint was, "Whose voice recorded those messages? I don't like it."

Educate Your Users on the Tool

Whether it is the agents who are using the tool or the customers, you really need to educate them on why the tool is there and the benefits that can be gained by the proper use of it. If they can understand why it is in place and what good can come from it, you will have gone a long way to using the tool better.

Your goals for the tool are always good to share. These are somewhat close to the Best Practices recommendation we discussed for products. This information allows the agent or customer to understand your intent for the product and the objectives you were hoping to achieve. By sharing this information, you should be able to properly set expectations for the tool. For example, you might tell your customers that the new ACD system was purchased to help route callers to the appropriate Help Desk agent. If your customers felt the agents were not answering the phones any quicker, they could have blamed the new phone system. While they still can, you can at least remind them that the original purpose of the system was better routing, not quicker answering. You may still need to fix the time to answer, but the tool should not be blamed.

Along with the purpose of the tool, you should also communicate its benefits, which could include increasing productivity, bringing in more revenue, or reducing costs. This information is good for a couple of reasons. First, it shows that the investment was worth it, and you may not receive complaints of your excessive spending. Second, it shows the customers that you are remaining proactive and continuing to look for ways to improve the service the Help Desk offers.

Expand the Areas That Need More Work

Now that your agents and customers understand why the tool was bought and what it should be delivering, they can provide you more focused feedback on it. Instead of general complaints (which you will always receive), you can begin to get better input on specific items. If the agents know that the call management package was intended to help them resolve more problems on their own, but the tool is not helping them do that, they can tell you that specifically. When you get this feedback, act on it. You may need to train the user more or work on the tool itself.

The tool may need to be changed either functionally or in its implementation. Functional changes may require the vendor's involvement. Perhaps they need to modify the programming or add new features that best fit your environment. The implementation of the tool might need to be changed as well.

The knowledge base in a call management package is a good example of an implementation to review. If the agents are not using all of its features, you should spend some time understanding why. It may be that one particular expert system needs an increase or update in its knowledge. The package was designed to help you solve problems and if it is not, you must resolve it to obtain the return on your investment. As mentioned earlier in the book, dedicating a knowledge engineer to be in charge of the knowledge within the software's database is a good idea and will help keep the agents productive.

Overcoming Bad People

Fixing weaknesses can be hard to do if it involves the agents themselves. The phrase "You can't teach an old dog new tricks" is appropriate. People are not above being changed, but it is difficult to influence core behaviors of people. Some say that a person's behavior is established by the teen years and only hardens after that. Making people something they are not may be worth the effort in some cases; you just need to be prepared for a long fight.

No matter how hard it is to deal with a problem person, it is one of the most important things you must do. The way you handle personnel issues will be seen by many people, both above and below you in the organization. These actions will set a precedent on how you manage and what is allowed and not allowed. There will be many other problems if you set rules and then do not apply them equally across the organization.

Think about a policy that states that your agents must be at their desks, logged into the system by a certain time each day. If Barbara routinely comes into the office 15 minutes late, you have a problem. If you ignore it for whatever reason, you set the precedent that it is an okay behavior. The first time you get on anyone else about arriving late, they could point out this fact. That is a poor excuse on their part, but one that should be recognized.

It is very easy to allow an agent to underperform or create bad customer service when he is one of a large group. There is so much going on in a Help Desk that one bad person might get lost in the shuffle. I urge you to not let this happen, especially if there is a large group. Many more people in this group will see bad behavior occurring with no consequences. There is no need to reprimand the person in public or with a lot of theatrics, but the issues need to be addressed. Other people in the group will recognize a change in behavior without you making a scene.

Keep in mind during all this that the situation may not be right for the person more than the person is just bad overall. In either case, you must act. It may be that you want to keep the person in the Help Desk but he or she needs to be moved to a different section. Again, their skill set may not be aligned well with their environment and a simple organizational move may completely turn the person around in the customer's perception.

Communicate Your Action Plan

Just as in conducting surveys, it is very important to communicate to the stakeholders what your plans are and the results you have seen to date. I think you will find that your prompt and resolved efforts to fix the problems will begin to ease the tensions from the beginning.

For example, let's say you hired a new agent and changed some processes in attempts to reduce the amount of time your callers are on hold. Figure 19-1 could be your chart that shows that your efforts in September have made a noticeable improvement. This communication can clearly demonstrate to your audience that you recognized a situation and made very good progress in making it better.

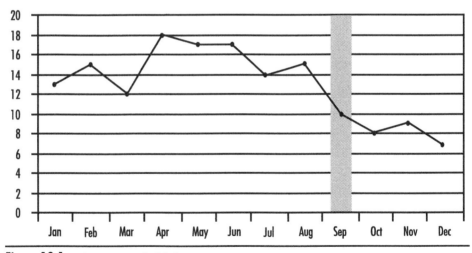

Figure 19.1   Average on-hold times

You might not have fixed a single thing yet, but if people know you are working on it that will count somewhat, too. I think you will find that your efforts will not just make your customers happier; they will make your agents happier as well. They don't like being screamed at or constantly complained about. Be a person of action, an agent of change, and the Help Desk will grow and thrive.

Quick Recap

- Do you have a good feel for how well your Help Desk is working? Do you stay in touch enough that if faced with customer issues, you can quickly determine the source of the problem? If not, find ways to get involved. Doing it regularly can save you a lot of time and frustration down the road.

- What are the top five things that your Help Desk does well? If you struggle to come up with that many, you need to look around some more. The five may not be the highest priority topics for you, but they surely exist and can provide you with strong building blocks for overcoming problems.

- Do you feel comfortable addressing problems head-on? Do you have a good relationship with your agents where you can work on problems without a lot of ill will or confusion? Problems cannot be ignored, and if they are ignored they will certainly turn into larger problems. Understand that most problems are resolved more easily early in the process, so taking the time to fix them when you hear of them is actually easier than delaying and hoping they go away.

CHAPTER 20

How Not To Be Outsourced

With all the talk about identifying and resolving customer issues with your Help Desk and its processes, there may be discussions about the outright replacement of your Help Desk with an outsourcing firm. We have discussed this as a strategy for selected functions you provide, but we did not cover the prospect that your senior management may choose this to completely replace you.

Have you been hearing rumors around the water fountain that senior management is looking at outsourcing? Noticed increased inquiries from them into your performance or operations? Have they called you in and flat out told you that outsourcing is coming? If so, and you still want a career, or a job even, then you need to get busy and make sure certain things are happening. This chapter will quickly cover some basic ideas that will help you keep the outsourcing committee at bay except in the areas you choose yourself.

What to Look For

- The first thing you must do to prevent a "hostile takeover" of your Help Desk is to fully understand your own operations. You need to know going into this process exactly where you are good and where you could use improvement.

- The second thing you must do is to ensure that others know about you. This ranges from your senior managers to your customers. If they do not know of your capabilities, they may look elsewhere for Help Desk functions without being fully informed of your own organization.

- Once you are finished gathering information, the task ahead gets pretty straightforward. To prevent your operations from being outsourced, you and your Help Desk need to do what you do better, faster, and cheaper than anyone else can.

Know Your Help Desk and Its Processes

You first need to fully know and understand everything about your Help Desk. You need to have reviewed the metrics of the operation and staff, and you need to understand the processes that are involved to get things done, the people that are performing them, and the costs to keep this Help Desk running.

By now, you must have caught on to the value of measurements. If for no other reason, I bet that using measurements to save your organization will reinforce their importance. Whether it is to fix processes that are broken or to have statistics on hand when speaking with senior managers, you need to know how well your group is doing. You need to be well versed in their speed, their quality, and their effectiveness. If you find things that can be fixed, then fix them! If you find no problems, good; just continue to keep yourself in the loop.

You need to know the processes as well. You designed them some time ago; make sure they are still in operation the way you want. Dig deep to find other rogue processes that may be affecting your Help Desk. Are your agents performing tasks in the name of customer service for someone who isn't an approved customer? Make sure your Help Desk is doing what it needs to be doing and not getting involved in things that take too much time and resources away from your main mission.

How do you review these processes? Although watching and interviewing people is good, reviewing your documentation of the processes is also good. If you do not have this documentation, you need to. The best way to maintain a standard and consistent process is to put it in writing so anyone can refer to it when needed. This documentation also allows a smoother transition for new agents entering your Help Desk as all agents will be reading from the same sheet of music, so to speak. Along the way if you find that your actual processes are different from what you once documented, you can validate which is the most correct for the times and amend the other.

Knowing your people may seem obvious, but it is good to review your agents and their respective jobs with an objective eye from time to time. Someone who might have once been perfect for a role may not have kept up with the changing technologies or needs of your customers. Or perhaps they have gone down the burnout phase of their career life cycles and are no longer performing up to your standards. These people need to be replaced or encouraged to increase their productivity. When management is potentially looking to outsource, they can substantiate their views by seeing agents in the current Help Desk not performing. You need to eliminate this problem before it becomes too big to fix.

Last in the *know your Help Desk* phase is understanding the costs of your operation. When times are good cost is not as big of an issue; however, when time are bad Help Desks suffer like everyone else, regardless of the cost-cutting measures you may take. We went over one measurement (cost per call) in Chapter 13 but this is broader. Compare your actual expenses to the budget you created or were given. Are you in line? Line items that are well over budget need to be researched to find out why. It may be that processes are not as efficient as they should be or you just plain missed some expenses in your planning. You need to at least know that before someone asks so you can have an adequate explanation and potentially a repair plan.

Line items that are well under budget should be reviewed just as much. Should you have spent a certain amount of money in areas and have not yet? Could you have job openings that are not filled? It won't look good to be criticized for not answering the phone and resolving problems quickly if you had a staff of six approved and you have only hired four.

Make Sure Others Know You, Too

If you are still at rumor stage, begin subtle promotions of your group. Hopefully, you have been sharing metrics all along, but if not, now is the time to start. Present them in a "Just thought you may want to see these numbers" kind of context. Make sure you are showing the right things in the right way also. Where in the past you may have shown 20 different metrics, now maybe you show only those that will differentiate you from any outsiders. I am not saying to hide bad measurements; I am saying to arrange the numbers and graphs to promote the things most important to your audience. Don't let your message get lost in the middle of a wide array of facts and figures.

If you are past rumors and are in the middle of outsourcing discussions, these promotions need to be more formal and directed. You will be more successful if you are not in defensive mode but provide the measurements in the true spirit of sharing information. You can distribute the numbers and then follow up with conversations. This way you can ensure your message is received as intended. This also gives everyone the opportunity to discuss plans while being fully informed of the situation. All you can ask is that any decision is made with complete knowledge of the environment and facts surrounding it.

One of the best advocates you can have is your customer base. If they are believers in your operations and can speak to your achievements, outsourcing will be much harder for anyone to prove beneficial. On that same note, if your customers see you as their technology advocate, they will do everything to keep you around. Having a customer fight for you to your management team is very powerful. You know that Help Desk customers can be a very demanding group, so if they feel good enough about you to speak for you, their message will definitely be heard.

As you are publishing measurements, include the results of any surveys you have taken. If you are delivering the quality service that you should be and have been conducting surveys, the results should praise you nicely. Even if there is not a good opportunity for your customers to speak out on your behalf, these survey results can speak for you. There can be items within your published results that are not all that great, and that is okay. Develop a strong plan to resolve those issues and attach it to the survey. Many times a valid plan to fix a problem can overcome any negative attention a bad survey creates.

Do Things Better, Faster, and Cheaper

This sounds obvious. Are you doing things well, quickly, and cost-effectively, though? A business manager once told me that he put his customers to the test by saying, "There is better, faster, and cheaper…you can have two of them." I know the point he was trying to make, and feel he was close, but not right on target. It may be right that to achieve higher goals you cannot have everything without costs going up somewhere, so I concentrate more on the "er" at the end of each word. You may not deliver more services better, faster, and cheaper, but know that every organization has opportunities to do better than in the past. I challenge you to look for ways to reach all your goals. If you need more than my challenge, look back at the water fountain or remember your conversations with senior management as incentives. I will not define what these words mean, but let's look at them in the Help Desk setting.

Do Things Better

Doing things better is a goal we should all reach for, and it ties into the suggestion of measuring and promoting your Help Desk. A good leader will always want to get better for the sake of improvement, but in times of strict review it is even more imperative. Resolve the root causes of problems to get your customer base more productive. Work with your management and customers to find ways to better serve them. Bring in your vendor partners and other consultants to aid in delivering the finest quality service possible. Communicate to your managers and agents to really concentrate on supporting the customer and their products in a quality fashion, both proactively and reactively. Tie up loose ends that have nagged you over time. Streamline your processes to make the best use of the resources you have.

Do Things Faster

Faster could be viewed as better, but I think it can stand well on its own. Answer the phone in two rings instead of three. Get your second-tier agents closer to the action so problems can be resolved in less time. Don't follow up with statuses every four days; try every three.

Okay, if you could do all that, you probably wouldn't have any concerns of outsourcing to begin with. I understand, but sometimes it takes a renewed sense of urgency for people to find quicker ways to do things. You need to keep a thumb on the pulse of the agents during all this. Speeding things up may be viewed as increasing workload and burnout will set in faster than normal. Achieve the speed increase through process efficiency. Analyze the workflow to make sure there is no unnecessary bureaucracy slowing things down. Empowering your agents to make certain decisions at the point of attack may provide you with a better customer experience. At the same time, you will discover those agents who can manage that responsibility and come up with creative solutions. You will also find those who reach too far past their capabilities and need to be brought back. Again, monitor the operations so that getting faster does not sacrifice quality.

Do Things Cheaper

Cheaper is viewed in money and noise. I got you wondering about noise, so I will start there. There is good noise and bad noise. Good noise is the marketing and promotion of your Help Desk's actions and effectiveness. Sharing metrics of the value the Help Desk adds to the organization is good noise that executives and customers like to hear. Bad noise is the talk of your Help Desk that is negative. Bringing senior management into situations that the Help Desk caused or could have prevented is an example of noise you want to avoid. "Why can't you...", "Why didn't you...", and "When will you finally..." are the beginnings of questions that are generally negative and not what a Help Desk manager wants to be answering.

The easier one to see is reducing costs. I didn't say easier to solve because that can be very hard to do, but you should be able to review costs relatively easily. In an outsourcing situation, you want your Help Desk to be as efficient and cost-effective as possible. Keep an eye on the high-ticket items like salaries. Are you incurring a lot of overtime? This should be as low as is feasible, for overtime can increase your salary expenditures at a rapid clip. Review any capital items you may be planning to purchase. It may be prudent to delay large purchases until things die down a bit, unless you are certain you will receive a strong and rapid return on the investment. Reducing a calculated cost per call will be hard to achieve in a short time period, but strive to do so. Outsourcing agencies will sell their services on call volume or flat fees so you need to be running a tight ship to compare favorably.

Your Overall Approach

While it is unhealthy to constantly walk around worrying about things that may or may not occur, it is healthy to keep a feeling in the back of your mind that you need to constantly improve. This mental exercise keeps you on your toes and makes you view your Help Desk from a different angle than you normally would. With this in mind, you now may react to bad people, processes, or tools more quickly than at other times. Managing a Help Desk can be a very time-consuming task that forces you to put out fires all day long, day after day. Know that you often need to rise above that to see the big picture. You must find time to review your operation with a critical eye and improve wherever it is needed. Your agents will thank you, your management will thank you, and your customers will most assuredly thank you.

Quick Recap

- How well did you do when you reviewed your own operations? Were you good where you thought you were?

- Do you think the other parties in your organization know about your abilities? If not, you must immediately begin a promotional campaign that demonstrates what you offer to the organization.

- It sounds pretty simple to do things better, cheaper, and faster, doesn't it? These are the goals you must establish and reach in order to keep your Help Desk employed by the customers. Without these factors, your customers will, and should, investigate other options. You must manage your Help Desk in a manner that keeps your customers from even considering looking somewhere else.

Action Plan Checklist

❑   Ensure you have good communications among you, your management, your customers, and your Help Desk agents.

❑   Continue to review metrics that show the progress of the Help Desk.

❑   Watch your Help Desk operations from a customer-centric view.

❑   When you receive complaints, listen carefully and with empathy. Try and understand the underlying causes of the complaints.

❑   Go after the resolution of customer complaints aggressively. This will help calm your customers, rebuild confidence in your management, and help keep the outsourcing bug away!

PART V

Taking Your Help Desk to Another Level

CHAPTER 21

The People

Taking care of your people has been a consistent theme of this book. We have organized them, trained them, and worked hard to retain them and grow their careers. All these are necessary to run a Help Desk.

This chapter will explore ways you can take this achieving, effective group and bring out even more growth and accomplishments. I will talk about ideas for your own agents and offer some suggestions for getting more out of your customers and other relationships.

What to Look For

- Empowering your Help Desk allows it to grow and become more valuable for its customers. Integrating other IT department functions into the Help Desk is a very effective way to achieve this.

- Growing the Help Desk also requires leadership within its ranks. While managers are necessary to coordinate and supervise the agents, leaders are needed to provide inspiration and role models for the agents to aspire to.

- Outsourcing is another way to grow your Help Desk and what it can offer. There are good opportunities for your Help Desk to use the resources of others to achieve its goals.

- There are many ways to compensate your agents. This chapter will discuss several options that will provide additional incentives for your agents to excel.

- Bringing your vendors together for formal meetings can be productive for your Help Desk and your customers. With everyone in the same room, you can share plans and ideas for the future.

- Don't forget your customers. Training them on the technology products and processes they use in their workplace can help them be more productive. This is a value-added process that your Help Desk can be very effective at providing.

Organizational Empowerment

A truly effective Help Desk is a proactive organization that does not just wait for problems to happen but goes after them and tries to resolve their root cause. It is involved in many aspects of the IS department and the business. Because every buggy program or bad hardware implementation comes back to haunt the Help Desk, it is imperative that they are involved. At the very least, a representative from the Help Desk should be a part of every project team that produces technology impacting the end user. They are invaluable sources of information.

I also found it very effective to empower the Help Desk wherever possible. In one instance, we moved elements of our Systems Administration group as well as LAN and WAN management under the Help Desk manager. This enabled the Help Desk manager to have strong input into decisions involving system downtime and maintenance planning.

I also think your training and documentation group should come under the Help Desk organization. Both groups come into play near the end of the development cycle and both have a vested interest in the product's impact on the end user. The groups can learn much from each other as well. The training can see what types of support calls are coming in and can focus its training efforts towards those calls. The Help Desk agents can also review training material to add tricks of the trade. They can bring their experience in the "real life" of the customers to ensure the training media is implemented in ways the customers will understand.

Another area that can work well with the Help Desk is your Quality Assurance or testing associates. Again, both groups are joined in the goal of assuring that any released product works well for the end user. A thoroughly tested product reduces load on the Help Desk, and the Help Desk can add testing guidelines that are beyond the pure development of the product and aimed more at the actual use of the product by the customer.

Developing Leaders

Haven't we already spoken about developing leaders? Close. We spoke of managers; leaders are different. They are mutually exclusive. Managers may or may not be good leaders just as leaders may or may not be good managers. Managers are jobs that people occupy; leaders are people that occupy jobs.

A leader does not have to be organizationally higher than a manager. Granted, you do not often see job titles with the word "Leader" in them, but they exist at all levels. A manager can have many subordinates under him, but some of the subordinates can command more respect and get more things done than the manager. Their personal attributes and value systems are positive and set a good example for others to follow. These people are leaders. They lead the team and the effort through their ideas and their actions. They do not rest on a job title to push things through. "Because I said so" is rarely heard from a leader.

Managers are very necessary in every organization because they see tasks and the actions that are required to get them done. However, they typically also spend a lot of time analyzing the process looking for small ways to do it better. Leaders see these tasks as well, but they also see the people who are performing them. Leaders care about the people involved and find ways to make the process better by inspiring the people within that process.

I titled this section *Developing Leaders* but I believe it is a misnomer. I really believe that leaders are out there already; it is your job to keep them in the organization and not let other aspects of the work environment push them down or away. While all natural leaders may not want to assume the official responsibilities of management, it is wise to keep, or put, them in positions where the most people can feel their influence. Leaders are imitated and you want your agents and your customers to notice them.

This position of recognition is sometimes quickly thought to mean promotion to a management job title. Some leaders cannot be effective with some of the administrative tasks and attention to detail that are required of a manager. If you put a leader in a position in which he is not comfortable, he will fail and you will have caused more problems than benefits. Putting leaders in a position to be recognized may not involve physically moving them or changing their jobs. It could be as simple as asking their opinion on matters either in front of others or in private. Use them for their ideas and vision to get new perspectives on growing your Help Desk.

Leading by example is a requirement. Leaders and leaders-to-be must be cognizant of this at all times. The best example in a Help Desk world is the ringing telephone. If the Help Desk agents see their boss walking down the hallway and passing a ringing phone without stopping, it will send a strong message. Apparently, it is okay to not answer a call if it is not at your desk. The next time the manager criticizes the Help Desk for not being customer-focused and not going the extra mile for the customer, he or she will be mostly ignored. The message needs to match the actions of the one speaking for it to be effective!

Can you imagine a better example than for a Help Desk manager to sit down at an empty desk to help agents answer the phone during extremely busy times? That manager would be acting correctly and the agents would appreciate his initiative and willingness to help. The Help Desk manager's motivation will be the difference between management and leadership. The manager within him helped out to keep metrics at a good level or because he felt he wanted to set an example. The leader didn't think about it. He knew the agents and customers were in need of help and he jumped in because it was the right thing to do.

Real-World Example

I was once in a program sponsored by my company entitled Legacy of Leadership. It entailed bringing in recognized leaders from across the company, regardless of job title, to see them in action, pushing them to make large-scale decisions in very short time periods and presenting corporate goals to the executive team. The participants didn't deal in how to get certain things done, but presented more of an overview of what direction the company should take and why that was important.

The program was a success. Those attending felt the recognition of doing their jobs well and many made positive impressions on the executive team. This is an example of nurturing the leadership qualities in people and hopefully encouraging them to pass those qualities along to people around them.

Outsourcing Revisited

With your Help Desk running full steam ahead and valued by your customers, it is time to revisit outsourcing. A Help Desk associate performs many functions on a regular basis that can be viewed as noncritical or adding little value to the company. These are the perfect candidates for outsourcing. Examples could include resetting passwords or answering spreadsheet software questions that are not part of your core business.

Another reason that outsourcing may be beneficial to you is staff augmentation. There are times when the market is not producing the quality of skill sets you are looking for. That skill may be in high demand and the talent too expensive for you to afford. These times are ripe for an outsourcing partner to help you. Perhaps your Finance department has just purchased an accounting package running on a database that you have not previously supported. Hopefully, you had prior knowledge of this transaction, but I know that is not always the case. You are still tasked with supporting it with a live date very close at hand. Bringing in an outsource partner to set up and manage this database until you can hire or train resources for it makes perfect sense. The department may scrap the project before it is fully implemented because it does not match expectations, and you will not be heavy in staff that is no longer needed.

Staff augmentation can also help you in time coverage in addition to skill sets. You may have staff in the office for most of the day but not overnight because the quantity of calls does not merit having someone sit around the office all night. Outsourcing partners can provide that coverage for you. The quantity may not justify a full-time person for you, but they will have many customers whose aggregate call volume makes it cost effective for them to offer this service.

Time coverage from outsourcers can also aid you in peak call periods. For some business reasons, your Help Desk may get a majority of its calls in a small block of hours. It would not make sense for you to hire staff for two to three hours a day just to handle this large influx so let your outsourcing partner help. Again, they can leverage their customer base needs to provide you the service you need at a cost you can afford.

Regardless of the reason, you must openly communicate to existing staff when you bring in an outsourcing partner. Their immediate fear will be that they are being replaced, so it is best to tackle that issue head on from the start. Here, I define "the start" not from when you first think of it, but when it is approved and will really happen. If the need goes away or is not approved, there is no need to stir the waters for nothing.

From the customer's viewpoint, the use of outsourcers can be published or not. Many outsourcing partners offer the capability to answer the phones as your company so the caller may not even know the difference. While not going all out to promote this, I would not actively hide it either. Outsourcing is a valid tool to help the Help Desk and can be very beneficial to all parties concerned.

Compensation Plans

It pays (come on, give me that one) to review your compensation plan every few years. While governmental or company policies will restrict you somewhat, there are still different ways to compensate your associates. However you decide to compensate your agents, you will find that there are two main areas where you can make an impact. The first is their normal base rate paid weekly, biweekly, or monthly. Because this is a straightforward approach that is fairly consistent everywhere, we will not address it here. What we will address are options for compensating agents that are in addition to this normal rate of pay. You can review this from a day-to-day angle or go after it to cover weekend and extra hours work, projects, or obtaining preapproved objectives.

Rules for Compensation Planning

No matter how you compensate your associates, you must follow some basic rules when you develop your plan. They include

- **The plan must be easy to understand.**   If the associates are expected to work towards goals that gain them more compensation, they must be able to understand how the plan works. Clearly defined compensation plans allow associates to see what is expected of them and there is not a lot of wasted time spent debating how it works. Complicated, hard-to-follow plans create much confusion and might even lead the associates to feel the plan has been designed that way to trick or fool them. That has to be the last thing you want your associates to think.

- **The plan must be easy to administer.**   This rule does not affect the associates directly, but is more for your own benefit. If the plan calls for significant work on your part to track, calculate, and report compensation amounts for the associates, you will be diverted from your main objectives each pay period. If the administration of the plan becomes too much of a burden, you may delay working on it or try shortcuts to get around all the effort. This will eventually lead to the demise of your plan and the associates will wonder what happened. The explanation "It was just too hard for me to do" will not go over well if the associates felt it was a valuable plan for them.

- **The plan must be fair.**   Any compensation plan you design must be fair to your associates. Many plans fall short because they impose objectives that your associates cannot meet in their environment. An example would be to reward an agent for accomplishing a certain amount of training within a deadline. A problem is created when you keep the agent so busy on the phone and working problems that she has no time to get the training. Now your plan has created frustration instead of incentive. It is one thing to not know you could be making $5,000 more; it is entirely another to know that $5,000 is available but out of your reach.

- **The plan must be aligned with your goals.**   Compensation plans will drive behavior as much as anything else. We spoke earlier about how measuring agents' activities will push them in a direction. Paying them money for this measurement will push them farther and faster still. Therefore, you need to be extremely careful when designing your plan. Unfortunately, something you should do at the end of the design is to attack the plan from an "opportunistic, greedy, selfish, borderline-unethical" view. Look at each and every point in the plan to see how someone could take advantage of it. Look everywhere to see how someone could act in ways to gain more money yet perform actions that are not in the interest of the Help Desk and its customers. While your agents probably do not match that description, you can never be too sure. If you find "loopholes" in your plan, make sure you close them before implementation.

- **The plan must be tied to performance in all cases.** There are certainly opportunities to compensate agents using subjective criteria, but all points of the plan need to be directed towards good performance by the agent. This could be working long hours, completing a project on time, or simply delivering consistently strong customer service. Pay your people well, but reward them for *doing* well, not just *being* good.

- **Make bonus plans a true bonus and not deferred compensation.** Your bonus plan needs to bring compensation to associates, which is in addition to their normal salary. It should reward performance and accomplishments that went above and beyond their normal workday. If you let your bonuses bleed into their regular salaries, it will begin to lose its special meaning. It will soon become *expected* and *owed* to the associate. The downside is that the extra work and accomplishments will still be deserving of recognition and the associate will want something for it. Keeping bonuses separate from regular salaries can be hard, but consistent management and communication of expectations will help a lot. It is okay when recruiting new agents to combine a salary with a bonus estimate if you think that compensation will be an issue with the recruit. However, you need to communicate strongly that this is an estimate, that it is entirely conditional on their performance, and should not be counted on without this in mind.

Bonus compensation can be based on many different goals and achievements. Some are tied to performance reviews and are pretty subjective in their calculation. Others are related directly to predefined objectives with some variance allowed for how well the associate worked along the way. Some bonus objectives you can use within the Help Desk environment are listed below.

- Project-based
- Continual goals
- Time off
- Certifications

Project-Based Compensation

One way to compensate a team is upon completion of a project or milestones within. Although this can work well in certain environments, the Help Desk is not as conducive to it. Each call to the Help Desk could be construed as a project and basing pay on this would be very high in administrative costs and low in return. You would also notice your agents spending as much time tracking project times as actually working towards resolving problems.

Continual Goals

Many bonus plans call for a year-ending payout based on the performance of the associate for the prior year. This is certainly easy to administer from a calculation view, but is hard to reward accurately because the achievements or failures might have occurred so long ago that they are forgotten. To help overcome this problem, think about implementing a continual goals program that sets expectations and reviews performance at several intervals throughout the year. Not only does this help you reward good things and discuss bad things more easily; it also gives you more flexibility in setting goals. Because your goals may very well change through the course of the year, this program gives you the ability to modify behavior by offering incentives at each decision point.

Define the Goals

Your first action in developing this continual goals program is to define the goals for the associates. These goals can vary by individual associate or by groups within the Help Desk, or you can apply them evenly for the entire Help Desk. The more homogeneous your agents are organized, the more you can apply the same goals for the whole group. These goals can include certain abandoned rates, call resolution times, or high levels of customer service. If you have tiered support levels or particular problems with a specific agent, you may use different goals for each group or associate. Tiered support groups may have incentives for low call transfer rates while problem associates may get bonuses for improved customer service feedback.

Define How You Will Measure the Objectives

The next step is to come up with how you will measure each of the goals you decided upon. Calculation methods are important any time you use and communicate measurements, but when a person's pay hinges on the outcome, you need to be especially certain you are measuring the actual and correct results. Not all the measurements have to be objective, however. You can use subjective criteria as long as you clearly show the people being measured how you plan to do it. At the end of the process, it is imperative that everyone is on the same page for the goals and the measurements. Your agents do not have to agree with the goals you laid out, but they need to understand them. If you can get understanding from all parties in the early stages, it will make things go much easier when it is time to pay your bonuses.

Determine Pay Amounts and Schedule

Given the goals you have established and the return they will bring the Help Desk, you can determine how much money will be available for the bonus program. It may seem logical to know the money first and to some degree that is true. You will probably know, or need to know, how much money is allowed in the budget for this program. You also need to fully understand how this bonus plan will impact the associates' total compensation. Remember that the bonus is a pure additional amount on top of the base salary and therefore should not be too high in proportion to their total compensation. For example, if the agent makes $30,000 a year in base pay and his potential bonus could total $15,000, his total compensation would be $45,000. His bonus is then 30 percent (15000/45000). If you are comfortable with a bonus plan being that high, then proceed. If you want bonuses to be a lower percentage, then you need to adjust the bonus plan accordingly.

Basically, bonuses can be viewed as "at risk" to the associates because the bonuses are not guaranteed unless the associates meet the objectives. The higher the risk, the more uncomfortable the agent will likely feel about his pay. Agents who can have the largest impact on the goals of the Help Desk and the company overall are the best candidates for higher levels of pay risk. However, until you are comfortable with the importance of your goals, it is wise to hold off announcing bonus compensation. Once you have defined the goals, though, you can announce the pay levels.

The last piece of the equation is the scheduling of the bonuses. The closer the bonuses are together, the more immediate feedback the associates get for their efforts. This also creates more administrative work on your part as you spend more time calculating their bonuses. Bonuses spread farther apart give less immediate feedback but there is also more time available for the agents to achieve their objectives. I would recommend a bonus schedule with quarterly payouts. Annual ones are too far apart and monthly ones create too much work just administering the bonus.

Figure 21-1 shows a sample continual bonus planning chart.

The continual goals bonus program offers associates opportunities for increasing their income by achieving objectives. Agents generally like this plan because they can clearly see how they can make more money and can get it periodically throughout the year.

Bonus plan for Parker Saunders				
Goals	1st Qtr	2nd Qtr	3rd Qtr	4th Qtr
Achieving 85% customer satisfaction	$1000	$1000	$1000	$1000
Join team for CRM implementation	$2500	$2500		
Serve as mentor to new hires		$500	$500	$500
To Be Decided			TBD	TBD

Figure 21.1   Continual bonus planning chart

Time Off

Time off for extra hours worked is good. If an agent has to work late into the night to resolve a problem or come into the office on Saturday to fix a down server, a good reward is time off one day that week. I stress the time off coming as soon as possible. Giving them time off sometime in the future diminishes the return, so go as far as requiring it to be in the next week or two.

Compensation overall is only as good as the value it brings the person being compensated. Sounds simple, right? Think about it, though. An hourly person works a day or so extra on the weekend to fix a problem that has occurred several times and caused much downtime. Giving her the next Friday off for a long weekend sounds like just the ticket, doesn't it? But what if time off is not as important as earning overtime pay for this associate? Now you have actually hurt the process instead of rewarding it.

Certifications

We discussed certification training in Chapter 12. This training is focused on certain technologies or skill sets and can add much value to your Help Desk. If the certifications can be identified that best help your Help Desk, you may institute bonus plans when an associate obtains the certification. We also discussed earlier that you must be careful with this type of bonus. The marketplace can place a lot of value on certifications and you don't want your company to fund the training for someone only to lose them to another company. Again, you cannot afford to not train your associates, so if you feel comfortable that the certification helps you, the bonus plan may be a good thing to try.

The success of any compensation plan is knowing your associates and what is important to them. Just as you surveyed your customers, remember to survey your associates, too. You may find that the smallest things make a large difference in an associate's happiness in the job. To some, job titles are a motivator, while vacation or recognition drives others. Talking with your group as a manager can uncover many good nuggets of information to help you both through your careers.

Vendor Councils

A good way to strengthen your Help Desk's effectiveness is to build and maintain relationships with your vendors. These vendors can be the manufacturers, resellers, consultants, contractors, and implementation partners. I recommend holding regular, formal meetings once or twice a year where you bring in all your vendor partners to discuss your coming plans and current issues. These meetings should take place more frequently in very large Help Desk environments. I am sure your vendors would love to hear this as it gives them insights into your company and where it is headed. They will be more than ready to present back to you all the areas where they can help you with your plans and issues. Don't expect this to occur during the meeting, however. If their competitors are in the room, they will hold their cards close to their chest until they can get you one on one. This is okay, but I still recommend that you hold the combined meeting because you only have to deliver your message once. It also shows each of the vendors that you do have choices and they should be alert in their dealings with you. A subtle way to ensure they see their competition is to provide all your vendors with an attendee list. Include the attendees' names and companies, and if you really want to push it, include the business you see doing with them!

If your vendors are from a wide variety of businesses you may want to have breakout sessions after the general presentation. That way you can drill down in areas without boring other listeners about areas they have no interest in.

You should also formalize the follow-up from the meeting. Inform each vendor that you would like a response back within some specified time period where they can show you how they can help you in your plans moving forward. These partners will show you how to improve your operations, augment your staff, or implement new technologies. They are key to your success so use them wisely.

Get a double reward from your meeting by videotaping the event. This way you can allow others in your department or company to see what happened even though they did not attend. You could also use this as a tool to see the soft skills of your presenters and possibly train them on presenting material while viewing themselves in action.

Customer Training

One way to further the importance of customer training is through certification. We discussed certification of your agents; why not certify your customers? You could develop a training and testing plan that covers important points and issues on new software or hardware being implemented. Once the user passed the test, they would be allowed to use it. The benefit to the Help Desk is that easy entry level questions might now be avoided because the user was forced to understand the product better from the beginning. The business should gain because their associates are better informed of the new product or service and can focus back on their jobs.

The implementation of a plan like this needs to be properly communicated and discussed with the business leaders from the outset. If you will not allow anyone to log on to the system until they pass a test, will the business allow that? If they were rushed to fill an open position and you stop that person from working, will that cause ill feelings? This shouldn't happen if they are bought into the process and involved in its design. Your entire goal is not to become the dictator of system use, but to become the teacher of it. Maybe you begin with smaller subsystems that don't directly impact the operation and profitability of the business. Over time you can monitor metrics that show the effectiveness of a well-trained associate versus the costs of supporting someone who isn't trained. This measurement may get the business leaders to demand this certification plan instead of being forced to live with it.

Real-World Example

A successful program we started in one Help Desk to help increase the technical knowledge of our business associates was called BASIC. BASIC stood for Branch Associates Supporting the Information Center and it brought in associates from the business to serve 12 to 18 months in the Help Desk. We felt that having these associates receive software questions concerning all levels of the business would help them grow into operation managers or branch trainers more quickly than going through the normal business career path. A side benefit was that it brought real-life business people into our Help Desk to help teach us how the business worked and bolstered our staff in terms of headcount as well. If possible I would encourage trying some version of this program. It may be an insignificant time period such as one day, but any face time the business and your Help Desk agents can share is very valuable. The business can see what you go through and hopefully empathize with the work, and your agents can learn how the business sees issues.

Quick Recap

- How empowered is your Help Desk to resolve the problems it receives each day? Are there opportunities to streamline processes to achieve a quicker resolution by combining any other IT groups?

- Do you fully understand the difference between managers and leaders? It is important that you recognize this so you can create an environment to develop and nurture the leaders within your Help Desk.

- We have discussed the pros and cons of outsourcing throughout the book. Do any of the ideas presented line up with the needs of your Help Desk? Are there services you provide to your customers that might be provided cheaper or even better by an outside organization?

- Compensation is a prime motivator for many people in a job. With the high turnover rates in the Help Desk industry, it is important that you create compensation plans that motivate your agents in the direction you, and they, need. Do you have any special compensation plans other than a biweekly or monthly check?

- Your vendors can be very valuable resources for your Help Desk. Do you have an opportunity to bring your strategic vendors in for a regular conference on the future of your relationship?

- Training your customers on the issues they encounter will benefit them and you. Your Help Desk and its database of problems can be a highly effective starting point for raising the technical skills sets of your customers.

CHAPTER 22

The Processes

A world class Help Desk is not created overnight. Instead, it is an evolution of trials and mistrials, new services your customers love, and some that are rarely used. The first parts of this book concentrated on the building blocks of your Help Desk and everything needed to lay a strong foundation for the future.

This chapter discusses some new processes and services that can bring even more value to your customers and agents. Whether it is these processes or others, it is important that you and your team are always looking for new things to offer your customers. Remember your mission statement from the very beginning, but also remember to grow as the needs of your customers grow.

What to Look For

- Your Help Desk is in a unique situation to be able to help the productivity and effectiveness of others by measuring them. There are measurements you can easily track that will help those you deal with become better at what they do.

- Procuring hardware and software for your customers is a service that relieves the customer of administration and complication. This relief enables them to concentrate on their own job and lets the Help Desk deal with the technology side more.

- On the other end of the technology life cycle is repair. There will constantly be a need for the repair of broken hardware for your customers. Field dispatch, depot, and cross shipping are three ways to handle this.

- Disaster recovery planning is a must in any organization. Your Help Desk can be an invaluable source of information and a resource to help your company create this plan. At the same time, there needs to be a plan for recovering the Help Desk itself in the event of a disaster.

- Telecommuting allows your agents to work remotely from the office. This is a strong recruiting and retention aid to get and keep good agents in the Help Desk. It does require some planning and there are rules you must follow for it to work effectively.

Measuring Others

One of the goals we set for ourselves from the early design stages was to become the hub of communication and information for the company. We spoke about the information the Help Desk could obtain and disseminate throughout the organization. Another piece of information that can be shown to others is measurements of their activities. You already have a measurements process in place because you must measure yourself to improve. This is taking the information that you are already capturing, displaying it from a different angle, and sharing it with people who may be interested. The two largest groups that could benefit from your measurements are your vendor partners and your customers.

Measuring Your Vendor Partners

Your vendors are the organizations that supply your Help Desk with hardware, software, or services. If the vendor is of any size, they are probably already measuring themselves for a variety of reasons. I cannot imagine any of them not wanting to see measurements from the customer's view on top of what they already get. Different views of the same processes are nice to have as they help eliminate subjectivity and can present opportunities for improvement that might not have been seen from viewing one single measurement.

Several measurements are easy to obtain that can be very valuable to your vendors. Some of these measurements are in the following list:

- Shipping timeliness

- Shipping accuracy

- Quantity of backorders

- Configuration accuracy

- Pricing comparisons to the market

- Technical expertise of their employees

- Mean time between failures of the product

- Customer satisfaction

I recommend you work with your vendors before you mail them reports on their products and performance. They need to know what you are measuring, how you are doing it, and, probably without wanting to ask you outright, why you are doing the measurements. Are you upset with their work and want to show them the results? Are you so pleased that you want to share the output with them? Is the vendor not performing up to an agreed-upon service level agreement and are they in violation of a contract? Whatever the reason, you should be very up front with the vendor on the process. You may find that they are eager to help you and might provide you pieces of information that would be hard for you to get on your own. If the vendor is not willing to participate in the process, you will have to wonder, or ask, why not. This information can be valuable to them in their dealings with other customers and may help solve problems that many others are enduring quietly.

Real-World Example

For a period of months, my Help Desk was receiving complaints from customers about the length of time it took them to get a PC they ordered. I heard people say it took weeks or months at times to get a PC when they were told it would arrive in 5 to 10 days. Our reseller of the PCs wasn't sure of the problem and they certainly never agreed that their part of the process was taking so long. We knew our process for taking the order for a PC could be a reason but nothing added up to the feedback we got from the customer. Therefore, we took the time to measure each segment of the process to see what was happening. The table below represents the report we developed and used with the vendor after about 3 months of tracking.

Action Phase	Average Duration	Factors
Customer request to order placed	2 days	Time spent confirming with requestor on their needs. Each order had to be approved by customer's manager.
Order placed to order shipped	12 days	Vendor spent much time configuring product before shipping. Backorders of parts were delaying shipping.
Order shipped to order received by customer	2 days	Normal shipping schedule.
Order received to product installed	5 days	Help Desk agents ranked installation as a lower priority.
Total Time	21 days	Validation of customer complaints on length of process.

The report was eye-opening for all of us. We saw that we could have a definite impact on the timeliness by streamlining the approval process and prioritizing the installation process higher. However, we also saw that the vendor was taking way too long to deliver the product. With this report in hand, they agreed to work on their own processes to speed up delivery. They had counted on their 12 days of order placed to shipping as an acceptable time, but could now understand the whole picture and how they were being viewed as a 21 day lead time versus a 12 day.

Measuring Your Customers

Odds are that if you can measure the relationship that is providing services to you, you can also measure the relationship you are providing services to—the customers. This needs to be handled delicately because they are the customers and you don't want to appear to be critical or condescending. However, if you present the information in a professional fashion and work with the customer on the interpretation, these measurements will be valuable and appreciated. Some of the measurements that could be shared include

- Volume of calls over time
- Volume of calls by person
- Volume of calls by type
- Subjective review of problem quality
  (should the customer have known the answer?)
- Subjective overview of process adherence
- Asset information

The first four measurements are good for understanding training opportunities at the customer's site. By knowing what the individuals are calling the Help Desk about, the customer can see areas or people who need additional training. Some customers may take a "that is why the Help Desk is there" approach. However, others will see the value of a trained workforce and how much more productive they can be if they are trained for certain situations. Your goal is not to punish or degrade the customer's knowledge but to show them where they could improve if they wish.

Subjective overview of process adherence can be a summary of the interactions between the customer and the Help Desk. It is your thoughts on how well the customer is performing on their end of the equation. Remember we discussed that the customer has responsibilities like providing detailed information, providing a single point of contact, and acting professionally to the agents? This overview can speak to how well the customer is accomplishing these things. I only recommend doing this if you feel entirely comfortable with that particular customer and you know they will listen to you in the correct manner. Otherwise, you may appear to be beating up the customer instead of handling your own affairs.

The asset management measurements can show the customer details on the computing technology they have. Examples could be inventory lists, what assets are being called in the most, and what assets may be due for upgrades. This will help the customer's management in their technology planning. If something is breaking frequently, the user is spending a lot of fixing it and is not using it productively. This may get the customer to replace the equipment proactively before it completely dies beyond repair.

Procurement Services

Providing procurement services to your customers means that you will buy the hardware or software that your customer will implement at their location. You don't necessarily have to pay for it; you just perform the act of procurement. This employs the centralizing of services methodology that says you can gain strong synergies by combining standard efforts in one place.

Procurement Options

There are many tasks involved in procurement. Areas where the Help Desk can assist the customer include

- Researching the best model or manufacturer
- Receiving quotes from multiple suppliers
- Tracking and following up on shipping issues
- Resolving discrepancies
- Handling returns or defective products
- Tracking warranties, licenses, and maintenance

The theory behind the Help Desk performing this function is that the Help Desk handles all things related to providing computing services so the customer can simply *use* the computers instead of worrying about acquiring and maintaining them. The Help Desk is staffed with technology professionals who are familiar with the various tools used by the customers and can therefore use their own knowledge to benefit the customer.

The whole process of providing procurement services to your customers must be designed, tested, and reviewed thoroughly with your customer before implementation. It would be wise to draw a flowchart that depicts the entire process from start to finish so everyone is comfortable with how things will work. Be sure to include the major buckets of work described in Table 22-1.

Category of Work	Items to Consider
Quoting	Who can send in a quote? How are quotes delivered? How are quotes replied to? Are there approval steps needed? Are there requirements for vendor selection?
Purchasing	Who is allowed to purchase? What documentation will be needed (purchase order number, etc.)? Is there an approval process?
Logistics	How will the order be shipped? Will there be a tracking mechanism for the shipment? How will incorrect shipments be handled? How to handle returns?
Accounting	How will the order be paid for? Will shipping or other charges be included? How to handle credits? How to handle late payments?
Administration	How can the requestor follow up on the order? How can you follow up on the delivery and customer satisfaction? What paperwork needs to be kept and for how long? Will you and how will you update an asset management database with this information?

Table 22.1   Process Categories for Procurement Services

There are definitely many things to consider and plan for when designing a procurement offering for customers. It is not impossible, though, and can be very beneficial for those who want it. There will be plenty of opportunity to fine-tune the process once it's implemented, but you should really try to get as many kinks as possible worked out of the process before you begin.

Benefits Gained by the Procurement Service

There are many benefits to be gained by offering this service to your customer. Some of them are listed here.

- **Standards control**   By providing a central procurement entity, you can more easily control the standards installed in your user community. Since you are the procurer of the order, you know what the customer is asking for and can guide them to the standards you have created. If the customer is going to go outside that standard, you at least know about it and can document it somewhere.

- **Better pricing**   You can also negotiate better discounted pricing if you are able to buy in larger quantities. By being a central procurement operation, you have the opportunity to combine many orders from customers and place larger orders with the vendor. In most all circumstances, you should be able to obtain a better price by buying more of a product at one time. Another way this helps get better pricing is if you are able to forecast future orders with the vendor. Over time you will learn the buying habits of the customers and can pass this information on to the vendors. Typically, the vendors welcome this and some form of value can be passed back to you.

- **Consolidated billing**   Accounting for the many invoices that can accumulate with technology purchases can take up many resources for a customer. However, if they use one vendor (your Help Desk) to procure their technologies, they should be able to consolidate their accounting needs as well. If you are able to combine the bills you incur for the various needs of a particular customer, you can invoice the customer on one statement. Now the customer can pay you once, and you disperse the funds appropriately.

Procurement Services Caveat

With all the benefits listed, why wouldn't all customers want this service? They may, but not all Help Desks can offer it. First, it is not generally a core competency of a Help Desk. Your mission statement probably did not list this offering, but concentrated more on providing support and fixing problems. It is for this very purpose that this service is listed so late in the Help Desk game. You should not offer this service until you are very established in the customer support business and have things well under control.

If you decide to offer procurement services to your customers you need to be prepared for the resources it will require. Not only will someone on your staff need to handle requests for a product but he or she will also be the clearinghouse for follow-up calls and status checks. This part of your Help Desk will now get "Where is my PC?" and "The box arrived with parts missing" calls that are high in administrative resources and lower in value.

If you want to proceed with this service, I urge you to automate as much as possible including putting order forms on the Web. You can create a front-end Web page that lists all the products you purchase. When the user clicks on that product, it can take him to the Web page of your supplying vendor. The user won't necessarily care as long as he gets the product when he wants it. Take it a step further and you might be able to sell advertising space on this front page.

Real-World Example

Another way to offer the service without committing your own agents to the task is to outsource it. After my first Help Desk had our PC technicians perform this function for a few years, I contracted with our supplier to put one of their staff on site to do the work for us. We liked it because we didn't have to do it, and the purchaser liked it because it gave them an automatic "in" on our buying habits. We found that the supplier could offer more technical knowledge and knew more about upcoming updates and upgrades. We kept a close eye on the processes along the way and ran reports of vendors used and prices paid. It never became necessary to formally audit the supplier, but the ability for us to check on them made all of us feel safer.

You are, after all, directing business traffic to vendors without them having to do the sales work.

Again, ensure this service is truly valuable to the customer. If they like it and you can measure some form of positive return on it, you will come out ahead.

Hardware Repair Services

Another service you can provide your customers is repair service for their hardware. I only recommend doing this if the volume of repairs is low, your geographic coverage is limited, or you feel very confident that you can make a profit from it. Much of any value-add from this service begins to erode if you have to constantly increase staff or other expenses. If you still feel you can offer this service, there are typically three types: field dispatch, depot service, and cross shipping.

While field dispatch involves technicians in the field, depot service and cross shipping involve hardware inventory and shipping. If logistics are an integral function of your company, these services can be incorporated nicely into your Help Desk. Otherwise, you want to be very careful how involved your Help Desk agents become in the boxing and shipping that will be required without outside assistance.

Field Dispatch

Field dispatch is the process of sending out an agent to fix the problem at the customer's site. The user calls into the Help Desk, and if they cannot resolve the issue over the phone, the Help Desk dispatches someone to the building or desk to fix it. This is helpful because there is no shipping involved and the user does not have to unplug a bunch of cables, box the equipment, and plug it back in when it arrives. The downside is that this can be expensive. The dispatched agents need to be well trained and the cost of travel can be high. You will also need a good tool to keep track of incoming requests, the whereabouts of your agents, and the availability of spare parts.

Depot Service

Depot service involves the customer shipping the broken piece of equipment to a depot, someone fixing whatever is broken, and then shipping it back to the customer. This is usually the cheapest method of hardware repair but it also keeps the customer without their hardware for the longest. If it is their desktop, and therefore their only access to the system, this could be a problem. The customer may keep a spare so they can still work while the original equipment is being repaired.

Cross Shipping

Cross shipping works a bit differently. Using this arrangement, the customer notifies the repair shop that they will be sending in a broken device. At the same time, the repair shop mails a working device to the customer. When the broken piece is repaired, the repair service keeps it in their spare pool. Since there is spare, therefore additional, equipment involved, the costs are higher than with depot service. However, the customer gets a working device faster.

Now that you understand these methods, Table 22-2 can help you decide what works best for you and your environment.

Disaster Recovery

All companies of any size should have a disaster recovery plan in place. Disaster recovery plans, sometimes called business recovery plans, are processes you would invoke if you lost computing service for some length of time. Depending on the extent and criticality of your computing system this plan could be quite complicated and expensive. While I do not necessarily suggest that your Help Desk be responsible for the development and upkeep of your disaster recovery plan, I do recommend that they play an important and ongoing role.

Remembering that the Help Desk is a proactive agency within your company, the Help Desk should be responsible for promoting business practices that will help the business resume operations as quickly as possible. This could range from reminding locations to print manual reports of pricing and inventories to working with vendors for backup lines and equipment.

	Field Dispatch	**Depot Service**	**Cross Shipping**
Issues	Fastest to resolve	Slowest to resolve	Faster shipping method
	More personal interaction	Minimal personal interaction	Minimal personal interaction
	Minimal work space needed	Work space required	Work space required
	Better for computer-illiterate customers	Customer needs to be able to disconnect and reconnect	Customer needs to be able to disconnect and reconnect
	No shipping to track	Must keep track of shipping	Must keep track of shipping and that customer returns the broken parts
	Travel costs incurred	No travel costs	No travel costs
	Unless your staff is dispersed, customers must be close by	Geography is not a factor	Geography is not a factor

Table 22.2   Decision Table for Hardware Repair Services

There are many types of disasters that can disrupt business and as many as possible should be accounted for in your planning. They can be acts of nature such as tornadoes, floods, hurricanes, or earthquakes. They can be caused by humans cutting power or phone lines. It can be very simple, such as the sprinkler system in your building going off and drenching your systems in water. Obviously there will always be disruptions of some type with various lengths of downtime. I would categorize these disruptions by expected length of downtime and build business cases around each for not only restoring service but planning for operations during the downtime. Your executives will make the final decisions on what risks they are willing to take for the costs, but that is their call. Your duty is to present options and, as much as possible, help guide them in the right direction.

Information I found very useful in setting expectations with the executives is presented in Table 22-3.

Percent Uptime	**Minutes of Downtime**	**Hours of Downtime**	**Days of Downtime**
99.999%	5.256		
99.99%	52.56		
99.9%		8.76	
99%		87.6	
95%			18.25
90%			36.5

Table 22.3   Downtime Calculation

This table was helpful because there is so much talk about "five 9s" of system availability these days. By showing the senior managers this table, I was able to equate this "number of 9s" availability expectation to actual minutes or days of downtime. They could then see what the percentages meant in terms they could better understand. From there, I was able to demonstrate the costs associated with each level of downtime.

Just as there are many types of disasters, there are many types of recovery options. They include

- Spare equipment or hot spares
- Cold site
- Hot site
- Business recovery partners

Spare Equipment or Hot Spares

A relatively inexpensive option is to keep spares of the critical parts of your systems. If a part goes bad, you have the part on hand to replace it with. Unless you have a spare for every thing that could break, you may become a victim of not having the exact right part. To combat this, you could keep an entire system on hand. Be careful not to let these parts gather dust in a closet somewhere, though. It would be a shame, and more, if a part broke and you confidently replaced it with one of your spares only to find out that the firmware had been upgraded and the spare no longer works in the system!

Cold Site

Having a room full of spares does no good if a tornado wipes out your production systems as well as your spares. A cold site helps in this regard because it is a computer room in another location that is equipped to handle your computing needs in all regards except the actual systems. A cold site may have the power, air conditioning, and space needed such that if you lost your computer room, you can arrange for duplicate systems to be shipped to the cold site, installed, and brought up.

Hot Site

Although a cold site has no computing power in it, a hot site does. Depending on the degree you equip this hot site, it may be an exact replica of what you have in production or somewhere close. Hot sites can bring you up faster but are much more costly to acquire and maintain. In general, a hot site is a room or building that has the computing power you need to run your business. The systems are powered up and loaded with any and all information that your daily systems have. They are available for switchover in a very short time frame. As you can tell, hot sites are expensive because they have all the machinery your regular computer room has. Their return on investment is low because no business is being conducted across them. As with insurance, you only need it when you need it. Just as you would not eliminate your insurance at home if you were working on your personal budget, you would not eliminate hot sites unless you had another option. You can cut costs in certain areas if needed. Take a good look at any development boxes, for example. Will these boxes be needed at a moment's notice if your computer room is demolished? Maybe for some companies it is okay to be without a development box for some time. Others may need it as much as their production boxes. It is not a definite one way or another, but is a good place to review when deciding how to set up your hot site.

Business Recovery Partners

You may find it less expensive to partner with a company that does nothing but provide computing services to customers in events of disasters. Firms like Sungard, Comdisco, HP, and IBM provide this as a regular service. They will guarantee to have whatever equipment you sign up for installed and live by the time your team arrives at their location. This requires a thorough plan, but if your business cannot survive extended periods of downtime, this option is well worth looking at.

The costs can be much lower using this method than building your own hot site. While you will pay the business recovery partner a monthly fee, you will not need to procure and maintain all the systems yourself as you would in a hot site. There are advantages and disadvantages in both scenarios, but strictly from a cost perspective you can easily find the cheaper solution or at least the timing when one becomes more expensive than the other. Take the total cost to buy all the hardware and software for the hot site. Divide that number by the recovery partner's monthly fee. That result is the number of months it will take for the hot site to become cheaper than the partner. This calculation is only from a cost view and should NOT stand on its own in your decision. Knowing it can help guide what you decide to do and when you decide to do it.

The Help Desk Itself

The business thanks you for helping with its business recovery planning. Drill down some levels and look at your own operation. Do you know what the Help Desk would do if disaster struck? The computer systems may be up and running five states away, but what about your staff? They need a plan as well. It needs to be formal, documented, communicated, and tested. The plan still works when broken down to the people, location, processes, and tools.

People

Your first goal in the planning is deciding what you are going to do with the agents. How will they communicate and with whom? How will they know where to go and what to do once there? In the middle of a disaster is no time to figure this out, so you must plan now. Getting to it next month may be easier, but that is one more month that disaster could hit and your Help Desk would be caught helpless.

Creating a communication plan is a good place to begin. You start with a central number everyone can call to get statuses and updates. Now, begin playing the "what if" games. If that phone system is down, what do your agents do? If a particular agent's home phone is down, how can she get information? Depending on the disaster, these are real possibilities. So, you start with a central number and then select another one as backup. You also create a communication tree as show in Figure 22-1.

This tree is useful because it creates a proactive way to alert your agents to news and statuses. In this example, George is the Help Desk manager and contacts two people, Dale and Mike. They in turn contact the people on their list. Instead of one person on the phone all day calling people, you have created a system that gets many people working on the same solution. Of course, with that many people involved, you run a risk of expanded exposure. This means that if one person cannot be found, there will be an increase in the number of people who will not be informed. Figure 22-2 shows the expanding lack of communication if one branch of the tree is missed.

If George cannot find Dale, then Dale will not be informed of what to do. Worse yet, the six other people in Dale's tree will not be informed, either. As with

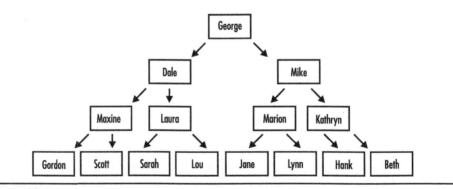

Figure 22.1   Communication tree

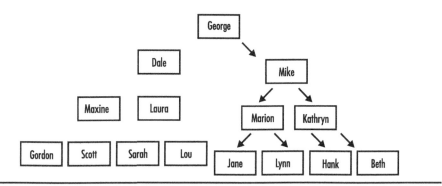

Figure 22.2 Effects of no communication

all of your disaster recovery plans, you always need a second option. In the communication tree, you first make sure all agents have a copy of the tree. They then know whom the person below them is responsible for. Now, if George cannot find Dale, he will know to call Maxine and Laura to get the tree working again.

Location

Okay, the staff has been contacted; where do they go? The place to go is where the phones are. Again, if your Help Desk was included in the business recovery plans, you will probably already know where to send your agents. If your disaster plans called for a hot site arrangement, it would be good to factor in some space for your Help Desk there. It may not provide enough room for all your agents, but it does give you a place to answer the phones and know the status of the systems. If you aren't in those plans, you need to find a place. Because you were smart enough to buy this book, I will assume you are smart enough to complete your disaster planning before the actual disaster hits.

One place to start may be in one of your existing customer locations. I doubt this would work for an external customer, but internal ones should want to help you out. Depending on the size of your Help Desk, you could rent office space close by or even rent out a hotel conference room for a while. Remember that whichever location you choose, you will need more than just space. You will need phone lines and data connections to wherever your systems are. Obviously, your best bet is to integrate your location planning with the systems work.

Processes

In the middle of recovering from a disaster, you will find that most of your processes will be in emergency mode. This means that only your most required processes and procedures will make sense. This is a good learning exercise for routine days. If the processes aren't worth doing in emergencies, are they really worth doing at all? I think this is a strict and overly tough look at your processes, but it is worth a quick thought.

Your call routing and problem handling processes should remain intact. While your resolution times may slide due to changes in staffing levels, your ability to receive calls and route them correctly should not change. In the beginning you may not have all the tools you are used to, so "going manual" needs to be built in to your plans. The customer may have sympathy for what you are going through and be more tolerant of issues. Your goal, however, should be that the customer does not notice. Wouldn't that stand out to the customer base, and senior management, if while disaster has struck and people are wondering what to do, your Help Desk was online and in business with minimal interruption?

So, what processes could slip? Asset and change management aren't day-to-day critical so perhaps they could. Catching up, or even knowing what to catch up, will be a challenge, though. I think it best to continue all your processes and let the timing be what takes a hit. In other words, keep up with changes as you normally would but don't be as strict in entering them in your system with the normal speed. Now, if your staffing is up to speed and all systems are in place, this is a nonissue. You have no reason not to continue on as before. Don't forget the customer and their problems are the main goal. All other work is good but should take a back seat to the customer if you have to choose.

Tools

The most critical tool you need working again is the telephone. It can take the place of walk-up traffic, e-mails, and Internet sessions so restoring the phone is a must. If the Help Desk was considered in the disaster recovery plan, odds are telephones and telephone lines will be available in the new location. If not, make sure your plan covers this. For quicker service, you may want to negotiate rates and procedures ahead of time with your local service provider. If your Help Desk has to move, the phone line move may be as easy as a call to the phone company to enact the plan.

If you have integrated a call management or other systems packages into your operations, you will need desktop devices, the software, and your data to run it. The desktops could be part of the overall recovery plan, but again make sure you have it in yours. As for the software and data, regular saves of the system should be made. On a periodic basis, perhaps weekly, send the saved tapes off site. That way, if your building is completely destroyed, you can get at least some data back when you retrieve the tapes.

Regular Testing

In any of the disaster recovery plans mentioned above, regular testing and evaluation are critical! This will be hard to do as you will always have more pressing items in front of you, but I urge you to find ways to prioritize this step. It will be very hard over time when you add new hardware, software, and services to remember to incorporate them into your disaster recovery plans. By testing and evaluating regularly, you should find these new items as well as discover plans that are no longer valid due to retirement, obsolescence, or upgrades.

Telecommuting

Chapter 11 discussed telecommuting to help reduce burnout in your agents. This chapter looks at telecommuting as a strategy in your Help Desk growth. Managing a team of telecommuting agents can be difficult for a beginning Help Desk because the agents are not physically together and developing a team will be hard. However, once you fully understand all the tricks of the trade for operating a Help Desk, telecommuting can be a valuable process.

Telecommuting saves energy, fuel, people's time, company money (because many people are willing to take less money to stay at home), and it reduces pollution. Additionally, you can get better and more experienced people and you are not limited to your geographic region or location. Telecommuting implemented correctly will also lead to higher morale among the participants and a lower absenteeism rate. With the amount of reliable communications and cost-effective ways for customers to communicate, this option is the option of the future and should not be overlooked.

Implementing a telecommuting strategy is not as simple as just proclaiming it. You must pass two tests before you can begin.

- Will it work for your customers?
- Do you have the technology to make it work?

Telecommuting Effects on Your Customer

How your customers reach you will determine the feasibility of telecommuting. If they always contact you by e-mail, who cares where you are physically located? The customer doesn't care where you are sitting as long as you resolve their issue. However, if the majority of your customers are co-located with your

Help Desk and walk into the Help Desk area for questions, telecommuting will obviously not work. So, the first test you must pass is the ability for your customers to find an agent when they need something resolved.

Technology for Telecommuting

Assuming your customers are comfortable (whether they realize it or not) with telecommuting agents occupying the Help Desk, you still cannot pull it off unless you have the technology that allows for offsite workers. This involves the ability of customers to reach the agent wherever he is, as well as the ability of agents to reach the customer or the computing system wherever they are.

I seriously doubt that your customers will want to dial many different phone numbers to reach your Help Desk. Therefore, your phone system will have to be capable of routing calls not just within the building but also to phone numbers associated with the remote offices of your agents. This is no longer overly complicated and the technology certainly exists; it is just a matter of your particular system having this capability. Taking it one step further, can the system coordinate the call so that it can be transferred *back* into the Help Desk office once the remote agent is done or needs additional help?

Your agents will also need to be able to reach your office to either access the call management packages, databases, and other tools that exist to run the Help Desk or access the systems used by the customer that may be the source of problems. This remote access will require a high-speed line for effectiveness as well as security to protect the data that may be viewed in resolving problems. Your Help Desk will need to resolve these issues well before implementing a telecommuting plan. The issues will be the cost to acquire the technologies and the subsequent installation and administration of them.

Telecommunication Implementation

Riding high on the success of passing the tests mentioned earlier, you are now ready to make telecommuting a reality for your Help Desk. You now need to develop a solid game plan for rolling it out. The three things you need to prepare for are

- Determining who can qualify for telecommuting
- Determining how it will be funded
- Tracking its progress

Who Can Qualify?

Depending on the organizational makeup of your Help Desk there may be agents who are a perfect fit for telecommuting and some who are not. Agents who take all their calls from customers over the phone or electronically will work well. Conversely, if you have agents who need to be near the data center for certain resolutions, telecommuting would not work. You will probably want your managers and any new agents to be in the office to aid in the development of the Help Desk and their skills.

Beyond the scope of the work performed by the agent, there are other considerations to resolve before choosing your remote team. For example, I highly recommend drafting a readiness assessment for both you and the associates wanting to telecommute before you begin. It prompts the associates to answer questions around their desire to work remotely. These questions can include why they want to work remotely, how they will achieve the objectives of the Help Desk, how they feel they can be managed remotely, and the measurements necessary to determine if telecommuting is right for them.

You may also want to require the telecommuters to have a dedicated work area that is used primarily for performing their job. It doesn't pass to have a PC in your den so that you can watch TV at the same time. Telecommuters should work from a private area. Reaching behind you to rock the baby's crib is not a prime environment for producing quality IT work.

Funding Telecommuting

Before you begin allowing your agents to work remotely, you also need to figure out how it will be paid for. There needs to be a consistent and published policy around who is responsible for what. There will be costs for a PC at the agent's remote site, a network connection through an Internet service provider or dial up line, and any necessary software. Some companies even pay for office furniture for the agent to use. You can see that telecommuting can get expensive if you have a large number of participants.

If funding is a problem in your budget, you may offer telecommuting as an option to agents who are willing to help pay for it. The agents should have an incentive to help because they get to work from home in a more relaxed atmosphere. They also save time in their day by not having to drive to work and back every day. Your company also has an incentive to help fund it, as they would be purchasing much of the same equipment if the agent were to work from the central office. The company also gets the benefit of having a happier associate in the Help Desk.

Tracking the Progress

The next challenge will be how to measure success. A fear of managers with people working outside the office is the inability to know if the worker is actually working or at least at the pace expected. To get past this, clear and well-defined measurements should be established so both parties can know what is expected. It would be nice to have measurements available before telecommuting begins so everyone has a baseline to compare with. Even without prior numbers, new numbers and expectations must be established. Metrics like number of calls handled, abandoned rates, and customer satisfaction should be closely monitored to ensure the success of telecommuting. There should be a clear understanding that if the measurements begin to fall after implementation of telecommuting, the program could be cancelled for a particular agent or for the whole team.

Telecommuting Overview

Telecommuting brings with it many challenges and obstacles. It can be a new experience for your company and prior thought patterns and management techniques will have to be modified. However, there are many advantages to telecommuting as mentioned earlier. With a good, well-communicated plan in place that is understood by all, telecommuting can be a strong driver to placing you in the world class Help Desk category!

Quick Recap

- I know that you have a consistent measurement process in place for your Help Desk. Do you see opportunities to expand the measurements to include others? I believe you will find that your customers and vendors will appreciate your knowledge of their own operations to help better themselves.

- Adding value to your customers should be an ongoing goal for your Help Desk. One way to do this is to offer procurement and repair services. Do you have the organizational setup to accommodate this? This is the beginning of expanding your core competencies to additional fields, but it can lead to a greater degree of customer satisfaction.

- Are you prepared for disaster? Hopefully the worst disaster you will have is an irate customer who demands to speak to your boss. However, you owe it to your company and your customers to have a well-developed plan in place to help you recover from a disaster that takes down your entire operation.

Without it, you may take months to regain your operation, if at all. Many companies never recover from a large-scale disaster and go out of business.

• Telecommuting can be a huge shift in the environment of your Help Desk. It will require you to plan for many things that an office-only Help Desk does not need. Have you been hearing a desire from your agents to telecommute? Do you have the technologies available to make it happen? If you do not, you may want to slowly look into what is needed in your operation. Telecommuting will only become more popular and allowing for it early may differentiate you in the marketplace for good talent.

CHAPTER 23

The Tools

The tools I've discussed so far are good and effective in keeping your Help Desk running smoothly and efficiently. I want to mention a few more that can take you even farther. They are not required, especially in smaller Help Desks, but are strong enablers of good processes and can return value to your customers.

Because of the proliferation of the Internet, the Web is taking over as a primary choice of communication between businesses and between businesses and customers. As this continues, more and more tools are being deployed that use the Web as an interface as much as the telephone used to be. Many of the tools described in this chapter run on the Web either exclusively or in conjunction with it.

What to Look For

- Keeping track of a Help Desk's operation and processes can be a daunting task for any manager. As the staff grows larger and the hours of operation increase, it becomes important to monitor and fine-tune your agents' schedules for maximum efficiency. A workforce management package can help you accomplish this task very effectively.

- Customer Relationship Management packages do just what the name implies. They help you manage the overall relationship between your Help Desk and the customer. Going far beyond an agent receiving a call and answering it, CRM packages look at the big picture of the customer needs and streamline the interaction in many places.

- Technologies are being integrated in many forms and all add increased value to the customer/Help Desk experience. As your Help Desk grows, these combinations will become more and more important to implement.

- Telephony practices are also adding value to the interaction between the customer and the Help Desk agent. Whether it is to train your agent or to get someone else's help on a problem, there are several telephony tools to look into.

- Monitoring and managing systems is a highly valuable, proactive process for a Help Desk. Used correctly, system management packages can alert a Help Desk agent to a potential problem before it impacts the customer. This behind-the-scenes work keeps your customers happy, although they may not be able to appreciate it without your promoting the fact that you are doing it.

Workforce Management

Your workforce in a Help Desk consists of your agents. You or someone under you is probably managing them. As long as you run a small Help Desk with a small number of agents, this arrangement will work absolutely fine. As your Help Desk grows, however, it will become harder and harder to keep up with the demands of your customers and agents while at the same time maintaining the high levels of service required. Enter workforce management software.

Workforce management is software that aids in the planning and scheduling of resources. Instead of a manager struggling with a spreadsheet trying to balance the agents and their workload, this software will do it for you. You simply enter parameters concerning your agents and historical call information and the software will plan the agents' days, hours, and costs. I will discuss the benefits of a workforce management package in the following sections.

Workforce Management Allows You to Be Proactive

The software can help you project future schedules based on information you enter. You do not need to be hit by an overworked or bored, underworked staff before you know you need to change your plans. Instead you can stay ahead of the curve to prevent these things from occurring.

Your Help Desk will constantly be faced with increases and decreases. For example, your agent count will go up and down. Your customer count will hopefully only go up as the technologies they use change. Some days and times will have a high spike in demand while other periods may be extremely slow. In fact, as your Help Desk evolves, even the ways your customers contact you will change.

These many changes will overtax even the best of a manager's plans without technology to help. Plugging in new information like changes in headcount can quickly be assimilated into the software and new results delivered.

Workforce Management Helps Align Agent Needs

If you are unable to keep up with plans for how many agents need to be in place during what times, you probably have no shot at allowing for individual agent skills and preferences. A Help Desk that is organized into technology sections will make a good first cut at putting individual agents in the right group. It stops there, though. With the right software you will be able to ensure that *within* your different groups, you have the right number of agents whose strengths and skills are aligned and available for customers.

By updating the software with the skills and competencies of your agents, the software will help you optimize the use of your staff. It will show you where you should schedule certain agents by the particular skills they possess or where multiskilled agents can be placed for maximum effectiveness. If you have service level agreements with your customers, a workforce management package can aid you in meeting the expectations agreed to in the contract.

Where the software gets even better is its ability to factor in agent preferences. Now you can input information around what days or times of day are most preferred by your agents. If you allow the software to plan everything for you correctly, wouldn't it be very favorable to the associates to schedule their times based on their own needs and wishes? It could account for holidays and vacations, too. This allowance is pretty unrealistic without software to help you. The return on the investment you will receive from increased agent satisfaction and lower turnover will be well worth the time and money to implement this software.

Workforce Management Provides Impact Analysis

Along with the basic capability to be proactive, workforce management allows you to create strategies for upcoming events whether you already know about them or not. Imagine being able to factor in an expected increase in call volume when your next implementation of technologies is begun. Instead of waiting for your agents to be overwhelmed with calls, you can plot a course ahead of time and have the right number of agents available from the beginning. Is a customer placing demands within a service level agreement that you are unsure about? If so, input these into the software and let it show you how the SLA will impact you.

Benefits

Having your Help Desk in the position it is to review workforce management options means you have really made it to the next level. You as a manager are able to see a bigger picture rather than concentrating on each incoming call. You are able to plan ahead and make your Help Desk become a more valuable and strategic ally of your customers. In addition to what has been mentioned before, this software can also

- *Produce staffing plans* you can review that will show you not just the number of agents you need but the skill sets necessary as well.

- *See different models* with which you can compare assumptions and facts. There is certainly more than one way to accomplish a goal and this software makes it easy to create multiple scenarios from which to make decisions.

- *Aid you in administrative planning* by reporting information that can be factored into budgets, capacity planning, and recruiting needs for the coming time period.

- *Reduce costs* by helping prevent overstaffing and only using resources where and when they are needed. It also helps prevent understaffing, which may push you to more drastic measures to overcome a heavier than expected workload.

- *Improve morale* of your agents because you can now consider their personal preferences like days of the week and hours of the day when creating your schedule.

| Note | *With all these features, it will be easy to stay locked in your office all day making grand plans for the future. As a leader of your Help Desk it is good to look to the* |

future, but you do want to get out and look for other opportunities to improve. Let the software do its thing and produce a solid plan for you for the times you need. When you have new ideas for increasing your service offerings, you can certainly plug them in to gauge an impact. The point is, the software is good but don't get so caught up in the "neatness" of it that you lose sight of the customer needs right in front of you.

Workforce Management Vendors

The number of vendors providing workforce management solutions is steadily increasing as the marketplace recognizes the need for technology to help it be more valuable to its customers. Here is a short list of software providers:

- Blue Pumpkin Software
- IEX Corporation
- Open Wave
- Portage Communications
- Simplex Workforce Solutions

This is by no means an exhaustive list of vendors, but it can serve as a strong beginning to research the solution that best fits your Help Desk.

Customer Relationship Management Packages

In the beginning chapters of this book, we spoke about call management packages and their importance in Help Desk operations. This software, or process, is critical to ensure customer calls are handled appropriately and effectively. As your Help Desk matures and your customers become more dependent on your services for their technology survival, you have an opportunity to move beyond basic call management packages to the next level. This next level is found in Customer Relationship Management (CRM) packages. While CRMs can be used in many other lines of business where a company interacts with a customer, Help Desks can benefit from them in many ways.

A CRM package provides a closed loop of information for a customer throughout the organization. It can handle incoming call information, route the caller to the appropriate organization, resolve the issue, and communicate back to the customer on the status. CRMs keep records all along the way of the issue and can report back to the user on status and resolution. This total integration of services within one package is very effective and gives the customer confidence that his issue is being handled very efficiently.

| Note | *The tools discussed in this chapter can also be implemented in parts and even from different vendors. They can then be integrated together to provide a seamless set of tools for your agents and customers. This modularity allows you to only implement the technologies as you need them.* |

CRMs can also be very expensive and complicated to implement, so I only recommend them in Help Desks that can afford them or can make good use of all their functionality. Examples of the functions a CRM can provide, in addition to traditional call management, include

- Collaboration
- E-mail management
- Customer self-service

We'll consider some benefits of each of these features in the following sections.

Collaboration

Collaboration is multiple people working together to achieve a common objective. Using the theory that two heads are better than one, collaboration tools allow customers and agents to work together or multiple agents working together to resolve issues or provide training. CRM packages that provide collaborative features are powerful tools that can bring people from different physical locations into the same issue at the same time or provide multiple people the same information over time to help each other. Examples of collaborative functions include

- Chat
- Follow me
- Information sharing
- Web call through

Chat

Think of Internet *chat* as an instant e-mail solution. Instead of typing a message, sending it, and waiting for the recipient to receive and respond, chat allows you to type a message and the recipient responds in real time. Imagine the difference between the postal service and a telephone. The postal service delivers messages with a delay in the delivery time and the time it takes the receiver to answer. A telephone call is begun as soon as the called party answers their phone.

Chat is therefore much faster than e-mail and is cost-effective because it uses the same Internet network connection already available to the customer. Within a collaborative environment, chat can also be queued with other incoming voice calls or other chat sessions so the customer's message is not lost. There are also features that allow a customer to initiate a chat session and receive a message when the next agent will be available. Once an agent comes free, the agent is notified of the chat session request and can begin "speaking" with the customer.

The benefits of chat are not confined to customer interactions, either. Chat can be very valuable within the Help Desk or IT department. If multiple levels of your organization can easily reach each other, even in different physical environments, the effectiveness of the group will be increased.

Follow Me

A *follow me* solution allows a customer and an agent to work with each other to see what is on the screen of the other. So if a customer is having trouble understanding a certain Web page, an agent can work with the customer by associating his browser with the customer's browser and walking him through the problem area. If you have documentation online you can also have the customer follow you to it. Now instead of referring the customer to page three of a document for the answer, you can actually show them right where the answer is on the page. What is shown on the customer's screen can be viewed by the agent and vice versa. The screens can be limited to the browser itself so confidential or nonpertinent information is not shared.

Information Sharing

Follow me technology connects two people together to resolve an issue. There are also other technologies that focus more on delivering the information *to* the customer instead of working *with* the customer. They include page push, file push, and forms sharing.

Page Push   *Page push* is the action of an agent pushing a Web page (really its URL) to a customer. If a customer is looking for information on your Internet or intranet site, the agent can send the page to him through the collaboration tool and have it show up on the customer's desktop immediately.

File Push   *File push* involves an agent sending a form or file to a customer. If a customer needs a certain document or spreadsheet, the agent can send the file to him much like the agent could send a Web page through a page push. Similar to e-mailing the file to the customer, forms pushing is quicker and allows the agent to continue working with the customer without interruption. This technology can also come in handy to send a version patch or bug fix to a customer to help them overcome a problem or upgrade their system.

Forms Sharing   *Forms sharing* is close to the follow me solution. The difference is that the follow me approach allows the agent to see what is happening, whereas the forms sharing solution allows the agent to take over the customer's screen and work with whatever form is causing an issue. An example of a form in question may be an application form to purchase some new equipment. If there are questions on certain parts of the form, the agent can link to the customer and have the customer point out the area of concern. If necessary, the agent can even fill out the form while the customer is watching. This will help the next time the customer needs to use that particular form.

Web call through

Another collaborative tool that is useful is Web call through. Using voiceover IP (VoIP), *Web call through* allows people to have conversations through their computers. Instead of e-mail or chat, a customer could click on "DME Help Desk" on an Internet page for example, and be passed through to a live agent. The agent would not respond by typing anything, but by literally speaking into his microphone. The two people could now speak to each other, which is obviously quicker than typing messages.

Queuing can also take place during Web calling. This means that the customer could choose the Help Desk and his "call" would be routed to the next available agent. An agent would receive a pop up message on his screen informing him he had a Web call. He could then accept the call and begin speaking or decline the call and the customer would wait for the next agent in line.

| Note | *The Web call tool works best when the people having the conversation wear headsets. Otherwise, the voice coming through the speaker may bleed over into the receiver's microphone and the conversation will become difficult to keep up with.* |

E-mail Management

Certain CRM packages also provide management capability for e-mail. Basically, this e-mail management gives you administrative control over incoming e-mail just as ACD and IVR systems provide for incoming phone calls. Six strong features available in packages offering e-mail management include

- Intelligent routing
- Auto response
- Auto suggest
- E-mail queuing
- E-mail monitoring
- Broadcasting

Intelligent Routing

For normal e-mail, the sender chooses the person they want to receive the mail, and sends it to them. That works in a Help Desk world if the customer knows the agent's name or can choose him from a list. However, if the wrong agent is chosen, the customer's problem may sit for some time before the e-mail is directed to the right agent. This causes delays and possibly creates an opportunity for the problem to be lost in the shuffle. Intelligent routing within an e-mail management solution fixes this problem.

Intelligent routing does just what it says; it routes the e-mail to the correct resource in an intelligent manner. Intelligent routing in e-mail management is similar to an IVR system for phones. The software uses various methods of artificial intelligence to discern which agent should receive the e-mail based on information in the subject and text of the e-mail message. With this information in place, the sender does not have to know exactly whom to send the e-mail to. He can just send it to the Help Desk and let the software figure out the recipient. This programming is "taught" the organizational layout of your agents and uses these rules to know where to route the e-mail.

Prioritized routing can also be included. Using information from your database, certain customers can be identified as having higher priority than others have, and their calls can be "bumped up" in line. Of course, all your customers are important, but due to service level agreements, past problems that need to be smoothed over, or just plain old size, it may be beneficial to give some customers an extra edge when they need assistance from your Help Desk.

Auto Response

Auto response is a feature that automatically sends the sender of an e-mail a set message without human intervention on the receiver side. This is beneficial because it allows the sender to feel comfortable that his e-mail was received at the Help Desk. For example, the customer could send in a problem and receive an e-mail in response like, "We at DME Help Desk have received your e-mail. One of our agents will respond to you within 24 hours. Thank you for using DME Help Desk services."

Technology is not perfect (or else the Help Desk's role would be greatly diminished) and there will be times when an e-mail that was sent was not received. The auto response feature gives that confirmation so there is no doubt about the successful transmission of the customer's issue. It will now be up to the Help Desk to work on and resolve the problem.

Auto Suggest

The next step in the evolution of e-mail management is an auto suggest function. *Auto suggest* is where an e-mail is sent in response to a customer with suggestions on how their problem could be handled. Auto response sends a standard message of acknowledgment. Auto suggest sends a message full of information to actually resolve the customer's problem.

For example, a customer sends the following e-mail:

To:	DME Help Desk
From:	Harrison Tyler
Subject:	Fuzzy monitor
Text:	My PC monitor is fuzzy and wavy. Everything on the screen shakes so much that I cannot read anything on it.

The auto suggest functionality reads key words in the subject and text and replies with:

To:	Harrison Tyler
From:	DME Help Desk
Subject:	Fuzzy monitor
Text:	Thank you for contacting DME Help Desk with your problem. We are familiar with this issue and suggest the following steps to resolve it. If these do not resolve your problem, please contact us again and we will have an agent call you personally.

1. Turn monitor off and back on.
2. Ensure the cables are plugged in securely.
3. Hit the side of the monitor with your hand.

Note *The third option seems to be a favorite of every computer user I have run into. I do not suggest you ever put that in your documented procedures, however.*

E-mail Queuing

IVR and ACD phone systems create a phone queuing system where callers are put in line waiting for an agent to answer the phone. Callers can be queued in the order they called in or by a rules-based prioritization system that you can define. E-mail management systems offer this as well where e-mails queue until an agent accepts them.

Historically, phone calls could be routed and distributed to agents who were flagged as available by the phone system. However, if an e-mail or Internet chat session was directed toward an agent, she was the owner of the problem. Therefore, a particular agent could be receiving an average number of phone calls compared to her peers, but be deep in an overflow of unread e-mails.

If you recall in Chapter 7, we spoke about different ways to organize your Help Desk, and grouping your agents by incoming media was an option. E-mail queuing works well in that environment because you can apply business rules and workflow procedures that direct the e-mails to the correct agent based on availability and skill set and the e-mails can wait for the best resource to handle the problem.

E-mail Monitoring

We have discussed in earlier chapters monitoring phone calls with agents to help train and develop their skills. A similar feature is available in e-mail. A manager can define a set of rules within the e-mail management system that then monitors outgoing e-mails from agents. If the subject or content of an e-mail falls within the parameters of the rules, the e-mail will be sent to the manager instead of the customer. Once the manager has proofread the e-mail and feels comfortable with it, the e-mail can be forwarded to its intended recipient.

You may want to use this feature for new agents or agents getting involved in new technologies. By searching for key words that are associated with the new topics, the e-mail monitoring software can pull out those e-mails that are related to the technology. As you become confident with the agent's knowledge on the topic, you can exclude him from future monitoring.

As with any type of monitoring, I suggest you fully inform your agents of your intent. Instead of seeming like "big brother" spying on your associates, create an atmosphere of full disclosure and trust. Explain to your associates about the monitoring and your reasoning behind it. They should understand that you do not have the time or the desire to read all their e-mails and you are only trying to maintain or increase customer satisfaction. Now, if you really are spying on someone, that is a different story.

Broadcasting

Broadcasting is proactively sending e-mails to a list of customers to convey a common message at one time. This is a very popular practice these days that allows the sender to blast a message to everyone on his list without having to identify each and every person to receive it. When used properly, this is a very convenient feature to spread your message. When used recklessly or without planning, it can be an extreme annoyance and your message will be lost among the bad feelings the e-mail created.

Some messages that may work well when broadcasted include

- Major program or hardware updates and revisions
- Upcoming schedules
- Changes to Help Desk procedures like hours of operation or phone numbers
- Hot news that affects the majority of your customer base

Please remember to use this feature wisely. It is too easy (read: lazy) to use broadcasting to send messages that may not be most effective for the entire audience. Use this tool judiciously; if you send too many broadcast messages, people will just ignore them. Also, make sure the audience cares about what you send. If you broadcast updates on certain hardware features to customers who do not have that hardware in their location, they will ignore the e-mail. That is okay, except they will grow to also ignore any e-mail from you that even looks like it is being broadcast. Now, what may be important will not be communicated at all.

Customer Self-Service

One of our original goals when building the Help Desk was to empower the customer where we could. This proactive process did not prevent the Help Desk from existing, but showed it could recognize situations where the value it could add was by giving the customer features to help themselves. Customer self-service tools within a CRM can go a long way to accomplish this goal.

Some of examples of how a self-service system can help are

- **Entering problem tickets**   Allows customers to place their own call ticket into your Help Desk package without agent intervention. This can be used for lower priority issues where an agent's time is not immediately required. Because the call has been entered directly into your management package, all the same workflow rules will be followed and the information needed will be gathered as if your agent had entered the call herself.

- **Help Desk assistant**   An automated process that "acts" like a real person when the customer calls. Keying off certain words and descriptions within the customer's entered call, the assistant can prompt for more and more information as it attempts to resolve the problem on its own. If it is unable to resolve the issue after a certain number of questions and answers, the assistant creates a call ticket with the Help Desk for a live agent to get involved. This solution is very good at resolving those 80 percent of recurring calls.

- **Knowledge base searches**   Allows customers to search through your resolution database to find answers to their problems. This powerful feature completely allows your customers to resolve their issues on their own.

- **Knowledge subscription**   A tool akin to a proactive review of call logs or other information sources. By "subscribing" or linking to a published issue, the customer is alerted to all actions taken by the Help Desk to update or change the defined solution. The subscription will typically e-mail the customer every time the published issue is modified. For example, a customer may be experiencing a problem with his sales application that generates a 402 error. If he searches your knowledge base for error 402 and finds the solution "This error message has been passed to our developers. We are anticipating a fix within 24 hours," he can subscribe to the published knowledge and each time there is an update, he is notified. This solution shows a more proactive approach to the Help Desk's processes.

  Another good example of using the knowledge subscription tool involves service level agreements or policy manuals. A customer can subscribe to the SLA and be automatically informed when anything within the SLA is changed. If the Help Desk offers different hours or new standards, the customer can be updated as soon as the new SLA is published. The customer doesn't have to wait for someone to think to tell him or go long periods of time operating under an outdated policy.

- **Requesting or scheduling an agent's call**   A nice self-service tool. Basically, it allows a customer to set up a time that is convenient to him for an agent to get online or otherwise contact the customer with a problem. Again, all by itself this technology is not spectacular in nature. Its benefit is found by being located within a suite of software tools that connects the customer and the Help Desk in many different places.

- **Self-healing**   A technology that allows a computer user to resolve problems on their own. Normally used with desktops and laptops, self-healing tools can be used to restore prior configurations from a saved copy. So if the customer had installed something improperly or something they should not have installed altogether, they can invoke this tool to "reset" their system to the way it was before the problem occurred. Self-healing can also allow users to download bug fixes or patches to their system when needed. It can even help a customer recover lost data when necessary. Overall, self-healing technologies are a powerful way to empower the customer to fix problems themselves without direct Help Desk intervention.

CRM Benefits

As you can see, customer relationship management offers a wide array of options for your Help Desk and its customers. It can be comprised of many tools to get the Help Desk job done better and smoother. A summary of its benefits follows.

Provides a 360-Degree View of the Customer

The name *customer relationship management* better mean a solution that provides a good way to manage your customers…and it does. A CRM package can incorporate the entire customer experience within your company even before the person is a customer at all! Wouldn't it be good to know for staff planning and budgeting when a person or company was considering doing business with your own company and Help Desk? Of course it would. Knowing of events prior to their happening allows for proper planning.

For example, your marketing department could log in information about a group of companies being targeted for a new strategic marketing campaign. This entry could be automatically e-mailed to your sales staff to ramp them up in their efforts to follow up. Once the sales staff qualifies the potential customers and begins to bring them into your company, the Help Desk can be made aware. Now the Help Desk can begin planning for the anticipated increase in call volume and the like. All this done automatically and with all the information available.

It can continue, though. As the Help Desk continues to log information about the customer through their interactions, the sales staff can be kept abreast of any recurring problems and follow up with the customer to ensure they are happy with what has been happening. Again, CRM provides a 360-degree view, an entire view, of the customer and its dealings with your company.

Business Logic and Rules Can Be Incorporated

By leveraging your database of information about the customer with business rules and workflow plans, you can keep the customer and others constantly informed. E-mails can be sent to the sales staff when a problem is older than a defined time. When an agent changes the status of a problem an e-mail can be sent to the customer. Escalation and notification processes can be performed automatically to ensure they are done on time. Instead of making policies and hoping your agents follow them, CRM packages always follow the rules and do so more efficiently.

Multiple Channels of Communication Can Be Incorporated

By combining the strengths and diversity of phone calls, e-mails, and chat sessions, CRM solutions can increase the ways a customer can reach you. The easier this process can be, the more satisfied your customer will be. This allows you to combine the information captured in your databases to be leveraged into these channels of communication. Through auto responses, auto suggestions, and follow me functions, you can use your database of solutions to help the customer get a quicker and more accurate resolution to their problems.

These different communications are improved overall as well. Chat sessions, information pushes, collaboration, and intelligent routing all combine to create a positive environment for the customer and agent to interact. It is becoming more and more important for a Help Desk to be organized to respond to multiple methods of communication because the customers are demanding it. No matter how the Help Desk is organized, it must use technology to leverage all these paths together and not lose information or time in the process.

Allows Customers to Help Themselves

Virtual assistants can guide a customer to the right answer based on the questions-and-answers interaction with the customer. Customers can search knowledge bases on their own to uncover problem resolutions. Customers can even request callbacks from an agent at the complete convenience of the customer. Instead of waiting for an agent to call you back when they are free, the technology allows you to "reserve" an appointment with an agent when the customer is free.

Technology Integration

As your Help Desk grows, you will need to take advantage of the advances in technology, which have combined different technologies into one solution. These combinations enable the Help Desk to be more productive and therefore more valuable to the customers. Three of these technology integrations are computer telephony integration, universal queuing, and unified messaging.

Computer Telephony Integration

Computer telephony integration (CTI) is the combination of desktop or server computing with telephone services. This integration ties together these two powerful tools to increase the effectiveness of your Help Desk and the productivity of your customers. Four advantages to CTI technologies in the Help Desk are

- **Screen pops**   *Screen pops* is a term that demonstrates a principal advantage of CTI technologies. Screen pops involve the population of fields within a software package when a call is received that is provided by linking your telephone system with a database. Its best example is seen when a customer calls the Help Desk. With CTI, the phone system can recognize where the customer is calling from, relate that to your database, and populate your call entry screen with the relevant information. This speeds up the process of logging calls and gets the agent working on the customer's problem faster.

  Any data you have stored can be included in this. It may be open incidents, inside tips on how to handle this particular customer, or even the caller's birthday. Any information you have can be brought up automatically so the agent can have it available before even beginning the conversation.

- **Intelligent routing**   Intelligent routing exists within CTI technology much like it does with ACD systems and e-mail management. Here it can route the incoming call to the party most likely to resolve the issue or even route to an agent who has a history with the caller and knows his environment. This also allows the customer to deal with someone they are more familiar with.

- **Screen transfers**   Screen transfers are possible through CTI as well. Using this feature, an agent can transfer not only the phone call to another agent if necessary, but the incident from within the call management screen as well. This allows the next agent working the problem to begin immediately on a resolution and not be bothered by re-keying in data about the customer and the call.

- **Outbound dialing**   Outbound dialing can also be found in CTI systems. This can be used for a proactive Help Desk to follow up with customers on open issues or surveys about past events. It can use the database you have developed over time to determine which customers are in need of contact from the Help Desk for a variety of reasons.

Universal Queuing

We have spoken about ACD systems queuing phone calls and e-mail management queuing e-mails. *Universal queuing* is technology that combines e-mail, voice, and Internet chat calls into a single queuing path for an overall coordination of your customers' calls. With this technology in place, agents work on what is truly the next call in line instead of choosing whichever media they want.

Think of your support day currently. You may have 15 e-mails from customers and 6 voice-mails when you come into the office. Which do you answer first? And I bet you don't answer either if your phone rings. By answering that ringing phone, you have automatically allowed customer #22 to go to the head of the line and pass the 15 e-mails and 6 voice-mails of customers who called earlier. This occurs every day but is inherently unfair. Universal queuing equals this out and provides a more first-come first-served process.

Unified Messaging

Universal queuing manages the incoming calls from your customers despite the media they use. *Unified messaging* is a technology that allows you to listen or read messages whether they came in via telephone, e-mail, or fax. This is extremely beneficial for traveling agents who may not have access to one of the communication methods. Using Telephone User Interface (TUI) technology, the agent can hear his messages even if they were originally sent through e-mail. If agents are on a desktop or laptop, they can view their messages instead of hearing them.

Unified messaging helps overcome the high level of administration that Help Desk agents spend performing the tasks of managing their incoming contacts. If a tool can be used to alleviate this work and allow the agents to work on the customer's problem instead of their method of communication, the agents will provide a higher degree of effectiveness and efficiency for their customer.

Telephony Practices

There are tools in existence today that are geared towards a more effective interaction between your customers and agents when speaking over the phone. They can be used for training or problem resolution. Three that are quite useful are coaching, silent monitoring, and 3 way conferencing. Each is a slight variation of the other.

Coaching is using technology to allow a person to be included in a phone conversation but only one end of the line can hear him. An example would be a customer calling Ingrid, a new Help Desk agent. As they converse, it may become apparent to Ingrid that she needs help with the problem being called in. Using coaching technology, another agent can come onto the line and hear what the customer is saying. He can then tell Ingrid what to do or say to resolve the problem. Think of it as having someone able to whisper in your ear for assistance without the other person knowing it is happening.

Silent monitoring is close to coaching but the third party cannot be heard by either party. The third party is, in effect, only able to hear, or monitor, the conversation. This can be useful in two ways. The first is having one agent sit with a newer agent to help him take phone calls. By sitting right beside the new agent, the silent agent can help out if a problem becomes real sticky. Coaching just allows this from any physical distance and with no chance of being heard.

The other way in which silent monitoring is useful is from a management view. If you have reason to believe that one of your agents is spending too much time on personal calls or is being rude to customers, you can silently join the conversation to hear what is occurring without anyone knowing.

Note *There may be legal ramifications to this practice. Please be fully educated on any requirements or restrictions around this practice.*

The *3 way conferencing* tool is a third telephony practice to increase productivity. Again, building from the coaching practice, 3 way conferencing is a technology that allows all parties to hear all other parties in a conversation. With this, multiple agents can be brought onto a call for a team approach to resolving a customer's issue.

System Management Packages

Just as call management and asset management can be achieved through software, so can the management of your systems, network, and the desktops themselves. There are all flavors of management packages in the market. Some are written by the hardware vendors themselves and some are created by independent vendors. Packages by Hewlett-Packard, Compaq, Cisco, and Tivoli are strong brand names in this line of business.

System packages can monitor your core systems and servers, alert you to problems or other scenarios you put in, and report back on any number of statistics. Network management packages can help you document your network, monitor its performance, and report problems potentially before your users even notice. Desktop management can do the same at the PC level. These management packages can also distribute software or upgrades from a central console, eliminating the need for you to perform an identical and time-consuming process multiple times.

As I recommended with call management, you should form a team to review the options available and decide on a solution. As with any review, you should know ahead of time what you are trying to solve with the package before you get too involved. The vendors will show you far more than you come up with but be as prepared as you can. If your needs align with it and your budget fits, I strongly recommend finding a common package that can perform all the functions mentioned. One package gives you instant integration that may take you much time and money to achieve yourself.

Be advised that the acquisition of the package is merely the beginning. The real work starts after you buy the package, both in terms of cost and time. All kinds of decisions need to be made about its implementation. I strongly recommend you hire a consultant to help you with this implementation. Management packages are a significant investment and without help the return on the investment will take months if not years to realize.

Real-World Example

One thing we learned early on in an implementation of a management package was that it did not reduce the need for administrative or network staff. In fact, we found that it created more work behind the scenes when done correctly. Why? Isn't this supposed to save you money? It does, but not in staffing. Picture a location of yours having data line problems. If there are only intermittent problems, the location may not even notice. With a management package, however, it will notice and it will alert you to the problem. Where in the past you would not have received a phone call, now in effect you have. The investment return comes in the fact that you can now perform preventative maintenance on the line to keep it running and not becoming worse. The business unit may never notice but it benefits anyway.

Quick Recap

- How do you plan the shifts and workload of your agents now? Do you use spreadsheets or notepads, or do you even have a formal system available? As your Help Desk grows in size or responsibilities, it will become more and more important to implement technology to make this process better and easier to administer.

- CRM packages can add a tremendous amount of value to your Help Desk. They can tie in many facets of your interaction with the customers and make the whole experience more productive for everyone involved. Are there particular features discussed that you can use in your Help Desk? If you already have some, are they integrated with other parts of your process?

- System management packages are a good way to reduce calls to your Help Desk. By monitoring the systems that run your customer's business, you can identify problems before they adversely affect the customer. Do your systems administrators have any such packages now? If so, you should work with them to obtain access. They should appreciate your wanting to offload some of their work while at the same time your customers will appreciate your involvement in the whole process.

Action Plan Checklist

❏ Look at the different departments around your Help Desk that you interact with frequently. Determine if there are opportunities to increase efficiency and productivity by bringing them within your own organization.

❏ Review your compensation plan if it has been around awhile. Make sure it is providing the correct incentive for your agents.

❏ Look for opportunities to leverage your relationships with your vendors and customers to increase the value you deliver.

❑ Look for opportunities to increase your service offerings into areas like technology procurement or hardware repair.

❑ Ensure you have a strong, regularly tested disaster recovery plan.

❑ Look for tools that can increase your effectiveness and that of your agents. Workforce automation, customer relationship management, and system management tools are a terrific start.

Sample Job Descriptions

Job descriptions can come in many shapes and sizes. Some are short and to the point and some are very lengthy and full of details. The key is to convey all the information needed for a prospective or existing employee to understand the job's requirements and expectations. Following are several examples of job descriptions to use as a starting place for your own Help Desk.

DME Help Desk

Help Desk Dispatcher

Reports to: Help Desk Supervisor

Primary Responsibility:
To receive incoming calls in a friendly, professional manner and route them to the most appropriate agent or group.

Job Duties:
- Answer phone calls and route to agent or group
- Read e-mails and route to agent or group in a timely manner
- Listen to voice-mails and route messages to agent or group in a timely manner
- Any other project assigned by the Manager of Help Desk Services

Qualifications:
- High school education or higher
- Some experience in a fast-paced office environment
- Able to handle multiple items at one time
- Experience with spreadsheets and word processors is beneficial

Objectives to Achieve:
- Become efficient at analyzing calls to best determine which group is best able to resolve
- Understand the Help Desk procedures to make the caller's interaction as effective as possible
- Continue to show high-quality customer service skills
- Continue developing strong interpersonal skills in dealing with people

Expected Career Length: 1–2 years

Possible Career Steps:
- Entry Level Help Desk Analyst
- Administrative Assistant
- Human Resources Specialist

DME Help Desk

Help Desk Analyst

Reports to: Manager of Help Desk Services

Primary Responsibility:
Work with end users to resolve their issues and answer their questions in a timely, professional, and effective manner.

Job Duties:
- Resolve customer issues or escalate when necessary
- Proactively look for ways to improve themselves, operations, or customer processes
- Take over dispatching duties if required
- Communicate to management on high-impact problems
- Any project assigned by the Manager of Help Desk Services

Qualifications:
- College degree in computer-related field is beneficial
- Intermediate level working with computer hardware and software is required
- 1–2 years of IT experience is preferred

Objectives to Achieve:
- Continue to develop superior technical troubleshooting skills
- Continue to develop strong customer service skills
- Develop complete understanding of Help Desk and IT department operations
- Understand business processes and their use of technology

Possible Career Steps:
- Senior Help Desk Analyst
- Manager of Help Desk Services
- Programmer—Entry Level
- Network Analyst
- Junior LAN Administrator

DME Help Desk

Manager of Help Desk Services

Reports to: Director of Information Systems

Primary Responsibility:
Manage the operations and agents in the Help Desk for maximum efficiency in the service to its customers.

Job Duties:
- Monitor daily operations of the Help Desk for possible issues
- Be available as 4th level support on problems
- Recruit, hire, and train Help Desk associates
- Communicate to business on problem status and measurements
- Any project assigned by the Director of Information Systems

Qualifications:
- 3–5 years of Help Desk experience required
- College degree in computer-related field is preferred
- 1–2 years of managing people is preferred
- Strong interpersonal skills preferred

Objectives to Achieve:
- Develop the Help Desk organization into a highly effective and efficient department providing high value to the business
- Develop superior team-building skills for the Help Desk agents
- Continue strong decision-making skills to achieve results
- Maintain a strong understanding of the business and its needs from the Help Desk
- Work with senior management to grow the Help Desk into an increasingly valuable asset to the business

Possible Career Steps:
- Director of Information Systems
- Business Operations Manager
- Project Manager
- Entry level position in any technical field in IS

DME Help Desk

Help Desk Analyst

Reports to: Manager of Help Desk Services

Primary Responsibility:
Work with end users to resolve their issues and answer their questions in a timely, professional, and effective manner.

Job Duties:
- Resolve customer issues when necessary
- Proactively look for ways to improve themselves, operations, or customer processes
- Take over dispatching duties if required
- Communicate to management on high-impact problems
- Any project assigned by the Manager of Help Desk Services

Qualifications:
- College degree in computer-related field is beneficial
- Intermediate level working with computer hardware and software is required
- 1–2 years of IT experience is preferred

Objectives to Achieve:
- Continue to develop superior technical troubleshooting skills
- Continue to develop strong customer service skills
- Develop complete understanding of Help Desk and IT department operations
- Understand business processes and their use of technology

Expected Career Length: 2–4 years

Salary Range:
$32,000–$35,000 at hiring
$50,000–$60,000 by end of four years

Possible Career Steps:
- Senior Help Desk Analyst
- Manager of Help Desk Services
- Programmer—Entry Level
- Network Analyst
- Junior LAN Administrator

Sample Service Level Agreement

**DME Help Desk
Service Level Agreement
September, 2001**

This Service Level Agreement will help familiarize you with necessary help desk information, such as hours, policies, and standards, and help define mutually agreed upon operating procedures. By reviewing this document, you will become more familiar with how to contact us, operating hours, call priority, and hardware and software standards. It should be used as reference when contacting the DME Help Desk.

Scope

DME Help Desk supports desktop computers, the software applications that run on them, and peripheral devices such as printers and scanners, servers, and networking equipment.

While the DME Help Desk will attempt to help with all technology issues, our support and training commitments will focus on the standard products listed in Appendix A.

This agreement will be formally reviewed each January and July for any necessary changes. No changes can be made to this document without the prior consent and sign-off of all parties affected.

Contacting the Help Desk for Assistance

You may contact the DME Help Desk for any issue by e-mail or by calling 757-555-2317. We also offer selected services over the intranet at dme.helpdesk.com. This service will then route your information or direct the call to the appropriate group, individual, or third party vendor for resolution. However, the following are guidelines for you to use when deciding whom to call for various issues.

Issue	Contact	Contact Method
Desktops and Printers	Hardware Support Group	E-mail or call 757-555-2317, option 1
Network and Connectivity	Hardware Support Group	E-mail or call 757-555-2317, option 2
Business Software	Software Support Group	E-mail or call 757-555-2317, option 3
Microsoft Office Software	Hastings Computer Services	Call 919-555-1937

Call ID numbers will be provided upon request for easier follow-up.

Hours of Operation

DME Help Desk   5:00 a.m. to 10:00 p.m. Monday–Friday Eastern Time
Emergency after-hours support is provided via pager during all other times.
Please refer to the Contact List in Appendix B for pager numbers. The Help Desk
is closed on all DME observed holidays.

Problem Severity Levels

Code	Customer Impact	Response Time to Customer	Resolution Time
1	Business halted	30 minutes	Until fixed
2	Business impacted	1 hour	24 hours
3	Software defect	2 hours	Tracked until fixed
4	Inquiry	Same business day	72 hours

Severity Level Definitions

- **Business halted**   The business systems are down or inaccessible.

- **Business impacted**   Multiple users in a location cannot access the systems but the systems are available and workarounds do exist.

- **Software defect**   An issue where our business software is not working correctly. Typically escalation requires programming involvement.

- **Inquiry**   Question on how things work, service request, etc.

- **Response time to customer**   The time between the initial request and the Help Desk's first response.

- **Resolution time**   The time between the initial call and the actual resolution of the problem. "Until fixed" means the IS staff will not leave until the problem is resolved.

Escalation

We recognize that the importance of calls can be subjective and many factors go into prioritizing them. As a guideline, however, we proactively escalate calls based on the codes above and inform increasingly higher levels of management when they remain unresolved.

We include the schedule of this internal prioritization below. Please refer to the Contact List in Appendix B for each contact name.

Code	Elapsed Time	Whom Notified
1	30 minutes	Manager of Help Desk Services
	1 hour	Director of IT
	2 hours	Chief Executive Officer
2	3 hours	Manager of Help Desk Services
	24 hours	Director of IT
3	3 hours	Manager of Help Desk Services
	48 hours	Manager of Applications Development (if a Trilogie issue)
	72 hours	Director of IT
4	72 hours	Manager of Help Desk Services

The Director of IT will receive a consolidated monthly summary of all open and closed calls for the previous month. This report will be sent via Internet mail no later than the 10th of each month. Customers wishing a copy may find each month's report on the intranet.

Notification

Because of the importance of the computing systems to DME Corporation, we will not only escalate issues internally but also notify and follow up with the DME contacts as well. For name detail, please refer to the Contact List in Appendix B. Included below is a schedule of notification based on problem severity.

Code	Notification from Time Issue Reported	Contact	Contacted by	Frequency
1	1 hour (if not resolved)	Store manager Division Head	Phone Phone	Every 1 hr Every 2 hrs
2	8 hours (if not resolved)	Store manager	E-mail	Weekly
3	8 hours (if not resolved)	Store manager	E-mail	Weekly
4	96 hours (if not resolved)	Calling customer Store manager	E-mail E-mail	Weekly Weekly

Notification of problem status can also be found on the intranet under dme.helpdesk.com. There is a problem status screen that will detail all open issues and notes.

Standards

As the technologies and services supported are constantly evolving with customer needs, we will maintain the standards officially supported in Appendix A. We will communicate changes to Appendix A through e-mail to each section manager 30 days before implementation.

Contact List

Appendix B will document the entire list of contacts alluded to in this master SLA. Their names, job titles, office numbers, and cell phone numbers will be included. As changes are made to this list, we will contact the section manager with 30 days' notice wherever possible. You are expected to update us with any changes on your side as required.

Service Performance Measures

Important to the process is to measure the actual performance against the service level agreement. As our current philosophy is not to staff for peaks in the workload, there will be times when we are unable to meet the agreement. Included below, however, are our commitments to the agreement despite unforeseen situations.

System availability   99.95% availability within the times stated.

| Note | *This relates to the computer systems being up and running. A location connecting to this system is a function of the phone company. To aid this, we provide all locations with a dial backup solution, which allows the location to reach the system through alternate means.* |

Problem management   90% resolved within severity level definition.

Those problems resolved outside these parameters will be included in our monthly report to the Director of IT and the appropriate customer manager.

Follow-up calls   All calls/e-mails returned within same business day.

First call resolution   80% of calls resolved during initial call.

Signatures

_____	_____
Manager of Help Desk Services	Date
_____	_____
Director of IT	Date
_____	_____
Hastings Computer Services Mgr	Date
_____	_____
Regional DME Vice President	Date

Glossary

In keeping with the nature of this book, this glossary will not be a formal dictionary version of word definitions. Instead, it will be a common sense explanation of terms used regularly in a Help Desk environment. Although many of these terms can be used in many settings, their definitions here will be as they relate to the Help Desk.

Glossary of Terms

abandoned rate   The number of times someone called your Help Desk but hung up before they reached an agent.

agent   A common term for a person who works in a Help Desk.

agent career life cycle   A graphical depiction of the career advancement for Help Desk agents over time.

as is   The current state of being of an environment.

asset management   A process that tracks, records, and reports on the various assets and technologies in an organization.

Automated Attendant   Technology that routes a customer's phone call to the resource he chooses.

Automated Call Distribution (ACD)   Technology that routes phone calls and other functions such as queuing and statistical reporting.

auto response   A feature that automatically sends the sender of e-mail a set message without human intervention on the receiver side.

auto suggest   A feature in which an e-mail message is sent in response to a customer with suggestions on how their problem could be handled.

average speed of answer   The average length of time it takes for an agent or automated tool to respond to an incoming call.

average talk time   The average length of time that an agent spends on the phone with a customer.

Best Practices   An established set of processes and procedures that are recognized as *the* correct way to do things.

Big Bang   Implementing a new technology or process all at once (see *phased implementation*).

broadcasting   A proactive sending of e-mails to a list of customers to convey a common message at one time.

burnout   A state of mind in which a person is no longer productive at his job and has lost the desire to better himself at it.

call   Any contact from a customer to the Help Desk, not limited to a telephone interaction.

call avoidance   A strategy in which processes are created to reduce the need for customers to contact the Help Desk.

call management system   Technology designed for Help Desks that helps agents and managers keep track of customer calls, problems, and resolutions.

case-based reasoning   A type of expert system that allows the user to enter information in any order. The system then returns suggested solutions based on the "case" made by the user.

change management   The process that tracks changes to the technologies, services, programs, or other items that your Help Desk supports.

chargebacks   A financial plan that charges customers for the services performed by the Help Desk.

chat   The typed equivalent of a voice conversation where two or more people communicate back and forth through their computers.

collaboration   Multiple people working together to achieve a common objective.

Computer Telephony Integration (CTI)   The combination of desktop or server computing with telephone services to enhance the customer-Help Desk relationship.

cost per call   How much your Help Desk costs per call taken.

cross training   Providing education on jobs and responsibilities not directly involved in an agent's day-to-day job.

customer   The user of your Help Desk services. It is particularly used to denote their importance to your organization.

Customer Relationship Management (CRM)   Technology that provides a closed loop of information for a customer throughout the organization. It begins with an initial contact by either party and includes each piece of information and every interaction point needed to maintain a strong customer-Help Desk relationship.

database   A collection of information stored for people to access at a later time.

decision tree   Technology that guides you through questions and branches out to possible resolutions depending on how you answer the questions.

disaster recovery   The plans and processes designed to recover a business from a disaster. It will include all plans for the people, the computing infrastructure, facilities, and processes needed for a business to reopen from a catastrophe.

dispatcher   A Help Desk position that receives incoming customer calls and routes them to the correct resource.

duration metrics   Used to keep up with the length of time that selected actions and processes are taking.

electronic display board   Electronic devices that allow you to display or scroll messages and statistics for your agents or customers to view.

ergonomics   The design of furniture and computing devices to provide ease of physical use to prevent chronic pain in the user's eyes, neck, back, knees, and elbows.

escalation   The process in which a problem's priority is increased in importance.

expert system   Technology that provides information from a knowledge base to its user to learn and resolve issues.

external customer   A user of the Help Desk who is not organizationally part of the Help Desk's company (see *internal customer*).

fax back   Technology that walks a caller through a menu of options and automatically faxes the caller with the chosen document.

first call resolution   The percentage of time a caller's problem is resolved during his initial call into the Help Desk.

flex time   A staffing strategy that allows agents to work a variable day or time schedule instead of a strict start and end time.

follow me   Description of collaborative technology that allows an agent or customer to "follow" the other within Web pages to show question areas.

follow the sun   Process in which the Help Desk location taking calls moves west as the time zones change.

frontline support   The organizational part of your Help Desk that receives the call and performs an initial diagnosis of the problem.

FTE   Abbreviation for Full-Time Equivalent. It is used when calculating the effort required to perform a task.

generalist   The term for a Help Desk agent whose skill set is broad in scope but who is not necessarily an expert in any technology or customer base (see *specialist*).

Help Desk   A formal organization that provides support functions to users of the company's product, services, or technology.

homegrown software   A popular term for software that was developed by the company using the software.

incident   An occasion that makes the customer realize there is a problem and thus a need to contact the Help Desk.

Intelligent Routing   Technology that uses rule sets and parameters to route customers to the correct resource without additional human intervention.

Interactive Voice Response (IVR)   Technology that allows a customer to use a telephone to choose a service and a computer performs that service for them.

internal customer   A user of the Help Desk who is organizationally part of the Help Desk's company (see *external customer*).

Internet   A collection of networks and gateways across the world.

intranet   A network of computers within an organization that uses the same tools and processes as the Internet.

IS   Abbreviation for Information Systems or Information Services.

IT   Abbreviation for Information Technology.

issues tracking   The act of keeping up with all events or items that crop up during the implementation so they can be followed until resolved.

knowledge base   A collection of information and processes that is used by expert systems to help a customer or agent.

knowledge engineer   A person dedicated to creating and maintaining a knowledge base.

Local Area Network (LAN)   A collection of computers on a network located in a select geographic area.

M&A   Abbreviation for Mergers and Acquisitions. It involves the planning and actions surrounding two or more companies combining operations or assets.

maintenance contract   A service agreement between a customer and a vendor that calls for the vendor to resolve issues found during use of their technology.

mentoring   A training technique in which a person serves as a resource for someone to help with issues and questions.

milestones   Established points on a timeline that reflect achievement of a goal.

mission statement   A declaration of the ideals you hold for your organization.

network management   Systems and processes that help monitor, notify, and resolve issues found within a network.

notification   A process that informs customers, agents, or management of events or changes.

off-the-shelf software   A common reference to software that can be purchased from a store. It therefore can be found on a shelf.

outsourcing   Hiring an outside resource to perform services instead of your Help Desk.

page push   Delivering a Web form to a customer.

phased implementation   Implementing new processes or technologies in pieces. This allows those being impacted to learn or uncover issues before the entire company is impacted (see *Big Bang*).

priority   A classification of a problem or process that establishes its importance when compared to other problems or processes.

problem   The root issue that makes a customer need a Help Desk's involvement.

problem life cycle   The process in which a problem is identified, reported, resolved, and its status captured for future reference.

problem subscription   A technology that allows a customer to be informed whenever their problem has a change of status within the Help Desk.

procurement   The act of purchasing technologies such as hardware or software.

qualitative measurements   Subjective measurements that reflect how well something is done in the Help Desk process.

quantitative measurements   Objective measurements that look at the numbers and times involved in the Help Desk process flow.

queue   A "line" where customer calls or requests form waiting for a Help Desk agent to handle.

screen pop   Technology that combines information from an incoming call and a database to populate a call entry screen automatically.

self-healing   Technology that identifies PC problems and attempts to resolve them.

self-service   Processes and technologies that empower a customer to resolve their own issues without the Help Desk being involved.

service level agreements   A formalized way to set expectations between your Help Desk and its constituents on what you will support and in what manner.

severity   A priority classification based on the problem's impact on the business.

shrink-wrapped software   A common reference to software that can be purchased from a store. It therefore can come in a box and might be shrink-wrapped for protection.

silent monitoring   A practice where someone uses telephony technology to listen in on phone conversations. This can be used for training or to review the productivity of the person being monitored.

SLA   Abbreviation for Service Level Agreement.

subject matter expert   A person who is extremely knowledgeable in a particular topic; he or she is the expert on that subject.

specialist   A term for a Help Desk agent whose skill set is focused on a customer or technology (see *generalist*).

standards   Established and published processes and technologies that should be used.

telecommuting   A computing user who works remotely from the main office, probably at home. Instead of commuting to work by transportation, the user commutes through a telephone line.

text searches   A feature that takes key words from the problem entry screen and matches them with key words already established in the database.

tiered support   Process in which one group of agents takes customer calls and a second or third group is available when the first group needs assistance.

total cost of ownership   A popular measurement that takes into account all costs involved in the purchase and use of a technology.

transfer   The act of passing a call or problem from one resource to another.

type metrics   Measurements around categories or classifications.

unified messaging   Technology that allows you to listen or read messages whether they came in via telephone, e-mail, chat, or fax.

universal queuing   Technology that combines e-mail, voice, and internet chat calls into a single queuing path for an overall coordination of your customers' calls.

version support   The practice of manufacturers and vendors to provide support only for current versions of their product.

volume metrics   Measurements that track the "how many" of things.

web call through   Technology that allows people to have conversations through their computers using VoIP.

workaround   A process that allows users to continue working through a different means to avert a problem they were having.

working manager   Someone assigned responsibility of managing a group of people while at the same time performing many of the same duties as the people she manages.

workforce management   Software that aids in the planning and scheduling of resources.

Index

INTERNATIONAL CONTACT INFORMATION

AUSTRALIA
McGraw-Hill Book Company Australia Pty. Ltd.
TEL +61-2-9417-9899
FAX +61-2-9417-5687
http://www.mcgraw-hill.com.au
books-it_sydney@mcgraw-hill.com

CANADA
McGraw-Hill Ryerson Ltd.
TEL +905-430-5000
FAX +905-430-5020
http://www.mcgrawhill.ca

GREECE, MIDDLE EAST,
NORTHERN AFRICA
McGraw-Hill Hellas
TEL +30-1-656-0990-3-4
FAX +30-1-654-5525

MEXICO (Also serving Latin America)
McGraw-Hill Interamericana Editores S.A. de C.V.
TEL +525-117-1583
FAX +525-117-1589
http://www.mcgraw-hill.com.mx
fernando_castellanos@mcgraw-hill.com

SINGAPORE (Serving Asia)
McGraw-Hill Book Company
TEL +65-863-1580
FAX +65-862-3354
http://www.mcgraw-hill.com.sg
mghasia@mcgraw-hill.com

SOUTH AFRICA
McGraw-Hill South Africa
TEL +27-11-622-7512
FAX +27-11-622-9045
robyn_swanepoel@mcgraw-hill.com

UNITED KINGDOM & EUROPE
(Excluding Southern Europe)
McGraw-Hill Education Europe
TEL +44-1-628-502500
FAX +44-1-628-770224
http://www.mcgraw-hill.co.uk
computing_neurope@mcgraw-hill.com

ALL OTHER INQUIRIES Contact:
Osborne/McGraw-Hill
TEL +1-510-549-6600
FAX +1-510-883-7600
http://www.osborne.com
omg_international@mcgraw-hill.com

Lightning Source UK Ltd.
Milton Keynes UK
UKOW06f2031080914

238251UK00003B/178/P